Child Language and Education

Courtney B. Cazden

Harvard University

Holt, Rinehart and Winston, Inc.
New York   Chicago   San Francisco   Atlanta
Dallas   Montreal   Toronto   London   Sydney

Preface

This book owes much to many people:

to Roger Brown, who remains for me, as for so many of his former students, the finest model of teacher, researcher, and writer;

to students in my course in Child Language at the Harvard Graduate School of Education, who will find many of their ideas and their questions in these pages;

and to my beloved aunt, Joyce Borden Baloković, in whose home and studio in the hills above Camden, Maine, this book was written in the summer of 1970, revised in April, 1971, and given its final editing during the last weekends of her life in the fall of 1971.

Some of the material in this book is adapted from previously published articles, some of which were written with colleagues. Grateful acknowledgment for permission to reprint is made to the following:

Ursula Bellugi	Eleanor R. Heider
Roger Brown	Vera John
Betty H. Bryant	Melissa Tillman

Academic Press
Aldine, Atherton, Inc.
Appleton-Century-Crofts, Inc., for "The Psychology of Language" in *Handbook of Speech and Pathology*, edited by Lee Edward Travis, 1971
Association for Childhood Education International
Basic Books, Inc.
Center for Applied Linguistics
Harvard Educational Review
Harvard Graduate School of Education Association Bulletin
Journal of Special Education
Merrill-Palmer Quarterly
National Association for the Education of Young Children
Philosophical Forum
Project Literacy
Society for Research in Child Development
Society for the Psychological Study of Social Issues
The Spastics Society
University of Illinois Press
University of Minnesota Press for Roger Brown, Courtney Cazden, and Ursula Bellugi-Klima, "The Child's Grammar from I to III" from *Minnesota Symposium on Child Psychology*, Volume II edited by John P. Hill. University of Minnesota Press, Minneapolis. © 1969 University of Minnesota

Permission to reprint is also acknowledged to

Holt, Rinehart and Winston, Inc., for selections from *Man's Many Voices: Language in Its Cultural Context* by Robbins Burling. Copyright © 1970 by Holt, Rinehart and Winston, Inc.
Liveright Publishing Corporation for selections from *The Role of Speech in the Regulation of Normal and Abnormal Behavior*, by A. H. Luria. Copyright renewed 1961 by Liveright Publishing Corp., New York

Contents

1

Introduction

It may be helpful at the very beginning to set forth some introductory ideas about the readers for whom this book was written, about child language, and about the book itself.

About the Readers

Usually, when we talk with someone, adult or child, we listen and respond to what they say. We aren't aware of how they say it, and we don't stop to think of the previous learning that it entails—learning of the structure or form of language, learning of the structure of conversation so that sentences spoken are not only grammatical but also appropriate, and learning to use language in social communication and private thought. One purpose of this book is to help its readers listen more reflectively to children by describing some of the ways in which behavioral scientists are studying child language, and by giving some examples of what they are finding out.

The book is written for anyone, researcher or teacher, who seeks to improve children's communicative adequacy through education. Researchers and teachers have different perspectives on their work, but what they need to know is much the same. Whether or not they think in these terms about what they're doing, teachers, like researchers, make judgments about what children can do, or need to do, with language; they plan strategies to bring about change, based on how they think language is learned; and they use observations and tests to evaluate their results. Hopefully, their work will be improved with better understanding of the work of linguists, psycholinguists, and sociolinguists. Hopefully, they will be provoked to become researchers themselves. The discoveries are too exciting to be left to someone else.

This book is for researchers, teachers, and teachers of teachers in all subject areas, not just those whose special interest or assignment is "language arts" or "English." All teachers are involved in language as a medium of communication; most of them accept responsibility for doing what they can to extend children's language ability.

At the least, the concept of "extension" implies a direction. In what direction do we want to extend children's language? In any particular situation, what kind of language, what ways of communicating, are of greatest worth? Unless a teacher has given serious thought to such questions, it seems unlikely that he will be aware of the most important directions for help. Teachers can only start from where the child is and then help him learn something new if they know about exciting places to go. Cremin said as much in his analysis of the progressive movement in the United States:

> For the resourceful teacher, all activities and occupations had an instrumental as well as an intrinsic value; they afforded opportunity for social and intellectual growth as well as more immediate satisfaction to the children.
>
> But there is a point to be made here, one that Dewey argued for the rest of his career but never fully communicated to some who thought themselves his disciples. A teacher cannot know which opportunities to use, which impulses to encourage, or which social attitudes to cultivate without a clear sense of what is to come later . . . with respect to intellect this implies a thorough acquaintance with organized knowledge as represented in the disciplines. To recognize opportunities for early mathematical learning, one must know mathematics. . . . In short, the demand on the teacher is twofold: thorough knowledge of the disciplines and an awareness of those common experiences of childhood that can be utilized to lead children toward the understanding represented by this knowledge. (Cremin, 1961, p. 138.)

It is easy for us as teachers to admit that we need to know more about mathematics. But because we all talk, we assume that we're all experts on language. The trouble is that the knowledge about language we require as teachers is one level beyond using it ourselves, no matter how richly we may do so. We need to know about language. And then we have to plan how to use that knowledge in the classroom.

About Child Language

From the moment of his birth, the human infant hears language all around him. It's not language in the form of monologs. Some of it may be language from a television set, but that source is remarkable for having so little demonstrable effect. We can say with very little qualification that the language a child attends to and learns from is the speech of significant persons in his world, addressed to each other and to him, in spontaneous but highly patterned social interaction. This interaction is both verbal and nonverbal, but we will be concerned here only with the part expressed in words.

As the child attends to this social interaction and gradually participates in it, he learns what Hymes (1971) calls "communicative competence." "Competence" here does not have the colloquial meaning of "adequacy"; it is a technical term, first used by Noam Chomsky, for the nonconscious, tacit knowledge that underlies behavior. Communicative adequacy is what teachers work toward; communicative competence is what every child has.

Communicative competence has two aspects. It includes both knowledge of language (in the more usual and narrow sense of syntax, phonology, and semantics) and knowledge of the social world and of rules for using language in that world so that speech is appropriate as well as grammatical and creative within both linguistic and sociolinguistic rules. Together, these aspects of communicative competence are realized in the child's actual speech behavior, or performance. This performance includes both speaking and comprehending.

In whatever terms, the distinction between knowledge and behavior is important. It has been familiar to psychologists in general terms at least since Lashley's 1929 review of the literature on learning. Language is knowledge in our heads; speech is the realization of that knowledge in behavior. Language consists of all the words in a person's mental dictionary, and all the rules at his (usually nonconscious) command for combining those words into an infinite number of novel sentences and for interpreting the equally novel sentences that he hears. Speech, by contrast, consists of his actual utterances spoken to particular people in particular situations. Language exists even in moments of silence and sleep; speech exists only in moments of actual speaking or listening, including the silent activation of language in thought. In this book, "language" will always refer to knowledge, and "speech" will refer to verbal behavior.

About this Book

As a title, *Child Language and Education* is twice misleading: first, because the book is really about both child language and child speech, and second, because questions will be raised about educational practice, but detailed analysis of curriculum will not be pursued.

Following this Introduction there is one chapter on language itself. The next group of four chapters deals with language development, divided into syntax, sounds and meanings, developmental processes, and environmental assistance. The third group of chapters deals with language differences and language use: dialects and bilingualism, communication styles, and the roles of language in cognition. The final chapter contains some thoughts on oral language education. The Appendix describes methods of analyzing child language, both from spontaneous speech and from tests.

Research methodology and substantive findings on these topics are uneven. Descriptions of language from the field of linguistics are more advanced than explanations of behavior. As yet, we know very little about the cognitive processes by which sentences are produced and comprehended. This is the focus of psycholinguistics. We also know very little about the distribution of acts of speaking—who says what to whom, how, when, and to what purpose. This is the focus of sociolinguistics. While psycholinguistics deals primarily with the processes of speaking and listening in an individual mind, sociolinguistics deals with the interactions of individuals in social settings. The two are related in important ways because any act of speaking necessarily involves decisions about function, topic, and form, which are affected by characteristics of the speaker and listener(s) and the setting both are in. Similarly, any act of listening is affected by the expectations set up in the listener about what he is likely to hear from particular persons at particular times. Methodology and findings from linguistics, psycholinguistics, and sociolinguistics will be interwoven throughout these pages.

2

The Nature of Language

The more we learn about human language ability, the more impressive the child's acquisition of language is seen to be. Computers that have guided man's trips to the moon cannot do as well, and there is increasing reason to believe that they will never be able to do so.

> Consider the simple sentence "Time flies like an arrow." . . . A grammar that pretends to describe English at all accurately must yield a structure for "Time flies like an arrow" in which "time" is the subject of the verb "flies" and "like an arrow" is an adverbial phrase modifying the verb. "Time" can also serve attributively, however, as in "time bomb," and "flies" of course can serve as a noun. Together with "like" interpreted as a verb, this yields a structure that becomes obvious only if one thinks of a kind of flies called "time flies" which happen to like an arrow, perhaps as a meal. Moreover, "time" as an imperative verb with "flies" as a noun also yields a structure that makes sense as an order to someone to take out his stopwatch and time flies with great dispatch, like an arrow.
>
> A little thought suggests many minor modifications of the grammar sufficient to rule out such fantasies. Unfortunately too much is then lost. . . . Anything ruling out the nonexisting species of time flies will also rule out the identical but legitimate structure of "Fruit flies like a banana."
>
> Semantics, the all too nebulous notion of what a sentence means, must be invoked to choose among the three structures syntax accepts for "Time flies like an arrow." No techniques now known can deal effectively with semantic problems of this kind. . . . We do not know how people understand language, and our machine procedures barely do child's work in an extraordinarily cumbersome way. (Oettinger, 1966, pp. 168–169.)

Any reader who glances at the dates in the list of references at the end of this book will notice that virtually all the research on child language listed there has been done within the past 15 years. *Syntactic Structures,* Chomsky's first published work, appeared in 1957. What we have learned about child language has been due largely to the powerful analyses of language that his work has stimulated. [See N. Chomsky (1968) for his least technical writing.] This fact points to an important characteristic of productive methods for studying any aspect of child development: The more we know about the characteristics of mature behavior in a particular culture—whether language or art or moral judgments—the more successful we can be in knowing both what to look for in children's spontaneous behavior and how to construct contrived situations called "tests" for eliciting aspects of behavior that would otherwise remain hidden. This is why a chapter on "the nature of language" cannot be avoided at the beginning of this book, no matter how much easier it would be to begin in a less theoretical way. For other excellent introductions that supplement this chapter in different ways, see Brown (1965, chaps. 6 and 7) on both language and its acquisition; Burling (1970) for a more anthropological introduction; Langacker (1968) and McNeil (1970, pp. 1138–1152) on transformational grammar; Slobin (1971) on psycholinguistics; and Fishman (1970) on sociolinguistics.

This chapter focuses on four characteristics of human language: its essence as creative but rule-governed behavior; its multiple levels of meaning and form; its hierarchical structure; and the transformational relations that linguists have discovered among sentences. Discussion of each characteristic includes an illustration of how it has influenced the study of child language in some important way. The chapter ends with speculation about how these characteristics of language may apply more generally to all human cognition.

Creativity and Rules

When a person knows a language, what does he know? What information does he have in his head, somewhere in the neurophysiology of his brain? A set of sentences from which he chooses the right one when he wants to say something? The meaning of a set of sentences from which he chooses the right interpretation for the sentences he hears? Even if the sets of sentences and interpretations were enormous, they would still be inadequate. Outside of a small and unimportant list of greetings like *Good morning,* clichés like *My, it's hot today*, and routinized statements like proverbs, few sentences are spoken or heard more than once. Each spoken sentence must be constructed anew to express and communicate particular meanings to particular individuals—oneself or others.

The heart of human language capability is creativity in expressing and understanding meanings, "free from control of external stimuli, and appropriate to new and ever-changing situations" (N. Chomsky, n.d., p. 66). It can be explained only if what we know in common with other members of our language community is a finite set of rules. These rules express the relationships that hold between meaning and sound in our particular language, and they channel our creativity within the limits of intelligibility and appropriateness for our speech community.

A description of such a set of rules is called a grammar. Like all descriptions of natural phenomena, grammars are subject to continuous revision and correction. In the range of phenomena they explain, the most powerful grammars of adult English are generative transformational grammars, first written by a group of linguists centering around Noam Chomsky. Although grammars are written by linguists, they constitute psychological theories about the organization of one aspect of human knowledge.

> At several levels the linguist is involved in the construction of explanatory theories, and at each level there is a clear psychological interpretation for his theoretical and descriptive work. At the level of particular grammar, he is attempting to characterize knowledge of a language, a certain cognitive system that has been developed—unconsciously, of course—by the normal speaker-hearer. At the level of universal grammar, he is trying to establish certain general properties of human intelligence. Linguistics, so characterized, is simply the subfield of psychology that deals with these aspects of mind. (N. Chomsky, 1968, p. 24.)

When we say that a person, either child or adult, knows a set of rules, we don't mean that he knows them in any conscious way. Usually, knowledge refers to something we are aware of knowing, something we could, if we wished, verbalize on demand. But linguistic rules are known only nonconsciously, out-of-awareness, as a knid of powerful but implicit, or tacit, knowledge. This is true for adults as well as for children. Few of us can state the rules for adding the sounds of /s/ or /z/ or /əz/ to form noun or verb endings. Yet, if asked to supply the plurals for nonsense syllables such as *bik* or *wug* or *gutch,* all who are native speakers of English can do so with ease, and most six-year-old children can too (Berko, 1958). Linguists infer the presence of rules from what adults or children can say and understand.

> By calling a rule implicit, we mean, among other things, that if it were formulated and offered for consideration to the persons concerned, they would accept it as codifying their previous practice, and that after such acceptance their behavior would not be substantially changed. (Black, 1962, p. 131.)

By calling a rule implicit, we also mean that when a rule is violated, we have a general sense that something is amiss. Hearing a waitress in Syracuse ask, *Anybody wants any?* as she removes the basket of rolls, most readers would register a mismatch between their rules and her speech. We might be hard put to explain the discrepancy, but we would be aware of its existence. Or we may, for expressive purposes, utter the imperative, *Tell it like it is,* and be aware in so doing that it comes from a dialect whose rules are slightly different from our own and derives its special expressive value from that source. Such acts of implicit evaluation constitute particularly strong evidence that we are obeying rules and not merely conforming to habits (Green, 1964).

Because it is hard to get children to evaluate sentences, the best evidence that children have learned rules is obtained when they say things they could not have learned from others. Sometimes this happens spontaneously, as when they say *He goed* or *She gots one*. Such evidence can also be elicited when a researcher asks children to incorporate nonsense syllables into their utterances, as Berko did. Children's errors of commission are important data in child language research. But we must always remember that they are only "errors" in terms of the adult model; in the child's language, they are representative expressions of his own linguistic rules and powerful evidence of the existence of those rules in the child's mind. Later chapters will include many examples of such evidence.

Levels of Structure

Sometimes, for purposes of analysis, language is divided into three aspects: syntactics, semantics, and pragmatics. Syntactics refers to the relationship of language forms to each other; semantics refers to the relationship of that syntactic system to the nonlinguistic world of objects, events, and ideas that we talk "about"; pragmatics refers to the relationship of forms and the ideas they express to the people who use them. This is not a wholly satisfactory division, and therefore the chapters of this book are not forced into that framework. But it does serve to connect two separate phenomena under a single heading. In both the syntactic and pragmatic aspects of language there are two levels of structure in a means-ends relationship: in syntactics, surface structure and deep structure; in pragmatics, form and function.

SURFACE STRUCTURE AND DEEP STRUCTURE

A grammar of a language is a formal representation of the implicit knowledge of a native speaker. One important attribute of that knowledge, which the grammar must reflect, is that it is not limited to the noises we speak and hear. We know that the unspoken subject of the imperative *Go home* is *you*; we know that the following three sentences say the same thing, despite different physical forms:

(1a)   The astronaut photographed the moon.
(1b)   The moon was photographed by the astronaut.
(1c)   It was the moon that the astronaut photographed.

And we know that the complex sentence like

(2)   The man fed the dog that belonged to his son.

is a combination of at least two ideas: a boy had a dog, and his father fed that dog.

Such facts as these reaffirm the existence of two distinct structures for each sentence: a deep (underlying and abstract) structure and a surface (superficial and perceptible) structure. The deep structure represents basic semantic relationships (such as actor-action, action-object, and modification) in the meaning being expressed. The surface structure represents grammatical relationships (such as subject of verb and object of verb) in the sentence as spoken.

Consider two more sets of sentences. First, three discussed by McNeill (1970b):

(3a)   They are buying glasses.
(3b)   They are drinking glasses.
(3c)   They are drinking companions.

Despite the superficial similarities of these sentences, particularly in their written versions, they differ in important ways. Say them aloud and note how different insertions of pauses affect them.

> With sentence (a), one might say *they—are buying—glasses*, but probably not *they–are–buying glasses*. It is the opposite with sentences (b) and (c). One could say *they—are—drinking companions* or *they—are—drinking glasses*, but not *they—are drinking—companions* or *they—are drinking— glasses* unless the reference was to cannibalism or suicide (McNeill, 1970b, p. 1146.)

A difference in the places where pauses can be inserted without distorting the meaning signifies a difference in surface structure. Sentence (3a) has a surface structure different from sentences (3b) and (3c).

Now consider possible paraphrases, or synonymous statements of meaning, for (3b) and (3c).

> Sentence (b) means "they are glasses to use for drinking," and sentence (c) means "they are companions that drink." Exchanging the form of the paraphrase between (b) and (c) leads to a nonparaphrase. Sentence (b) does not mean "they are glasses that drink" anymore than sentence (c) means "they are companions to use for drinking." (McNeill, 1970b, p. 1147.)

A difference in possible paraphrases signifies a difference in deep structure. Sentences (3b) and (3c), while alike in surface structure, differ in deep structure.

It was not a new idea that each language can be regarded as a particular relationship between sound and meaning. In fact, the existence of two levels of structure—deep and surface—is a traditional notion. (Blumenthal, 1970, documents with extensive quotes the history of this and other ideas about language.) The special contributions of contemporary transformational grammarians have been more elegant and formal ways of representing the relationships between sound and meaning.

In studies of the child's acquisition of syntax, it is possible to ask at what point in the child's development one can assert that deep and surface structures are separably present. To answer this question, the researcher must have information from which the child's intended meaning can be inferred. Bloom (1970) systematically incorporated that information into her analyses of the language of three children, and her work has contributed to an important shift in our thinking.

One can begin analyzing grammatical structure when children put two words together into a single utterance. Consider utterances that in adult language terms are often Noun + Noun (N + N). Bloom found that when one of her three subjects, Kathryn, was 21 months old, N + N utterances could be interpreted with five different structural meanings (Bloom, 1970, p. 62):

(4a)   *Conjunction:* Umbrella boot (*two referents with no connection between them*).

(4b)   *Attributive:* Party hat (*the first noun is an attribute of the second*).

(4c)   *Genitive:* Kathryn sock (*possessor and possessed object*).

(4d)   *Subject-locative:* Sweater chair (*referent and place it is*).

(4e)   *Subject-object:* Cat meat (*the subject and object of an action*).

Except for the first meaning, conjunction (4a), these utterances cannot be considered simply as two aspects of a situation combined into a composite name, because order in the other four cases (4b–e) is invariant. When possession seems intended, as judged by the mother's response or the researcher's intuition, the possessor is always given first; when location seems asserted, the place is given last.

One two-word utterance spoken by Kathryn is particularly informative because the identical form, *Mommy sock*, was uttered in two different nonlinguistic contexts: (a) when Kathryn was picking up her mother's sock, and (b) when Mother was putting Kathryn's sock on Kathryn. Here are the two sections from Bloom's protocols, with her discussion.

To represent the description of a single utterance with two different meanings, Bloom gives two different structural descriptions, in tree-diagram form (Figure 1). S stands for sentence, N for noun, NP for noun phrase and VP for verb phrase. A dotted line indicates a postulated constituent that is not actually spoken—in (b), a verb.

When meaning is considered, as in Bloom's analysis, the result imputes to the child a distinction between surface structure and deep structure, as in context (b) where the presence of an unspoken verb is assumed. It can be assumed because Bloom knows that verbs occur in Kathryn's speech in other utterances with either subject or object alone. Presumably a verb is not spoken here, with both subject (*Mommy*) and object (*sock*), because of a limit on the complexity of an utterance which the child can

Table 1　　**Two Utterances of *Mommy Sock* from Kathryn I**

Description of Speech Event and Mother's Utterances	Kathryn's Utterances
(a)	
(79)　(*M holding M's sock*) Here's Mommy's dirty socks. Wash. We'll do the laundry and we'll wash 'em. We do the laundry on Thursday too.	
You help me do the laundry? (*K pointing to M's socks*)	
	Mommy sock
Yes	
	də dirty.
They're all dirty. I know.	
(b)	
(88)　(*M putting K's sock on K*)	
	Mommy sock.
There.	
	Mommy sock.
That's not Mommy's sock.	
	Kathryn sock.
That's your sock. There.	

Source:　Bloom, 1970, Table 3.5, pp. 47–48.

It should be observed that Noun + Noun constructions could be ambiguous in context as they occurred—notice that Mommy interpreted (88) *Mommy sock* as a "mistake" on Kathryn's part, which Kathryn subsequently "corrected." Mistakes are certainly plausible but not likely in this instance. The occurrence of the homonymous form in (79) *Mommy sock* and the remainder of the Noun + Noun sentences provided strong evidence that Kathryn recognized the difference in syntactic relationship in these different situations. Moreover, Kathryn seemed to have learned the possessive relationship between people and objects—she never said *Kathryn cottage cheese* or *Kathryn slipper* when looking at Mommy's cottage cheese or Mommy's slipper (Bloom, 1970, p. 55.)

construct. Discussion of the relationship between a child's linguistic knowledge and his cognitive ability will return in Chapter 3.

The ability to construct ordered sequences of words to express structural meanings rather than just composite names turns out to be a critical difference between human beings and animals. One of the most successful efforts to teach language to an animal was the Gardners' attempt to teach manual sign language to Washoe, a chimpanzee raised as a child from the age of one year (Gardner and Gardner, 1969). Washoe's signs have been compared with child language by R. Brown (1970) and Bronowski and Bellugi (1970). The following summary is taken from their accounts.

> Washoe's intellectual accomplishments are impressive. She generalized the meaning of signs beyond their original context. For example, the meaning of *more* generalized from more tickling (and other actions involving Washoe herself) to more soda (and other substances she wanted) to more acrobatics (and other events she wanted to see). She also constructed sign sequences of gradually increasing length:

> > Hurry open.
> > Listen dog.
> > Key open food.
> > You out go.

But at least up to the age of 36 months, she had shown no evidence of combining signs in particular orders to express particular structural meanings. Combinations seemed to occur in all possible orders, unrelated to the non-linguistic context. In short, Washoe had not demonstrated that she knew the difference between *Me Tickle* and *Tickle me*.

FORM AND FUNCTION

A single communicative intent can be expressed in multiple forms that may not be synonymous in their literal meaning at all. For example:

(5a)   Please turn on the lights!   (*Imperative*)

(5b)   Are the lights out?   (*Question*)

(5c)   My, it's dark in here.   (*Declarative*)

Conversely, a single sentence can express two different intents. For example, *I am hungry* would convey different meanings and therefore elicit different responses when spoken by a beggar at the door or by a child who hoped to delay bedtime (example from Hymes, 1964, p. 6).

The same word may even have different communicative functions at

Figure 1   **Tree-Diagram, Single Utterance with Two Different Meanings.**

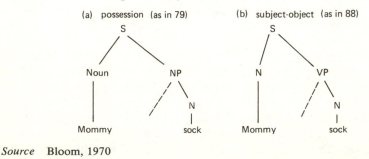

Source   Bloom, 1970

different points in a single conversation. Consider the two functions of the single question word *what* in the following conversational sequence analyzed by Speier (1969):

Child (C) is talking with his father (A):

C: Dad?
A: What?
C: At the end of all the counting there is an 8 on its side.
A: What?
C: At the end of all the counting there is an 8 on its side.
A: Where did you learn that?

Following the child's summons to obtain the adult's attention, the first *what* is understood correctly by the child as permission from the adult to proceed with the conversation. The second *what* following the child's substantive comment is understood, again correctly, as a request for repetition.

We can use the same diagrammatic form (Table 2) to show the relationships between surface and deep structures and between form and function. Both pairs express means-ends relationships.

Understanding in the full complexity diagrammed in Table 2 entails several processes. Understanding of ambiguous sentences (6) and (7) requires the use of the linguistic or nonlinguistic context to select among alternative meanings. Understanding of synonymous sentences (8) and (9) requires retrieval of the underlying meaning or communicative intent from the sentence, plus interpretation of the additional information conveyed by the particular form (a, b, or c) that the speaker has selected. In (8), that additional information consists of subtle aspects of ideas presupposed or negated. In (9), that additional information is about attitudes of politeness or sarcasm. In both cases, one form—maybe (8a) and (9a)—must be accepted as unmarked or "normal" for a particular speaker or setting; then the marked form conveys additional meaning as a deliberate contrast.

The knowledge that makes this performance as speaker or listener possible is not knowledge of language alone; in addition to linguistic rules, our tacit knowledge must include sociolinguistic rules that relate speech, and the interpretation of speech, to social variables such as sex, age, or relative rank of speaker and listeners, topic, setting, etc. (see Ervin-Tripp, 1971a and 1971b). This more inclusive knowledge is what Hymes calls "communicative competence."

We don't know at what age children learn that form and function do not correspond exactly. In the case of the two functions of *what* in Speier's protocol, it is not even clear what cue the child is responding to. Does he understand the different functions of *what* from their place in the conversational sequence? Or does he understand them from differences in stress or intonation? Spectrographic analyses of the two utterances of *what* might

Table 2 **Means-Ends Relationships in Language Structure (Syntactics) and Language Use (Pragmatics)**

	Syntactics		*Pragmatics*	
	Means, Surface structure	Ends, Deep structure	Means, Form	Ends, Function
AMBIGUITY	(6) They are eating apples.	(statement that apples are object of action, *eating*)	(7) I am hungry	(beggar's request for food)
		(identity statement about a kind of apple)		(child's attempt to delay bedtime)
SYNONYMY	(8a) The astronaut photographed the moon.		(9a) Please, turn on the lights!	
	(8b) The moon was photographed by the astronaut.		(9b) Are the lights on?	
	(8c) It was the moon that the astronaut photographed.		(9c) My, it's dark in here.	

be informative. So would an experimental situation in which intonation and place-in-sequence were pitted against each other. Imagine saying the first *what* with intonation appropriate to the second, or vice versa. Would intonation or sequence be more influential in determining the child's response?

Occasionally, in spontaneous speech, errors of commission display a child's lack of understanding of some particular form-function equivalence. In an Albany, California, kindergarten, the following interchange occurred:

Teacher to child₁ :   Speak up! No one can hear you.
Child₂ (*from the back of the room*):   I can.

At other times, teacher-talk itself calls attention to form-function disparities. One first-grade teacher in Santa Barbara, California, said *Excuse me* when children continued to talk while she was speaking to the class. It was obvious to the observer (and evidently also to the children) that her intended meaning was not a request for forgiveness, but rather a directive to be quiet.

In a classroom where one person controls the behavior of others, and where the controller may want to avoid flaunting her authority, nonimperative forms may often be used for directive intent. In being socialized to school, children thus have to learn three relationships in increasing degree of specificity: that form and function do not always correspond; that, in school, nonimperative forms frequently express a directive intent; and that particular teachers use particular form-function equivalencies and expect appropriate responses to them. We know very little about when this knowledge becomes part of children's communicative competence.

Hierarchical Structure

The rules of a language represent the ways in which an idea that is simultaneously present in the mind (meaning) becomes a sequential structure of linguistic units (sound).

> Subjectively, we seem to grasp meanings as integrated wholes, yet it is not often that we can express a whole thought by a single sound or a single word. Before they can be communicated, ideas must be analyzed and represented by sequences of symbols. To map the simultaneous complexities of thought into a sequential flow of language requires an organism with considerable power and subtlety to symbolize and process information. (Miller and Chomsky, 1963, p. 483.)

One characteristic of this "sequential flow of language" is its organization in a hierarchical, not linear, form. Try dividing sentence (1a) into progressively smaller constituent units. Just on the basis of what seems

Figure 2   **Hierarchical Structure of a Sentence.**

Sentence	The astronaut photographed the moon.							Sentence (S)
Clauses and phrases	The astronaut		photographed the moon.					Noun phrase (NP) + verb phrase (VP)
	The astronaut		photographed		the moon.			NP + verb (V) + NP
Words	The	astronaut	photographed		the	moon.		Article (ART) + Noun (N) + V + ART + N
Morphemes	The	astronaut	photograph	ed	the	moon.		ART + N + V + TENSE + ART + N

intuitively right, most English speakers would probably agree with the sequence of divisions shown in Figure 2, at least down to the last level of morphemes (the smallest meaningful units). Level of unit is given on the left, and labels used by linguists for particular units are given on the right.

The same hierarchical relationships can be depicted in three other forms. First, the familiar outline:

I. Sentence
   A. Noun phrase
      1. article: *The*
      2. noun: *astronaut*
   B. Verb phrase
      1. verb: *Photograph-*
      2. tense: *ed*
      3. noun phrase
         a. article: *the*
         b. noun: *moon*

Second, (as in transformational grammar) by a branching-tree diagram (Figure 3) in which the left branch is always the subject noun phrase and the right branch always includes the verb and the object noun phrase, if there is one;

Third (also in transformational grammar) by a set of "phrase structure" (PS) rules that specify permissible substitutes. With an arrow ($\rightarrow$) to mean "can be replaced by," the PS rules for sentence (1a) are:

$$S \rightarrow NP + VP$$
$$VP \rightarrow V + TENSE + NP$$

Figure 3   **Branching-Tree Diagram of Linguistic-Unit Relationship.**

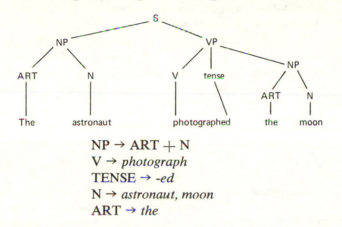

$$NP \rightarrow ART + N$$
$$V \rightarrow photograph$$
$$TENSE \rightarrow \text{-}ed$$
$$N \rightarrow astronaut, moon$$
$$ART \rightarrow the$$

Jacobs and Rosenbaum (1968) and Burt (1971) give detailed presentations of English transformational grammar.

Note that the labels on the right of Figure 2 refer to constituent types such as NPs (*the astronaut* or *the moon*) and not to grammatical relationships such as subject of verb (*the astronaut*) or object of verb (*the moon*). These two kinds of labels refer to two dimensions of structure for any unit except the smallest or largest: internal structure (what the NP consists of) and external structure (what relationships a particular NP bears to other units in the sentence).

At least during development, there is a relationship between the two dimensions. At any point in a child's development, object NPs are longer than subject NPs. A child will say sentences like *I saw that big red truck* while he is not yet saying *That big red truck is mine*. In tree-diagram terms, left-branching sentences, in which modifying words, phrases, or clauses are attached to the subject, are developmentally behind right-branching sentences, in which such modifiers are attached to the object. It may be true even for adult speakers of English that left-branching sentences are less frequent and/or somehow psychologically more complex. Maybe we share a psychological disposition to "get to the verb" as soon as possible, and tend to avoid constructions such as left-branching sentences in which the verb is delayed. This is one question that psycholinguists study.

In their analysis of the development of the noun phrase in two children called Adam and Eve, Brown and Bellugi (1964) found that child language has a hierarchical structure at an early stage. When Adam was 27 months old and Eve was 18 months old, the internal structure of their NPs consisted of an undifferentiated class of modifiers (M) plus an undifferentiated class of nouns (N). The phrase structure rule representing NPs in these children's language was

$$NP \rightarrow M + N$$

This rule describes utterances such a *a coat*; *a Becky*; *two sock*, and *my Mommy*. At that time these NPs were almost always spoken as separate utterances, not as components of larger units.

Sixteen weeks later, Brown and Bellugi found distributional reasons for separating articles and demonstrative pronouns from the modifier class. The children said *a blue flower* and *that my cup* but not *blue a flower* or *my that cup*. This differentiation could result from learning linear word order alone. But, simultaneously, Brown and Bellugi found an "integrative process" at work:

> From the first, an occasional noun phrase occurred as a component of some larger construction. At first these noun phrases were just two words long and the range of positions in which they could occur was small. With time the noun phrases grew longer, were more frequently used, and were used in a greater range of positions. The noun phrase as a whole, in all the permissible combinations of modifiers and nouns, was assuming the combinational privileges enjoyed by nouns in isolation. (Brown and Bellugi, 1964, p. 21.)

Following are examples of some of the sentence positions in which both nouns and noun phrases occurred in Adam and Eve's speech (from Brown and Bellugi, 1964, Table 8, p. 149):

Noun Positions	*Noun Phrase Positions*
That (flower)	That (a blue flower)
Where (ball) go?	Where (the puzzle) go?
Adam write (penguin)	Adam eat (the breakfast)
(Horsie) stop	(A horsie) crying
Put (hat) on	Put (the red hat) on

This kind of external structure, in which NPs are substituted by the child for Ns alone, is evidence that his language is organized in a hierarchical way.

Transformations

Relationships between surface forms and the underlying deep structure (which presumably is closer to a simple, active, declarative sentence) can be formally represented by transformational rules. According to these rules, sentence constituents are combined, interchanged, substituted, or deleted. The rules do not refer to psychological processes of speaking or understanding, as the label "transformations" implies. It is usually stated that the rules represent changes in form only and not in meaning—in other words, that meaning is determined by deep structure alone. This is true in general, but exceptions exist.

Three transformations can serve as examples: verb-particle separation, passive sentences, and indirect objects. More examples will be given in

Chapter 3. In the examples, a double-shafted arrow (⇒) in a transformational rule indicates that one structure can be transformed into another structure. This form of arrow contrasts with the single-shafted arrow (→) used in phrase structure rules in the preceding section to indicate that one constituent may be replaced by another one.

SEPARATION TRANSFORMATION

Certain verbs and their particles form a single unit of meaning, but can be separated in a sentence under certain conditions.

(10a)   Don't wake up the baby   ⇒   (10b)   Don't wake the baby up

This separation transformation is usually considered obligatory if the object of the verb is a pronoun. That is, we say *Don't wake her up,* but not *Don't wake up her*.

So, when a child in an East Boston Headstart classroom said to me about the school bus driver, *He picks up us,* I inferred that the child had not yet learned the special obligatory rule for separating particles around pronouns. A context can be imagined, however, in which one wished to stress that it was *us*, and not someone else, whom the driver picked up. With that meaning, when uttered with stress on the final word, the supposedly ungrammatical sentence would be entirely appropriate.

The Headstart child's utterance shows how stress affects meaning. Since stress is an aspect of the surface structure of a sentence, we must qualify the statement that deep structure alone determines meaning whereas surface structure changes only form. That is true under normal, unmarked conditions of stress. But when particular meanings are presupposed or negated, marked stress can affect meaning. An example used by linguists is—

(11)   When he entered the room, Mary kissed John.

Say it to yourself, stressing first *kissed* and then both *he* and *John*. Can you hear the referent of the pronoun *he* shift from *John* to some unnamed third person?

The Headstart child's utterance also points to a frequent occurrence in child language research: more than one inference about a child's language can often be made from his speech. When that happens, it is important to weigh evidence for each alternative.

In the case of separation transformations, some child language data indicate that "noun phrases with separable verbs occur in transformed [separated] position well before they occur in untransformed position" (Brown and Hanlon, 1970, p. 50). If one could refer to longitudinal records on the Headstart child's speech instead of hearing him only as a one-time visitor, it might be possible to determine whether this child had learned the separated form first. If so, then one could hypothesize that he had now learned the nonseparated option and had temporarily overgeneralized it to the one case, with pronoun objects, where it doesn't fit.

Alternatively, perhaps the child had learned all the relevant grammatical rules but had deliberately chosen to "violate" them for expressive purposes, to stress that it is *us* and not someone else whom the driver picks up. A tape recording of the utterance would show whether stress on *us* makes this inference plausible. If so, then the child's response is a sign of expressive maturity and not of grammatical immaturity at all. Teachers and researchers must often seek additional evidence before evaluating a child's language from a single utterance.

PASSIVE TRANSFORMATION

Many active sentences have passive counterparts:

(12a)   The boy chased the dog.   ⇒   (12b)   The dog was chased by
the boy.

It is easy to find out whether children understand this transformation by presenting toys and asking them to enact the meaning of passive sentences like (12b). During the preschool years, children tend to interpret any sentence, active or passive, in an agent-action-object order and ignore the extra morphemes in the passive sentence (*was, -ed,* and *by*) as irrelevant noise. They would make the boy chase the dog in response to both sentences, (12a) and (12b), thus interpreting (12a) correctly but getting (12b) wrong.

Functionally, passive sentences are one form of topicalization in English, one way of manipulating the relationship between "topic" (psychological subject) and "comment" (psychological predictate). The comment is defined contextually as new information that the speaker wishes to convey. What means are available to the speaker of English to focus the listener's (or reader's) attention on this new information? In an active sentence such as *The boy chased the dog*, more attention is naturally given to the grammatical object of the action, the dog, because it comes at the end. But what if the speaker wishes to emphasize the subject *boy* instead? Among the means available to him are the following:

(13a)   The *boy* chased the dog. *Contrastive stress*
(in oral language only)
(13b)   The dog was chased by the boy. *Passive sentence*
(13c)   It was the boy that chased the dog. *Cleft sentence*

Instead of studying the child's production or comprehension of one particular form of topicalization, such as passive sentences, one can determine instead how children of different ages accomplish the more general function.

Children's earliest utterances, such as *more* or *all gone*, have been considered as "holophrastic" or one-word sentences that are topic-comment constructions with the topic omitted (McNeill, 1970b) or topic-comment fusion (Sinclair, 1970). Later, children express both topic and comment but in variable word order: *All broken, wheel* and *Dump truck, all fixed* (Gruber, 1967). Still later, topic and comment become fixed as the grammatical subject and predicate of simple, active sentences. From this point on, development proceeds through the child's adoption of the means indicated above in sentences 13a–c for manipulating the topic-comment relationship to achieve particular communicative purposes.

To study the course of this development, Hornby and Hass (1970) presented four-year-old children with pairs of pictures that differed in three ways:

Actor: a boy or a girl riding a bicycle
Action: a man washing or driving a car
Object: a girl petting a cat or a dog

The children were asked to describe the first picture and then the second. Analysis focused on the children's descriptions of the second picture. Hornby and Hass found that these children used contrastive stress to express the new information: *The* girl *is riding the bicycle*. Furthermore, they used it most frequently (80 percent of the time) to comment on a new subject, only 56 percent of the time for a new action, and 44 percent for a new object. These percentages indicate what these four-year-old children had already learned: "By virtue of the fact, in English, that the predicate generally carries the role of comment, contrastive stress is a particularly valuable technique for drawing attention to (making a comment of) the subject" (Hornby and Hass, 1970, p. 398). In a related experiment, Hornby (1970) found that first, third, and fifth graders still used contrastive stress as the most common means of topicalization, but that transformational means increased with age.

Studying the linguistic forms through which basic language functions are achieved should be a particularly informative way of comparing child language development across different dialects of languages as well as across ages. Bruce Fraser's suggestions (Fraser and Roberts, 1969) for doing this are described in the Appendix. See Goodenough (1970) for a general discussion of the value of functions as a basis for comparison in cross-cultural research.

INDIRECT OBJECT TRANSFORMATION

Often, prepositional phrases following transitive verbs can be transformed into indirect objects:

(14a)   He gave the book to her.   →   (14b)   He gave her the book.

McNeill, Yukawa, and McNeill have studied the child's acquisition of direct and indirect objects in Japanese.

> In Japanese the direct (DO) and indirect (IO) objects of the verb are marked by postpositions [Author's note: something added at the end, in contrast to *pre*positions which come before.]. The order of the DO and IO is accordingly variable. Thus, *the turtle-ni-(IO) the fish-o-(DO) push* and *the fish-o-(DO) the turtle-ni-(IO) push* both mean "push the fish to the turtle." In contrast to English, therefore, word order in Japanese does not indicate the DO and IO; the DO as well as the IO is marked by a particle; and both the DO and IO must be marked in all sentences. (McNeill, Yukawa, and McNeill 1971, p. 238.)

Japanese sentences also differ from English because the verb must be at the end.

In order to find out how children select the DO and IO in interpreting sentences, McNeill and his coworkers made up sentences in which the order of IO, DO, and verb, and the marking of IO and DO, were systematically varied. They gave these sentences to 31 children, two to five years old, and asked them to manipulate toys according to the story. In effect, the children were expected to move the DO to touch the IO. The results are complicated, but one finding is of special interest. The 12 children who received the highest scores on the entire test performed best when only the IO was marked, next best with fully marked sentences (which are correct Japanese), and poorest when only the DO was marked.

McNeill and his associates relate this finding to two issues of theoretical interest in the study of language. First, they use the term "supernormal stimuli" to label non-Japanese sentences that elicited more correct responses than those that nature (the Japanese language) provides. This term was first used by the ethologist Niko Tinbergen in his study of the behavior of newly hatched herring gulls, who somehow know just where in their parent bill in which these characteristics were exaggerated. As he predicted, studies, Tinbergen found that the baby gull's pecking is "released" by sign stimuli that call his attention to the parent's bill. These signs are characteristics of the bill tip, such as its elongated shape, downward-pointing position, and a patch on the tip that must be red and contrast in color with the surrounding bill. Tinbergen then constructed a supernormal dummy parent bill in which these characteristics were exaggerated. As he predicted, baby gulls preferred it to a true copy of their parent. The important point is that although language is a form of communication specific to man, some of the processes involved in acquiring and using it may be vestiges of instinctive sign recognition remaining from man's evolutionary past.

The second issue raised by McNeill and his associates is the concept of primary and secondary forms. In a book first published in 1941, but translated only recently, Jakobson (1968) suggested that at all levels of linguistic structure, there are contrasting pairs of features, shared by all languages, which can be identified in three ways:

A component of this system (i.e., a part of speech, a case, a verbal category), which, with respect to some other component (another part of speech, case, or verbal category) proves to be necessarily secondary, arises in children after, disappears in aphasics before, and does not occur in the languages of the world without, the corresponding primary components. (Jakobson, 1968, p. 92.)

Both the passive-active contrast and the indirect-direct object contrast may be secondary and primary forms in this sense.

Sometimes the contrast is made explicit because the secondary form is a "marked" version of the primary form. An obvious example is plurality. To my knowledge, all languages that mark this contrast do so by marking the plural, not the singular. That is why McNeill and his colleagues' finding on the supernormality of sentences in which only IO is marked is so interesting.

Sometimes the same scheme of unmarked-marked pairs is applied to word meanings as well (Lyons, 1970, p. 17). For instance, Clark (1970) points out that pairs of adjectives in English like *long-short, deep-shallow, high-low* share an interesting characteristic: One "unmarked" member of the pair has both the general meaning of physical extension along a dimension (length, depth, height) and the particular meaning of the extended or positive end of that dimension (long, deep, high). Young children use the word correctly for the extended or positive end earlier than the word for the unextended or negative end (short, shallow, low) (Donaldson and Wales, 1970). One wonders, therefore, if Jakobson's other two criteria apply: Is the meaning for the negative end lost earlier in aphasia? And in languages around the world, do languages have a word for the negative end of a scale (short) only if they have a word for the positive end (long)?

The work of McNeill and his colleagues shows how research on the child's acquisition of one language can raise important questions about universal aspects of language and language acquisition. Some researchers suggest that what is universal about the acquisition process are certain information-processing strategies, functional characteristics of the way young minds deal with complexity in their environment; others suggest that more specific hypotheses about linguistic structure are somehow also "innate." See Brown (in press), Slobin (1969, 1970), and selections in Bar-Adon and Leopold (1971) for further discussion.

Beyond Language

In this chapter and those to come, we are talking primarily about child language. But generalizations from these ideas may extend beyond language to other aspects of cognition and to ways of deliberately planning for them in education. The new look in linguistics represented by transformational grammar has stimulated new looks at the study of human intelligence in general. Questions about such general implications will be raised throughout the book, starting here with the five main ideas of this chapter but in reverse order, that is, from most specific to most general.

TRANSFORMATIONS

Many of our concepts can be understood as examples of transformations. Consider just three examples. First, in auditory perception we have no trouble recognizing a melody across changes in pitch, as in switching from a man's voice to a woman's voice, or across shifts in musical key. Second, acquiring the concept of "conservation" in its cognitive (not ecological) meaning entails the recognition that number remains the same, despite different physical arrangements:

$$..... = ... = :: .$$

Similarly, volume remains unchanged when one cup of water is distributed among two narrow containers (in which the water level would be high) or two wide containers (in which the water level would be low). Third, in mathematics, transformational rules express the equivalence between

$$5 + 3 = 8 \quad \text{and} \quad 3 + 5 = 8 \qquad (\textit{commutative rule})$$
$$\text{or between}$$
$$5a + 5b = c \quad \text{and} \quad 5(a + b) = c \qquad (\textit{distributive rule})$$

In both cases, transformations relate the constant underlying substance to perceptually different superficial forms. Some psychologists (for example, Beilin and Spontak, 1969) are studying the relationship in a child's development between acquiring a transformation in language and in other areas of thought.

HIERARCHICAL STRUCTURE

Hierarchical structures characterize much of human behavior, not just language.

The necessity for analyzing a complex idea into its component parts has long been obvious. Less obvious, however, is the implication that any complicated activity obliges us to analyze and to postpone some parts while others are being performed. A task, X, say, is analyzed into the parts Y_1, Y_2, Y_3, which should, let us assume, be performed in that order. So Y_1 is singled out for attention while Y_2 and Y_3 are postponed. In order to accomplish Y_1, however, we find that we must analyze it into Z_1 and Z_2, and those in turn must be analyzed into still more detailed parts. . . . While one part of a total enterprise is being accomplished, other parts may remain implicit and still largely unformulated. The ability to remember the postponed parts and to return to them in an appropriate order is necessarily reserved for organisms capable of complicated information processing. Thus the kind of theorizing we have been doing for sentences can easily be generalized to even larger units of behavior. (Miller and N. Chomsky, 1963, p. 484.)

The infant's skill in grasping is later incorporated into the more complex skill of catching a ball. Scales on a musical instrument are run off as part of a larger phrase. In both cases, processes of differentiation of one unit and its integration into larger units are at work. See Lashley (1951) for one of the first discussions of hierarchical structures in behavior; and Miller, Galanter, and Pribram (1960) for applications to many kinds of problem solving.

If this is indeed the way the human mind deals with complex tasks, both in muscular skills and cognitive problems, how can we help children in their education to use their natural capacities with greater consistency and power? This question will return in Chapter 5.

LEVELS OF STRUCTURE

Does the distinction between deep and surface structure levels obtain outside of language? Here one must not overgeneralize too far. Hymes reminds us that "a level (or component) of linguistic structure is to be recognized when there appear systematically two one-many relations." Ambiguity and synonymy in Table 2 are examples of one-many relationships. Further, "It would wholly miss the point of Chomsky's linguistic theory to regard 'deep structure' as simply a more abstract set of patterns of the same sort as patterns of surface structure. The point is that the levels of structure are related by a finite system of generative principles" [Hymes, in press (a)].

Mathematics is one area of knowledge in which the concept of levels seems to fit. A student at Harvard, Pearla Nesher (1970), considered in these terms the problems encountered by children in learning mathematical language. The following analysis is taken from her work.

Of the two deep structure-surface structure relationships, ambiguity is not present in mathematical language, but synonymy is. Ambiguity does not exist because brackets are always used to make divisions into immediate constituents completely clear. For example, the English phrase *one third of some number decreased by three* is ambiguous. But the two possible mathematical sentences (15a) and (15b) are not:

(15a) $\quad\quad\quad\quad\quad\quad \frac{1}{3}X - 3$

(15b) $\quad\quad\quad\quad\quad\quad \frac{1}{3}(X - 3)$

Mrs. Nesher relates synonymy to school problems in arithmetic. Consider the following mathematical relationship (deep structure meaning), which is presented to the child as a problem in finding the missing subgroup when the whole and another subgroup are given:

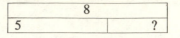

This relationship can be expressed in eight mathematical sentences:

(16a) $5 + \underline{} = 8$ (16a′) $8 = 5 + \underline{}$

(16b) $\underline{} + 5 = 8$ (16b′) $8 = \underline{} + 5$

(16c) $8 - \underline{} = 5$ (16c′) $5 = 8 - \underline{}$

(16d) $8 - 5 = \underline{}$ (16d′) $\underline{} = 8 - 5$

Each of these mathematical sentences can in turn be translated into innumerable English sentences. In five arithmetic textbooks, Mrs. Nesher found nine English sentences for mathematical sentence (16d) or (16d′).

(17a)   Five is subtracted from eight. The difference is three.

(17b)   Five less than eight is three.

(17c)   Eight decreased by five is three.

(17d)   The difference of eight and five is three.

(17e)   Three is five less than eight.

(17f)   Eight minus five is three.

(17g)   Three is five shorter than eight.

(17h)   Eight, take away five, is three.

(17i)   Remove five from eight, three are left.

The whole set of relationships can be diagramed as in Figure 4.

For the child trying to solve "word problems," however, the relationships have to be processed in a different order (Nesher, 1970):

> For the child the picture is more complicated. First he gets information in his native language. . . . In order to translate correctly the English sentences into mathematical sentences he must grasp the deep structure. Then he has to choose among the various mathematical models the one he prefers. . . . The real process for the child in school is . . . something like:

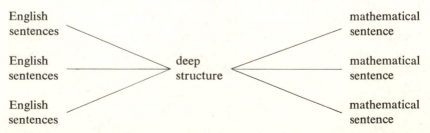

Nesher's analysis highlights two questions in arithmetic education. First, how can we best use concrete materials to express mathematical relationships (deep structure)? Second, how can we help children cope with the multiple ways these relationships are expressed in words (surface structure)?

CREATIVITY AND RULES

The notion that behavior is systematic and rule-governed suggests that children's "errors" are often important clues to child thought. Children take the problems we pose and deal with them in their own ways. Researchers and teachers either measure how well the children have learned to see the world "our" way or they try to discover how children see it for themselves. To Piaget, "errors" are an important source of information on qualitative changes in intelligence as the child's mind develops (Ginsberg and Opper, 1969). Clinchey and Rosenthal (1971) suggest how classroom teachers can learn from children's errors, too.

Finally, the creative quality of human language is one aspect of creative intelligence. N. Chomsky speaks directly to educators:

> There are strong pressures to make use of new educational technology and to design curriculum and teaching methods in the light of the latest scientific advances. In itself, this is not objectionable. It is important, nevertheless, to remain alert to a very real danger: that new knowledge and technique will define the nature of what is taught and how it is taught, rather than contributing to the realization of educational goals that are set on other grounds and in other terms. Let me be concrete. Technique and even technology is available for rapid and efficient inculcation of skilled behavior, in language teaching, teaching of arithmetic, and other domains. There is, consequently, a real temptation to reconstruct curriculum in the terms defined by the new technology. And it is not too difficult to invent a rationale, making use of the concepts of "controlling behavior," enhancing skills, and so on. Nor is it difficult to construct objective tests that are sure to demonstrate the effectiveness of such methods in reaching certain goals that are incorporated in these tests. But successes of this sort will not demonstrate that an important educational goal has been achieved. They will not demonstrate that it is important to concentrate on developing skilled behavior in the student. What little we know about human intelligence would at least suggest something quite different: that by diminishing the range and complexity of materials presented to the inquiring mind, by setting behavior

Figure 4 **Relationship Among Sentences 17a–17i.**

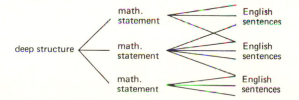

in fixed patterns, these methods may harm and distort the normal development of creative abilities (N. Chomsky, n.d., pp. 66–67).

A truly educative environment is one from which the child is most likely to
learn the regularities, patterns, or rules that make this creativity possible.
Maybe the child is such a powerful consumer that the nature of the environment matters little as long as certain ingredients are present; maybe teaching
specific primitive responses will even ultimately retard the development of
more advanced processes. See Glick (1968) and H. Werner (1937) for
further discussion.

Language is part of human cognition. As we learn more about language,
we should always consider possible implications beyond language itself.
Of course, these implications are only hypotheses that must be tested for
their more general application. The reader is encouraged to speculate about
such implications for himself as he reads the rest of this book.

3

The Acquisition of Syntax

This chapter, the first of three on language development, discusses the acquisition of syntax. Chapter 4 is about the acquisition of the system of language sounds and meaning, and Chapter 5 is about more general aspects of the dimensions and processes of language development as a whole.

Proceeding in this way has two disadvantages. First, it starts with one part of what must eventually be understood as an integrated whole: a child learning to control all aspects of language for private expression and social communication. Second, syntax—the first part to be discussed—is in one sense least important in education. It seems to be the aspect of communicative adequacy that develops with least deliberate attention. Why then, not start with the development of meaning, or of particular communicative skills? The answer is simple: we have more sure knowledge about the development of syntax. So we start here, hoping to tell the story in such a way that from a detailed description of the development of a few syntactic elements the reader can start thinking about characteristics of the whole.

It may help the reader to be aware of some themes presented in Chapter 5, on dimensions and processes of development. "Dimensions" refer to the systematic deviations of child language from the adult model, the simultaneity of differentiation and integration at work, increasing freedom from control by (or dependence on) the immediate context, and the "metalinguistic" ability to reflect on language as well as use it. "Processes" include the roles of imitation and practice, and interactions between language and more general cognitive abilities. These themes can serve the reader as mental organizers of some of the details in this chapter and Chapter 4.

Because syntax is the focus of most recent research on child language development, there is now so much to say that it is hard to know how best to tell the story. A monograph published by the Society for Research in Child Development (Bellugi and Brown, 1964) reports a conference held in 1961 at which early data from contemporary studies were critiqued by Chomsky, Hymes, and others. Since then, excellent reviews have been written by Ervin-Tripp (1966, the most complete); John and Moskovitz

(1970, which includes a review of early childhood language programs); and McNeill (1970b, the most theoretical). Bar-Adon and Leopold (1971) have assembled an excellent book of readings that complement both this chapter and Chapter 4. This chapter focuses more narrowly and does not attempt to supplant these sources. It concentrates on only two elements of syntax: noun and verb inflectives, and questions.

Inflections are a part of morphology—the rules for combining meaningful units, called morphemes, into words. Inflections are "bound" morphemes that cannot occur alone but must be attached to "free" morphemes like nouns and verbs. They serve either to "modulate the meaning" of a word, in Brown's (in press) felicitous phrase, as with the plural -*s* or past tense -*ed*, or to encode relationships between two words, as with the possessive -*s*. These same meanings can, of course, be expressed in other ways—by numerical adjectives for plurality, by adverbs like *yesterday* for past tense, and by the preposition *of* for possession.

Questions, by contrast, are a part of syntax proper—the rules for combining words into sentences—in this case so as to serve a specific communicative function. Sometimes the acquisition of morphology and syntax together are termed "the acquisition of grammar." In this book, use of the term "grammar" is restricted to the descriptions that linguists write, and the term "syntax" is applied to what children learn.

Most of the data on the development of inflections and questions presented in this chapter were obtained from one study of three children— Adam, Eve, and Sarah—who were the subjects of a longitudinal study at Harvard by a group centering around Roger Brown. When the study was started, Adam's and Eve's fathers were graduate students at Harvard; Sarah's father was a clerk in a local supermarket, and neither of her parents had gone beyond high school. We worked from typed transcriptions of tape recordings of spontaneous parent-child conversation made weekly (for Sarah) or biweekly (for Adam and Eve) in each child's home. The primary goal of the project was a description of the course of language acquisition. Secondarily, we sought hypotheses about underlying developmental processes.

Figure 1 gives a small-scale view of the language development of the three children for the period discussed here. The horizontal axis is age. The vertical axis is mean length of utterance in morphemes (MLU). Roman numerals on the graph indicate five points in the developmental continuum at which Brown (in press) wrote grammars to describe the children's language. In addition, we tracked some features of the three language systems throughout the entire period, including the acquisitions of five nouns and verb inflections (Cazden, 1968a) and the development of question forms [e.g., Bellugi (1965) and Brown (1968)]. The letters A–D in Figure 1 are stages that Bellugi identified in her analyses.

Figure 1 **Mean Utterance Length and Age in Three Children.**

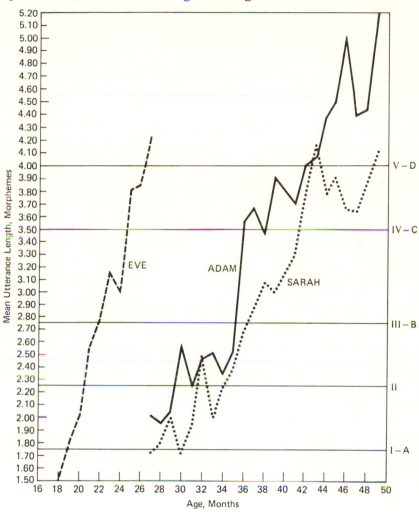

Inflections

In the research on Adam, Eve, and Sarah's language development, inflections were selected for intensive analysis more for methodological than linguistic reasons. When analyses of language development are based on a corpus of spontaneous speech, the researcher must question the representativeness of his corpus. If a particular construction does not appear in a certain transcription of the child's speech, is it missing from the child's linguistic competence or only from this sample of his performance?

One way to separate the absence of a construction in the child's competence from the rarity of that construction in his performance is to look for the frequency of forms in contexts that make them obligatory. Each of these contexts in the child's speech can be considered a learning trial, and we can compute the proportion of times in which the child performs appropriately as that proportion changes over time. For such analyses, one needs features for which clearly defined contexts exist even in the telegraphic speech of young children. Noun and verb inflections fit this criterion well.

First, the course of development of five inflections will be charted:

> On nouns
> > *Plural*: two dog*s*.
> > *Possessive*: Mommy*'s* hat.
> On verbs
> > *Present progressive*: I'm go*ing*.
> > *Past* (*regular*): He walk*ed*; (*irregular*) He *rode*.
> > *Third person present indicative*: He look*s*.

Then individual differences in development will be discussed. Finally, a way of categorizing errors will be suggested.

THE DEVELOPMENTAL SEQUENCE

To begin with, criteria had to be established for asserting that each inflection was required. Following are the criteria for plurality, with examples of omitted inflections from the three children's speech.

Number (required after all numbers except 1): *Two minute.*

Linguistic (required on count nouns after such modifiers as *more* or *some*): *More page.*

Interaction (required for discourse agreement): *Shoe* in response to mother's question, *What are those?*

Plural referent: *Put my slipper on*, uttered just after child had taken off both slippers.

Expansion: Child's singular morpheme expanded to plural by mother as her interpretation of child's meaning: *Lion* followed by mother's response, *The lions, yeah.*

Imitation (child presumably attempting an imitation of preceding parent word, which was pluralized): *Shoe?* immediately following mother's utterance *Shoes.*

Normally plural: *stair* ("upstairs").

Routines: either public, like nursery rhymes and the names of TV cartoon characters: *Mr. Ear* ("Mr. Ears"); or private, like Eve's version of her mother's often-repeated explanation of father's work: *Make penny Ema' Hall* ("He's making pennies in Emerson Hall.").

Comparable criteria were established for the other inflections. Any one criterion was considered sufficient, but multiple coding was frequently necessary.

The entire set of transcriptions from I and V was used. On the preceding criteria, inflections were coded as supplied correctly when required (S_c), supplied in inappropriate contexts (S_x), or required but omitted (O). Overgeneralizations in form (OG)—*Somes* or *I seed it*—were also coded. In some analyses the relations between S_c, S_x, and O were charted as they changed over time. In other analyses a point was established at which a certain inflection could be said to have been acquired. Those points were then compared within each child's language system and across the set of three subjects. Point of acquisition was defined as the first transcription of three, such that in all three the inflection was supplied in at least 90 percent of the contexts in which it was clearly required.

Noun Inflections

Of the two noun inflections, plurals reached the point of acquisition before possessives in Adam's and Sarah's speech. In Eve's speech, they reached the criterion for acquisition at the same time, suggesting that for Eve the limiting factor may have been a pronunciation difficulty with final *s*.

Table 1 summarizes data on the acquisition of plurals by the three children. The fourth column gives the ratio of S_c to the total required; the fifth and sixth columns give the ratios of S_x and OG to the total supplied. The first two rows for Eve thus read as follows: at 18–19 months, which include I on the graph, Eve used no plurals. At 20–22 months, which include II, she used them 15 percent of the time they were required, with no errors and no overgeneralizations.

In Table 1 the development continuum for each child has been broken at three places to yield four periods. These have been labeled W, X, Y, and Z to avoid confusion with A, B, C, and D in Figure 1. Period W is defined by the absence of the inflection. Adam and Sarah had gone beyond this point when our research began. Period X is defined by occasional production with no errors or overgeneralizations. This period is present in all three children's development. In period Y, production increases markedly, and errors and overgeneralizations appear. Finally, in period Z, the inflection attains the arbitrary criterion of 90 percent correct use.

These three divisions do not have the same status. The break between Y and Z is clearly arbitrary. The meaning of the break between W and X, signaling the onset of the inflection, is unclear. But the break between X and Y represents a significant developmental phenomenon, because systematic errors and overgeneralizations provide convincing evidence that the child has a productive rule. Werner (1957) differentiated between quantitative change (no matter how abrupt) in the frequency of some behavior

Table 1 Periods in the Development of the Plural Inflection

Period	Age, Months	Point(s), Fig. 1	$S_c/(S_c + O)$	$S_x/(S_x + S_c)$	$OG/(S_x + S_c)$
			EVE		
W	18–19	I	0.00	0.00	0.00
X	20–22	II	0.15 (14/(14 + 78))	0.00	0.00
Y	23–24	III	0.86 (136/(136 + 22))	0.07 (10/(10 + 136))	0.05 (8/146)
Z	25–27	IV–V	0.98 (217/(217 + 4))	0.005 (1/(1 + 217))	0.03 (7/218)
			ADAM		
W	...	...	...	...	0.00
X	27–29	I–II	0.36 (32/(32 + 57))	0.00	0.00
Y	30–32	...	0.68 (142/(142 + 67))	0.15 (25/(25 + 142))	0.01 (2/167)
Z	33–42	III–V	0.94 (927/(927 + 58))	0.06 (54/(54 + 927))	0.04 (40/981)
			SARAH		
W	...	...	...	...	0.00
X	27–30	I	0.13 (11/(11 + 74))	0.00	0.00
Y	31–33	...	0.86 (124/(124 + 21))	0.03 (4/(4 + 124))	0.00
Z	34–49	II–V	0.98 (722/(722 + 12))	0.04 (28/(28 + 722))	0.03 (23/750)

and qualitative change. Later, he described the "de-differentiation (dissolution) of existing, schematized or automatized behavior patterns" (1957, p. 139) as one of the processes by which simple behavior is reconstructed into more complex behavior. Such a dissolution of existing behavior patterns seems to be taking place in the qualitative break between periods X and Y.

Tables 2 and 3 give finer details of two developmental patterns and, correspondingly, more striking examples of regularities across the three children. Table 2 shows an enlarged close-up of one subset of plurals, those required on linguistic criteria. The linguistic criteria can be divided into requirements that are contained within the noun phrase and requirements that extend across the noun-phrase boundary. For example, in the noun phrase *some crayons*, *crayons* must be pluralized because it is a count noun following *some*. That is a requirement within the noun phrase. In *Those my crayons*, however, *crayons* must be pluralized because it is a predicate nominative, which must agree with the subject *those*. Here the requirement extends across the noun-phrase boundary. With striking consistency, the three children temporarily supplied the plural correctly when the requirement was within the noun phrase more often than when the requirement extended across the noun-phrase boundary. These data suggest that one aspect of language development is the extension of linguistic dependency relations across larger units in the hierarchical structure (across greater distances in tree diagrams).

Because plurals, possessives, and third-person-singular verbs all take the same inflectional ending (*-s*), sequence of acquisition within this set of three must be based on factors other than pronunciation. Jakobson (lecture, Feb. 29, 1968) suggested that, on the basis of structural distance or level of unit in the hierarchical structure of a sentence, linguists with no knowledge of developmental research would predict the following order of acquisition by children: plurals (which need not depend on any linguistic context); then possessives (which depend on a word within the same phrase); and lastly verb endings (which depend on words within a larger unit, the clause). This sequence fits our findings (see Fig. 2, p. 36). It also fits the results of the Berko (1958) type of test in which children are asked to supply inflectional endings for nonsense syllables.

Table 2 **Provision of Plural Inflection in Two Linguistic Contexts**

	Age, Months	*Within Noun Phrase*	*Across Noun-Phrase Boundary*
Eve	18–27	0.89 (48/54)	0.30 (3/10)
Adam	27–42	0.77 (124/162)	0.43 (26/61)
Sarah	27–49	0.83 (67/81)	0.54 (12/22)

Figure 2　**Comparison of Acquisition of Inflections in Terms of Age in Months.**

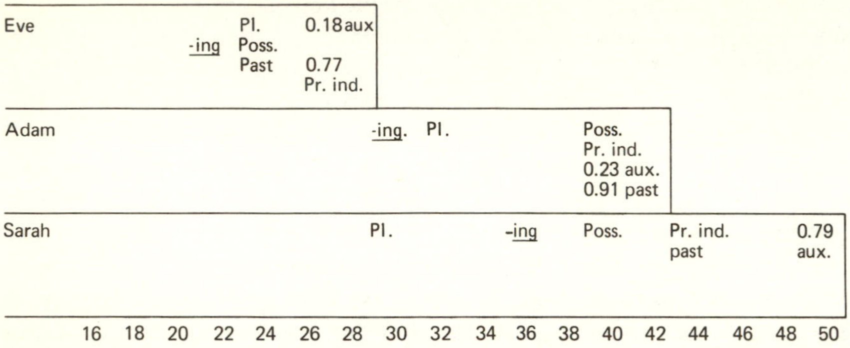

```
Eve                    Pl.    0.18 aux
              -ing   Poss.
                     Past   0.77
                            Pr. ind.

Adam                             -ing.  Pl.          Poss.
                                                     Pr. ind.
                                                     0.23 aux.
                                                     0.91 past

Sarah                       Pl.        -ing   Poss.   Pr. ind.    0.79
                                                      past        aux.

        16  18  20  22  24  26  28  30  32  34  36  38  40  42  44  46  48  50
```

A related but simpler hypothesis was not confirmed by our data. Because a child's programming span is limited, it seemed possible that, during the learning period, the utterances that included plurals would be on the average shorter (not counting the plural morpheme itself) than their counterparts with plurals omitted. Supporting examples were found of isolated noun phrases that included plurals and noun phrases in longer utterances that did not. But computation of mean length showed no clear pattern across the three children. The hypothesis suggested by Table 2 still assumes a limit on programming span, but it does not assume that the limit is on the accretion of morphemes of equal unit, like beads on a string. Rather, it assumes that morphemes have differential cognitive weight depending on structural complexity.

In Table 3, the evidence shifts from plurals to possessives. Here we find another regularity in the contexts in which an inflection first appears. The normal form for expressing possession is noun plus possessive inflection plus noun: *That's Daddy's hat.* In the alternative elliptic form, the final noun is deleted: *That's Daddy's.* Table 3 shows that for the period up to the criterion of 90 percent accuracy, all three children were more apt to supply the possessive inflection in the elliptic context.

The data are particularly clear on this point for Sarah because of a conversational routine that served to test Sarah's use of the possessive in-

Table 3　**Provision of Possessive Inflection in Two Linguistic Contexts**

	Age, Months	*With Noun*	*Elliptic*	*OG*
Eve	18–24	0.07 (9/138)	0.69 (11/16)	5
Adam	27–33	0.16 (21/130)	0.86 (37/43)	36
Sarah	27–39	0.06 (2/33)	1.00 (8/8)	2

flection at intervals. Sarah's mother frequently asked *Whose girl are you*, to which Sarah was supposed to reply *Mommy's girl*. The first time she answered correctly was at 38 months. Before that we found the following:

Only one instance of possessive inflection plus noun, and that's an imitation of her mother's preceding utterance

10 instances of the routine answer *Mommy girl*

21 other instances of omitted inflection, all with final noun

8 instances of inflection supplied, all elliptic

2 (the only two) instances of overgeneralizations: *Where mines* and *I drink hims*

This finding is particularly interesting because the three mothers used the normal form 7 to 20 times as often as the elliptic form. The proportion of elliptic to all possessives in a sample of 2800 utterances from each mother is: Eve's mother, 3 of 62; Adam's mother, 3 of 37; Sarah's mother, 7 of 50. Two possible reasons for this discrepancy between what the children hear and what they produce are confounded. First, even though the children hear the elliptic form much less frequently, the inflection may be more noticeable in that context. Second, the elliptic form is less redundant and more critical to meaning. The relative importance for unambiguous communication was shown by a remark of Sarah's after a trip to get an ice cream cone. She told her mother *I shared Daddy's*. Only the inflection signifies that it was the ice cream cone and not Daddy that was divided up.

Verb Inflections

In the analysis of verb inflections, numerous decisions had to be made about what to include and exclude. For example, the *-ing* form was counted only when it was attached to the main verb in the child's utterance. Not counted were gerunds, where a verbal form is used as a noun (as in *Stop crying*), or present participles where they are used as an adjective (as in *camping trip*). *Got* was excluded entirely because its past status is uncertain, and its colloquial uses make syntactic interpretation difficult. Often, the child used an unmarked verb for which some inflection was clearly required. But unless it was also clear which particular inflection had been omitted, these cases were not included. The appearance of *be* auxiliary forms with the present progressive (*I'm going* or *we're playing*) was added to the analysis because the required contexts were clear and errors of interpretation therefore unlikely.

Despite these simplifications, the findings on verb inflections are fragmentary, perhaps because the verb system is generally one of the most complicated parts of English grammar. There is no one-to-one relation between linguistic forms and temporal reference, and so application of requirement criteria probably produces more wrong interpretations with verb inflections than with nouns. For example, we can say *Tomorrow we'll go to the movies*, or just *Tomorrow we go to the movies*. Furthermore, verb inflections cannot be easily separated from the complex system of English auxiliaries. For example, the past and present indicative inflections appear only in declarative sentences. In both questions and negatives, the markers for tense and person shift to the dummy auxiliary *do*:

He walked.	*Did he walk?*	*He didn't walk.*
He walks.	*Does he walk?*	*He doesn't walk.*

Parenthetically, note that the relation of verb inflections to the auxiliary system complicates the child's learning as well as the researcher's analysis. Sometimes, an adult model is not helpful:

Mother:	Did you write it already?
Child:	Write already.

And sometimes the parent's utterance even leads to regression in the child:

Child:	Because I caught . . .
Mother:	What did you catch?
Child:	I catch my bicycle.

To the extent that the child's learning is helped by adult speech that precedes as a model or follows as an expansion, the past and present indicative inflections pose special problems. Parent speech uttered with identical intent cannot provide the same assistance as it may for other constructions.

Of the three verb inflections, the present progressive appeared first in all three children, reaching criterion between points II and III (Figure 1). The sequence of acquisition for regular past and present indicative was less consistent. At point V, Sarah had attained the criterion of 90 percent accuracy on both, Eve had attained only the past, and Adam only the present indicative. None of the children had attained the 90 percent criterion on the auxiliary by point V. The percentages of auxiliaries supplied in the final three transcriptions ranged from 0.18 for Eve to 0.79 for Sarah. Eve supplied auxiliaries in questions first, but this seems to be an idiosyncratic phenomenon. Adam was more apt to include them in declaratives, and Sarah showed no tendency either way.

Adam and Sarah both occasionally used a form of *be* without *ing*, while Eve did not. These utterances seem to have different structural descriptions in the two children's language. In Sarah's speech there were nine instances, all containing *I'm* plus verb, such as *I'm play with it* and *I'm twist his head*. These constructions are probably reduced catenatives ("I'm going to play with it"), conveying intention rather than referring to ongoing action. The same form appeared in the speech of lower-class Black children in Roxbury (Cazden, 1965). In Adam's speech, only one utterance was counted as auxiliary without *ing*: *Dey are stand up*. But there were many instances of *Its* plus verb: like *Its go up* and *Its went away*. Brown, Cazden, and Bellugi (1969), analyzed Adam's use of *its* as a temporary segmentation error that led him to consider *its* as a variant of *it* in subject position, presumably because in his mother's speech *it* was followed much more often by *is* than by a main verb.

INDIVIDUAL DIFFERENCES IN RATE OF ACQUISITION

Any comparison of developmental phenomena across children requires a metric for that comparison. The conventional metric is chronological age (CA). Because Adam, Eve, and Sarah were equated at five points on MLU, comparison on this basis is also possible. The three children's acquisition of inflections have been analyzed on both cases of comparison. Holding CA or MLU constant in this research is comparable to holding CA or mental age (MA) constant in studies of intellectual development. Like MA, MLU is a single global measure. Equating children on such a measure yields additional information on the relative development of more specific abilities.

Figure 2 and Table 4 compare the three children's rate of acquisition on the basis of CA and MLU. When we compare the children on CA in Figure 2, the order of development is clear: Eve far ahead, Adam second, and Sarah third. This is what one would expect from Figure 1. But if age is ignored, the order changes, as shown in Table 4. By point II, when all three children had an MLU of 2.25, only Sarah had achieved criterion on one of the inflections (plurality); by IV, when all three children had an MLU of 3.50, she had five inflections, Eve had four, and Adam only two. Where criterion was not reached by V, the percentage of supplied inflections to total required is given in the last column. Note the much higher percentage for Sarah's auxiliaries with the present progressive.

An earlier paper (Cazden, 1968) reported that Sarah acquired plurals

Table 4 **Comparison of Acquisition of Inflections on Basis of MLU**

	I	II	III	IV	V
Eve	...	...	*ing*	Plural Poss. Past	0.77 pres. indic. 0.18 aux.
Adam	...	...	Plural *ing*	...	Poss. Pres. indic. 0.91 past 0.23 aux.
Sarah	...	Plural	*ing*	Poss. Past Pres. indic.	0.79 aux.

before Eve and Adam (in terms of MLU) and suggested a relationship to the higher density of plurals in her mother's speech. With later evidence, this suggestion must be amended. The relative advancement of Sarah at particular MLU values is not restricted to plurality.

Several additional pieces of evidence are now available on the relative syntactic knowledge of the three children when MLU is held constant. Bellugi (in press) found that the auxiliary verb system developed earlier in Sarah (before point IV) than in Eve and Adam (at point IV). She also found that, of the three children, only Sarah used tag questions (*Now you can see, can't you?*) by point V. "Tag questions are of particular interest in the language acquisition process, since they involve knowledge of a good deal of [grammatical] apparatus . . . and very little meaning" (Bellugi, in press). Brown and Hanlon (1970) studied the development of negatives, questions, and truncated utterances (*We did.*). They report that ". . . in respect to the sentence types with which we are concerned, she [Sarah] was ahead of the others relative to the mean length of utterance . . . Sarah's age tells, and she knows more relative to the length of her sentences than do the other children" (Brown and Hanlon, 1970, p. 33).

Finally, Brown tabulated the presence and absence of required functors at points I and V. Functors include inflections and also articles, prepositions, etc.—everything except content words (nouns, verbs, adjectives, and adverbs). At both points, Sarah supplied required functors a higher proportion of the time than did Adam and Eve. At V, the percentage of functors still missing was: Eve, 0.33; Adam, 0.26; and Sarah, 0.21 (Brown, in press).

In interpreting this evidence, consider only the two extremes, Eve and Sarah. If, at a particular MLU value, Sarah supplies more required functors, then Eve's speech contains proportionately more content words. An abnormal proportion of content words to functors characterizes what we call telegraphic speech (Brown and Bellugi, 1964), used by adults in note taking and telegrams (*Arrive Saturday* instead of *I will arrive on Saturday*), and generally by young children. It is a highly informative language, since functors can be guessed from context whereas content words cannot. Eve thus conveys more information for the same overall mean utterance length than Sarah does. Her utterances are a more telegraphic version of a more informative and less predictable utterance, whereas Sarah's utterances are a less telegraphic version of a less informative and more predictable utterance.

These two patterns can be labeled "macro" development and "micro" development, respectively. Macrodevelopment refers to the elaborateness of the semantic intention or plan for speaking; microdevelopment refers to the successful execution of whatever plan has been formulated. They represent relative advance in more cognitive or more strictly grammatical aspects of the total acquisition process. Evidently, synchronization of the two aspects can vary in ways that are masked by the global measure of mean length of utterance. Eve had undoubtedly caught up in the provision of functors by the time she reached Sarah's age, probably long before. But Sarah was less behind in the provision of functors than in what she was trying to say.

Alternatively, and perhaps more simply, prediction of level of language development on the basis of MLU, a measure of performance, may have underestimated Sarah's linguistic knowledge. Perhaps communication patterns in her home provided less stimulation for Sarah to use whatever linguistic knowledge she had acquired. If so, this would help explain the interesting differences in the straightness of the lines for Eve and Sarah in Figure 1. If we think in figure-ground terms again, Eve's straighter line can be interpreted as a stronger "figure" of developmental change in language knowledge, while the more zigzag line for Sarah can be interpreted as a noisier "ground" of other influences on her speech behavior. Eve may have been more consistently stimulated to use everything she knew about language structure, while Sarah was only intermittently stimulated to operate at her full capacity.

Further evidence of individual differences appears in later pages. While much current research is concentrated on discovering similarities across children and even across languages, individual differences in learning strategies, as well as in rates of success, must eventually become part of a complete picture. Nelson (1971) provides a comparison of two children. But generally in research, as in education, they are still too little understood.

INFLECTIONAL ERRORS

The foregoing analyses have been based on errors of omission, on utterances in which inflections were required but not supplied. The systematic errors of commission which children make are also guides to their linguistic knowledge.

In order to compare these errors in a larger and more varied group of children, the data of Adam, Eve, and Sarah have been supplemented by data on 11 lower-class Black children in Boston. These children were the subjects of an experiment (Cazden, 1965) to determine the effect of adult-child conversation patterns on the child's acquisition of syntax. That experiment will be described in detail in Chapter 6, but data on the Black children's inflections are included here because there are still few descriptions of the language of young lower-class children. The development of inflections of these children could not be charted as it was for Adam, Eve, and Sarah because their speech was tape recorded only at the beginning, middle, and end of a three-month period, but since even a single error can be informative, their errors are included here.

Of the 12 children, 11 (9 girls and 2 boys) fall within both the age and MLU range for Adam, Eve, and Sarah. During the experiment, their ages ranged from 28–41 months, and their MLU ranged from 2.29–3.86 morphemes. One boy, 33 months old, had an MLU above 4.0 morphemes, and so is excluded from this analysis. His language is of special interest for other reasons, and will be discussed in Chapter 8.

Figure 3   **Mean Utterance Length and Age in 15 Children.**

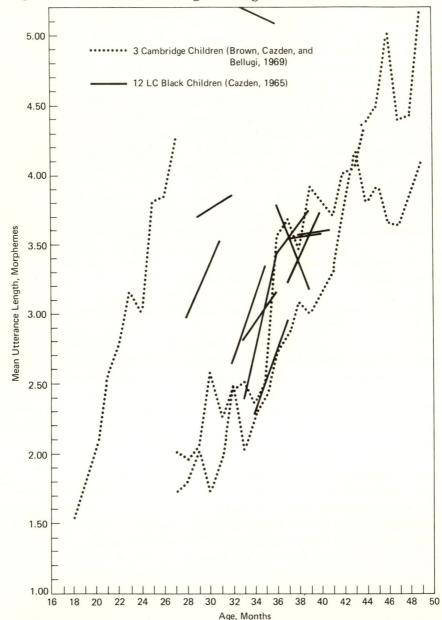

While the MLU was computed by different investigators for the two groups, the rules for computing it were very similar (described in the Appendix). In Figure 3, these 12 children have been added to the graph for Adam, Eve, and Sarah given in Figure 1.

One way to categorize inappropriate inflections is to look at noun and verb inflections separately, and further subdivide each set according to the rule being overgeneralized. This is done in Table 5.

Another way to categorize the errors is to start with the levels of N. Chomsky's (1965) grammar and fit to them the rules that the children violate. The levels constitute subsets of rules, parts of the adult speaker's knowledge of his language. The syntactic component of the grammar has four levels: phrase structure rules (described in Chapter 2), lexical subcategorization rules, transformational rules, and morphophonemic rules. Inappropriate inflections fall into the last three categories and these will be discussed in turn. Table 6 gives frequencies by level for the two groups of children. All of the overgeneralizations in Table 5 are included in Table 6, plus other errors that occur in the construction of sentences (syntax) rather than in the formation of words (morphology). Occasionally, errors that do not involve regular inflections are discussed, but they are not included in Table 6. The many aspects of number agreement, a complicated source of error, are not included at all.

Subcategorization Rules

According to N. Chomsky, each word in a person's lexicon or mental dictionary has a set of tags or syntactic features that govern the slots in the phrase structure in which that word can be placed (strict subcategorization rules), and the words in other slots with which it can co-occur (selectional rules). For example, the noun *boy* is a count noun (and so can be pluralized), a common noun (and so can be preceded by an article), and a human noun (and so can be the object of a verb like *frighten*). When a word enters a child's lexicon, it does not enter with the full set of syntactic features correctly attached. Vocabulary development in children involves both acquisition of new words and addition of new features (with their restrictive implications) to words already learned. Morphological overgeneralizations, or more accurately "underdifferentiations," can serve as tracers to linguistic categories that are still immaturely formed.

The first major division among words in a child's lexicon is the division into parts of speech: noun, verb, etc. Children so rarely violate these boundaries that we may fail to notice how easy this learning seems to be, despite ever-present opportunity for error. While noun and verb inflections are being learned, one would expect children to add them to words that are not nouns and verbs. Instances of such errors are rare, and where they do occur other interpretations are possible. In Table 6, three tokens of plural inflections were added to adjectives. This would be appropriate in

Table 5 **Overgeneralizations of Noun and Verb Inflections**

Inflections	Eve	Adam	Sarah	Lower-class Black Children (11)
A. PLURAL INFLECTIONS				
Nouns with no plural form	peoples sheeps	deers peoples reindeers	deers fishes reindeers	reindeers
Nouns with irregular plural	mans snowmans	firemans mans milkmans	childs knifes toothes	
Pluralizing irregular pls.	mens	feets firemens mens	feets teeths	
double plurals		auntses schoolses	pantses	sockses toeses toyses
Mass nouns		coffees dirts honeys ketchups milks moneys sugars	knittings milks	breads coffees
Words used as pronouns	somes twos manys	somes threes twos	thems	somes twos
Words used as adjectives		greens slipperys	pinks	
B. POSSESSIVE INFLECTIONS				
	mines	mines	mines hims	mines hes

Table 5 (*Continued*)

C. VERB INFLECTIONS

-ing	seeing(?)	having(?)		
-ed, added to verb having irreg. past	comed	falled	comed	doed
	doed	feeled	goed	falled
	drinked	growed	growed	flyed
	falled	maked	heared	maked
	goed	taked	hurted	
	seed	throwed	maked	
	throwed	waked up	runned	
	weared		swimmed	
			taked	
			throwed	
			waked up	
			winned	
-ed, added to irreg. past	tored	broked	caughted	
		felled	flewed	
Third-person singular, -s		doos	stand ups	doos
		fells		
		gots		
		wents		

French but not in English unless the adjective is functioning as a noun. Color names can function that way, and *greens* could correctly refer to crayons or vegetables. The only instance of a misplaced verb inflection is *Stand ups*. Because violations of part-of-speech boundaries were just as rare in Miller and Ervin's (1964) records, it is all the more curious that one of their subjects, Susan, added a past to the same verb phrase: *stand up-ed*. A segmentation error may make *stand up* a single unit to the child. Or the adverbs of separable verbs may tend to take on a verbal force. At an earlier stage, Susan used *off* and *on* as verbs, and one of the Roxbury children used *off* twice as a verb: *I can't off that*.

In the subcategorization of nouns and verbs, four kinds of rule violations occurred. Plurals were extended to pronouns (a subdivision of nouns, complementing common nouns and proper nouns) like *somes,* and to mass nouns like *sugars.* There were five instances of a possible violation of the process-status distinction among verbs, all with *seeing* or *having* as in *I seeing Fraser*. These are verbs to which *-ing* can be added with some meaning but not others: *I'm having lunch,* but not *I'm having a dress on.* There were no overgeneralizations to status verbs that can never take *ing*, not even to verbs of high frequency in the children's speech like *want* or

Table 6 **Inflectional Errors in Two Groups of Children**

INFLECTIONS	Group 1*		Group 2†		EXAMPLES
	NO. OF CHILDREN	NO. OF TOKENS	NO. OF CHILDREN	NO. OF TOKENS	
Parts of speech:					
Adjectives	2	3	0	0	*Dat greens.*
Adverbs	1	1	1	1	*Look how she stand ups.*
Noun and verb subcategories:					
Noun: mass-count	2	11	2	6	*Going put some sugars.*
Noun: pronoun	3	10	2	2	*Let me have somes.*
Verb: process-status	2	5	0	0	*I seeing Fraser.*
Verb: transitive-intransitive	1	1	0	0	*I falled that down.*
Transformational Rules					
Wh question	3	5	1	3	*It doing dancing.*
No. and tense markers in question and negation	3	15	0	0	*Does it works?* / *I didn't spilled it.*
Compound nouns	1	3	0	0	*Streets lights.*
Morphophonemic Rules					
Wrong allomorph	2‡	5‡	1‡	1‡	*You pull my pantses down.*
Regular-irregular:					
Plural	3	32	1	1	*Two mans.*
Possessive	3	43	1	1	*Where mines?*
Present indicative	1	4	6	6	*The milkman doos*
Past	3	50	4	7	*Why Paul waked up?*

* Adam, Eve, and Sarah.

† Eleven lower-class Black children.

‡ Only inappropriate provision of /ɪz/ allomorphs included

know. (In British English the rules are different; in England and Scotland one frequently hears *wanting* and *needing* as in *If you get a skirt, you'll be needing a sweater to go with it,* or, in the words of Eliza Doolittle's father, *I'm willing to tell you, I'm waiting to tell you, I'm wanting to tell you.*)

Finally, there was one instance of an intransitive verb used transitively: *I falled that down.* In this case, the inflectional error itself belongs in the morphophonemic category below, but the presence of the inflection confirms the structural analysis of the utterance. Three Roxbury children also used *fall* as a transitive verb, as in *I don't wanna fall him.* But without the inflection, someone could make the (far-fetched) claim that the utterance was a telegraphic reduction of *I don't wanna make him fall* with the order also wrong. We do *fell* trees, but the children use *fall,* and it's unlikely they know about lumbering operations anyway. Of these four subcategorization errors, violation of the mass-count subcategorization of nouns is the most common. Why it should be more difficult for children to learn than the process-status division among verbs is unclear.

Transformational Rules

Inappropriate inflections can result from missing or inadequate transformational rules that govern the permutation and deletion of linguistic units. First, the rules for answering Wh-questions are overgeneralized to the one kind of question where the rules don't work: *What is X doing?* or *What is happening (going on,* etc.)? While a complete answer to *What is he eating?* is *He is eating candy,* the answer to *What is it doing?* is not *It doing dancing.* But that is the kind of answer given by four of the children. Second, failure to shift inflections for number (in the present indicative) or tense (in the past) to the auxiliary verbs in questions and negatives produces utterances like *Does it works?* and *I didn't spilled it.* One Roxbury child provided two additional examples with irregular inflections: *I didn't took him.* Third, Adam's utterance *Streets lights* may represent violation of the rules for forming compound nouns.

Morphophonemic Rules

Morphophonemic rules govern pronunciation. Two kinds of violations occur: first, provision of the wrong form of the plural morpheme—*knife-es* or *toyses*; second, failure to observe the division between regular and irregular forms of the plural (*mans*), possessive (*mines*), present indicative (*doos*), and past (*maked*). *Mines* is a particularly understandable error. All the other possessive pronouns end in -*s* (*ours, yours, his, ours,* and *theirs*)—why not *mines*? Presumably children make so many errors with these irregular forms because the division between the regular and irregular forms is an arbitrary one, and so rote learning is required for each one.

In general, analyses of children's errors are an important source of insight into their language development. But the particular analyses offered here must be considered only a first approximation. Any categorization of errors necessarily involves some basis for grouping a list into categories. How much any particular categorization scheme contributes to our understanding depends on the validity of the scheme on both psychological and linguistic grounds. Transformational grammar is itself a subject of continuing controversy and development. But even if it were stabilized, questions about the psychological reality of a linguistic construct like "levels of the grammar" would remain. Such questions are important topics in current psycholinguistic research.

Two final comments on similarities among the two groups of children and differences among individual children: The overgeneralizations made by the two groups are strikingly similar in kind, though not of course in absolute numbers. The Roxbury children not only make the same kind of errors; they even make them with some of the identical words. While we cannot assume that similar or even identical forms necessarily have the same status in different language systems, the similarities across these 14 children, despite differences in their home dialect, are too numerous to be dismissed. In projecting her research plans, Ervin-Tripp said: "For various types of rules, we would like to know whether the children in different dialect communities have identical grammars up to a point (though their parents do not). These might be rules which in fact disappear in later stages of development" (1966, p. 42). To the extent that analogical errors indicate children's syntactic rules, these data suggest that dialect differences do not make much difference at these early stages. It seems likely that those parts of the structure of English which children learn first are the same across dialects, and it seems even more likely that the strategies or processes by which children learn that structure are also the same.

Just as striking are individual differences in error rate. Adam is more prone to overgeneralizations than are Eve and Sarah (see Table 5), and one of the Roxbury children had a similar quality. Adam also produced more anomalous sentences. For instance, he said *Dey talking* about two irons that face each other on the ironing board. This may indicate late learning of the restrictions on subjects with which *talking* can co-occur, or it may be a deliberate metaphorical extension. Generalizations before and after differentiation are different phenomena, but one wonders if the roots of childish error and mature creativity are in this case somehow related.

Questions

Before turning to the development of question forms in children's language, it is necessary to make clear what knowledge this particular part of English syntax requires.

QUESTION FORMS

Questions are asked in four common forms: yes-no questions (*Can the boy drive a car?*), Wh-questions (*Where is he going?*), tag questions (*Mary's coming, isn't she?*), and indirect questions (*She asked me if the boy can drive a car*). Let's consider in a simplified way what syntactic knowledge each requires.

Yes-No Questions

Take the simple declarative sentence, *The boy can drive a car*. In the now-familiar tree-diagram form, this sentence can be analyzed as in Figure 4.

Figure 4   **Tree-Diagram Analysis of "Yes" Assertion.**

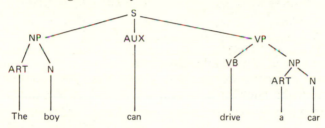

Now consider that instead of asserting that *the boy can drive the car*, we want to question that same proposition. In other words, the meaning of the sentence includes a question constituent (Q), as in Figure 5. What changes, or transformations, must be made in the form of the sentence to convert it to a question? For yes-no questions, one transformation is required: The auxiliary *can* must be exchanged with the subject-noun phrase *Peter*, as in Figure 6. This process is called the interrogative transformation. Like all transformations, it can be applied to constituents of certain types (here, NP + AUX) regardless of the particular words in

Figure 5   **Transformation of Assertion to Question.**

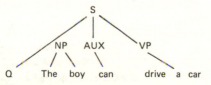

Figure 6   **Interrogative Transformation.**

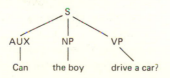

that constituent in any particular sentence. If there is no AUX (such as the modal *can* or a form of the verb *to be*) in the declarative sentence, the "dummy" AUX *do* is supplied in the question

Peter drives a car: *Does Peter drive a car?*

Wh-Questions

Consider next a Wh-question such as *Where is he going?* What transformations have to be made to obtain this question from the nearest declarative sentence *He is going somewhere?* First, the appropriate question word (*where, when, what, who, which,* or *how*) has to be substituted for the indefinite pronoun *somewhere* and preposed, or placed at the beginning of the sentence. That transformation yields *Where he is going?* Then, if the same transformation required for yes-no questions is applied—transposing auxiliary (here a form of *be*) and the subject-noun phrase—the final form is *Where is he going?* Thus, yes-no questions require one transformation and Wh-questions require two.

The Function of Yes-No Wh-Questions

Turn for a moment from questions of grammar to questions of function. In the search for knowledge, yes-no questions and Wh-questions place different cognitive burdens on speaker and listener. One day a colleague and I were observing at the Brandeis University nursery school. We had identical small cassette recorders hanging from our shoulders and carried a microphone for dictating murmured notes as we watched. Several children noticed and asked questions. Some asked very general Wh-questions: *What's that for?* and *What's she doing?* Others asked yes-no questions that reflected considerable relevant knowledge: *Are you going to play that for us today?* and *Can you talk to her?* (thinking we had intercom equipment). Yes-no questions and Wh-questions are often called "general" and "specific" questions, respectively, but these labels seem appropriate only when applied to the expected answer. If one considers the knowledge required on the part of the speaker, the labels might better be reversed. In other words, with yes-no questions, the cognitive burden falls on the speaker (which is why teachers are admonished to avoid them); with Wh-questions, the burden falls on the listener.

Tag Questions

Tag questions follow the speaker's own statement and ask for confirmation of it: *Mary's coming, isn't she? Daddy won't be late, will he?* Briefly, the transformations required to obtain the correct form of the tag from its declarative sentence *Mary's coming* are

Pronominalization:	She's coming (*unless subject of sentence is already pronoun*)
Negation:	She isn't coming (*or deletion of negation if declarative sentence is negated*)

Interrogation: Isn't she coming?
Truncation: Isn't she?

Simpler forms that remain invariant for all sentences do exist for the same purpose: *N'est-ce pas* in French, and *Right?* or *Huh?* in colloquial English.

Indirect Questions

Both yes-no and Wh-questions can be embedded in the noun phrases of other sentences—for instance, as the object of the verb ask: *She asked me if the boy can drive a car.* The main difference in formation between these indirect questions and their simple counterparts is that in indirect questions the question transformation that inverts AUX and subject NP is not applied. Then, in indirect yes-no questions, the question constituent takes the form of *whether* or *if. Is he sick? I don't know if he is sick.*

THE DEVELOPMENT OF QUESTION FORMS

Is there a sequence of stages by which children develop mature question forms? The simplest way to ask a question is by intonation alone. To mature speakers, a question asked in that way may differ slightly in meaning from the same question asked in the usual form: *You're going home?* versus *Are you going home?* But on a more primitive level, intonation is enough, and children start out by asking questions in this way.

Menyuk and Bernholtz (1969) recorded the speech of a child age 18 to 20 months who was producing primarily one-word utterances. They wanted to find out if various utterances of a single word *door* were simply repetitions of a name, or if they were one word (holophrastic) sentences with differentiated meanings:

That's a door.   (*Declarative*)
Is that a door?   (*Question*)
Shut the door!   (*Emphatic*)

These three sentence types are distinguished by prosodic features of stress and intonation that can be determined by the judgments of human listeners, or by spectrographic analysis that converts speech into a visual representation of sound frequencies. Menyuk and Bernholtz analyzed the child's one-word utterances in both ways. Two listeners reached 81 percent agreement that all three types of sentences did exist, and their reactions were supported by the spectrograms. What they considered declarative utterances ended with a falling-frequency contour, questions ended with a rising contour, and emphatics rose sharply and then fell. These data are given in Table 7, and the spectrograms are reproduced in Figure 7.

Menyuk and Bernholtz conclude:

Although the data are extremely limited there appear to be indications that the child's single word utterances are not simple names of objects and

Figure 7   **Spectograms of a Child's One-Word Utterances.**

Fig. 7a
Statement "door"

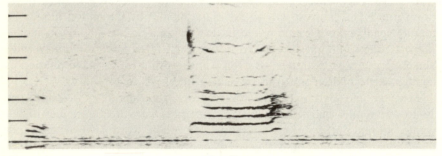

Fig. 7b
Question "door"

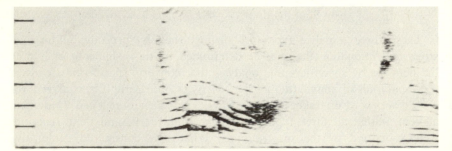

Fig. 7c
Emphatic "door"

Source   Menyuk & Bernholtz, 1969, p. 218

Table 7 **Measurements of Spectrograms of the Utterance "Door"**

Type	Total Length	Fundamental Frequency		
		BEGINNING	MIDDLE	END
Statement	.60 sec.	350	426	213
Question	.53 sec.	382	560	560
Emphatic	.72 sec.	455	1010	255

Source: Menyuk and Bernholtz (1969, p. 219).

events and that the child uses prosodic features generatively [productively, or creatively according to rules] to create sentence types rather than merely imitating prosodic features or including these features as part of the speech sound composition of a particular word. (Menyuk and Bernholtz, 1969, p. 219.)

Menyuk is now continuing this work to see whether other one-word utterances of this same child follow the same pattern, whether other children make the same differentiations at this stage in their development, and whether the responses of the mothers indicate that they respond differentially to the different sentence types. Spectrographic analyses of children's speech may provide a way of substantiating interpretations of what children are trying to say while their utterances are still too primitive to provide clear syntactic evidence.

Once children begin to put two words together, charting the development of mature question forms can begin. This development has been charted for Adam, Eve, and Sarah. Capital letters A–D in Figure 1 indicate periods (or stages) that Bellugi found in her analysis of the development of questions and negations (Bellugi, 1965, 1971a in press; Klima and Bellugi, 1966). In all cases, periods A–D include, and extend beyond, the time of the corresponding Roman numeral. For example, point III for Sarah includes the transcription for three weeks (long enough to get 700 completely intelligible utterances), and period B for Sarah covers ten weeks, which include the former three. Whereas I–V were points set in advance by the arbitrary selection of mean length of utterance, A–D were periods discovered from the analysis of the children's language. Bellugi's later periods E–F extend beyond this graph, and refer to Adam and Sarah only.

Table 8 outlines Bellugi's and Brown's analyses of the development of the question forms described above: yes-no questions, Wh-questions, and also tags and indirect questions. While the ages at periods A–F and all examples of child speech are those of one child, Adam, the descriptive statements apply to all three children. This means that the basic sequence with which the children learned to ask questions was the same for all three. But, as Figure 1 makes clear, the ages of the three children at any one period of their language development, and the interval from

Table 8 **Stages in the Development of Question Forms**

Ages for Adam	*Yes–No Questions*	*Wh–Questions*
PERIOD A (28 MOS.)	Expressed by intonation only: *Sit chair?* *Ball go?* *Dat black too?* *Mom pinch finger?* *You can't fix it?*	Limited number of routines: *What('s) that?* *Where NP go?* *What NP doing?*

More complex sentences being questioned, but no development of question forms themselves except the appearance, probably as routines, of two negative auxiliaries *don't* and *can't*.

		What soldier marching? *Where my mitten?* *Why you waking me up?*
PERIOD C (38 MOS.)	Development of auxiliary verbs in the child's entire grammatical system. Inversion of AUX and subject NP in yes–no questions, but not in Wh-questions. *Are you going to make it with me?* *Will you help me?* *Does the kitty stand up?* *Can I have a piece of paper?*	*What I did yesterday?* *Which way they should go?* *Why the Christmas tree going?* *How he can be a doctor?*
PERIOD C–F (42–54 MOS.) Period D + E	Development of tag questions from *Huh?* to mature form: *I have two turn, huh?* *We're playing, huh?*	Inversion of AUX and subject NP, first in affirmative questions only: *Why are you thirsty?* *Why we can't find the right one?*
Period F	*That's funny, isn't it?* *He was scared, wasn't he?* *Mommy, when we saw those girls, they were running, weren't they?*	Later, starting in Period F, in negative question also: *Why can't they put on their diving suits and swim?* Development of complex sentences, including indirect Wh-questions: *You don't know where you're going.* *He doesn't know what to do.* *We don't know who that is.*

Source: Adapted from work of Bellugi, 1965, 1971a, in press; Brown, 1968a; Brown and Hanlon, 1970; Klima and Bellugi, 1966.

one period to another, varied dramatically even in this small group. In the most extreme comparison, Eve had reached point V (in terms of MLU) or period C (in terms of the development of her question forms) at the age of 26 months, when Adam and Sarah were at point I and period A.

Does this mean that individual differences in the acquisition of syntax exist only in the *rate* of development whereas the *sequence* of development is invariant? This is an important question, and many more children will have to be studied before we have a definite answer. But even from the analyses of the development of question forms in these three children, a "yes" answer must be qualified.

In periods A–C, there are striking commonalities in the developmental sequences for these three children. The clearest example comes with the appearance of auxiliary verbs. While they enter the child's entire language system in a very short span of time, they are treated differently in yes-no questions and Wh-questions by all three children. There was a period of time (period C) during which AUX and subject NP were inverted in yes-no questions while this transformation was still missing from Wh-questions: *Will you help me?* but *How he can be a doctor?* And there was a later period (D–F) when affirmative Wh-questions were inverted while negative ones were not: *Why are you thirsty?* but *Why we can't find the right one?*

Even during the A–C periods, however, idiosyncratic forms were present in the speech of individual children. Adam, for example, relied extensively in period B on one form of yes-no questions, which neither Eve nor Sarah used: *D'you want + pronoun + VP* (Bellugi, 1965).

> D'you want it's turn?
> D'you want me tie that?

And in the same period, Adam had his own form of negative Wh-questions: Why not + pronoun + VP [Bellugi, in press (a)]:

> Why not he take bath?
> Why not me careful?
> Why not you looking right place?

Both idiosyncratic forms seem to be unanalyzed chunks, unrelated to other forms in the child's language system. Whether it is generally true that in this early period the individual differences lie more in the addition of such routine chunks than in parts of the productive system, we cannot say.

Later, in periods D–F, there was evidence that individual differences in the sequences of development became more important [Bellugi, in press (a)]. For instance, tags appeared in Sarah's speech in period D, but not in Adam's speech until period F.

Because the foregoing analysis of the development of question forms is based on transcriptions of spontaneous speech, it is subject to one important question: What basis is there for believing that what the child happens to say is all that he is capable of saying? Is this particular sample of his speech performance a valid expression of his language competence? The only way to be sure is to supplement natural conversations with more experimental tests.

Bellugi (1971a) did this with Adam. One test situation that even two-year-old children can understand is a request to imitate. The experimenter tells the child, "You say what I say." During period C, when Adam was inverting AUX and NP in yes-no questions but not in Wh-questions, Bellugi gave Adam such an imitation test:

Adult: Adam, say what I say: "Where can he put them?"
Adam: Where he can put them?

This evidence strengthens the assertion that Adam's language system could not cope with the inversion transformation in this linguistic context.

Later, in period E, when affirmative Wh-questions were inverted but negative Wh-questions were not, Bellugi, with the help of another adult, gave Adam a different and more difficult test:

> One of us had the glove puppet figure of an old lady, and responded to the child's questions with a quavering voice of an elderly puppet. The other adult gave the child instructions in the form of indirect questions (which preserve word order). We had a set of twenty questions, half affirmative and half negative which we mixed randomly and interspersed with other games and conversation during the session. The game went like this:
>
> Adult: Adam, ask the Old Lady what she'll do next.
> Adam: Old Lady, what will you do next?
> Old Lady: I'll fly to the moon.
> Adult: Adam, ask the Old Lady why she can't sit down.
> Adam: Old Lady, why you can't sit down?
> Old Lady: You haven't given me a chair.
>
> In the course of the game, Adam inverted all the affirmative questions (*What will you do?*) and did not invert any of the negative questions (*Why you can't sit down?*), although they were presented in random order (Bellugi 1971a, pp. 100–101).

Customarily, a summary would appear at the end of this chapter, but—as pointed out at its beginning—the subject of language development is discussed in three parts, in Chapters 3, 4, and 5. Chapter 5 will serve as a summary by integrating the essentials of Chapters 3 and 4 into a more general discussion.

4

The Acquisition of
Sounds and Meanings

For the child, learning about sounds (phonology) and meanings (semantics) is no less important than learning about syntax, and for education, one could easily argue that meaning—whatever that is—is the most important of all aspects of language. Discussions about sounds and meaning are combined in one chapter here because less is known about their development and therefore there is less to tell. In each section, discussion of phonology and semantics is combined with a discussion of children's development.

Phonology

The child's acquisition of the sound structure of his language has two aspects. One is the ability to discriminate and pronounce the sounds of his native language. The second is knowledge of the rules that govern how sounds are combined into words and larger units. While discussions of both aspects will necessarily get technical at points, each has implications for matters of practical importance such as speech therapy and learning to read.

SPEECH SOUND DISCRIMINATION AND PRODUCTION

A phoneme is a class of sounds that a native speaker considers functionally equivalent and discriminates from other classes of sounds. The sound system of each human language consists of a unique set of phonemes. These sounds, or phonemes, will be bracketed in the text by slanting lines. So, in English we distinguish between voiced /b/ and unvoiced /p/ as in *bet-pet*. In Arabic, this distinction does not exist, whereas in Bengali "not only are /b/ and /p/ differentiated by the ordinary speaker of Bengali, but in addition, an unaspirated *p* (as in English *spin*) is differentiated from an aspirated *p* (as in English *pin*). Similarly an unaspirated /b/ is regularly differentiated from an aspirated /b/" (Fishman, 1970, p. 9). The same variations among languages exist in vowels. English makes no distinction between vowels according to length, nasalization, or tone, but Navajo does. "Like musical scales, phonemic patterning is an intervention of culture in nature, an artifact imposing logical rules upon the sound continuum" (Jakobson and Halle, 1956, p. 17).

Each phoneme may be defined as a simultaneous bundle of distinctive articulatory features. Figure 1 diagrams the relationships among eight English phonemes that are combinations of three features: voiced or unvoiced; stops or fricatives (depending on the continuousness of the sound); and apicals or labials (depending on place of articulation: mouth or top of the tongue). One day Sarah demonstrated the psychological reality of this way of conceptualizing phoneme relationships. She wanted a banana from the top of the refrigerator and tried, for a while unsuccessfully, to get her mother's attention. In her childish repetitions of the word "banana" Sarah's pronunciation varied through four initial consonants, all closely related in distinctive features, as Figure 1 shows:

> banana
> panana
> fanana
> vanana

Jakobson (1968) proposed a detailed hypothesis about the sequence of phonemic development in terms of distinctive features which fits into his larger analysis of primary and secondary linguistic forms mentioned in Chapter 2. In his theory, the same laws determine the order in which the child's sound system develops, the order of its mirror-image dissolution in aphasia, and the distribution of features in all languages of the world. For example, according to Jakobson, fricatives like /f/ necessarily entail the corresponding stop /p/; this means that fricatives would appear later than stops in a child's speech, be impaired first in aphasia, and occur only in

Figure 1   **Distinctive Feature Analysis of English Consonants.**

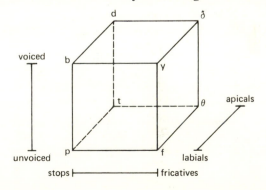

those languages that also have stops, but the reverse would not be true. McNeill (1970a) reviews the evidence for this theory, and Moskowitz (1970) presents many ideas for further research.

We used to think that learning to discriminate the speech sounds of one's native language was as slow and gradual as learning to produce them seems to be. Research now being done indicates how wrong that notion may be. Infants are notoriously intractable subjects for any scientific experiment, but conditioning procedures provide a means of determining which discriminations they can make. Presentation of an auditory stimulus to an infant produces an increase in his sucking response, and this effect diminishes as the infant becomes used to the sound. The critical question is this: How different does the sound have to be to restimulate the response? Using this experimental procedure, Eimas and his colleagues (1971) made some surprising findings:

> In this study of speech perception, it was found that 1- and 4-month-old infants were able to discriminate the acoustic cue underlying the adult phonemic distinction between the voiced and voiceless stop consonants /b/ and /p/. Moreover, and more important, there was a tendency in these subjects toward categorical perception: discrimination of the same physical difference was reliably better across the adult phonemic boundary than within the adult phonemic boundary. . . .
>
> Another way of stating this effect is that infants are able to sort acoustic variations of adult phonemes into categories with relatively limited exposure to speech, as well as with virtually no experience in producing these same sounds and certainly with little, if any, differential reinforcement for this form of behavior. The implication of these findings is that the means by which the categorical perception of speech, that is, perception in a linguistic mode, is accomplished may well be part of the biological makeup of the organism and, moreover, that these means must be operative at an unexpectedly early age. (Eimas et al., pp. 303, 306.)

With such findings, it is not surprising that research on infants is becoming increasingly important in our attempts to understand the nature of human intelligence.

We also used to think that learning to produce speech sounds developed by a process of gradual shaping from the randomly produced sounds of infant babbling. It now seems more likely that a discontinuity exists between prelinguistic babbling and true speech behavior. Frequently, in a child's development, there is a period of silence between babbling and speech. Furthermore, MacDonald (1967) points out that the sequence of emergence of sounds is incompatible in the two developmental phases. In the period of babbling, or vocalic play, from about 4 to 11 months, the back consonants /k/, /g/, and /x/, and the front vowels /i/ and /u/ are most common; once speech starts, these sounds do not reappear until after the front consonants /p/ and /m/. Parenthetically, it is interesting to consider whether this early production of /p/ and /m/ may account for the initial sounds for "papa" and "momma" in many languages (Jakobson, 1939).

Because distinctive features provide a metric for measuring the distance between phonemes, they can also be used to analyze the articulation errors that children make. In 1968–1969, a national sample of more than 38,000 children in grades 1 to 12 were tested in the National Speech and Hearing Survey. Williams and associates (1970) analyzed the errors made by a subsample of 384 children in Marshalltown, Iowa (all of whom spoke standard English), using the Goldman-Fristoe Test of Articulation. In a few minutes of connected discourse, 15 phoneme substitutions accounted for 196, or 87%, of all substitution errors on the Goldman-Fristoe test. These substitutions involved the following number of feature changes (adapted from Williams et al., 1970, Table 11, p. 62):

No. of Feature Changes	*No. of Substitutions* ("types")	*Total Frequency* ("tokens")
1	9	144
2	3	15
3	1	6
4	1	31

Clearly, the distribution of substitutions does, in general, support the psychological validity of a feature analysis.

Williams and his associates refer to one clinician (Compton, in press) who suggests how a theoretically based analysis of the articulatory disorders of two children can provide insights for appropriate therapy.

One more finding from Williams's research deserves attention. Contrary to the researchers' expectations, more phonemes were mispronounced on the Goldman-Fristoe test than in connected talk. The authors comment—

> In view of these results, perhaps the hypothesis should be entertained that the speech production mechanisms operate more accurately when given an abundance of contextual cues. Under this hypothesis the context provided by a section of discourse provides cues and feedback for the muscles of the vocal apparatus, thus making individual phonemes more likely to be correctly articulated. This situation would be analogous to that of the speech perception mechanism, which, it is known, operates far better as context introduces redundancy into the speech signal. (Williams et al., 1970, p. 59.)

Our knowledge of complex phenomena frequently proceeds by the isolation of some aspect of that complexity for more carefully controlled study. But we must never forget that, ultimately, that aspect must be understood in its interaction with all its natural co-occurrences, and that isolation from that interaction may even be misleading in some cases. The same methodological problem arises in research on environmental assistance discussed in Chapter 6.

Two facts about speech sound discrimination and production have implications for education. First, intelligibility in real life must meet a shifting criterion. At any one time, an utterance is either understood correctly by the listener or not. But identical pronunciation can be intelligible to one listener and not intelligible to another, depending on the degree of shared background of experience between speaker and listener, and the availability of extralinguistic cues to what the child is talking about. This fact is important in planning for the care of young children by people outside their family. For instance, if a young child is cared for in a day-care center by one of a large group of adults, those adults may be less likely to understand all his speech and therefore be less able to respond meaningfully to him than if there were greater continuity in the adult-child relationship. Usually the benefits of such continuity are considered in affective terms alone. Increase in the range of listeners to whom the child's speech is intelligible can be used as a measure of his development (Sapon, in press).

Second, both speech therapists and teachers must distinguish between developmental deviations in pronunciation and dialect differences. A child needs speech therapy only if his speech deviates from the norms of his own community. Fortunately, this distinction is becoming more frequently recognized in professional education and practice.

COMBINING SOUNDS INTO WORDS

In the course of development, children learn how the sounds of English can be combined. Most obviously, they learn what can be called the transition probabilities that characterize sound sequences. Bruner (1957) relates an experiment by William Hull in which pseudowords were presented to good and poor fifth-grade spellers. After a very brief exposure to the words, the children were asked to write them down. Some of the pseudowords were random strings of letters; others reflected the sound structure of English but were not actually in the dictionary—words like *pokerson* and *vernalit*. For the random sequences, there was no difference between the good and poor spellers. But with the close approximations to English, the good spellers wrote down more words correctly. They had somehow learned the general system.

Less obviously, our knowledge of language is not limited to the noises we speak and hear, and this generalization applies to our knowledge of the sound system of our language as well as to its syntactic structure. If our knowledge of the sounds of English words were limited to the phonemes present in words as spoken, all knowledge of morphemic relationships would be lost. That is, a phonemic system of spelling would ignore sound relationships among such words as the following:

(18a) histor-y, histor-ical, histor-ian
(18b) anxi-ous, anxi-ety

(18c)   courage, courage-ous

(18d)   tele-graph, tele-graph-ic, teleg-ra-phy

Yet the changes in pronunciation from one of these words to another is regular and can be explicitly formulated in rules.

The only way to account for this system of sound relationships is to postulate a deep and surface structure distinction for sounds as well as for syntax. The deep structure consists of a single and highly abstract "lexical representation" of each morpheme. This underlying representation (for example, of *courage*) is related to the surface phonetic representation of the morpheme, in isolation or in combination, by a complex set of phonological rules. [N. Chomsky and Halle (1968) describe these rules. See Langacker (1967) and O'Neill (1969) for as readable introductions as the technicalities of the subject permit.] Somehow this system of rules becomes part of the implicit linguistic knowledge of the native speaker, at least of the speaker of a rich version of spoken English.

Read (1970, 1971) found one way to study young children's mental representations of speech sounds. He analyzed the invented spellings of a small group of preschool children who knew the names of the letters and tried to write words before anyone had taught them conventional English orthography. It is striking that with sounds, as with syntax, children construct their own rules in unique, but not idiosyncratic, ways.

Consider two examples of invented spelling, one of vowels and one of consonants. As one would expect, the children whom Read studied used vowels to spell the sounds of their names (tense or, as we would say, "long" vowel sounds). In the following examples, the children's spelling is given in capital letters:

DA (*day*)   LADE (*lady*)   TIGR (*tiger*)

For the lax (or, as we would say, "short") vowel sounds, the children's solution was more novel. Say the name of the vowel very slowly, and notice that you're really saying a diphthong—a combination of two sounds:

tense A is   e-y.
tense E is   i-y.
tense I is   a-y.

The children's invented spellings indicate that they were aware of this phonetic relationship. They spelled the lax vowel with the tense vowel whose initial segment it matches:

FALL (*fell*)   FES (*fish*)   GIT (*got*)

The children's spellings of consonants is also consistent and interpretable even if unconventional. For example, the spellings of /t/ and /d/ before /r/ become *ch* and *j*, respectively:

AS CHRAY (*ash tray*)   JRAGIN (*dragon*)

Like the vowels, these inventions have a phonetic basis because the stops /t/ and /d/ do become released more slowly (affricated) before /r/; in this sense they are indeed closer to the affricates *ch* and *j*.

To determine the perceptions of a larger number of children than the small group who invented their own spellings, Read asked 80 kindergarten children questions such as these: Which pictures start like *train: teddy bear, chair, tie, track, chicken, tree*? He reports that "it was a surprise to the teachers of these kindergartens to find that many of their students hear the first sound of *truck* as that of *chair*, and the first sound of *dragon* as that of *jacks*" (1970, p. 104). Read concludes:

> We have examined evidence that some children perceive certain fine phonetic differences and that these perceptions are reflected in their original spelling. These same phonetic distinctions are not perceptually real to most adults, including, usually, the children's parents and teachers. This suggests that the children have learned facts about English, and perhaps general strategies, that they have not been taught. (Read, 1970, p. 74.)

In education, the reconceptualization of phonology by transformational linguists may have important implications for the teaching of reading.

> The educational importance . . . seems clear enough, at least in general. We can no longer assume that a child must approach reading and writing as an untrained animal approaches a maze—with no discernible prior conception of its structure. . . . Evidently, a child may come to school with a knowledge of logical categories and relations; without conscious awareness, he may seek to relate English spelling to these in some generally systematic way. If this inference is correct, some long-neglected questions turn out to be crucial for understanding and facilitating the process of learning to read: what levels of phonological analysis do individual children tacitly control at various stages of development; how do these analyses relate to the lexical representation that generally corresponds to standard spelling; and how can reading instruction build on this relationship, while encouraging children to extend and deepen their notion of the sound system of the language? (Read, 1971, pp. 32–33.)

N. Chomsky (1970) and C. Chomsky (1970) suggest several directions for further thought and research.

First, while the beginning reader may expect a one-to-one relationship between phonemes (sounds) and graphemes (letters), to become a successful reader the child must abandon this early hypothesis and shift "from a phonetic to a lexical interpretation of the spelling system" (C. Chomsky, 1970, p. 297). We don't know why some children make this shift so easily, nor do we know how to help those who don't.

Second, reading out loud may be more a hindrance than a help to the beginning reader by impeding the shift to a lexical interpretation. Readers of this book may have learned new words while reading it, as I did while writing it. An example is *paraphrastic*, which occurs in the next chapter as a characteristic of special sets of sentences. Reading it aloud is no problem, but visual cues will be more helpful to comprehension by suggesting the related word *paraphrase*.

Third, enrichment of the child's vocabulary may have important benefits for his ultimate success in learning to read.

> . . . it ought to be given serious consideration in light of the close tie that exists between English phonology and English orthography. The orthography assumes a fairly sophisticated degree of internal organization of the sounds system of the language. Extending the child's vocabulary to include Latinate forms and polysyllabic derived forms is one of the best ways to provide him with the means of constructing the phonological system of his language more fully as he matures. . . .
>
> In general, connections should be brought out among words that he already knows but may not yet have classified together, and new words should be introduced for the purpose of establishing new connections. . . . Literacy acquisition from this point of view may well extend over a much longer period of time than ordinarily assumed, and be closely interrelated with these other aspects of the child's linguistic development. (C. Chomsky, 1970, p. 302.)

Usually we think that reading may be a source of vocabulary growth. Perhaps the influence extends in both directions.

Fourth, with examples from her three-year-old son who first spelled "Kate" in plastic letters as K-T, C. Chomsky (1971a) urges that children begin learning to read by creating their own spellings for familiar words. Parents and teachers needn't worry that such invented spellings will remain as bad habits hard to unlearn. Read (1971) found that none of the children he studied had trouble shifting from their invented spellings to conventional orthography, despite some parental fears. So that this suggestion will not be dismissed as applicable only to children who are unusual in intelligence or family background, Read's comments on his larger kindergarten groups are important: "The children who spelled spontaneously were better than most at becoming conscious of their phonological judgments" (1971, p. 15). One important function of education for all children is to bring their own implicit knowledge to self-awareness. C. Chomsky (1971a) suggests that such a program of "write now, read later" might have a generalized effect of encouraging and rewarding the child's active role as learner.

Finally, new questions about the value of the Initial Teaching Alphabet (ITA) come to mind. According to Chomsky and Halle's theory (1968), the ITA would be a disastrous substitution for adults, just because all morphological relationships are lost in exclusive concern for similarities in superficial sounds. The same evaluation would apply to spelling reforms using our conventional alphabet, such as the recommendations of G. B. Shaw. But if children are both more attuned to sounds and less knowledgeable about morphological relationships, the ITA may briefly serve its intended purpose for them. Empirical research on this point is still equivocal (Warburton and Southgate, 1969). Read suggests a rather different and more "fringe" benefit of the use of the ITA. Even though it does not fit his findings about what children do in fact perceive and try to represent, its use in classrooms "would seem to have institutionalized a distinction between children's initial efforts and standard spelling, making the former more acceptable" (Read, 1970, p. 196).

Meaning

While meaning is the most important aspect of child language for education, it is also the most difficult to study and describe. Three aspects are discussed: the meaning of words; combining of word meanings into sentences; and the propositions that sentences express. Discussion of the meaning of words is further divided into three parts: component meanings, awareness of word meanings, and individual differences.

THE MEANINGS OF WORDS

Component Meanings

In order to utter or understand a sentence, a person must have a mental dictionary that contains the words in that sentence. He must also have a set of rules for combining dictionary entries into a meaning for the sentence as a whole. In the mental dictionary, all that we know about the meaning of a word must be organized and represented in some economical form. Katz and Fodor (1964) present one form of organization such a dictionary could have.

Consider their example *bachelor*. Its meaning can be represented as in Figure 2.

The unenclosed marker "noun" is a grammatical marker, in this case of the lexical category or part of speech to which the word belongs. This marker reflects knowledge of the slots in a sentence in which the word can appear. Markers of lexical subcategories such as "count noun" could have been added as a further specification that *bachelor* can appear in the slot *some* + _____ + plural *s*, which a mass noun like *rice* cannot. The markers enclosed in parentheses are semantic markers. Some of these, like "human" (or "animate," which could have been included), restrict the words with which *bachelor* can co-occur. For instance, as an animate noun, *bachelor* can be the object of a verb like *frighten*, whereas an inanimate noun like *stone* cannot. Other semantic markers like "male" express

Figure 2   **Diagrammatic Representation of Bachelor.**

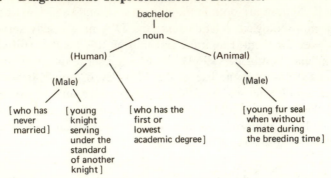

Source   After Katz and Fordor, 1964, p. 496

part of the meaning of the word. Together the semantic markers exhibit the relations between different dictionary entries—for example, between *bachelor* and *spinster*, which would have identical entries except for sex. Katz and Fodor point out one interesting mismatch between grammatical and semantic markers. We say *The baby dropped its rattle.* While *baby* is clearly an animate noun, it is marked grammatically as taking, at least optionally, the inanimate pronoun *it.*

The items enclosed in brackets are called distinguishers by Katz and Fodor, and each expresses an idiosyncratic meaning of the word. "The distinction between markers and distinguishers is meant to coincide with the distinction between that part of the meaning of a lexical item which is systematic in the language and that part of the meaning of the item which is not" (Katz and Fodor, 1964, p. 498).

Analysis of word meaning into semantic markers is similar to distinctive feature analysis of speech sounds given in Figure 2 and the componential analysis of kinship terms in anthropology. Figure 3 shows that

Figure 3   **Componential Analysis of Eight Kin Terms.**

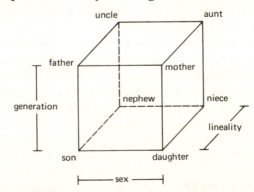

Source   Reprinted with permission of The Macmillan Company from *Social Psychology* by Roger Brown. Copyright © 1965 by The Free Press.

analysis of eight English kin terms in the same diagrammatic form. Just as distinctive features represent universal potentialities of the human articulatory system from which a unique selection is used in each language, so the dimensions of a componential analysis (or the semantic markers in transformational grammar) may represent universal ways of categorizing reality from which a unique selection is expressed in each culture.

Until very recently, it was widely assumed that the assignment of labels to any semantic domain (such as color) varied in an arbitrary way across languages. As part of contemporary interest in universal aspects of language and cognition, Berlin and Kay (1969) analyzed the color terms in 20 languages from a number of different language groups. Instead of arbitrariness, they found a predictable sequence. If a language had only two color terms, they were *white* and *black*; if there were three, the third was *red*, and so on through the following list (asterisks added for later discussion):

2 terms:	white and black*
3 terms:	red* added
4–5 terms:	either green* and then yellow* or vice versa
6 terms:	blue* added
7 terms:	brown* added
8–12 terms:	purple,* pink,* orange,* and gray added in any order or combination

The degree of differentiation of the color lexicon in any language seems related to the technological complexity of the society where it is spoken, but not at all to the perceptual abilities of its speakers.

Because of the obvious resemblance of these findings to Jakobson's (1968) theory about the progressive differentiation of sounds, Berlin and Kay speculate about whether the individual child learns color names in this sequence. They could find only one study (Istomina, 1963) and that did confirm this order. From my experience as a teacher in first grade, when many children are still learning color names, I have no evidence on the order of their acquisition. But I do remember the yearly archaeological evidence of children's color preferences. Boxes of eight crayons issued to each child at the beginning of the school year contained those marked with an asterisk in the list above. As children used up their crayons, new boxes were issued, and leftover bits were collected for general use in a single classroom container. As the year went by, that container became more and more densely filled with unused pieces of just two colors: purple and orange, both at the end of Berlin and Kay's list.

Heider (1971) investigated another possible universal aspect of color naming: the tendency to pick particular "focal colors" as the best exemplars of basic color names. Having found the same focal colors—a particular "red," for example—selected in several languages, she hypothesized that if those colors were more salient to young children, there might be a developmental explanation for the universality. She found that three- and four-year-old children did more frequently pick focal colors to show to the experimenter, more often correctly matched them to a model, and more often chose them to represent a color name. Heider (1971, p. 447) concludes that "The color space, far from being a domain well suited to the study of the effects of language on thought, appears instead to be a prime example of the influence of underlying perceptual-cognitive factors on the formation and reference of linguistic categories." Heider did not find in her experiment, however, that the order of effects across colors matched Berlin and Kay's proposed evolutionary sequence. We have more to learn.

So far discussion has been restricted to the denotation of a word, the criterial or essential parts of a word's meaning that are shared by members of a given language community. Words also have connotations, aspects of meaning that are more idiosyncratic to individual persons because they reflect individual experience—whether dogs are loved or feared, whether the mention of spinach arouses anticipation or disgust.

Undoubtedly, Katz and Fodor's conceptualization of word meanings will yield to other formulations as the semantic part of linguistic science proceeds. But some way of representing a word's component meanings should continue to be useful in thinking about development and individual differences.

Notice that all words except proper names can be conceptualized in this way. Proper names are special just because they have a precise referent—the person named—but they have no meaning. Even when a name like Ronald or Alicia is known to apply to several different individuals, no composite meaning is built up. Possibly a positive or negative connotation becomes attached to the name, but that is all. All other words have meaning, without exception, and many sets of words can be analyzed through the relationship of their semantic features. This is as true of articles, pronouns, prepositions, and verbs as of nouns.

Sometimes children's spontaneous speech gives clues to the absence of semantic markers or to their relative importance. When Sarah asked her mother to draw a letter, the listener can infer that in her language the semantic marker was missing that restricts the use of *draw* to nonsymbols (except in the special case of calligraphy). Presumably, learning the word *write* added the markers for this distinction to both words. Once Sarah asked, *"Where's my birthday?"* Unless she had been looking at the calendar at the moment (which she wasn't), the question word should have been *when*, but the distinction between spatial and temporal absence may not be easy to learn. And when a three-year-old says of the ring she cannot find, *"Maybe it's hiding,"* the listener wonders if she hasn't yet learned that *hiding* can be done only by an animate object.

While visiting nursery schools in England, I watched a nursery school director draw large chalk shapes on the playground for the children to identify and then march around. The children enjoyed anticipating and calling out the names before the teacher had finished. In the case of the triangle, they called correctly when she had finished only one line, even though it could have been the beginning of a square or a rectangle as well. That one line was diagonal to the seams in the playground cement and diagonal to the school building wall. Evidently, in those children's concept of a triangle, diagonality was a more important marker than three-sidedness.

To establish the presence of semantic markers, carefully controlled experiments are needed. Maratsos (1972) experimentally investigated young children's understanding of the distinction between *a* and *the*. The children were seated at a table with a group of identical toy cars in front of them. The experimenter sat facing the child across the table. At the experimenter's request, the child handed him one of the cars. The adult then asked two questions:

(19a)   Do you have a car?

(19b)   Do you have the car?

The questions were asked in random order, with normal intonation. To (19a), most children as young as three years old answered *yes* or nodded their heads; to (19b) they said *no* or shook their heads. Whether children as young as two possess this knowledge is unclear; they are such intractable subjects that experimentation becomes nearly impossible. But somehow, at least by three years of age, many children have learned the contrast in meaning which we usually label as indefinite versus definite. That particular semantic marker is itself a very abstract relational concept which no one tries to teach a child directly.

As part of the cross-cultural research on language acquisition conducted at the University of California (Berkeley), Stross (1969) studied the acquisition of names for a wide variety of plants by Teneljapa Tzeltal children in Mexico. He selected plant names for study because a detailed analysis of the adult semantic system had already been made. Stross wanted to find out the order in which plant names were learned, which attributes were used in identification by children of different ages, what children called plants whose names they didn't know, and who taught them names and how. He arranged a test situation by laying out a special plant trail. "My assistant would walk ahead with the child, pointing out prearranged plants and asking the child to identify them while I stayed behind writing down the responses" (Stross, 1969, p. 99). Twenty-five children from 4 to 13 years old, and 10 adults from 15 to 60 years old were taken along the trail, one at a time. Stross concluded that the order of acquisition of names follows two dimensions: location—from those seen *in* the house to *near* the house and then to more distant plants; and cultural significance—from the most important to least. There was also regular change in the attributes by which children made their identifications: first by the fruit; then by location; and only later by the various growth stages, conditions of health, and morphological attributes other than fruits. In general, learning proceeded to greater and greater differentiation of categories, but both differentiation and generalization proceeded together.

A particularly interesting case study in the psychological reality of semantic features comes from research in still another culture—Hale's (in press) analysis of a secret language known as tʸiliwiri, which the Walbiri men of central Australia use in certain rituals. It depends on the use of opposites, which are words that share all semantic markers except one. Here is Burling's summary of Hale's analysis:

> Boys first encounter tʸiliwiri when they are about 13, after their first initiation. At first they are unable to understand it. Its principles are never abstractly explained, but boys must infer them by listening to older men speak. Unlike pig latins, *which attain their secrecy by distorting the phonology, tʸiliwiri distorts the meaning. Its most general principle is that all nouns, verbs, and pronouns are replaced by their semantic opposites.* The phonology follows regular Walbiri conventions, and the grammatical markers are left intact, so the structure of the sentences is not obscured, but there is wholesale substitution of nouns and verbs. The youth who has not yet inferred the principles by which the language is derived from normal Walbiri may fail to realize that a sentence like "that one is small" should be interpreted as "this one is big" or that "another is standing on the sky" must be understood as "I am sitting on the ground."
>
> For words such as "big," "small," "hot," "cold," and so forth, the principle seems easy enough to apply, but only a few words in any language have transparent opposites. Nevertheless, the Walbiri are able to find opposites for all of the words of the major form classes of their language, and they even describe tʸiliwiri as turning ordinary Walbiri upside down. The most interesting aspect of the language is to see how the Walbiri settle upon opposites for concepts that do not have real polar antonyms.
>
> Terms for plants and animals can hardly be described as having real opposites, and the Walbiri solution is to exchange the names of the most closely related species. Two terms are substituted for each other when they stand for animals that are differentiated by only a single characteristic. Thus the terms *wawiri* and *kanʸala*, which refer to two different kinds of kangaroos, can be substituted for one another as can *wakulʸari* and *yulkaminʸi*, two kinds of wallabys. . . . As a matter of fact, we even recognize real polar opposites by a similar principle, for terms like "hot" and "cold" are very close in meaning, being differentiated by just one feature.
>
> Kinship terms are also switched with as closely similar terms as possible. Walbiri kinship terms are differentiated by criteria such as sex, relative age, and kinship-group membership, and it might be possible to move across any one of these dimensions of contrast or even some combination of them in finding an opposite. Indeed, the most opposite term of all might be supposed to be the term that is most differentiated from the intended meaning, con-

trasting with it on every possible semantic dimensions. The Walbiri, however, choose to concentrate upon the single principle of relative age and generation. Terms for "older brother" and "younger brother" are substituted for each other as are terms for "older sister" and "younger sister" and the terms for "father" and "son."

Synonymous and even partially synonymous terms may be replaced by the same opposite term when speaking *tʸiliwiri*. The Walbiri words for "hole" and for "creek bed" are both replaced in *tʸiliwiri* by the word that ordinarily means "even ground." "Before" and "after" are both replaced by "now." The general context will usually be sufficient to resolve any resulting ambiguity. In some respects, however, the *tʸiliwiri* version may actually be somewhat less ambiguous than the normal Walbiri. The term *nalapi* can mean either son or daughter in normal Walbiri and is, therefore, ambiguous as to sex. Since terms for the older generation in normal Walbiri are not ambiguous in this way, the *tʸiliwiri* substitutes for *nalapi* are *kidana* "father," when a male is to be spoken of, but *pimidi* "mother," if one intends the sense of "daughter." In cases like this, *tʸiliwiri* is less ambiguous that the normal Walbiri from which it is derived.

The way in which Walbiri makes substitutions can sometimes clarify the structure of a term's meaning. Thus *rampaku* can mean either "weak" or "light in weight." *Wakutudu* means "strong" and *pirtʸidi* means "heavy," these two terms being opposites of *rampaku* in its different senses. When the normal Walbiri would have *rampaku* in the sense of "weak," the *tʸiliwiri* substitute is *wakutudu*, but when *rampaku* would be used in the sense of "light" the *tʸiliwiri* is *pirtʸidi*. Clearly it is semantic features that govern the substitution of terms rather than mechanical rules based upon arbitrary pairing of morphemes.

A few substitutions are dependent upon particular concepts of Walbiri culture. The terms for "fire" and "water" are exchanged, reflecting the pairing of these terms in much Walbiri mythology. *Tʸiliwiri* also makes use of a number of idiosyncratic pairs that must simply be learned. However, in spite of all these complexities, a skilled speaker of *tʸiliwiri* can speak as rapidly as when he speaks normal Walbiri, and beyond its ritual associations Walbiri men take great pride and pleasure in their ability to produce skillful *tʸiliwiri*. (Burling, 1970, pp. 154–156.)

Playing word games with children could be a profitable research technique. Pig Latin would show how children perceive word boundaries and the Walbiri opposites game might show aspects of older children's semantic systems otherwise hard to tap.

Awareness of Word Meanings

As with sounds, so with word meanings—there is a metalinguistic aspect of development in which children become in some sense conscious of what they know. Then they can separate conceptually a word from its referent and reflect upon word meanings as well as use them in speech behavior.

Bever (1970) suggests that one of the basic linguistic capacities is "the capacity to recognize (and often to say) the names of some objects and actions—that is, the capacity for *reference*." But he adds a qualification: "Of course it is not clear whether they [children] understand the arbitrary nature of the acoustic-referential relationship or whether they believe that the names of objects and actions are intrinsic and indivisible from the objects and actions themselves" (Bever, 1970, p. 303). Recall the moment in Helen Keller's life when she understood that a particular tactile sensation in her hand was the name for water. It was not the first time she had learned a name-object association, but it was the first time she was aware of the name as a name. Vygotsky makes the same distinction:

> Before continuing, we want to clarify the term *consciousness* as we use it in speaking of nonconscious functions "becoming conscious." (We use the term nonconscious to distinguish what is not yet conscious from the Freudian "unconscious" resulting from repression, which is a late development, an effect of a relatively high differentiation of consciousness.) The activity of consciousness can take different directions; it may illumine only a few aspects of a thought or an act. I have just tied a knot—I have done so consciously, yet I cannot explain how I did it, because my awareness was centered on the knot rather than on my own motions, the *how* of my action. When the latter becomes the object of my awareness, I shall have become fully conscious. We use *consciousness* to denote awareness of the activity of the mind —the consciousness of being conscious. A preschool child who, in response to the question, "Do you know your name?" tells his name lacks this self-reflective awareness: He knows his name but is not conscious of knowing it. (Vygotsky, 1962, p. 91.)

Vygotsky's particular example can be interpreted in other ways. The child who says *David* when asked "Do you know your name?" may, as Vygotsky says, be immaturely lacking in "self-reflective awareness." Or he may be maturely aware of sociolinguistic rules for translating what people say into what they mean. Usually, the intent of such a question is to find out what the name in fact is. More evidence would be needed for proper evaluation.

Another manifestation of the separation of words from their meanings is the ability to give definitions. To the young child, only the use of word meanings is possible. When asked to define words, a five-year-old child will respond with a demonstration of use. If asked what a hole is, a child will answer *a hole in the ground*. Later, children can respond in the form *A hole is X*, where X is some attribute or synonym.

The nature of the attribute or synonym is itself of interest in studies of development or social class comparisons. For example, in a study of intermediate-grade children's verbal comprehension, Carson and Rabin (1960) categorized six levels of meaning for *wagon*:

Categorization: A vehicle.
Synonym: A cart.
Essential description: A wooden thing.

Essential function: You ride in it out West.
Vague description or function: It bumps into people.

In a study of "abstract thinking," Lundsteen (1970) categorized the definitions of fifth-grade children for a word like *experience*:

Concrete: Like going to the beach.
Functional: You feel something that happens to you.
Abstract: Living through an act or happening.

It is often assumed that giving a category label (*vehicle*) is somehow better than giving a function (*you ride in it out west*). The best validation for this assumption is that development does progress in that direction. But there may be strong cultural reasons why one kind of definition is preferred over another, and Leacock (in press) reminds us that scientists work with operational (functional) definitions all the time.

Regardless of the nature of the attribute given, there remains an important contrast between a demonstration of use and some statement of equivalence between a word and a synonym or paraphrase. When a child can give some statement of equivalence, entries in his mental dictionary are no longer limited to examples, and explicit comparison of word meanings becomes possible.

Individual Differences

Individual differences in word meanings take several forms. Word meanings are changing and growing sets of component features, and individual mental dictionaries will vary in completeness. Semantic development includes both learning new words and learning new markers, or aspects of meaning, for words already familiar. Readers of this book will know the two human meanings of *bachelor,* but few will know the animal meaning included in Fig. 2 as well. A child may understand that *father* is male, but not understand the generational meaning and so ask a woman if the man with her is her father.

Alternate possible meanings for a single word, such as paths in the diagram for *bachelor* (Figure 2), probably also acquire differential weightings, depending on frequency of occurrence in individual experience. In Webster's dictionary, entries for a word are listed in historical order from archaic to contemporary slang. But in mental dictionaries they must be organized to reflect differential experience in the past and, as a result, differential expectations in the future. Depending on our experience, we may be more likely to think of a *bachelor* as an unmarried man or as a college graduate; depending on our experience, we may think first of *father* as a label for a biological relationship or a role in a religious order. These weightings can facilitate or impede communication, depending on whether speaker and listener, or author and reader, have had shared or contrasting experience.

Word association tests provide one method of tapping these differential weightings. Entwisle (1970) found that Black inner-city fifth-graders associated a medical connotation with the word *examine* (*x-ray, operate, doctor*), while suburban fifth-graders associated it more often with words such as *test* and *check*. Entwisle considered the latter responses less restricted to a specific context, but one could say that the responses of suburban children were also specific; they simply reflect preoccupation with examinations given in school rather than by a doctor.

There are also differences among people in connotative meanings. *Cheap* may have a good connotation to people of limited means—synonymous with "not expensive"; it may have a bad connotation to the affluent—meaning sleazy or poorly made. For some people the adjective *black* is changing now from a bad connotation (reinforced by such expressions as "black magic") to a good one such as "Black is beautiful." Entwisle's research turned up one indication of the psychological reality of this shift: "Differences between Negro and white responses to 'black' are particularly interesting. No responses that pertain to human beings are given by white children, whereas Negro children respond 'child,' 'girls,' 'hand,' 'man,' and even 'yes' to the stimulus word 'black.'" (Entwisle, 1970, p. 133).

Violations of semantic restrictions by children can be distinguished from poetry only on the assumption that children act out of ignorance while poets act deliberately and in full knowledge. When the child says *Coffee dancing* as the cream swirls in his mother's cup, we assume he does not yet know that dancing properly takes an animate subject; when used by an adult, as in poetry, we call such rule-breaking metaphor. The distinction represents the difference between generalization before and after differentiation.

In general, vocabulary tests fail to tap these many aspects of word meanings. They test only for the presence or absence of "a particular semantic association with the word, in the form of a pictorial image or another word" (Roberts, 1970, p. IV–8). Multiple meanings are not tapped, and syntactic aspects of meaning, such as whether a "ring" can "hide," are completely overlooked.

COMBINING WORD MEANINGS

In addition to a knowledge of dictionary entries, people know rules for combining word meanings into a meaning for a sentence. Each word contributes to the sentence one of its meanings (a single path in the dictionary entry for *bachelor*); each word also contributes to the elimination of all but one of the possible paths for the other words in the sentence. For example, *man* can have a concrete meaning of an individual man, or it can have the abstract meaning of *mankind*. In the sentence

(20)   The man hits the ball.

man must have the concrete meaning because *the* is marked for restriction to use with nouns that are concrete in this sense.

Note that combining word meanings into a sentence meaning is what the computer cannot do in interpreting "Time flies like an arrow," but here certain meanings of words are eliminated by our knowledge of the real world. *Like* cannot be a verb because, if it were, then *time flies* would have to be a noun phrase containing *adjective + noun*, and we know that no such insects exist. Katz and Fodor (1964) explicitly set out only to describe our ability to understand sentences apart from our knowledge of the settings in which they occur. But, as emphasized in an earlier chapter, in a full description of human language ability, the notion of "understand a sentence" must be expanded beyond the kind of literal interpretation that Katz and Fodor discuss—"beyond" in the sense of further removed from the actual perceptible utterance.

PROPOSITIONS THAT SENTENCES EXPRESS

In previous chapters the construction of sentences was separated from the meaning of words. Bronowski and Bellugi (1970) suggest that this separation is artificial and that both aspects signify one general human ability:

> . . . the human practise of naming parts of the environment presupposes and rests on a more fundamental activity, namely, that of analysing the environment into distinct parts and treating these as separate objects. That is, there is implied in the structure of cognitive sentences a view of the outside world as separable into things which maintain their identity and which can be manipulated in the mind, so that even actions and properties are reified in words. . . .

> Learning the word for objects like *chair* is considered to be one of the simplest problems of language learning. Yet for the child to understand his parents' sentence, "The chair broke," he must first analyze out the state of being of the chair at the time of the utterance, and then interpret the meaning of the word *broke* . . . from this. . . .

> The match between a sentence and the reality that it maps strikes us now, when we know the language, as made by putting the sentence together; but it begins in the first place, in the beginning of language, by taking reality apart. (Bronowski and Bellugi, 1970, pp. 672–673.)

This connection between taking reality apart and putting sentences together is seen clearly at the earliest stage of the acquisition of syntax, when basic semantic relations are being expressed in two-word utterances. Brown suggests that these meanings "seem to be extensions of the kind of intelligence that has been called 'sensory-motor' by the great developmental psychologist, Jean Piaget . . . [in which] the child 'constructs' the world of enduring objects and immediate space and time." (Brown, 1970, p. 223.)

Later, Brown (in press; Table 8) classified the semantic relations expressed in children's two-word utterances into four "operations of reference" and seven "relations":

I.   Operations of reference.
    Nominations: *That* (or *It* or *There*) + *book, cat, clown, hot, big,* etc.
    Notice: *Hi* + *Mommy, cat, belt,* etc.
    Recurrence: *More* (or *'Nother*) + *milk, cereal, nut, read, swing, green,* etc.
    Nonexistence: *Allgone* (or *No-more*) + *rattle, juice, dog, green,* etc.

II. Relations.
    Attributive: Ad + N (*Big train, Red book,* etc.)
    Possessive: N + N (*Adam checker, Mommy lunch,* etc.)
    Locative: N + N (*Sweater chair, Book table,* etc.)
    Locative: N + V (*Walk street, Go store,* etc.)
    Agent-Action: N + V (*Adam put, Eve read,* etc.)
    Agent-Object: N + N (*Mommy sock, Mommy lunch,* etc.)
    Action-Object: V + N (*Put book, Hit ball,* etc.)

The child's primitive questions are also indications that objects now endure and that out of sight is *not* out of mind. *Where Dad,* or even the more primitive *Daddy?* asked in Daddy's absence, signifies the child's growing conceptual ability to evoke in his mind representations of things in his world not present in any immediate sensation.

Once language is used, it stimulates the development of thought beyond what was possible nonverbally.

> The meanings of the first sentences pre-suppose the sensory-motor constructions, but they also go beyond them. The aim of sensory-motor intelligence is practical success, not truth; sensory-motor intelligence is *acted* not *thought.* The ability to create propositions which can be expressed in sentences must mature near the end of the sensory-motor period. (Brown, 1970, p. 223.)

Once the children start asking questions, the conversation that ensues can contribute to the child's thought.

> The chief result of obtaining replies to his Where-questions is this, that the child finds that through these questions he can take the initiative in causing another person to refer to something within their common environment and yet beyond the immediate situation. By securing social cooperation of this kind, he extends his area of reference, building up a structure of symbolization of what is absent. (Lewis, 1964, p. 92.)

Discussion of the relationship between the development of ideas and of language returns in Chapter 9.

5

The Developmental Process

It is now possible to characterize in more general terms the dimensions of language development, and the processes by which it seems to take place. Details presented in Chapter 3 and 4 will be supplemented by the results of other research.

Dimensions of Development

Four dimensions of development have been illustrated in Chapters 3 and 4: deviations of child language from the adult model; simultaneous differentiation and integration; increasing freedom from immediate context; and the development of metalinguistic awareness.

CHILDISH RULES AND THEIR EXCEPTIONS

In Chapter 2 knowledge of a language was characterized as tacit knowledge of a set of rules. Children learn this set of rules gradually. One might assume, therefore, that the stages a child passes through on his way to mature knowledge could be characterized as partial versions of adult knowledge. But this is clearly not true. One of the most dramatic findings of studies of child language is that these stages show striking similarities from one child to another, but equally striking deviations from the adult model. Hopefully, the adjective "childish" will convey this uniqueness without any negative connotation of condescension.

Recall the errors that children make. In morphology, while children are learning to form noun and verb endings, they temporarily say *foots* instead of *feet*, *goed* instead of *went*, *mines* instead of *mine*. Children do not hear *foots* or *goed* or *mines*. The child hears *his*, *hers*, *ours*, *yours* and *theirs*; and he hypothesizes that the first-person singular possessive should be *mines*. These invented words are based on regularities that each child is somehow extracting from the language he hears. These stages on the way to the child's acquisition of mature behavior may seem for the moment to be regressions, new errors in terms of adult standards, and yet actually be significant evidence of intellectual work and linguistic progress.

Rules for the formation of questions show the same kind of deviation. When Adam asks *What he wants?* or *Why you can't open it?*, it is clear that these are forms that he has not heard from his parents and which cannot be derived from their questions by any telegraphic reduction. This is important evidence for the child's constructive activity. When a child asks, *What you want?* one could assert that he is simply imitating an adult question but omitting the dummy AUX *do*. *What he wants?* and *Why you can't open it?* cannot be explained in this way.

A child's speech that does look like or sound like a telegraphic reduction of adult speech is probably also constructed by rules, though one cannot be as sure. "Telegraphic" is an accurate characterization of a product—an utterance like *Mommy sock*—which is constructed at a particular stage in development before function words have been acquired and while the child's programming span is severely limited. But "telegraphic" should not be understood as a characterization of the process by which such utterances are produced.

As with morphology and syntax, so with sounds. Remember that Read (1970, 1971) discovered that, unknown to each other or to their parents or teachers, a group of preschool children "agreed" that the sounds of *tr-* and *ch-* were closely related. They also "agreed" that "short" vowels should be represented in writing by the letter of the alphabet whose initial sound it matches, and so wrote *fall* for *fell*.

One should not assume, however, that everything a child says is constructed by rules. Isolated bits of surprisingly advanced constructions often appear in a child's speech, and one should not automatically credit the child with knowledge of the rule that such behavior would imply in an adult. Among inflections, common irregular forms like *went* and *saw* are learned first, presumably as isolated vocabulary words, and temporarily coexist with the overgeneralizations that indicate acquisition of a productive rule. For example, the age span, in months, over which Sarah used *went* and *goed* was as follows:

Went	27	32	47	48	49	50
Goed			47		49	

The same phenomenon occurs in the formation of questions. For example, Table 8, Chapter 3, shows that the negative auxiliaries *don't* and *can't* appear in questions like *You can't fix it?* before any affirmative auxiliaries appear. Because there is such a striking contrast between the use of these two isolated forms and the later and quite sudden use of a wide variety of both affirmative and negative auxiliaries, Bellugi (1965) argues that *don't* and *can't* probably enter the child's language first as un-analyzed wholes, which are only later reconstrued as part of the total auxiliary system. The same argument can be made for *What dat?*, which precedes all other wh-questions and is very frequent even at stage I (Brown, 1968a). It can also be made for the longer form *D'you want . . .* , which Adam used as a question introducer for a brief period. Spoken with an invariant pronunciation, it was followed by a wide range of pronouns and verb phrases, as in *D'you want me have birthday?* (Bellugi, 1965).

In children's production of sounds, the course of development is also in general systematic, but seemingly isolated bits of extrasystemic complexity may appear. Moskowitz (1970) discusses the premature pronunciation of *pretty* by one-year-old Hildegarde (Leopold, 1939–1947):

> The existence of *príti* in the lexicon . . . is a very nice example of what Jakobson meant when he said that there are often some extra-systematic phenomena in children's speech. . . . As an isolated, memorized item, its encoding is incommensurable with that of any other part of the system . . . [Hildegarde] has no other consonant clusters, and even no other examples of either *p* or *r* in any other syllables. After a long tenure, the isolated *príti* gives way to *píti*, which seems superficially to be simpler but is actually far more complex, precisely because this new item is a concession to the system . . . and is generated by the same phonological rules which operate everywhere else. (Moskowitz, 1970, pp. 39–40.)

These examples of extrasystemic complexity share two characteristics: Their appearance is not accompanied by related structures in morphology, syntax, or phonology, and they are rigidly set in a single form. Brown points out that adults also learn this way when, without knowing another language, they control "what might be called Operatic Italian or Lieder Deutsch" (Brown, 1968a, p. 283). This phenomenon will be discussed further in Chapter 6.

According to the analysis of inflectional errors in Chapter 3 lower-class Black children seemed to share learning strategies, and even specific over-generalizations of rules, with Adam, Eve, and Sarah. The same conclusion appeared from another comparative analysis of these 15 children's language development. A student at Harvard, Donald Moore (1967) analyzed the emergence of forms of the copulative verb "be", contracted or not, in sentences like Sarah's *He's cute* and *My teeth are black*. The auxiliary use of "be" as in *I'm going*, which was included in the analysis of inflections, was not included; nor was a particular "habitual" meaning of "be" in Black English (discussed in Chapter 8).

Since it could be claimed that the experimental treatments (discussed in Chapter 6) that 8 of 12 children received would influence their language in the direction of the Cambridge children, Moore confined his analysis to the spontaneous speech samples collected before treatment began for all 12 children, and to only the 4 control children for the entire three-month period. Therefore, his conclusions about similarities among the 15 children are stronger than about inflections where that limitation on the speech samples was not observed.

Briefly, Moore found that Adam, Eve and Sarah first began using copulatives in sentences that started either with pronouns or with *where, here,* or *there* before using them in sentences that started with noun phrases (NPs). For example, Eve said *That's hot* while still saying *Finger stuck.* Moore combined pronouns and the three locational words into a single category of "introductory words" (Int.). "A period exists for each child (Adam, 7 months; Eve, 4 months; and Sarah, 5 months) in which Int. words are sometimes followed by "be" while initial NPs never are" (1967, p. 10), despite the presence in the protocols at this period of more than 100 utterances with initial NPs in which "be" could have been included. At the next stage, "be" appears after NPs, and in the third stage, it reaches the criterion of "supplied 90 percent of the time, clearly required" in all contexts. Only Sarah attained this criterion by stage V (see Figure 1, Chapter 3), at which point Moore ended his analysis.

Of the 12 Roxbury children at pretest time, 5 were in the initial stage: some copulatives after Int. words, and examples in their protocols of utterances with subject NPs but without "be." Three other children used no NPs in the initial position (recall the comment in Chapter 2 that subject NPs seem to be more complex in general that object NPs), and so no determination of their stage of development could be made. The remaining four children all included "be" some of the time after both Int. and NPs. Of the children in the control group whose language was analyzed for the entire three-month period, two reached the 90 percent criterion and one other was close to it. Table 1 gives the ages and mean length of utterance (MLU) for all 15 children.

All 15 children made similar "errors" with copulas as they did with inflections. For a time, Adam sprinkled *s*'s on third-person singular impersonal pronouns, producing utterances like *Its fell* and *Its works.* Brown, Cazden, and Bellugi (1969) suggested that this might be a segmentation error, caused by Adam's thinking that *its* was simply a variant pronunciation of the pronoun itself. Moore noticed that three of the Roxbury children made the same kind of error, though with different Int. words, producing utterances like *Thats a Andy* (about a Raggedy Andy doll), *Hes fall down* and *Whats is this*? A segmentation error interpretation would fit here, too.

The importance of the child's active intelligence in constructing rules evidently applies beyond verbal language to the acquisition of other symbolic systems. At least that generalization is suggested by Bellugi's current research (1971) on a deaf child's acquisition of sign language from her deaf parents. In sign language, the subject-object relationship can be expressed with some verbs, but not all, by a gesture of directionality. In perfect analogy to verbal overgeneralizations like *goed,* this deaf child

Table 1 **Age and Mean Length of Utterance (MLU) at Three Stages of Copulative Development**

Stage	Eve		Adam		Sarah		Children	
	AGE, MONTHS	MLU	AGE, MONTHS	MLU	AGE, MONTHS	MLU	AGE, MONTHS	MLU
"Be" after Int. only	20½	1.95	29½	1.75	32	2.25	34½*	2.99*
"Be" after both Int. and NP	24½	4.00	37½	3.75	37	2.85	35†	3.38†
"Be" supplied to 90% criterion	not by 26	4.00	not by 41	4.00	48	3.95	40½‡	3.68‡

Source: (D. Moore, 1967.)
* Five children with "be" after Int., but not after NP in initial protocol.
† Four children with "be" after both Int. and NP in initial protocol.
‡ Two children in control group.

overgeneralized this gesture for irregular verbs to which it did not apply and which she could never have seen.

DIFFERENTIATION AND INTEGRATION

Differentiation and integration characterize development at the level of lexical categories and the level of rules. Brown and Bellugi (1964) described the child's gradual differentiation of the category of modifier into articles, demonstrative adjectives, and so forth. Each differentiation entails greater restrictions on possible linguistic contexts. The same is true of rules. When we say that children overgeneralize rules, we should say more accurately that they have underdifferentiated them. We saw how this is true of rules for forming plurals and for forming questions.

Later syntactic development can also be characterized in this way. C. Chomsky (1969) studied the acquisition during the elementary school years of several aspects of syntax which require very specific knowledge. On the basis of a linguistic analysis, she proposed several hypotheses about the sequence of development: First, consider the following two sentences:

(21a)   Bozo [*the clown*] tells Donald [*Duck*] to hop up and down.

(21b)   Bozo promises Donald to hop up and down.

In both sentences the subject of the complement verb *hop* is not expressed and must be supplied by the listener. In (21a) the subject is *Donald*, the noun nearest to the verb, following what C. Chomsky calls the "Minimal Distance Principle (MDP)"; in (21b) the subject of *hop* is *Bozo*. The majority of English verbs act like *told*, whereas *promise* is the rarer exception. Chomsky hypothesized that when "the syntactic structure associated with a particular word is at variance with a general pattern in the language" (C. Chomsky, 1971b, p. 7), that structure will be learned later. She found that when asked to demonstrate the appropriate actions, younger children make Donald do the hopping in both cases.

Second, whereas the syntactic structure associated with *promise* always violates the MDP, *ask* can take both kinds of structures:

(22a)   Ask X to stand up. (*Subject of* stand up *is* X.)

(22b)   Ask X what to feed the doll. (*Subject of* feed the doll *is speaker, not* X.)

Here "a conflict exists between two of the potential syntactic structures associated with a particular verb," and learning to interpret *ask* correctly in all possible syntactic structures should occur later than learning to interpret *promise*. When told sentence (22b), younger children said *The cucumber*.

Third, consider the referent for the pronoun *he* in the following two sentences:

(23a)   Pluto thinks he knows everything.

(23b)   He knows that Pluto won the race.

In most sentences with both a noun phrase and a pronoun, as in (23a), the pronoun *he* can refer either to the NP *Pluto* or to someone else not mentioned in the sentence. In certain sentences, however, as in (23b), *he* must refer to someone else, not *Pluto*. Chomsky hypothesized that when "restrictions on a grammatical operation apply under certain limited conditions only," the restricted structure should be learned later. In fact, young children, when asked *Who knows?* repeated the NP or pointed to that toy in both cases.

As differentiation of categories and rules proceed, increasing integration is also taking place. Noun phrases are being integrated into more varied slots in utterances. And more rules are being combined in a single utterance. In some cases, this integration is probably due to some lifting of cognitive limitations, as when children combine the inversion transformation and the preposing transformation and finally form mature wh-questions: *How can he be a doctor?* In other cases, this integration is probably a matter of greater linguistic knowledge.

One dimension of development is the ability to pack a greater density of ideas into a single sentence by embedding one sentence in another. Hunt (1965), and O'Donnell, Griffin, and Morris (1967) have followed the increase in written language, from childhood through professional writers, in the number and length of clauses combined in a single sentence. Consider the following sentence from a fourth-grade composition:

> The captain said / if you can kill the white
> whale, Moby Dick / I will give this gold to the
> one / that can do it.

As Hunt points out, "Within the main clause is embedded a noun clause [what the captain said] and within it is both an adverbial *if* clause and an adjective clause" (1965, p. 21). Other means to the same end are the rich possibilities for nominalization in English. Here are three sentences with increasingly complex nominalizations, all taken from captions dictated by preschool children in Berkeley, California, for their drawings.

(24a)   My friend's house *or* Some big kids. (*Noun with preceding modifier.*)

(24b)   My little brother opened his mouth to drink some *water from the rain.* (*Noun modified by prepositional phrase.*)

(24c)   Once upon a time at the Oakland International Airport *a dog named Cricket who rides a motorcycle* was on the airplane. (*Noun modified by a participial phrase and a relative clause.*)

We need research on how this aspect of language structure develops in children.

FREEDOM FROM CONTEXT

N. Chomsky (n.d.) spoke of human language as "free from the control of external stimuli." In one sense, this is true of child language from the very beginning. In comparing the language of child and chimpanzee, Bronowski and Bellugi remind us that the monologs spoken by Weir's two-year-old son in his crib (Weir, 1962) were free of any immediate nonlinguistic context.

> His monologues show a great deal of syntactic play, arrangements and re-arrangements, transformations of sentence types, substitution of words in fixed sentence frames, and so forth. It is not just idle chatter, although it has no social function, no content to instruct someone else, and consists in large part of explorations of structure. It is in fact the extreme form of that "distancing" from any immediate context. (Bronowski and Bellugi, 1970, p. 671.)

But in other ways, one characterization of development is a progressive freeing of language from dependence on support from the nonverbal context. This does not mean simply that as children develop, their sentences are more interpretable apart from the context in which they occur, though that is true; disambiguation by context is indeed gradually replaced by disambiguation by vocabulary and sentence structure. But it is also true that as development proceeds, the child's own language comprehension and production requires less nonverbal support. Several examples can be cited.

Huttenlocher and Strauss (1968) asked children to create a pile of two blocks in response to a description like *The red block is on top of the green block*. One of the two blocks was fixed on the middle rung of a ladder. The task was much easier when the block that was free for the child to manipulate was the grammatical subject of the sentence (the red block). Evidently when the green block was the free one, children had to transform the statement to correspond to the extralinguistic situation before they could understand it.

Slobin and Welsh discovered one suggestive phenomenon when they were asking a two-and-a-half-year-old girl, "Echo," to imitate sentences.

> Often Echo will spontaneously produce a fairly long and complex sentence [e.g., *If you finish your eggs all up, Daddy, you can have your coffee.*] and if this utterance is offered as a model immediately after its production, it will be (more or less) successfully imitated. However, if the very same utterance is presented to the child ten minutes later—i.e., the child's own utterance—she will often fail to imitate it fully or correctly. . . . It would seem that the child has "an intention to-say-so-and-so"—to use William James' phrase—and has encoded that intention into linguistic form. If that linguistic form is presented for imitation while the intention is still operative, it can be fairly successfully imitated. Once the intention is gone, however, the utterance must be processed in linguistic terms alone—without its original intentional and contextual support. In the absence of such support,

the task can strain the child's abilities, and reveal a more limited competence than may actually be present in spontaneous speech. Thus whatever we discover in systematic probes of imitation must be taken as a conservative estimate of the child's linguistic competence. (Slobin and Welsh, 1971, p. 175.)

In the longitudinal study of Adam, Eve, and Sarah's speech, we noted that the first verbs that seemed to receive a past tense in the children's speech were verbs like *smashed, banged, dropped*. It seemed possible that the instantaneous quality of the referent actions, and the fact that they were inevitably completed by the time they were talked about, may have helped trigger the use of the past tense. Chapter 6 discusses how *what* and *who* in parental speech may focus attention on the distinction between inanimate and animate parts of the nonlinguistic world. Here, the reverse relation is suggested—a characteristic of certain actions in the nonlinguistic world may focus attention particularly effectively on the means for encoding the past-present distinction. When this suggestion was made to Piaget's colleague Sinclair, she corroborated the suggestion from her analyses of child language in Geneva:

> At a much later age when we ask children to describe actions which we have just performed in front of them, the question is always put in the same way: "Tell me what happened"—that is to say it is put in the past tense. We find that the children introduce some kind of distinction between duratives and non-duratives. That is to say, all the actions that take some time, like *laver*, are put in the present. I will say: "Tell me what has happened" and the child will say: "The boy washes the car" or rather in English: "is washing the car." Whereas when it was *breaking*, he would say: "the boy broke the stick" and the distinction is quite clear, five to six year olds always seem to answer with the past tense when the action was momentary or non-durative and in the present when it was durative action, even though the question was always put in the past. (Discussion in Huxley and Ingram 1971, pp. 75–76.)

Finally, there seems to be an iconic quality to some aspects of human language whereby the simplest constructions parallel experience in some way. Jakobson (lecture, 5/14/64) suggested that the subject-verb-object word order is the simplest form in most languages of the world. In English, as we have seen, the passive construction in which that order is reversed is learned later by children.

Language is also iconic when temporal clauses are spoken in the same order as the events they describe. Hatch (1969a, b) found that this temporal order is easier for children to understand than reversed temporal order. That is, sentences (25a–c) are easier than sentences (25d–f).

(25a) Fill this and then set the fish in it.

(25b) It made a last goggle and glug before it went to the street.

(25c)   After I sell the eggs, I will get a silk dress.

(25d)   You can go to the moon, but first talk to your father.

(25e)   He knows he will get something to eat after he gets the ball.

(25f)   Before Tom got to town, he saw nine mules.

Hatch also compared the children's language with the language in their readers. She found all the above sentences (25a–f) in the primers and pre-primers of four reading series, even though they pose unequal problems in comprehension for six-year-old children. She suggests that language structures in texts should be selected to fit the children for whom they are intended.

DEVELOPMENT OF METALINGUISTIC AWARENESS

As a child's language develops, so does his conscious metalinguistic awareness of that language. Think of each addition to the child's linguistic knowledge as written in his mind in magic ink or recorded in his mind in magic sound. As these additions are growing in number and complexity of relationships, they are also becoming progressively more visible, or audible, to the child himself.

While trying out some new beginning reading materials, Mackay and Thompson (1968) uncovered one aspect of this metalinguistic development: a developmental progression in the child's awareness of the structure of his own spoken sentence. Mackay and Thompson's materials are designed so that the child's first reading materials are the child's own compositions and so that the conceptual aspect of composition is separated from the mechanical skill of handwriting. Each child has a "word folder" with a preselected store of words plus some blanks for his personal collection. He also has a stand on which words from the folder can be set up as a text. Mackay and Thompson found that in their awareness of words in a sentence, children go through several stages (condensed from Mackay and Thompson, 1968, pp. 112–115):

Stage 1:   The child simply lists words with no apparent link—*Dad boy girl* —and reads them as isolated words.

Stage 2:   The child composes on his stand a telegraphic sentence—*Children school*—but reads it as a complete sentence—*The children go to school.*

Stage 3:   The child realizes that words are missing from the Stage 2 sentences and either adds them at the end—*Mum home my is at* —or selects the missing words after the nouns and verbs but then inserts them into their proper place.

Evidently, when they're five to six years old, children recapitulate at the metalinguistic level of conscious awareness the development from telegraphic to complete sentence that they went through when they were two to three years old at the linguistic level of nonconscious oral speech. When materials such as these are used, the developmental progression is laid bare for the teacher to see. But as Mackay and Thompson point out, progress in this conceptual abiilty will not be revealed if the child only copies from a model that the teacher has written from the child's dictation, and it will be confounded with problems in handwriting and/or spelling unless he has whole words in some form to work with.

While watching children using the Mackay and Thompson materials, I realized how much they must be learning *about* language. For example, in a short visit to one Infant School I noticed the following:

Morphology: A child adding a separate card for *s* to verbs like *take* and nouns like *picture*; composing *coming* by adding a card with *ing* to *come* so that the *e* is covered.

Syntax: A child shoving to the right a previously constructed sentence, *The movie-camera man is coming*, and inserting *on Tuesday* as a chunk at the beginning.

Orthography: A child using a combination of small words and separate letters to compose longer words such as *h-it-s,* as one boy in the six-year-old group did.

In using these materials, children are stimulated to monitor their own language behavior, objectify it in words and/or letters on the stands, and then operate on it in various ways. This, too, is part of the metalinguistic level of language ability.

Metalinguistic awareness is not confined to grammatical structure. Whereas all children [even infants, according to Eimas et al. (1971)] learn in some nonconscious way which speech sounds are alike and which are different, subsequent training in school in auditory discrimination and analysis of words into component sounds is training in the metalinguistic ability to reflect upon sounds in the words one speaks and hears and to make deliberate, conscious judgments. Read's (1970, 1971) research on children's invented spellings suggests that individual differences may be greater in metalinguistic awareness than in language ability per se.

Chapter 4 discussed a distinction between using words correctly and being able to discuss their meaning and give synonyms or paraphrases. Another aspect of word knowledge, which seems to shift from nonconscious to conscious, is part-of-speech (or form-class) membership. Word-association research has repeatedly shown that sometimes during the early elementary school years the associations children give shift from words that could appear sequentially in an utterance like *dark-night* to words that could substitute for each other, like *dark-light*. These two kinds of associations have been labeled *syntagmatic* and *paradigmatic,* respectively. Anglin (1970) applied the same labels to the groupings that children make when asked to sort words into categories. As previous research has also shown, younger children tend to make thematic (syntagmatic) groupings, such as *needle, doctor, suffer, weep*, and *sadly*, while older children and adults are more likely to group (paradigmatically) by part of speech: *white, dark, cold, soft, sweet*, and *hard*. Anglin reported his own research in which children in grades 3 to 4 and even many in grades 7 to 8 did not group words according to parts of speech, and concludes that "young children cannot grasp the abstract semantic concepts in terms of which parts of speech are taught." His monograph ends with "A Remaining Puzzle":

> . . . there remains a single but ubiquitous phenomenon that can be viewed as counter evidence. The young child speaks the language and, specifically, the parts of speech are given proper grammatical treatment. . . . within the child's own body of utterances there exists a potential indicant of the most abstract semantic relations among words. . . . How does one reconcile this ability with his apparent inability to treat them as equivalent in our other tasks?
>
> Perhaps there is a parallel here . . . with the finding that use of rules of grammar in spontaneous speech appears much earlier than the ability to describe those rules. Employing principles and being cognizant of them may reflect very different cognitive capacities. . . . Viewed in this way the developmental trends reported in this book may be inextricably linked to the growth of an aspect of consciousness. (Anglin, 1970, p. 101.)

Anglin is right in contending that from the beginning "the parts of speech are given proper grammatical treatment" in child speech. The rarity of violations of part-of-speech categories was noted in Chapter 3. But becoming aware of knowledge one has acted on is probably a continuum, not a none-then-all phenomenon. And the experimental condition in which the child is asked to think about that knowledge will make a significant difference in research results.

A student at Harvard, Martha Bronson (1971) didn't believe that preschool children couldn't sort words according to parts of speech because she had been a Montessori teacher and knew that such lessons were part of the standard Montessori curriculum. In barest outline (which doesn't do the teaching procedure justice) you train children to associate "thing words" with a particular cardboard shape (Montessori recommended a large black triangle), and then to associate "action words" with a very different shape (Montessori recommended a large, red circle). After an initial period of training, the children are asked to group new nouns and verbs. Mrs. Bronson proved her point with a group of four-year-olds. She does report, however, that at this age children have trouble categorizing some nouns and verbs like *idea* and *grow*, because the "thing" or "action" is less perceptually obvious, and she suggests that their concepts of adjective, adverbs and prepositions might be even less accurate.

Two points should be noted about the Anglin and Bronson work. First, the nature of the test situation is extremely important. One problem in all language research with young children, which Mrs. Bronson solved, is finding a task appropriate for their understanding and span of attention, in which they can display their linguistic knowledge. The Appendix discusses this problem further. Second, if Mrs. Bronson's children can only categorize the more perceptual (concrete) things and actions, then Anglin is still right in asserting a gap between linguistic knowledge that children nonconsciously use in speech behavior and metalinguistic knowledge that they can apply in other verbal tasks.

As Dixon says, we know very little about "the conditions and the stages in which the children and young people become aware of language they have learnt to use; and the effects of such awareness or knowledge on their further learning and operating of language" (1967, p. 76). We do know that awareness of language is not easy and may account for more differences among children in school language tasks than can be accounted for by language abilities themselves. In Kelkar's words, "talking about language, using language about language, is about as easy as burning wood in a wooden chulha [a wood-burning stove in India]" (1969, p. 11).

Presumably, metalinguistic awareness develops unevenly from one aspect of language to another. Collections of the games children play with words should yield insights into this progression.

> When we notice that a child has started to play with some newly acquired component of understanding, we may definitely conclude that he has become full master of this item of understanding; only those ideas can become toys for him whose proper relation to reality is firmly known to him. (Chukovsky, 1963, p. 103.)

Doesn't the manipulation of sounds in a game like pig Latin precede the appreciation of multiple word meanings in puns? Doesn't delight in name-calling, which assumes the arbitrariness of names, precede the delight in semantic absurdities like the following (Opie and Opie, 1959, p. 25)?

> I went to the pictures tomorrow.
> I took a front seat at the back.

Apart from the functions that any such games serve in a peer culture, they must take different forms and depend on awareness of different aspects of language at different ages.

For some children, metalinguistic awareness may be hastened by knowing more than one language. At least Leopold thought that bilingualism helped his daughter Hildegarde become aware of the arbitrariness of names:

> The most striking effect of bilingualism was a noticeable looseness of the link between the phonetic word and its meaning. The child never insisted on stereotype wording of stories, as monolingual children often do, and even made vocabulary substitutions freely in memorized rhymes and songs. The unity of phonetic word and meaning . . . was definitely not a fact for this

child, who heard the same thing constantly designated by two different phonetic forms. (Leopold, 1971a, p. 141.)

Metalinguistic awareness is one aspect of general cognitive development. In Chapter 4, Vygotsky (1962) was quoted on the awareness of names. An extension of that quotation describes the more general process.

> Piaget's studies showed that introspection begins to develop only during the school years. This process has a good deal in common with the development of external perception and observation in the transition from infancy to early childhood, when the child passes from primitive wordless perception to perception of objects guided by and expressed in words—perception in terms of meaning. Similarly, the school child passes from unformulated to verbalized introspection; he perceives his own psychic processes as meaningful. But perception in terms of meaning always implies a degree of generalization. Consequently, the transition to verbalized self-observation denotes a beginning process of generalization of the inner forms of activity. The shift to a new type of inner perception means also a shift to a higher type of inner activity, since a new way of seeing things opens up new possibilities for handling them. A chess player's moves are determined by what he sees on the board; when his perception of the game changes, his strategy will also change. In perceiving some of our own acts in a generalizing fashion, we isolate them from our total mental activity and are thus enabled to focus on this process as such and to enter into a new relationship to it. (Vygotsky, 1962, p. 91.)

In a provocative essay extending this process into adult education and radical social change, the Brazilian educator Paulo Freire describes "conscientization" as the way by which men—not as recipients, but as knowing subjects—achieve a deepening awareness both of the social-cultural reality that shapes their lives and of their capacity to transform that reality. Whereas "animals are simply in the world, incapable of objectifying either themselves or the world," man's "consciousness is never a mere reflection of, but a reflection upon, material reality" (Freire, 1970, pp. 453–454). It is easy to provide children with opportunities for experience—with language and beyond. Finding ways to help them become consciously aware of and reflective about those experiences seems harder, but perhaps it is the heart of true education.

Processes of Development

If the development of language structure can be characterized in the ways described above, what is implied about the processes by which it takes place? The rest of this chapter is devoted to three processes: imitation, practice, and the interaction of knowledge of language and cognitive capacities, with a postscript on neurological research.

Throughout, discussion focuses on *how* child language develops, not why. Questions about causality in any biological system can be asked at many levels. See Mayr (1961) for one particularly clear discussion. Questions about "why" are particularly difficult to answer at the level of propellants acting within the organism. They remain unanswered in theories of more general cognitive development (for example, Piaget's); and they also remain unanswered in theories of language development. What propels the child, inexorably so it seems, toward the language norms for his community? Is he propelled by specific expressive and communicative needs? That cannot be the whole answer because, as we have noted, immature forms often do the job: Yes-no questions can be asked by intonation alone; the confirmation sought by tag questions can be requested by *OK?* and *right?*; topicalization can be accomplished by stress without resorting to a passive construction. Is the child also propelled by what K. Goldstein calls "actualization"—"the drive to actualize inborn capacities" (Freedman, 1968). And what is the relationship between the two?

THE ROLE OF IMITATION

The general question of how child development is at once independent of adult behavior and simultaneously dependent on it is not unique to language. In all aspects of development, children behave in uniquely childish ways because they are children, and yet they are influenced (some would say "shaped") toward the standards of behavior in their community. But if we compare the acquisition of language with the acquisition of a cognitive operation like the conservation of mass or volume, the special interest of the question about language becomes apparent. Consider the proverbial child growing up alone on a desert island. From his own manipulative activities, with no models of mature behavior available, a child would probably achieve conservation. But without such models of mature language behavior, he could not acquire a full human language. Yet, given such a model, he seems to create it anew for himself, using what he hears as examples of language to learn from, not samples of language to learn.

The commonsense view of how children learn to speak is that they imitate the language they hear around them. In a general way, this must be true. A child in an English-speaking home grows up to speak English, not French or Hindi or some language of his own. But in the fine details of the language-learning process, imitation cannot be the whole answer. Examples from Chapters 3 and 4 of children's creative but rule-governed "errors" in inflections, questions, and invented spellings attest to an active, nonimitative construction process.

Sometimes we get particularly dramatic evidence of how impervious to external alteration the child's rule system can be. Jean Berko Gleason's conversation with a four-year-old is an example (Gleason, 1967, p. 1):

> She said, *My teacher holded the baby rabbits and we patted them.*
> I asked, *Did you say your teacher held the baby rabbits?*
> She answered, *Yes.*
> I then asked, *What did you say she did?*
> She answered, again. *She holded the baby rabbits and we patted them.*
> *Did you say she held them tightly?*, I asked.
> *No*, she answered, *she holded them loosely.*

Impressed by the confidence with which the child continued to use her own constructions, despite hearing and comprehending the adult form, Gleason conducted a variation of her older test (Berko, 1958) with first-, second-, and third-grade children. She asked the children to give irregular plural nouns or past-tense verbs after she had supplied the correct form as she asked the question. "In the case of the verbs, they were shown a bell that could ring and told that yesterday it rang; then they were asked what the bell did yesterday" (Gleason, 1967, p. 3). Even under these conditions, only 50 percent of the first-graders (7 of 14) said *rang*; 6 said *ringed*; and one said *rung*. Gleason concluded—

> In listening to us, the children attended to the sense of what we said, and not the form. And the plurals and past tenses they offered were products of their own linguistic systems, and not imitations of us. (Gleason, 1967, p. 8.)

When sophisticated parents try deliberately to teach a child a form that does not fit his present rule system, the same filtering process occurs. The following conversation took place when a psychologist (McNeill, 1966, p. 69) tried to correct an immaturity in her daughter's speech:

> C.:   Nobody don't like me.
> M.:   No, say "Nobody likes me."
> C.:   Nobody don't like me.
>   (*eight repetitions of this dialogue*)
> M.:   No. Now listen carefully; say "Nobody likes me."
> C.:   Oh! Nobody don't likes me!

Writing in 1907, Clara and William Stern posed a question about the role and limits of imitation, one that is still unanswered today:

> It might be assumed, of course, that there is an observable correlation between a child's speech and its environment, and that consequently the process of language acquisition by a child would be considered simply as the mechanical acceptance of external speech forms and meanings through imitation. In contrast, those who emphasized the internal contributions a child makes to its own speech looked for productions having nothing to do with imitation. They sought so-called "word inventions" or early manifestations of self-produced logical activity. Both views are capable of obscuring the real situation. . . .
> We believe that the proper position is a synthesis of these two opinions.

In his form of speech a child learning to speak is neither a phonograph reproducing external sounds nor a sovereign creator of language. In terms of the contents of his speech, he is neither a pure associative machine nor a sovereign creator of concepts. Rather, his speech is based on the continuing interaction of external impressions with internal systems which usually function unconsciously; it is thus the result of a constant "convergence." The detailed investigations pertaining to the development of speech and thought should determine the relative participation of both forces and also show how they accommodate each other. (Reprinted in Blumenthal, 1970, pp. 86–87.)

At most, imitation guarantees that the child's language system will converge, in superficial forms, on the language of his speech community. But it cannot account for the child's acquisition of the system of which those forms are the external expression. In the case of *a* and *the*, for example, the child can learn those two forms by imitation, but he must learn by some other process the abstract contrast in meaning that underlies their appropriate use.

In analyzing the role of imitation in the developmental process, it is important to distinguish between imitation as a cognitive process and identification as an attitudinal stance. While imitation seems to be less important in language acquisition than is often assumed, identification may be more important. See Bruner (1966) for a discussion of identification as one source of the will to learn. The influence of attitudes will be discussed further in Chapter 8 on dialects. Where multiple models are available to the child, the question of why one model is chosen instead of another is more sharply posed.

THE ROLE OF PRACTICE

Speaking grammatically has been likened to other skilled behavior such as piano playing (Lashley, 1951), and skills are usually aided by practice. Practice can be defined as repeated trials that result in increasing mastery. What can be said about the role of practice in speaking and comprehending? It is a bit of folklore that, in the course of language acquisition, children have extensive opportunity for practice. This can mean simply the uninteresting fact that children talk a lot and gradually acquire the adult grammar of their speech community. At the more interesting level of particular features, it is certainly the case that children repeat features such as the addition of plural morphemes or the inversion of noun phrase and auxiliary in questions. But what behavior should be considered as "practice in speaking"? Until a child uses a certain feature, he can't be said to practice it; and after he begins to use it, examples of repeated use can be considered practice only if some kind of progress can be shown.

The acquisition of many parts of the child's language system does happen gradually, over some period of time. This is clear from longitudinal data.

For example, in the acquisition of inflections shown in Table 1, Chapter 3, periods X and Y together constitute the period between the first appearance of an inflection and the attainment of the 90 percent criterion, which for plurals required four months for Eve, five months for Adam, and six months for Sarah. Do opportunities for practice influence the length of these periods?

The same phenomenon of variable performance during a phase of the developmental process appears as unreliability data in Cromer's (1970) cross-sectional research on children's interpretation of ambiguous adjectives. Given a toy duck and a toy wolf to manipulate, children were asked to show that "The wolf is happy to bite" versus "The wolf is tasty to bite." The youngest children, three to five years old, consistently showed the named animal doing the biting; Cromer calls these children "primitive rule-users." An intermediate group of six-year-olds gave some right answers and some wrong answers. The oldest children, seven to ten years old, were consistently correct. In an experimental procedure too rarely used, Cromer retested 19 of the 41 children one day later and found that 83 percent of the primitive rule users gave exactly the same answers on both days, but 89 percent of the intermediates changed one or more of their answers between the first day and the second. What determines the length of the intermediate stage? Does practice in any sense make a difference? It seems less likely here than with inflections because of the rarity of such ambiguous adjectives in everyday speech.

Children add the plural morpheme consistently and correctly to familiar words before they extend the rules to nonsense syllables (Ervin-Tripp, 1966). One dimension of development is the range of contexts in which a rule is used. If we consider application to nonsense syllables as the end of that continuum (when a child can apply them to nonsense syllables, presumably he can apply them to any real words), then we could correlate the number of times a child uses a plural morpheme with the time interval between first using it for familiar words and later generalizing it to nonsense syllables. At least theoretically, looking for such a relationship makes sense.

There is one major problem, however, with any research that depends on counting frequency of practice in speaking: A child may practice by himself in covert, silent rehearsal, and the frequency of such repetitions is not available for study. Experiments that do not depend on frequencies of occurrences in spontaneous speech, but only on frequencies within the experimental situation itself, may be a better source of information. For example, Olds (1970) asked six-, eight-, and ten-year-old children to give paraphrases of sentences as evidence of comprehension. She was studying the effect of absence or presence of relative pronouns and or presence of semantic constraints. Examples of her sentences were—

(26a)   The lion that the tiger chased was ferocious.
(26b)   The ring that the queen bought was gold.

Of interest here is her finding that all of the children showed improvement over the course of the trials. Improvement in Olds' study was indicated by an increasing number of correct paraphrases. It could also be indicated by shorter latencies, evidence that children are able to do the necessary mental processing more quickly. It is hard to explain the improvement Olds found. If the children did not have the requisite rules in their linguistic knowledge, they would fail. Yet something changed in their ability to use those rules. Did practice make the rules become more accessible? Or was the improvement only in the children's understanding of what the experimenter wanted?

As part of the picture of the role of practice, we should consider Elkind's (1967) reminder that children engage in a great deal of spontaneous repetitions by themselves. In language, this repetitious behavior is often outside communicative contexts in the forms of expressive, verbal play. Weir's (1962) study of the bedtime monologs of her two-year-old son Anthony provides many examples. In a rare "discourse" analysis of child language beyond the unit of a single utterance, Weir (1963) includes the following combination of grammatical analysis and sound play:

> Bobo's not throwing.
> Bobo can throw.
> Bobo can throw it.
> Bobo can throw.
> Oh (2x)
> Go (3x)

Such self-generated repetitions presumably serve some important cognitive function. According to Elkind (1967) "Repetitive behavior in the child is frequently the outward manifestation of an emerging cognitive ability and the need to realize that ability through action." Such behavior may play an important role in the integration of units of behavior into the larger hierarchical structures discussed in Chapter 2. If so, two aspects of the child's own repetitions may be critical in accomplishing that end. First, they are more variations on a theme than exact repetitions; second, the child is repeating behavior natural to his own stage of development, not imposed bits of behavior that conform to adult norms. The second characteristic contrasts sharply with much of the practice we ask children to do in school, such as pattern drills in second language teaching.

So far we have been talking about practice in speaking. Children also get practice in listening, chances to comprehend particular features again and again. In his discussion of repetition in listening, Friedlander contrasts the infant's auditory and visual experience:

> Listening experience differs markedly from visual experience in the very important respect that the listener can very seldom control the repetition of a stimulus array, while most (but not all) visual displays are available for repeated examination. The infant or young child inspecting his visual environ-

ment and learning its major features has an almost infinite number of opportunities to examine and re-examine his spatial surroundings. . . . But in the auditory world, almost all stimuli are beyond the infant's jurisdiction to regulate repetition at times and places of his own choosing except for the sounds the baby can produce himself, or the sounds he can prompt his parents to repeat on cue. (Friedlander, 1970, p. 31.)

Is there a relation between frequency of hearing a feature and the rate at which it appears in the child's spontaneous speech?

Brown, Cazden, and Bellugi (1969), as part of the longitudinal study of Adam, Eve, and Sarah, looked at the relationship between frequency of occurrence of particular features in parent speech (which could be considered opportunities for practice in comprehending) and sequence of acquisition of those features by the child. This evidence will be reported in Chapter 6.

There is also evidence that children seek opportunities for repetition in listening. In natural circumstances they ask for the same nursery rhyme or story again and again. For research in this area, Friedlander devised an imaginative piece of equipment, called Playtest. Infants as young as nine months can turn on one of two tape recorded segments. In a set of experiments Friedlander (1969, 1971, in press) documented both the infants' appetite for hearing the same few sentences over and over and changes over time in the kinds of selections that they preferred. In one experiment, the two Playtest channels played selections from the same child's story edited to two different lengths. One channel repeated itself after 20 seconds (high-redundancy version), and the other repeated itself after 140 seconds (low-redundancy version). There was an interesting shift in the preference of babies about 14 months old:

> Six of the babies showed a very conspicuous "crossover" effect. They first selected the short, high redundancy story as the preferred feedback to listen to, and then switch to the long, low redundancy story segment, with its richer informational content. This response pattern lends itself to the interpretation that the babies first prefer the simpler material they can more easily assimilate and then reorganize their preference in favor of the longer, more complicated story segment—showing a kind of psychological appetite for more nourishing fare. (Friedlander, 1971, in press.)

In summary, on the role of repetitions in learning to speak and comprehend, we are left with a set of questions:

1. Does practice in hearing a linguistic feature affect the schedule of acquiring it as a rule for speaking?

2. Is there any psychological continuum underlying the availability of rules for activation—that is, does the notion of availability for use have any validity in linguistic knowledge? If so, once a rule is in some sense acquired, does practice in using it play any role in extending it to the widest

range of linguistic contexts? (See articles by Flavell, Wohlwill, and Pinard and Laurendeau in Elkind and Flavell (1969) for related discussion.

3. Is there any psychological difference between using rules separately and using them in combination such that repetitions may not affect the acquisition of each rule, but may affect the ease of combining them into more complex structures?

INTERACTION OF LINGUISTIC KNOWLEDGE AND COGNITIVE CAPACITIES

Bever asks "How does the instinct to communicate integrate the distinct components of perception, cognition and motor behavior into human language?" (1970, p. 282). A twelve-year-old can play basketball, but a five-year-old cannot. The difference between them is only partly a matter of learning the rules of the game. It is also the case that the twelve-year-old has gained some general maturational characteristics that are necessary conditions of play—such as strength, endurance, and even height. The same is probably true for language. Although development is certainly characterized by the acquisition of additional rules for constructing sentences, more general changes in cognitive development are probably also required.

One such change that is frequently cited is the child's ability to construct longer and longer utterances. Being able to repeat longer and longer strings of numbers is a standard part of intelligence tests, and it is true, as Figure 1 in Chapter 3 made clear, that children do gradually speak longer sentences, at least for the period shown there. Ability to deal with increasing length cannot be the only relevant aspect of cognitive development, but other relevant aspects are still unknown.

Nor is it known what role is played by the child's understanding of the nonverbal referent or context. Bever and Macnamara offer contrasting arguments. Bever (1970) reports that two-year-olds are better than three-year-olds at demonstrating comprehension of the following two sentences by making appropriate actions with toys:

(27a)   The mother pats the dog.
(27b)   The dog pats the mother.

Older children are apt to make the mother do the patting in both cases, but, according to Bever, two-year-olds are less misled by probabilities of events in the real world.

Bever argues from these unusual data on the comprehension of very young children:

These results were found initially with only two sentences of each type, but have been replicated in a second experiment with five sentences of each type. These experiments show that the two-year-old child is relatively unaffected by semantic probabilities. The implication of this is to invalidate any theory of early language development that assumes that the young child depends on contextual knowledge of the world to tell him what sentences mean, independent of their structure.

It is obvious why the young child cannot make use of contextual probabilities: he does not have enough relevant experience to know what the probabilities are. For example, the young child may know the meaning of the word "pat" but may not have heard it enough, or done it enough, to know that usually people pat dogs and not the reverse. (Bever, 1970, p. 306.)

To my knowledge, no one has yet replicated this finding that two-year-olds are relatively superior in at least certain aspects of linguistic knowledge because they have not been misled by the probabilities inherent in worldly experience. If it should be replicated, the older children's behavior will represent another example of errors that indicate developmental progress.

Macnamara sets forth a different argument in a review of C. Chomsky's work. Remember that one of the syntactic structures that she investigated was the child's understanding of such sentences of *Bozo promises Donald to hop up and down* [sentence (21b)]. Macnamara suggests that—

. . . one might know many things but not everything about promises. Furthermore, one might not have complete mastery of all the implications of what one knows about them. In particular one might not fully appreciate that one can usually promise only for oneself, not for others. Perhaps this is all that there is to the syntactic feature associated with the verb *promise* which indicates that the succeeding proper noun is usually an indirect object and that it is usually not the subject of the complement which expresses the promise. The point derives added force when we recall that fathers used to promise their daughters (direct object) in marriage. (Macnamara, in press, p. 8.)

More generally, Macnamara argues:

I have hinted above [that] the non-linguistic cognitive development is a necessary prerequisite for syntactic learning. In fact, I want to argue that meaning is the clue to language rather than language the clue to meaning, at least at the point where a new linguistic fact is being learned. In other words, the child acquires most of his linguistic knowledge by guessing, largely independent of language, that which is expressed in language, and by mapping his guess onto the speech code which he has heard. . . . Unless I am greatly mistaken, an investigation of the acquisition of several of the relationships which Carol Chomsky discusses would reveal just this process. The child learns more about promises and human cognition and the like; he also appreciates the implications of such knowledge better. Under certain circumstances he can guess what is meant by a particular sentence even though there is no surface marking to indicate it. Then he realizes that in this language, that is how one expresses this meaning. (Macnamara, in press, p. 13.)

In other words, according to Macnamara, a child expresses or understands in language what he already knows.

From a different perspective, the mere fact of learning a language demonstrates possession by every speaker of complex and abstract conceptual abilities. This is true at the level of word meaning and of utterance construction. As stated in Chapter 4, every word that has meaning—(and that is every word except proper names)—refers to a concept, not to a single thing. "Knowing a word is never a simple association between an object and an acoustic pattern, but the successful operation of those principles, or application of those rules, that lead to using the word 'table' or 'house' for objects never before encountered" (Lenneberg, 1969, p. 640). See Levi-Strauss (1966) for an analysis of the elaborate classification schemes underlying the labels used in nonliterate societies, and see Leacock (in press) for another anthropologist's view.

As with word meanings, so with sentence construction—the processes are just as abstract and complex. Labov has analyzed one English rule in these terms as a demonstration of this point:

> Let us consider what is involved in the use of the general English rule that incorporates the negative with the first indefinite [*anyone can go* negated becomes *No one can go*]. To learn and use this rule, one must first identify the class of indefinites involved, *any, one, ever* which are formally quite diverse. How is this done? These indefinites share a number of common properties which can be expressed as the concepts "indefinite," "hypothetical" and "non-partitive." One might argue that these indefinites are learned as a simple list by "association" learning. But this is only one of the many syntactic rules involving indefinites—rules known to every speaker of English, which could not be learned except by an understanding of their common, abstract properties. For example, everyone "knows" unconsciously that *anyone* cannot be used with preterit verbs or progressives. One does not say, **Anyone went to the party* or **Anyone is going to the party*. The rule which operates here is sensitive to the property [+hypothetical] of the indefinites. Whenever the proposition is not inconsistent with this feature, *anyone* can be used. Everyone "knows" therefore that one can say *Anyone who was anyone went to the party*, or *If anyone went to the party . . .* or *Before anyone went to the party. . . .* There is another property of *anyone* which is grasped unconsciously by all native speakers of English: it is [+distributive]. Thus if we need one more man for a game of bridge or basketball, and there is a crowd outside, we ask, "Do any of you want to play?" not "Do some of you want to play?" In both cases, we are considering a plurality, but with *any* we consider them one at a time, or distributively. (Labov, 1969, pp. 74, 169.)

In short, "one cannot attribute to people a cognitive capacity that is less than is required to produce the complex rule-governed activity called language." (Cole and Bruner, 1971, p. 868.) The full implications of this argument for psychology and education remain to be worked out.

THE NEUROLOGICAL BASE

Nothing has been said so far about language learning at the neurological level. Eventually, our understanding must be grounded there. Now there are only bits of data and provocative hypotheses from men like Lenneberg (1967), Soviet psychologists like Luria (1969), and those represented in Pribram (1969).

Luria's data came from neuropsychological studies of the effects of lesions in different parts of the brain on the patient's behavior "that will lead to better understanding of the components of complex psychological functions for which operations of different parts of the brain are responsible" (1970, p. 66). He found, for example, that phoneme recognition and speech-sound articulation are controlled by different parts of the brain. Patients with lesions in one area cannot distinguish /p/ from /b/, or /t/ from /d/, whereas people with lesions elsewhere confuse sounds like /b/ and /m/, which are made with similar lip movements. Luria also suggests a new basis for categorizing behavioral processes. Surprising as it may seem, he found that perception of musical sounds and of speech sounds are controlled by different parts of the brain. On the other hand, orientation in space, arithmetical operations, and "dealing with complexities of grammar logic" are all affected by lesions in one place, presumably because they share a dependence on representations of spatial relationships in some way.

6

Environmental Assistance

Discussion of the process of language development in Chapters 3, 4, and 5 has been limited to characteristics of the child's mind—whether they are specific to language or apply to cognitive development more generally. Language development must also be influenced, in rate if not in course, by influences from the external environment. These influences can be called "environmental assistance."

As the previous chapters point up, children easily and rapidly learn the language of their parents and home community at an age when other seemingly simpler learnings, such as color identification, are absent. Questions about the kind of help children naturally receive are therefore especially intriguing, and may carry important implications for education. Education may be conceived as more deliberate attempts to duplicate, extend, supplement, complement, or change the effects of the spontaneously provided assistance available outside the school. In a book on "child language and education," therefore, it is not surprising that this chapter is the longest of all. It raises questions about education at many points and ends with a fuller discussion of three educational issues: outward form versus the inner substance of child behavior; sequencing instruction; and the transferability of conclusions from oral language to other educational goals such as literacy.

In research terminology, this chapter shifts from descriptions of the dependent variable—child language itself—to a hunt for the independent variables—aspects of the child's environment which make some difference. In other terms, the discussion is about antecedents (in the environment) of particular consequents (in child language). Such research is possible only when a detailed description of the dependent variable, child language, is available. Without it, there is no basis for evaluating environmental factors. That is why the most specific research on environmental assistance is about assistance to the child's acquisition of syntax.

It is important to realize how severe this limitation is. One can suggest many aspects of child language for which the nature of the environment must make a difference (see Ervin-Tripp, 1971(b) for one good list). Children differ in the language or dialect they learn, and it is too simple an explanation of this fact to say that they learn whatever rule system they hear. Many, perhaps most, children are exposed to multiple models—in a bilingual community or between home community and television—and we need to understand how and why they choose one model to learn, or some particular combination of two. Children differ in their sociolinguistic knowledge—in the way they categorize speech situations and in the rules they follow for speaking appropriately in each one. We know nothing about how such categorizations and such sociolinguistic rules are learned. Moreover, and this is a critical point in planning research, we will not be able to do productive research on these questions about environmental assistance until we have more adequate descriptions of these aspects of child language itself. And that in turn depends on the availability of descriptions of adult communicative competence in the child's community.

Consider first two general issues: pervasive versus differential environmental variables, and whether environmental assistance influences the course of development or only the rate. Eventually, we will probably find two kinds of social variables: one that has a pervasive impact on the development of language and cognition in general, and another that has a differential impact on language in contrast to its impact on other aspects of cognitive development. Nutrition deficits in pregnant women are probably one example of a pervasive factor, whereas relative opportunities for conversation with adults may be a differential factor.

The terms "pervasive" and "differential" are taken from the study by Lesser, Fifer, and Clark (1965) of social class and ethnic differences in primary mental abilities. Their purpose was to examine the pattern of four mental abilities (verbal, reasoning, numerical, and space) among first-grade children in New York City from middle and lower social-class groups and four ethnic backgrounds—Chinese, Jewish, Black, and Puerto Rican. Verbal ability was measured by a 60-item vocabulary test, one-half pictures and one-half words, administered in the child's native language, or English, or a combination of both.

One important finding was that ethnic background and social class have different effects. Ethnic background affects the pattern of mental abilities, while social-class status affects the level of scores across the mental-ability scales. Specifically, Jewish children ranked first on verbal ability (being significantly better than all other ethnic groups), Blacks were second, and Chinese third (both being significantly better than Puerto Ricans), and Puerto Ricans fourth. On spatial abilities, by contrast, the rank order was Chinese, Jewish, Puerto Rican, and Black children. But in all four ethnic groups, on all scales and subtests, the middle-class children were significantly superior to the lower-class children. As Lesser and his coworkers observe:

Apparently, different mediators are associated with social-class and ethnic-group conditions. . . . The importance of the mediators associated with ethnicity is to provide differential impacts upon the development of mental abilities, while the importance of mediators associated with social class is to provide pervasive (and not differential) effects upon the various mental abilities. This conclusion allows selection among several explanations offered to interpret cultural influences upon intellectual activity. (Lesser *et al.*, 1965, p. 83.)

The same investigators also found that social-class position has more effect on mental abilities for Black children than for other groups, and that on each mental-ability test the scores of the middle-class children from the four ethnic groups resemble each other more than do the scores of the lower-class children.

When Lesser and his associates use the term "language ability," they mean vocabulary. That is the only language subtest in their test battery. The terms "pervasive" and "differential" may also apply to different aspects of language itself. One useful distinction may be between universal versus language-specific features of any given language. Consider these as ends of a continuum rather than as a simple dichotomy:

language   language
universals   specifics

The components of language knowledge can then be placed along this continuum. On one level of discussion, grammatical structure as a whole can be considered more universal than vocabulary, which is more language-specific; on another level, within grammatical structure, aspects of word order, such as subject-verb-object, may be more universal than details of noun and verb morphology, which are more language-specific.

In reporting her research (discussed in Chapter 5) C. Chomsky suggests a further but analogous distinction between language rules that apply to all words and those that apply to particular words. In the case of the rule of pronominal reference, she found that "with very few exceptions children above 5.6 [years of age] in our sample knew the construction and children below 5.6 did not" (1969, p. 116). With the rules for interpreting *promise*, *ask*, and *tell*, however, the learning pattern was quite different. There was an extended period of several years during which some children knew them and others did not. Here, some as yet unknown aspects of individual experience seem to make more difference. In Chomsky's words, "The basic principles of the language may be acquired more uniformly across children, perhaps at a certain level of maturation, whereas the more specialized constructions vary more with the individual" (1969, p. 116). Whether or not C. Chomsky's particular finding will be substantiated by further research, her method of comparing language structures in this way should be informative.

I think we will eventually find that variation in a child's experience will affect acquisition along the preceding continuum in different ways or to different degrees. The acquisition of knowledge toward the left, or more universal, end of the continuum should require less exposure to samples of speech, show less variability across children, and be reflected in a shorter learning period and fewer errors on the part of any one child. Conversely, acquisition of more language-specific knowledge, toward the right end of the continuum, should require more exposure, show greater variability across children, and be reflected in a longer learning period and more fluctuation and errors by each child.

Aspects of the child's experience may affect either the course or the rate of the child's development, or both. In a fashion similar to Piaget's descriptions of an invariant sequence in the development of logical operations (Piaget and Inhelder, 1969), N. Chomsky (1965) argues against the notion that linguistic or nonlinguistic aspects of unique individual experience can in any way determine the course that the acquisition of a given language takes, whatever their effect on rate. About the linguistic aspects of individual experience, he says:

> Certain kinds of data and experience may be required in order to set the language acquisition device into operation, although they may not affect the *manner* of its functioning in the least. Thus it has been found that semantic reference may greatly facilitate performance in a syntax-learning experiment, even though it does not, apparently, affect the *manner* in which acquisition of syntax proceeds; that is, it plays no role in determining which hypotheses are selected by the learner. (N. Chomsky, 1965, p. 33.)

The critical word is "manner," underlined in the original. Differences in individual language experience will not affect the course of acquisition, but may facilitate or retard it. Chomsky goes on to imply that nonlinguistic aspects of experience may be facilitating or retarding as well:

> To take one of innumerable examples from studies of animal learning it has been observed . . . that depth perception in lambs is considerably facilitated by mother-neonate contact, although again there is no reason to suppose that the nature of the lamb's "theory of visual space" depends on this contact. (N. Chomsky, 1965, p. 34.)

Chomsky's comments are limited to the child's acquisition of language structure. It is possible that other aspects of language may be influenced in course as well as in rate.

Aspects of the child's environment to which researchers have paid some attention can be grouped into three categories: (1) characteristics of the language which the child hears; (2) characteristics of the patterns of interaction which he engages in; and (3) characteristics of the nonlinguistic environment or context. From the results of this research, knowledge of social factors can also be categorized according to its certainty, from the weakest to the strongest: (A) discovery of an interesting and theoretically plausible feature of the child's environment; (B) correlations between

Table 1 **Nature of the Evidence**

Aspects of the Environment	Discovery of Feature in Environment	Correlational Data	Manipulative Experiment
Language child hears	1A	1B	1C
Interaction	2A	2B	2C
Nonlinguistic environment	3A	3B	3C

such features and some aspect of the child's language; and (C) causal relationships tested in a manipulative experiment. Combining the three categories of social factors and three degrees of certainty yields a 3 × 3 table (Table 1) with nine cells into which all the research in this area can be placed.

Brief examples of substantive findings and/or methodological problems of research in each cell will be given, drawing largely on the research on Adam, Eve, and Sarah. That research is especially important in this chapter because it is the one research project with both detailed analyses of child language and transcriptions of mother-child conversation. 1A and 2A, 1B and 2B, and 1C and 2C will be considered in that order, leaving till the end more speculative comments on nonverbal characteristics of the environment (3A, 3B, and 3C).

As in the rest of this book, no attempt is made here to provide a complete research review. The section on "mediating variables" in Cazden (1966) includes discussion of additional studies, as does Ervin-Tripp (1966). Here the focus is on selected research studies that specify variables of child language or its environment in detail, or suggest provocative new hypotheses about their relationship. If the result seems fragmentary, that is a realistic picture of how little we understand.

Aspects of Language the Child Hears (1A)

At least by the age of one year, verbal stimuli become more powerful for the child than other forms of auditory stimulation. We still know little about characteristics of those verbal stimuli to which the child is exposed, and so arguments about the development process have proceeded on different assumptions about them. See, for example, the arguments between Braine, and Bever and associates in Bar-Adon and Leopold (1971, pp. 242–274).

There is probably a qualitative difference between language directed to the child and other language he overhears. The former is what is called (somewhat condescendingly in our society) "baby talk." We usually think of baby talk as distortions in pronunciation (such as simplification of the initial consonant cluster in saying *tummy* for *stomach*) or special lexical

choices (like *choo-choo* for train). Ferguson (1964) broadens the definition to "any special form of a language which is regarded by a speech
community as being primarily appropriate for talking to young children"
(1964, p. 103) and includes syntactical modifications like the switch from
first-person pronouns to nouns (as in *Daddy wants* instead of *I want*).

More recently, there have been several detailed studies of the ways in
which mothers modify their speech patterns to young children. Slobin
(1968) reports Kerry Drach's analysis of the language of a Black mother in
Oakland, California. The mother's utterances to her child were simpler and
shorter than those spoken to a neighbor. Baldwin and Frank (1969) found
that Black lower-class and middle-class mothers from Harlem and Caucasian
mothers from Washington Square (New York) reduced the grammatical
complexity of their sentences when speaking to their three-year-old
children as compared with their sentences in an adult interview. Phillips
(1970) found the same simplification for mothers in Baltimore hospital-
staff families. Snow (1971) compared the amount, complexity, and density
of repetitions in the speech of college-educated mothers to two-year-old and
ten-year-old children in two conditions—when the children were actually
present, and when the mothers were asked to tell a story or explain something to a tape recorder for later playing to the child. The mothers talked
more, simplified more, and repeated parts of all phrases more to the two-
year-old children, and the younger child's actual presence had more effect.
In a second experiment, Snow found that the same adjustment was made
by women who were not themselves mothers. She concludes that this kind
of simplification for young children is partly a component of adult communicative competence and partly a response to cues provided by the
child—cues of inattention when the speech addressed to him becomes too
complex.

Snow further suggests how some of the forms of modification and repetition may be particularly helpful to the child's acquisition processes. Partial repetitions like *Put the red truck in the box now. The red truck.* may
provide information on the boundaries of grammatical units (in this case
the NP). Similarly with partial repetitions in new frames: *Pick up the red
one. Find the red one. Not the green one. I want the red one.* The mothers
also frequently use paraphrases, which could display relationships between
deep and surface structures. In all these cases, the simpler, more repetitious
speech may give the child valuable linguistic information as well as provide
a particularly effective guide for his action.

Where some aspect of mothers' speech has been tracked over a period of
time, it has been found to increase gradually in complexity as the child's
speech does. On general measures of speech complexity and length, the utterances of the mothers in Phillip's study increased as their children developed
from 18 to 28 months. On a more specific measure of NP complexity, Moore
(1967) found that from periods I–V (see Figure 1, Chapter 3) the
mothers of Adam, Eve, and Sarah increased the length of their predicate

NPs, but not of their subjects NPs, as their children did too. Presumably, the lack of change in subject NPs for both mothers and children is an artifact of the high proportion of Introductory words in all speech, as noted in Chapter 3. On the basis of everything known about learning, this kind of maternal accommodation to the child's growing language knowledge and ability should be extremely helpful.

It is important to remember that the child's linguistic environment is not limited to speech. Children are read to, and later they read to themselves. Reading to the young child may be a particularly potent form of language stimulation. As usually done, with the child sitting on the adult's lap, it brings a special relationship of close physical contact, easily shared visual focus, and adult speech about that focus spoken directly into the child's ear. Furthermore, reading aloud is likely to stimulate meaningful conversation about the pictures to which both adult and child are attending. Once children learn to read for themselves, what and how much they read may also be a significant source of variation in environmental assistance to their language development. C. Chomsky is now investigating the relationship between individual differences in knowledge of complex structures like *ask-tell* and the reading done by elementary-school children.

Because language in books differs from speech in both structure and distance from nonverbal context, it may have qualitative as well as quantitative significance. I heard a preschool teacher reading a book about worms to a small group of children who had just found a large worm on the playground. One passage read: *"The worm's mouth is at the fat end. The worm's tail is at the thin end."* Had the teacher been talking instead of reading, the children probably would have heard something like this: *"His mouth is here* (as she points), *and his tail is here"* (as she points again). Children's books also include unusual idiomatic expressions. For instance, another book about a worm was based on the use of the worm's body as a unit of measurement; it ended with the sentence, *"He measured and measured, inch by inch, till he inched out of sight."*

In short, writing is not just speech written down (Kolers, 1970). Chapter 8 explores the cognitive implications of this fact for writers. Here, the important point is that listeners and readers probably benefit from the difference too.

Aspects of Verbal Interaction (2A)

Two suggestive aspects of parent-child interaction came to our attention in the study of Adam, Eve, and Sarah. During the very first recording session at Sarah's home, Sarah and her mother played "the naming game." Sarah was just 26 months old, and her mother was understandably anxious about her expected role in getting Sarah to talk for the Harvard researchers. Her solution was to play "the naming game," asking Sarah *What's this?* or *What's that?* of objects around the room or in books. After a sequence of 37 questions beginning with *what* about inanimate objects, the mother shifted to *who* for a picture of a lady. This shift in her mother's words may have signaled to Sarah a feature to be attended to in the non-linguistic environment—namely, categorization of the world into animate and inanimate.

Note that in this spontaneous conversation it is not possible to get unequivocal information about the child's knowledge. If Sarah answered correctly, as she usually did, she might be responding to the most obvious referent and not specifically to *what* and *who*. And if she answered incorrectly—for example, *What's that? A peanut butter*—she might still understand the animate-inanimate implication of the pronoun, but be attending to more salient aspects of the total verbal and nonverbal stimulus.

Two questions asked of Sarah by her mother at other times raised questions about the contribution of routinized interactions to the child's development. *What's the doggie say?* is one of the familiar set of adult questions by which associations between names for animals and names for their sounds are taught—*cat-meow, cow-moo,* etç. *What did Bugs say?*, on the other hand, refers to a Bugs Bunny doll who actually emits intelligible words, such as *Take it easy,* when the recorder inside him is started by pulling a cord on his back. The answer to the first question, *What's the doggie say,* can be learned only as a routine, since no child ever really hears a dog say *bow-wow.* When the same question was asked about Bugs, however, the answer was audibly presented to Sarah a few seconds before, and the child could answer from her own experience.

The same contrast fits the questions *How old are you?* or *How old is Mike* (the dog)? versus *How many fish in there?*, asked about fish in the fishbowl present on the table. Questions about age can only be routines because there is nothing for the child to count, no physically present referent for the numbers at all. It is not surprising, therefore, that when Sarah was asked *How old is Mike?* and the answer *Mike two* was rejected as wrong, her next attempted response was not another number but another well-practiced routine—*Mike gone.* Sarah's conversation with her family seemed to contain a denser proportion of what could be considered meaningless routines. One wonders if this may be part of the explanation for the contrast between Eve and Sarah, reported in Chapter 3—that Sarah was less behind in grammatical knowledge than in what she had to say.

Correlational Data on the Influence of Language the Child Hears (1B)

In analyses of Adam, Eve, and Sarah's conversations, we found a correlation between the frequency of certain linguistic structures in the child's environment and the order of their acquisition by the child. Questions have been raised by others about the significance of frequency as a language variable. Discussion in this section is divided into these two parts.

DATA ON FREQUENCY AND ACQUISITION

Note first that the danger of confusing performance and acquisition of knowledge exists when we are looking for environmental assistance, as when we describe sequence of emergence in the children's language itself. Brown, Cazden, and Bellugi (1969) discuss this danger in interpreting data on the children's use of possessives.

> One of the first individual differences we noted was Eve's tendency to use N + N constructions far more often than Adam or Sarah did. At point I in Fig. I, Ch. 3, the frequencies of N + N in 700 utterances were: Eve, 66; Adam, 40; Sarah, 10, of which 8 were imitations. In looking for an explanation, we thought it possible that the speech of the three mothers might differ in the frequency with which sentences were spoken from which N + N constructions might be telegraphically derived. The best match to the rank order of the children was the particular subset of parental N + N constructions that express possession, such as *Daddy's chair*. In the first 1,253 utterances of each mother, these frequencies were: Eve's mother, 31; Adam's mother, 24; Sarah's mother, only 6. This is an extremely interesting relation. One can hypothesize that territoriality and property rights are more important in homes where father is a graduate student, and that this is related to the child's tendency to use the N + N construction. But it is not sufficient evidence that greater frequency in parent speech produces earlier learning in the child. It is the antecedents of grammatical *knowledge* we are seeking, not influences on performance. (Brown, Cazden, and Bellugi, 1969, pp. 65–66.)

Two examples of possible antecedents of grammatical knowledge involve Adam's errors with *s* and Eve's learning of prepositions (Brown, Cazden, and Bellugi, 1969). As noted in Chapter 5, for a brief period Adam seemed to think that *its* was simply an alternative pronunciation of *it*. When we looked for features of his mother's speech which might be responsible for such a segmentation error, we found a simple matter of frequency: Adam's mother was more apt to follow *it* with a form of the verb *to be*, usually *is* in contracted form, and more apt to follow other pronouns with a main verb: *It's blue* but *She went home*.

Frequency in parent speech is also related to Eve's order of acquisition of prepositions. When Eve was 18 to 21 months old, her mother used *in* and *on* approximately three times as often as she used *with, of, for*, or *to*. Later, when Eve was 22 to 24 months old, she supplied *in* and *on* correctly 90 percent of the time, while the proportion correct for each of the other prepositions was between 0.67 and 0.77. Note that it is not sufficient to demonstrate that *in* and *on* appear first in the child's speech. Because they are more common in English in general, they would be likely to appear first in our transcriptions even if in fact all prepositions had been learned at the same time. That's why we computed the percentage of prepositions supplied when they were required.

As an interesting addition to this finding, it turned out that it did not matter in what particular prepositional phrase Sarah had heard *in* or *on*. Once she started using a particular preposition, it popped into all phrases requiring it—*in the wastebasket, in the book*, etc. The child thus could not have been imitating particular phrases as whole chunks. If frequency in the child's environment had been influential, it must have been operating by providing the child with more ample raw material for the induction of rules.

Brown and Hanlon's conclusion has important implications for environmental assistance in general:

> Our guess is that [the relation between parental frequency and order of emergence among well-formed constructions] is an incidental consequence of the relation between frequency and complexity, and that frequency, above some minimum level, does not determine the order in which structural knowledge emerges. What would happen if the parents of a child produced tags at a much higher rate than is normal? We have some basis for a guess.
>
> The parents of Adam, Eve, and Sarah did produce certain wh-questions at a very high rate in a period when the children did not understand the structure of wh-questions. What happened then? The children learned to produce the two most frequently repeated wh-questions, *What's that?* and *What doing?*, on roughly appropriate occasions. Their performance had the kind of rigidity that we have learned to recognize as a sign of incomprehension of structure: they did not produce, as their parents of course did, such structurally close variants as *What are those?* and *Who's that?* and *What is he doing?* When, much later, the children began to produce all manner of wh-questions in the preposed form (such as *What he wants*) it was interesting to note that *What's that?* and *What are you doing?* were not at first reconstrued in terms of the new analysis. If the children had generated the sentences in terms of their new rules they ought to have said *What that is?* and *What you are doing?* but instead they, at first, persisted with the old forms. . . .
>
> We suggest that any form that is produced with very high frequency by parents will be somehow represented in the child's performance even if its structure is far beyond him. He will find a way to render a version of it and will also form a notion of the circumstances in which it is used. The construction will become lodged in his speech as an unassimilated fragment. Extensive use of such an unanalyzed or mistakenly analyzed fragment probably protects it, for a time, from a reanalysis when the structure relevant to it is finally learned. Such we suspect, are the effects of frequency. (Brown and Hanlon, 1970, pp. 50–51.)

Brown and Hanlon found that unanalyzed fragments, even if mature in outward form, are relatively impermeable to more active reanalysis by the child. Moskowitz reports the same fate for many extrasystematic pronunciations that, unlike Hildegarde Leopold's *príti*, often remain in their immature form, even "when the child's advancing phonological system would allow for a more complex representation" (1970, p. 40).

Rule-governed errors, on the other hand, seem to be open to shedding when the child is in some sense "ready" to move on, no matter how well practiced they may be. This was true of overgeneralizations like *goed* and *mines* in the acquisition of inflections and of invented spellings in the learning of standard orthography. The implication for education is that teachers may be interfering with the child's learning process by insisting on responses that superficially look or sound "correct." This issue will be discussed again in the final section of this chapter.

Adam, Eve and Sarah were exposed to different frequencies of particular structures within a single language. In a bilingual (or bidialectal) environment, children are exposed to different frequencies of two or more language systems. Friedlander (in press) describes the role of one father's speech in his bilingual child's development. Although this father contributed only 4 percent of all the utterances spoken within earshot (more exactly "microphone shot") of his infant while Friedlander's recording equipment was turned on, he was responsible for almost 25 percent of the utterances directed to the baby herself.

> This difference between the personal and the total language environments is important in practice as well as in theory. It happens that the Jones father . . . set out to teach his baby Spanish by speaking only Spanish in her presence. According to the sampling information on infant-directed utterances the baby heard about one-third as much Spanish from the father as she heard English from the mother. Though there are no formal tests on which such judgments can be made, observation by tape recorder and by visits to the home when the child was 22 months old suggest that she was almost as fluent in her use of and response to Spanish as she was to English. It is certainly noteworthy that the father obtained this actualization of his bilingual objectives *while occupying so small a percentage (only 4%) of the infant's total language environment samples* when she was 12 months old. (Friedlander, in press, emphasis in the original.)

ISSUES CONCERNING FREQUENCY AND COMPLEXITY

One problem in determining the effect of frequency is that it is usually confounded with some other aspect of language such as semantic or syntactic complexity.

For example, Brown, Cazden, and Bellugi (1969, p. 67) looked at the relationship between the frequency with which mothers of Adam, Eve, and Sarah asked four kinds of wh-adverbial questions and the proportion of a given type that elicited semantically and grammatically appropriate answers from the child.

For all three mothers at [point] II, the order of frequency is locatives first (about three-fourths of the total), then causal, manner and time—in other words, *where, why, how,* and *when.* This rank order matches the rank order of proportion of appropriate responses from the children at [point] V except for questions about time, for which the data are too few to be reliable. Pooled data for the three mothers and children are presented in the accompanying tabulation.

	Frequency of Mothers' Questions	*Proportion of Children's Appropriate Responses*
Locative	228	0.64 (29/45)
Causal	29	0.40 (14/35)
Manner	18	0.11 (1/9)
Time	7	0.50 (1/2)

In this instance, frequency of occurrence is confounded with semantic complexity. There seems little doubt that *where*-questions are easier for the child to answer than *why*- or *how*- or *when*-questions. When someone asks where something is, the answer can often be given here and now in physical terms by pointing or fetching. But if he asks when something will happen, the answer must be given in words alone, and frequently in words like *Tomorrow,* which are themselves relational words with a shifting referent. For *How* and *Why* questions, the answers are also more conceptual than perceptual, and accordingly more difficult for young children. Therefore, little can be concluded from the above table about the effect of frequency alone. See Ervin-Tripp (1970) for further research on how children learn to answer questions.

Frequency of occurrence can also be confounded with gramatical complexity. Brown and Hanlon (1970) counted the average frequencies of simple, active, affirmative, declarative sentences (SAAD), and four question forms in 700 maternal utterances:

SAAD: 139
Affirmative yes-no questions: 53
Truncated questions: 2
Negative yes-no questions: 4
Truncated negative questions: 4.

Of these five types, SAAD did appear first in the child's speech, then affirmative yes-no questions, and then the remaining three types. But one cannot thereby conclude that frequency in parental speech has any influence because, on any criteria of complexity, frequency and complexity are confounded in these structures.

In their discussion of the relation between frequency and complexity, Brown and Hanlon (1970, p. 40) suggest that Zipf's "Principle of Least

Effort" may apply. According to Zipf (1949), that principle "causes our frequently used tools to be kept simple and close to hand." In his comment on the Brown and Hanlon paper, Watt (1970) analyzes the possible application of the least effort principle (LEP) in considerable detail. If frequency determined complexity, one should find relevant evidence in historical change within languages. Watt found none. If complexity determined frequency, then speakers would be selecting constructions on the basis of structural characteristics rather than on what they wanted to say. Watt concludes that SAAD's simplicity and frequency are not related as cause and effect in either direction. Instead he suggests that both simplicity and frequency are effects of the same cause: the iconic nature of the subject-verb-object order of elements. He suggests further that only in selecting among paraphrastic alternatives that do not differ in subject-verb-object order could stylistic choices be said to follow LEP. For instance, (28a) is both simpler and more frequent than (28b):

(28a)   Henry wanted to present the best paper at the Conference in order to win the Pulitzer Prize in linguistics.

(28b)   Henry's wanting to present the best paper at the Conference was due to his wanting to win the Pulitzer Prize in linguistics.

Correlational Data on the Influence of Verbal Interaction (2B)

Two different sets of correlational data exist on the influence of mothers' patterns of interaction on their children's language development: first, from the study of Adam, Eve, and Sarah; second, from correlational studies which compare mother-child interaction among different social-class groups.

ADAM, EVE, AND SARAH'S ACQUISITION OF SYNTAX

Brown, Cazden, and Bellugi (1969) examined the role of three aspects of mother-child interaction: adult expressions of approval or disapproval of what the child said; differential communication effectiveness of the child's mature and immature utterances; and adult expansions of the young child's telegraphic speech.

Approval and Disapproval

Just as the commonsense view holds that the child's process is basically imitation, so it holds that the adult's contribution is to shape the child's speech by correcting him when he is "wrong" and reinforcing him when he is "correct." Here, too, the commonsense view is invalid. Because child speech deviates from adult norms in so many ways, opportunities for parental instruction are always present. It is striking, therefore, to note how infrequently such opportunities are taken up. So far, no evidence exists to show that either correction or reinforcement of the learning of grammar occurs with sufficient frequency to be a potent force. Analysis of conversations between only a few parents and children are available, but that generalization holds for them without exception.

Consider correction first. Evidence on the role of correction in the child's learning of syntax is wholly negative. In hundreds of hours of recordings of Adam, Eve, and Sarah talking with their parents, we found corrections of misstatements of fact, but no correction of immature syntactic forms.

Data on the role of corrections are not limited to research on Adam, Eve, and Sarah. In her analysis of two full days of parent-child conversations of two lower-class Black children, Horner (1968) found seven instances of corrections: two of vocabulary items, one of counting, two of "bad language" such as *pee-pee*, one of the the pronunciation *yeah*, and one an admonition to say *thank you*. Horner's study is particularly interesting in this regard because, unlike many current investigators of child language, her initial theoretical framework is from behaviorist (Skinnerian) psychology, and she presumably was looking for evidence of shaping of the child's verbal behavior by external pressures. Finally, students documenting the acquisition of language in such far-flung corners of the world as Kenya (Blount, 1969), Samoa (K. Kernan, 1969), and Mexico (Stross, 1969) also produced no evidence of parental corrections of immature syntax (summarized in Slobin, 1968).

The investigation of reinforcement is more complex. Parental reinforcement of mature constructions by the child could be expressed in many ways. Brown and his colleagues looked for two forms of reinforcement: verbal signs of approval and disapproval, and differential communication effectiveness (Brown, Cazden, and Bellugi, 1969; Brown and Hanlon, 1970). In either case, the critical requirement for the operation of reinforcement is that it must be supplied contingently—that is, supplied when the child speaks maturely and omitted when he speaks in an immature fashion. Without that contingent relationship, the adult behavior cannot reinforce the child's mature utterance and make it more likely to occur again.

Here are the details on verbal signs of approval and disapproval as reported by Brown, Cazden, and Bellugi:

> It might be supposed that syntactically correct utterances come to prevail over those that are incorrect through the operation of positive reinforcement and punishment on the part of adults. Because events subsequent to a child's speech are infinitely various, one can never be sure that there is no event which functions as a reinforcer or punishment. In practice, however, we know that certain events such as signs of approval or disapproval are likely to function in this way. The proposition "Syntactically correct utter-

ances come to prevail over syntactically incorrect utterances through the selective administration of signs of approval and disapproval" is a testable one. . . .

For this analysis, we worked with samples II and V. The general plan was to contrast the syntactic correctness of the population of utterances followed by a sign of approval—*that's right, very good,* or just *yes*—with the population of utterances followed by a sign of disapproval: *that's wrong* or *no.* The results are simply stated: there is not a shred of evidence that approval and disapproval are contingent on syntactic correctness.

What circumstances did govern approval and disapproval directed at child utterances by parents? Gross errors of word choice were sometimes corrected, as when Eve said *What the guy idea.* Once in a while an error of pronunciation was noticed and corrected. Most commonly, however, the grounds on which an utterance was approved or disapproved in Levels I–V were not strictly linguistic at all. When Eve expressed the opinion that her mother was a girl by saying *He a girl,* her mother answered *That's right.* The child's utterance was ungrammatical, but her mother did not respond to that fact; instead, she responded to the truth of the proposition the child intended to express. In general, the parents fitted propositions to the child's utterances, however incomplete or distorted the utterances, and then approved or not according to the correspondence between proposition and reality. Thus, *Her curl my hair* was approved because the mother was, in fact, curling Eve's hair. However, Sarah's grammatically impeccable *There's the animal farmhouse* was disapproved because the building was a lighthouse, and Adam's *Walt Disney comes on on Tuesday* was disapproved because Walt Disney came on on some other day. It seems, then, to be truth value rather than syntactic well-formedness that chiefly governs explicit verbal reinforcement by parents—which renders mildly paradoxical the fact that the usual product of such a training schedule is an adult whose speech is highly grammatical but not notably truthful. (Brown, Cazden, and Bellugi, 1969, pp. 70–71.)

Relating Brown and his colleagues' examples back to the universal-specific continuum presented at the beginning of this chapter, it seems that the acquisition of syntax and of meaning may benefit from different kinds of environmental assistance. Certainly, in spontaneous mother-child interaction, that distinction is very clear in parental response. Two anecdotes from Eve's conversations with her mother sharpen this contrast.

Once Eve noticed her mother rubbing her face and asked, "What you was having on you nose?" This utterance has no less than four grammatical immaturities: failure to reverse auxiliary and pronoun in a question, the wrong auxiliary with *you,* an *-ing* added to a verb that is never "inged" with this meaning, and failure to add the possessive inflection on the pronoun. Yet the mother responded, "What I was having on my nose? Nothing, I was rubbing my eyes." Contrast that reaction with what happened after a walk to watch construction on the William James Center for the Behavioral Sciences at Harvard. Eve, reporting her experience, said, "Watching the men—building hole." This time the mother said, "Well, they aren't building a hole, sweetie. They're building a building now. First they dug the hole and now they're building the building."

Linguists may argue that Eve's mother is in fact teaching Eve about syntax, about the semantic markers that prevent the co-occurrence of *build* with *hole*. Without entering the controversy among linguists over the dividing line between syntax and semantics, it may be pointed out that this is one focus, limited but still present, where mothers do spontaneously "teach." Note, too, that in light of developmental changes in children's definitions described in Chapter 4, Eve's mother correctly, though probably nonconsciously, adapted her teaching strategy to the child's developmental level. Her correction was given in the form of contrasting usage rather than definitional equivalence.

Differential Communication Effectiveness

Brown and Hanlon (1970) investigated a form of reinforcement less obvious than overt approval or disapproval: selective communication effectiveness of the child's well-formed utterances. At a time when children's speech is oscillating between immature and mature forms—for instance, of questions and negative statements—one can look for evidence that the mature forms communicate more successfully in the sense of accomplishing their intended purpose. Such evidence could indicate selective communication pressure toward the mature forms. At such a developmental period, Brown and Hanlon categorized adult responses to Adam, Eve, and Sarah's questions:

Sequiturs: clearly relevant and comprehending answers.
Non sequiturs:
a) Queries. Child: *Where's my spoon?* Adult: *Your spoon?*
b) Irrelevancies. Child: *Where ice cream?* Adult: *And the potatoes.*
c) Misunderstandings. Child: *What time it is?* Adult: *Un-uh, it tells what time it is.*
d) No response.
e) Doubtful classification.

In the case of the children's negative statements, Brown and Hanlon considered as sequiturs all "continuations strongly suggesting comprehension of the child's utterance" (Brown & Hanlon, 1970, p. 43).

Table 2 gives the combined means for sequiturs and non sequiturs for yes-no questions at points III and V, Wh-questions at points III and IV, tag questions at point V or later, and negatives at points III and IV. So, for example of Eve's primitive utterances, 61 percent were followed by sequiturs and 25 percent were followed by non sequiturs. For well formed utterances, the corresponding percentages were nearly the same: 53 and 27 percent respectively. Data for each construction separately are given by Brown and Hanlon in their Table 1.10 (1970, p. 44).

Table 2 **Sequiturs and Non Sequiturs Following Primitive and Well-Formed Constructions**

	Means	
	PRIMITIVE	WELL FORMED
Eve		
Sequiturs	0.61	0.53
Non Sequiturs	0.25	0.27
Adam		
Sequiturs	0.31	0.36
Non Sequiturs	0.62	0.49
Sarah		
Sequiturs	0.42	0.45
Non Sequiturs	0.55	0.50
Means for Three Children		
Sequiturs	0.45	0.45
Non Sequiturs	0.47	0.42

Brown and Hanlon conclude:

> The obtained difference on Non-sequiturs should be interpreted in the light of the fact that a great many of the Non-sequiturs were "No responses" and it is not clear that these should all be considered unsatisfactory responses. In some cases the child was talking fast and scarcely seemed to expect or leave time for an answer. When Non-sequiturs were counted more narrowly— as instances of genuine misunderstanding—we found precisely one instance (the example given earlier) for all children and all constructions. In general, the results provide no support for the notion that there is a communication pressure favoring mature constructions. (Brown and Hanlon, 1970, p. 45.)

In her more general comment on these same mother-child conversations, Bellugi expresses the only reasonable conclusion:

> The mother and child are concerned with daily activities, not grammatical instruction. Adam breaks something, looks for a nail to repair it with, finally throws pencils and nails around the room. He pulls his favorite animals in a toy wagon; fiddles with the television set; and tries to put together a puzzle. His mother is concerned primarily with modifying his behavior. She gives him information about the world around him and corrects facts. Neither of the two seems overtly concerned with the problems that we shall pursue so avidly: the acquisition of syntax. (Bellugi, in press.)

The preceding argument against the role of differential communication pressure is limited to its effect on the syntactic structure of child language that is virtually all intelligible. One criterion used in selecting Adam, Eve, and Sarah as subjects for longitudinal study was their clear articulation from the very beginning. For research to be possible, the children's speech had to be intelligible to the Harvard researchers; presumably it was even more intelligible to their own mothers. From the data on Adam, Eve, and Sarah, therefore, nothing can be said about whether shaping by means of differential communication effectiveness operates up to the threshold of parental comprehension.

Parental Expansions

One common form of parental response that could play a corrective role in the child's acquisition of syntax is what have been called "expansions." The narrative of research efforts to determine the extent of their influence is long, and draws heavily on previous discussion by Brown, Cazden, and Bellugi (1969). But ideas expressed in that paper are now so interwoven with my own later thoughts that it is impossible to keep the credit clear for every sentence.

When the study of Adam, Eve, and Sarah began several years ago, one of the first things we noticed was the frequency with which their parents responded to the young child's telegraphic utterance by echoing what the child said and filling in the missing parts. If the child said *Eve lunch* or *Throw Daddy*, the parent often responded with the nearest complete sentence appropriate in the particular situation: *Eve is having lunch* or *Throw it to Daddy*. Brown and Bellugi (1964) called such responses "expansions," and suggested that they might provide optimal data for the acquisition of grammar. They did not mean that the child learned grammar by storing the expanded versions of his telegraphic utterances, since he could not in this way learn more than the finite set of sentences he had at some time attempted to produce. Brown and Bellugi recognized that expansions were only raw data for the child's mental processes and that syntactic knowledge was a system of rules somehow derived from those data. They argued simply that the data provided by expansions might be particularly relevant and seemed to be delivered with ideal timing. One could argue that a child's language development is affected simply by the amount of well-formed sentences that he hears. Without further qualification, that label would apply to language heard over TV or overheard in conversations of which the child is not a participant. The first qualification may be "well-formed sentences which are simultaneously paired with meanings the child can understand." If this pairing is important, it seems likely that conversation in which the child is a participant would be more likely to provide it. A second qualification would be "well-formed sentences which the child can understand and which are closely related to meanings to which he is spontaneously attending at the moment." If, as is certainly the case, the human mind is always spontaneously active, then any environmental stimulation must be considered in its relationship to the child's preexisting thought. Based on this criterion, the relevancy and timing of expansions assume importance.

Expansions are an intriguing phenomenon from at least two other points of view. Compare them first to "reflections" in psychotherapy. In both expansions and reflections, one person is interpreting the feelings, behavior, and ideas of another person, and then expressing his interpretations in explicit verbal terms. But there is also a difference. When reflecting, the adult encodes his interpretation of the other person's underlying intent. When expanding, the adult encodes his literal interpretation of an utterance by building on the child's partial formulation of it. Of the two interpretations, the expansion is probably more likely to be correct.

Now compare expansions to teacher's corrections. Parental expansions may be like corrections in effect, but they are notably different in affective tone. The difference may lie only in intonation patterns and in an optional initial *yes* or *no*. Yet that difference may have great significance for the child. Suppose that while looking at a book a child says *He fall down.* Let the reader say to himself the following alternative responses:

(29a)   *Expansion:* Yes, he fell *down.*
(29b)   *Correction:* No, he *fell* down.

The warm, confirming quality of the expansion contrasts with the critical and impatient manner of the correction. The expansion, in substance and tone, focuses on how much the child has already achieved, while still pointing the direction for further growth; the correction stresses the gap still remaining between where the child is and where he is supposed to arrive.

In our sample of three parents, expansion rate was confounded with other possibly beneficial aspects of interaction. The mothers of Adam and Eve responded to the speech of their children with more expansions, but they also talked more in general. Note also, in Table 2 (p. 117), differences in frequency of quotations "sequitur" responses to both primitive and well formed utterances among the three children. Therefore the research took two different directions. One was a more detailed comparison, from the longitudinal data, of the effect of expansions versus frequency on the emergence of particular features of child language. That will be reported here. Second was a manipulative experiment that fits into the C column of Table 1 and will be reported in the next section.

Before turning to the emergence of inflections, a comment on method is in order. For relating child behavior to parental behavior in a sample of more than one child, two approaches are possible. Let's call them Method A and Method B. In Method A, the child's language (CL) is related to antecedents in his mother's speech (ML), and this relation is then compared across the mother-child dyads; no direct comparison of the children is made. The correlational analyses of prepositions and answers to Wh-questions described in section 1B were of this type. Alternatively, in Method B, differences in the language of the children (C_1L vs. C_2L vs. C_3L) are related to differences in the languages of their parents (M_1L vs. M_2L

vs. M_3L). The analysis of $N + N$ constructions in section 1B was of this type. The two methods can be diagramed as in Table 3.

In Method B, direct comparison of the children is required, and the experimenter must select a metric such as chronological age (CA) or mean length of utterance (MLU) for that comparison. The emergence of inflection was analyzed in both ways (Method A and Method B) and on both metrics for Method B.

Recall that in the research on inflections, each child utterance was coded S_c (supplied correctly), S_x (supplied incorrectly, or O (omitted). Each child utterance was also coded for the adult utterance that followed immediately. If a child's utterance that contained an omitted or inappropriate inflection was followed by an adult utterance that contained the appropriate inflection, it was coded E for expansion, whether or not the entire utterance was an expansion of the child's utterance. For the particular purpose of this analysis, expansions were thus defined less restrictively than usual (cf. Brown and Bellugi, 1964). If the child's utterance was followed by an adult utterance that contained the noun or verb in the same form as the child's utterance, it was coded M for imitation. Finally, if the child's utterance was followed by an adult utterance that did not contain the relevant noun or verb at all, it was marked N. From these analyses it was possible to determine the percentage and absolute frequency of parental expansions.

In order to compare expansions with noncontingent models of mature forms in parental speech, the latter had to be counted as well. Because of their greater density in a given period of time, noncontingent models of the five inflections were counted in only a sample of parent speech. This sample consists of the four sets of 700 parent utterances that immediately precede points II, III, IV, and V in the children's speech, and is the same as that used in the comparison of normal and elliptic possessives in parent speech reported in Chapter 4.

First, rank-order correlations were computed for each child separately

---

Table 3 **Methods of Relating Parental Response to Child Behavior**

	Method A			Method B	
C_1L	is related to	M_1L			
	vs.				
			C_1L *vs.* C_2L *vs.* C_3L		
C_2L	is related to	M_1L	is related to	M_1L *vs.* M_2L *vs.* M_3L	
	vs.				
C_3L	is related to	M_2L			

(Method A). For all three children, order of emergence within the child's language system was more strongly related to the frequency with which the inflection was modeled by the parent than it was to the proportion or frequency of expansions. The only statistically significant positive correlation was with frequency of modeling for Sarah, $p = 0.90$ ($p < 0.05$).

We also considered relationships between differences among the children and differences among their parents (Method B). Table 4 shows the relationship between order of emergence of the five inflections ranked on two metrics—age and MLU—and the provision of parental expansions and models. Order of emergence is given in summed ranks, which range from 5 to 15—first to last of the three children on the five inflections.

The difference in modeling frequency among the parents is small. This finding was anticipated because of prior evidence of common patterns of maternal speech in the three homes. But the difference in proportion and frequency of expansions is considerable. Sarah's telegraphic utterances, which omit inflections, were followed much less frequently by a parental utterance that included the appropriate inflections than was the case for Adam and Eve. Previous observation had shown that Sarah's mother provided the lowest density of expansions. In fact, discovery of the relation between rate of parental expansions and rate of child language development in terms of chronological age was one basis for the hypothesis that expansions aid the acquisition of grammar (Brown and Bellugi, 1964). Table 4 shows that Sarah received fewer expansions in absolute frequency as well.

The negative relation between expansion rate and order of emergence in terms of MLU is surprising. Sarah received the fewest expansions, yet her language system was relatively the most advanced in the provision of inflections. It is hard to reconcile this finding with the hypothesis that expansions should provide the most usable information for the acquisition of syntax. Comparison of Eve's and Sarah's development suggests that particular forms of parent interaction may have less effect on more strictly grammatical aspects of the total language-acquisition process than on the more

Table 4 **Acquisition of Inflections and Two Features of Parent Speech**

	Summed Ranks of Order of Emergence on Basis of Age	*Summed Ranks of Order of Emergence on Basis of MLU*	*Proportion of Parent Expansions I–V*	*Frequency of Parent Models in 2,800 Utterances*
Eve	5.0	11	0.45 (191/427)	499
Adam	12.5	12	0.51 (348/679)	576
Sarah	12.5	7	0.29 (86/294)	471

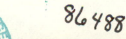

cognitive aspects. Basic grammatical structures seem to be learned despite differences in the child's linguistic environment, whereas how children use language to express ideas may be more vulnerable to environmental variation.

SOCIAL CLASS COMPARISONS

More general cognitive aspects of language use are the focus of most of the social-class comparisons of mother-child interactions. The work of Hess and his associates (1968, 1969) will be considered first as an example, and then important questions that have been raised by others about the validity of this body of research will be discussed.

The work of Hess and his associates (1968, 1969) in Chicago was planned as a test of Bernstein's (1961) hypothesis of a relation between a child's cognitive development and his mother's verbal ability, maternal teaching style, and characteristic mode of family control. In the Hess study, measures of maternal behavior included observations of mother-child behavior in structured tasks as well as from interviews. 163 Negro mothers from four socioeconomic levels were interviewed, tested, and brought to the university with their four-year-old children for a structured session of mother-child interaction. Each mother was taught three tasks—two sorting tasks and the use of an Etch-a-Sketch board—and then asked to teach those tasks to her four-year-old child. Her maternal teaching style was monitored and analyzed. The children were subsequently given the Stanford-Binet IQ test, the Columbia Mental Maturity Scale, and the Sigel Sorting Task, the last specifically selected as a measure of the child's ability to use language as a cognitive tool. They were also followed through their first two years in school. Hess and his colleagues found that aspects of the mother's behavior—such as the specificity with which she gave directions (positively related) or the tendency to use imperative statements (negatively related)—correlated more highly with preschool measures of the child's performance ($r — 0.67$) than did a combined index of mother's IQ, child's IQ, and social class ($r — 0.47$) (Hess and Shipman, 1968).

To 56 of these 163 children, Stodolsky (1965) administered the Peabody Picture Vocabulary Test (PPVT) one year later when the children were five years old. She then correlated the children's scores with a selected set of maternal variables from the year before and obtained a multiple correlation of 0.68. The best single predictor of the children's PPVT scores was the mother's vocabulary score on the Wechsler Adult Intelligence Scale. Aspects of the maternal teaching styles which added most to the prediction were amount of reinforcement and a "discrimination index," which measured the extent to which the mother isolated task-specific qualities of the environment.

Finally, when the children were followed into the primary grades, Hess et al. (1969), found that maternal teaching styles during the preschool years were significantly related to school performance, with a higher relationship to standardized achievement tests than to teacher's ratings, and a higher relationship for girls than for boys.

Recently, criticism of research that compares children or families from different subcultural groups has increased; see, for example, Baratz and Baratz (1970) and Sroufe (1970). Sroufe has written "a methodological and philosophical critique" which should be considered one aspect of the important issue of the nature of objectivity in social science research. As Myrdal (1969) makes clear, it is impossible for social science research to be "objective" in the sense of "value-free." All social science research will be influenced by the moral and political valuations of the researcher. But these values should be made explicit rather than hidden, so that they can be challenged and discussed.

Sroufe criticizes the implicit values in research on mother-child interaction that is then used to justify educational attempts to change maternal behavior. The particular research he criticized is by Bee and associates (1969). (This research differs from that by Hess and associates (1969) in that Hess's families were all black, and social class comparisons were less important than analysis of significant maternal variables across the entire social class range.) No attempt will be made here to evaluate Bee's research; see Bee, 1970 for her answer. Rather, the questions raised by Sroufe will be categorized so as to alert readers to significant issues in evaluating any research of this kind.

First, questions must be raised about the underlying assumption that the poor performance of lower-class children on intelligence tests or in school is a fact to be explained by limitations in the child home environment:

> Programs in this area generally include some assessment of "deficits" in lower-class children and "limitations" in some aspect of the lower-class family environment, and a causal connection between the two is implied. (Sroufe, 1970, p. 140.)

Second, once a particular research question has been selected, bias may intrude in the methods used to answer it. Implicit biases may affect the design of the experimental situation by preventing the researcher from considering how a setting or task would be perceived by members of another group. Do all aspects of the assessment situations carry the same meaning for all subjects? That is, are they functionally equivalent in the behavior they elicit? Sroufe mentions such aspects as race of examiner, ability of the other to understand the examiner's dialect, the mother's reaction to being in a university waiting room (where the mother-child interaction was observed), her perception of the house-building task, and the effect of this on her directiveness of the child. Implicit biases may also affect how the researcher categorizes the behavior of the people he is

observing. The question of whether middle-class investigators can make
valid categorizations and ratings of the behavior of lower-class (especially
Black) subjects should at least be raised. ". . . unwittingly bias is not
ruled out by the establishment of high inter-rater reliabilities. Such agreement may only indicate similarities in meaning system, point of view, or
training" (Sroufe, 1970, p. 142).

Third, faulty or biased interpretations may be made from the data. Is
the distinction between a construct and a measure of that construct
observed?

> As just one example from the Washington Project . . . it was concluded that
> lower-class communication patterns were less complex and less rich than
> those of the middle-class mothers. But number of clauses per sentence is not
> the only possible measure of linguistic complexity, nor are number of words
> and adjective/verb ratios the only measure of richness. (Sroufe, 1970, p.
> 142.)

Are alternative interpretations of the data considered? For example, on
one of Bee's tasks, LC children made fewer key taps during a 2-minute
interval. Instead of the MC children's performance being valued, Sroufe
suggests that it could represent "rigid persistence in a meaningless, boring,
key-tapping task merely because of instructions to do so from an adult"
(1970, p. 143).

Finally, is the critical distinction between correlation and causation
remembered? Do the correlations hold within each social class group?
That is, "within the lower-class group, did mother-child interaction scores
account for a significant portion of the variance on the cognitive task?"
(Sroufe, 1970, p. 141). As Sroufe points out, when descriptive research
is used to justify a subsequent home-training program, a causal link is
indeed being inferred from correlational data.

A Manipulative Experiment (1–2C)

A manipulative experiment (Cazden, 1965) was originally conceived
to separate the effect of expansions (section 2C) from the effect of sheer
quantity of well-informed speech (section 1C) more sharply than they
could be separated in analyses of spontaneous speech. But I now realize that
the experiment as actually conducted contrasted two specific forms of contingent interaction (2C alone). This reconceptualization is important because of the implications of this particular research for education.

The subjects of this experiment, who have been referred to in previous
chapters, were 12 Black children, aged 28 to 38 months. They were all
attending a private day-care center in Boston, where 30 children less than
four years old were cared for by one teacher, with occasional help from

the cook and the owner-director. We assumed that these children were sufficiently language-deprived by being in this environment 8 to 10 hours a day that the stimulation added in this research should make an observable difference. Four matched trios were formed on the basis of each child's chronological age, talkativeness, and initial level of language development, as judged by his mean length of utterance in spontaneous speech during an orientation period. Within each trio, the children were randomly assigned to one of two treatment groups or a control group.

One treatment group received 40 minutes a day of intensive and deliberate expansions. If the child said *Dog bark* when a dog was barking, the adult said *Yes, the dog is barking*. The second treatment group received exposure to an equal number of well-formed sentences that were not expansions. Since the adult tried to maintain a reasonable discourse agreement, the child's comment *Dog bark* would in this treatment be followed by a nonexpansion such as *Yes, but he won't bite*, or *I guess he's mad at the kitty*.

We called this second treatment "modeling," but I now believe that label to be seriously inaccurate. Because the adult tried to maintain as much conversational relevance in this second treatment as in the first, while suppressing the expansions that come almost automatically to mind, the second treatment was characterized by a higher density of what Brown (personal communication) called "extensions" in the longitudinal study of Adam, Eve, and Sarah. Both expansions and extensions are adult responses that are contingent on the child's previous utterance, but the nature of the contingency is slightly different in the two cases. Expansions in their purest form express the meaning of the child (as the adult understands it) in syntactically complete form. Extensions presuppose a particular expansion, but then build out from it along some dimension of meaning. It is this very limited contrast that was tested in this manipulative experiment (Cazden, 1965). In the discussion that follows, the second treatment will be labeled "extension," rather than "modeling."

Expansions and extensions are both provided spontaneously by parents. Frequently they occur in the same utterance. To the child's *Dog bark*, the parent might respond *Yes, the dog's barking at the kitty*. Interpretation of the results of the experiment will return to the question of what happens when expansions and extensions are artificially separated. But, first, back to the experiment itself.

Two tutors were trained for this research, and the children randomly assigned to them. Each child in the expansion and extension groups had an individual play session with one of the tutors every school day for three months. The sessions were held in two small rooms in the day-care center normally used only for naps. Both rooms were equipped with toys and books selected to stimulate conversation. In the expansion treatment, pictures in the books were used as stimuli for talk. In the extension treatment, the books were read, one each day. I did not try to determine whether qualitative differences between spoken and written language played any part in the results. The play sessions were monitored at regular intervals during the three-month period to ensure the separation of the critical interaction variables. Children in the control group received no treatment, but they were brought into the treatment rooms every few days so that they would maintain familiarity with the materials and the tutors.

Tape recordings were made of each child's speech at the beginning, middle, and end of the three-month period. The tapes were transcribed by a secretary who was trained by a staff linguist and who was ignorant of the treatment assignment of the children. The transcriptions were then coded according to strict rules. The dependent variables were six measures of syntactic development: one was a sentence imitation test, and five measured aspects of the child's spontaneous speech—mean length of utterance in morphemes, noun-phrase index, verb complexity, copula index, and type-of-sentence index. The last four indexes were devised for this research. These measures are discussed in more detail in the Appendix.

Two statistical analyses were used to test the hypothesis that expansions would provide the most effective treatment. In neither analysis was there any evidence that expansions aid the acquisition of grammar. Contrary to our basic hypothesis, semantic extension proved to be slightly more helpful than grammatical expansions.

Three reasons can be suggested for these results. First, the richness of verbal stimulation (within limits of the child's comprehension) may be a critical variable. A treatment that focuses on grammatical structure tends to limit the ideas to the presumed meaning of the child, and tends to limit the grammatical elements to those used by the child; focus on the idea, by contrast, extends that idea beyond the presumed meaning of the child and introduces more varied grammatical elements to express those related meanings. If the learning of syntactic rules is akin to concept formation, then learning may be aided by variation in noncriterial attributes—for instance, the particular noun in the case of inflection for plurality. If the process of first-language learning is akin to construction of scientific theory, in which hypotheses are tested against available data, then a meager set of data may be disadvantageous. An impoverished language may be harder —not easier—to learn.

McNeill (1970) suggests an alternative explanation. When an adult attempts to expand a child's telegraphic utterances far more often than parents spontaneously do, some of the expansions probably misinterpret the child's intended meaning. Instead of facilitating the acquisition of grammar, such erroneous expansions may mislead the child and interfere with his learning. It is also probable that dialect differences between children and tutors may have produced erroneous expansions and therefore more syntactic interference in the expansion treatment. Researchers were not as sensitive to the syntactic aspects of dialect differences in 1965 as they are today.

Still a third explanation is possible, separately or in conjunction with either of the other two. Artificial elevation of the expansion rate may depress attentional processes in the child. We know from many current studies of child development that stimuli of a certain degree of novelty—not too familiar and not too strange—command the greatest attention. The acquisition of language should be facilitated by those environmental events that enhance the child's attention to the adult's utterance and to relevant features of the verbal and nonverbal context in which it is spoken. In these particular experimental treatments, a greater degree of novelty may have been attained in the extension treatment.

There may be an important lesson here for attempts to isolate specific features of the environment that affect a child's development. Campbell and Stanley describe the strategy that was the pattern for this experiment.

> The actual X [independent variable, here treatment] in any experiment is a complex package of what will eventually be conceptualized as several variables. Once a strong and clear-cut effect has been noted, the course of science consists of further experiments which refine the X, teasing out those aspects which are most essential to the effect. (Campbell and Stanley, 1963, p. 203.)

Trouble arises when isolation of an aspect of X distorts it. This may have happened when expansions were separated from the extensions with which they so frequently and naturally occur. As a refined conversational diet, they become uninteresting and may invite inattention. But one cannot conclude that they are necessarily also impotent in their natural environment. Moerk (in press) offers a good discussion of this point.

To my knowledge, no manipulative experiment has tested the effect of increased or more systematic exposure alone (1C). In her study of how Adam, Eve, and Sarah learned to say no, Bellugi (in press) discovered that the children learned the complex system of English auxiliaries from very fragmentary data and suggested that perhaps the acquisition of that system could be aided by more systematic presentation, in natural conversation, of all the forms that auxiliaries can take. Lavatelli (1970) suggests how the modeling of particular syntactic structures can be incorporated into a Piagetian preschool curriculum. But neither suggestion has been experimentally tested.

There is an interesting question about the timing of environmental assistance. Does either exposure or contingent feedback, using a particular grammatical structure, make more difference when growth in knowledge of that structure is actively taking place? The growth curve for language development in general is steepest between the ages of two and four years.

For particular features, the curve would be steepest at shorter intervals during that period. One hypothesis is that exposure to examples of those features would be particularly potent at that time. Imagine an experiment as follows: Child A hears lots of plurals before his language system is at the stage of incorporating them. Then (somehow) plurals are eliminated from his environment for a period of some months. Child B hears them only during the one period when he is likely to be learning them. Child C hears them throughout, as in normally the case. Would the course or rate of acquisition of plurals by the three children be different as a result?

An alternative hypothesis is possible. If perception is more separated from production, input from the environment may be undistorted by the filter of the child's momentary level of language structure and somehow stored intact for later cognitive use. That is a possible implication of Piaget's experiments on the child's spontaneous improvement in memory of a series of sticks graduated in height (Inhelder, 1969). We don't know how the capacity to make use of experience is related to the capacity to respond to it.

On the effects of interaction on the acquisition of syntax, Brown, Cazden and Bellugi (1969) conclude:

> . . . It seems likely that the many kinds of grammatical exchange in discourse will prove to be the richest data available to the child in his search for a grammar. It may be as difficult to derive a grammar from hearing unconnected static sentences as it would be to derive the invariance of quantity and number from simply looking at liquids in containers and objects in space. The changes produced by pouring back and forth and by gathering together and spreading apart are the data that most strongly suggest the conservation of quantity and number. We suspect that the changes sentences undergo as they shuttle between persons in conversation are, similarly, the data that most clearly expose the underlying structure of language. . . .
>
> Perhaps we shall someday find that linguistic environments at home do vary significantly in structural richness but that any single form of response is an unreliable index of this variation, even as age of weaning has proved an unreliable index of something more important—general child-rearing attitudes (Brown, Cazden, and Bellugi, 1969, pp. 72–73.)

It is important not to overgeneralize the negative results of the experiment on the role of expansions. I suggested earlier that interpretation of it should be restricted because of the narrowness of the independent variables and the possible distortion introduced by separating expansions from extensions. The dependent variables may also be too narrow and further distortions may have been introduced by looking for effects on syntactic measures of development alone. Reeves (1965) presents a beautiful discussion of the attempts by human infants to "calibrate" their observations with those of another person, and to seek evidence that their calibration has been made. Visually, when an adult points, the child follows the adult's movements and then looks back to check his response. Verbally, calibration is achieved by contingent adult responses—expansions or extensions. From the beginning, Brown and Bellugi suggested this broader view:

> The meanings that are added [in expansions] by functors seem to be nothing less than the basic terms in which we construe reality. . . . It seems to us that a mother in expanding speech may be teaching more than grammar; she may be teaching something like a world-view. (Brown and Bellugi, 1964, pp. 142–143.)

Bruner has many times (1966, for example) emphasized the importance of such reciprocal relationships for cognitive development in general.

In the section on correlation data (1B) the probable importance of environmental assistance to the development of syntax was contrasted with the development of meaning. Two recent manipulative experiments confirm that contrast. Ammon and Ammon found that "vocabulary training" was more effective than "sentence training" with preschool Black children in the San Francisco Bay area. Two separate groups of children were each randomly divided among a vocabulary treatment, a sentence structure treatment, and a control group.

> Children who received vocabulary training recognized and produced more of the target words than children in the sentence training and control groups. Sentence training did not affect performance on a Sentence Imitation Test containing the target constructions. There were no transfer effects from vocabulary to syntax or vice versa, but vocabulary training did increase the general variety of words produced in an interview. (Ammon and Ammon, 1970, p. 7.)

Moore (1971) contrasted an extension treatment with what he called "patterning," adapted from Bereiter-Engelmann (1968), for four-year-old Black children in Roxbury. While there were treatment differences on intelligence test scores and measures of communication effectiveness, there were no treatment differences on the one measure of syntactic development, a sentence imitation test, despite the fact that one of the treatments (patterning) included a great deal of practice in imitation itself.

Note that in contrast to the acquisition of language structure, acquisition of meaning is never finished. With accelerating social change, adult lexicons are probably growing even more rapidly than in the past. Consider just the recent shift from frequency of space terms like *module* to conservation terms like *biodegradable.* At least with regard to this aspect of language development, interesting questions about environmental assistance continue to apply at all ages.

Research that differentiates among the many aspects of language development and tests their differential vulnerability to environmental differences is extremely important. But ultimately we will understand how the environment affects any aspect of language only when we understand more fully how language is in turn related to other aspects of cognition.

The Nonlinguistic Environment (3A–C)

The nonlinguistic environment may affect the child's language development in two ways. It certainly affects the nature of the language the child hears and the patterns of interaction he engages in; that is, part of the effect of row 3 (Table 1) will be mediated through rows 1 and 2. The nonlinguistic environment also has an effect more directly by influencing the ways in which the child attends to and processes whatever language he hears.

INDIRECT EFFECTS

Nonlinguistic aspects of the child's environment can be influential in at least three ways: differences in who speaks to the child, differences in characteristics of the context or situation in which the conversation takes place, and differences in attitudes of the speaker toward language and toward the child.

Consider under the general label "speaker" anyone who speaks in the presence of the child or directly to him. Whether that person is an adult, another child, or a voice from the TV will affect patterns of speech and interaction. The difference between adult and child has been hypothesized as one source of social-class differences in child language. On the other hand, Bar-Adon suggests that "children seem to possess a special sense for 'speech analysis' of their younger siblings or friends" (1971, p. 445). We need analyses of interaction among siblings and peers.

Friedlander (in press) is one of the few people who actually has collected data on the infant's language environment (3A). Using a time-sampling, voice-activated tape recorder system, he made recordings in the homes of two graduate-student families with 12-month-old infants. Table 5 gives his analysis of the source of all utterances spoken within hearing range of the microphone, and the source of those utterances directed to the infant. It is striking how different the two families are in the role of "other"—in all utterances—and how similar they are in who actually talks to the baby. The Jones family has the bilingual father described above in section 1B.

As part of a study of residential nurseries in England, Tizard et al. (in press) discovered organizational conditions that affect how often high-quality conversations take place between adults and children. The adult-child ratio is not the only factor, though that is important. Nurseries in which the children's language development was highest were also characterized by a smaller proportion of children under three years of age, greater staff stability, and greater staff autonomy. Where the proportion of very young children was high, the staff was preoccupied with the burdens of physical care. Where staff turnover was high, the adults were less apt to know the children well enough to understand their immature speech. Where staff autonomy was low, the adult saw her job more as " 'minding' the children under the eye of her supervisor." Finally,

Table 5 **Percentages of Systematically Sampled Utterances in the Homes of Two 12-Month Infants, Showing the Source of All Utterances and the Sources of Infant-Directed Utterances**

Source of Utterance	Smith Family, %	Jones Family, %
ALL UTTERANCES		
Mother	22	11
Father	18	4
Baby	35	15
Other (guests, radio, TV)	25	70
INFANT-DIRECTED UTTERANCES		
Mother	67	73
Father	30	24
Guests	3	3

Source: Friedlander, 1971.

within any given adult-child ratio, conversation was affected by how staff responsibilities were allocated. "When two staff were on duty with a group of six children, the junior of the two tended to talk less and interact less with the children than when she was alone in charge of the group" (Tizard et al., in press). Adults as well as children are influenced by power relations inherent in speech situations. We sorely need more studies of how features of complex organizations influence behavior and thereby affect the child's development.

Row 3 affects rows 1 and 2 (Table 1) if the speakers in the child's environment have different beliefs about language and children. Whether adults talk to children at all before the children themselves begin to talk, whether they try to respond to the child as often as possible, how much they simplify their speech—all these behaviors will be influenced by parental beliefs as well as by how busy the parents are at other activities.

Parental attitudes toward language can be inferred from their behavior or tapped directly in interviews. Friedlander describes one of his subjects:

> One mother often became involved in rather long and complicated dialogues with her baby in which the baby's only participation consisted of occasional coos, babbles, or grunts. This observation does not necessarily imply that the mother was indifferent to the probability that the baby did not understand the meaning content of her speech and that the dialogues were essentially non-reciprocal. Perhaps a more suitable interpretation would be that she appeared to regard the baby as a perfectly satisfactory conversational companion who did not need to speak at length in order to be regarded as a peer (Friedlander, in press).

Expansions can be reconstrued here, too. They seem to express parental conviction that the child means something when he talks and parental concern to communicate successfully with him. Maybe the correlation that we initially found between rate of language development and frequency of expansions (section 2B) should be interpreted as a correlation between development and such attitudinal variables as parental conviction and concern (section 3B), of which expansions are only one expression.

In his large research project on the role of language in primary socialization in London, Bernstein obtained information on maternal attitudes toward language through interviews with the mothers before the children started school at five years of age and again in the last year of the infant school when the children were seven (Brandis and Henderson, 1970; Bernstein and Henderson, in press). Two indices of maternal behavior were established: the Communication Index (CI) and the Index of Communication and Control (ICC). Two questions in the first interview asked how the mother would respond when her child wanted to chat in various settings—*when you're around the house* or *when you're in a shop*—and how she would answer or evade a set of difficult questions such as *Why do leaves fall off the tree?* or *Where do I come from?* The mother's responses were scaled to yield the CI. A mother with a high score on this index encourages her child's conversation and questions. For the ICC, the answers to these two questions were supplemented with the answers to three others, which asked the mother how she controlled her child, whether she explained the reasons for her actions, and what value she saw in toys.

Bernstein and his colleagues predicted that measures of the child's language and intellectual ability would be more highly correlated with such indices of the mother's behavior and attitudes than with the more global variable of social class. This prediction was borne out for the 174 children within the working-class schools, where most of the parents were in the lowest four categories of a 10-point social-class scale based on parental occupation and education. Within the middle-class schools, on the other hand, the ability test scores were more related to social class, either because the social-class range was greater here or because a more sensitive maternal-behavior index was needed to discriminate among MC families (Brandis and Henderson, 1970). Table 6 gives the correlations within the working-class area between four "ability" tests and social class (in the first column) and the maternal index (in the second column). The first three tests were given when the child entered school at age 5: the Raven Progressive Mat-

Table 6 **Ability Tests: Working-Class Area**

Test	Correlations with Social Class	Correlations with Maternal Index Score
Matrices	0.179	0.192
Crichton	0.163	0.231
EPVT	0.137	0.251
WISC	0.25	0.38

rices (nonverbal IQ), the Crichton Vocabulary Scale, and the English version of the Peabody Vocabulary Test (EPVT). One year later, the children were given the Wechsler Intelligence Scale for Children (WISC).

The correlations in Table 6 are independent of number of children in the family or the sample child's ordinal position. Brandis and Henderson conclude that a child's measured ability, particularly on more verbal tests, is related to the extent to which mothers respond to their child's questions and give explanations—in short, to the mother's orientation toward "the *relevance* of language" (1970, p. 106).

Bernstein's second questionnaire also tapped maternal attitudes toward the use of language in different domains of family life. The mothers were asked to imagine "If parents could not speak, how much more difficult do you think it would be for them to do the following things with young children who had not yet started school?" (Bernstein and Henderson, in press). Eleven statements were presented, of which four dealt with the transmission of skills (for example, "Teaching them everyday tasks like dressing, and using a knife and fork"); five dealt with aspects of social control (for example, "Helping them to work things out for themselves"); and two were "dummies," included to make the purpose of the interview less obvious. The responses of 50 MC and 50 LC mothers were analyzed:

> Although greater emphasis was placed on the difficulty of dealing with the situations described in the *person* (social control) area by *all* the mothers, the difference between the responses of the middle-class mothers in relation to the two areas of statements was significantly greater than the difference between the responses of the working-class mothers. Middle-class mothers place much greater emphasis upon the difficulty of doing the things described in the *person* area than the working-class mothers, but they placed much *less* emphasis upon the difficulty of doing the things described in the *skill* area than the working-class mothers. This highly significant interaction effect illustrates the polarisation of the responses of middle-class mothers in relation to the two areas of statements. (Bernstein and Henderson, in press.)

The mean scores presented by Bernstein and Henderson (1970) are graphed in Figure 1 to help make these relationships clear.

Like other environmental variables, adult attitudes may have a pervasive effect on a child's general development or a more differential effect on language alone. In a study of mother-child interaction in two white social-class groups during the baby's first year of life, Tulkin (1970) found examples of both. Middle-class mothers both initiated more vocalizations to their infants and responded more frequently and more quickly to them. In seeking explanations for these results, Tulkin and Kagan (1970) comment—

> It appeared that one source of variance in maternal behavior was the mother's conception of what her infant was like. Some working-class mothers emotions or to communicate with other people; hence, they felt it was futile did not believe that their infants possessed the ability to feel adult-like

Figure 1   **Relevance of Language to Socialization.**

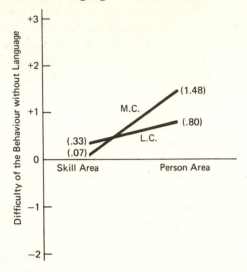

Source   Bernstein and Henderson

to attempt to interact with their infants. One working-class mother who constantly spoke to her daughter lamented that her friends chastised her for "talking to the kid like she was three years old." A common working-class philosophy appeared to be that only after the child began to talk was it important for the mother to speak back.

Secondly, working-class mothers tended to feel that they could have little influence on the development of their children. . . . This philosophy may be indicative of a general sense of fatalism which develops when working-class people find that they are often powerless to effect changes in their environment. (Tulkin and Kagan, 1970, pp. 5–6.)

Tulkin and Kagan's two explanations suggest a differential and a pervasive influence respectively.

For all research on parental attitudes and beliefs, Friedlander's comments apply.

It must be evident that variables of this nature are very hard to specify, and perhaps impossible to express in terms of "clean" relationships between cause and effect. Yet the door must be open to recognize these attitudinal sources of variation as being among the most powerful there are in establishing the quality of the communication in which the infant and young child serves his linguistic apprenticeship. (Friedlander, 1970, p. 46.)

DIRECT EFFECTS

Turn now to hypotheses about more direct effects of the nonlinguistic environment on the children's reception of whatever language he hears.

Some researchers have speculated about differences in the signal-to-noise-ratio in different homes, and have suggested that this may be a source of social-class differences in child language. Again Friedlander provides us with rare and valuable data that suggest that poor signal-to-noise ratios may be a very general characteristic of normal family environments. After listening to tape recordings made in homes, Friedlander comments:

> Careful analysis of home language interactions, well recorded on quality audio equipment, tends to breed an enhanced respect for the awesome intricacy of the language learning process in its natural habitat. As one listens to such recordings, it seems altogether inexplicable how so delicate a fabric as language can be woven from such crude, chaotically tangled, poorly organized, and seemingly random raw materials as the natural sounds that surround an infant in a bustling household. . . . Among the American families we have studied, speech articulation in adult and sibling conversation is almost uniformly poor. . . . Speech messages and language signals are deeply embedded in background noise; sound intensity levels are often inaudibly low or assaultively high; the speech stream flows with great rapidity; two or more people are often speaking at one time; and grammatical structures are often incomplete or very distorted. In such a mess, what is the stimulus? (Friedlander, 1970.)

Before retreating completely to nativistic interpretations of how language learning takes place under such conditions, consider three cautions. First, it may not be valid to generalize from what even the best recording equipment picks up to what the human ear can attend to. What the human ear and brain can do through selective attention, perhaps especially with language signals, is part of the miracle of being human. Unfortunately, the only way we can capture environmental moments for subsequent analysis is to record them on nonhuman, mechanical equipment. But, as a result, some distortion in the sound and thereby in our interpretation seems almost inevitable.

Second, another comment by Friedlander excepts from this dismal description "the most intimate one-to-one encounters between parent and child, such as the bath, dressing, and feeding" (1970, p. 44). If children can learn language from a small set of data, then these moments of intimate encounter may play a critical role and the remainder of the day recede in importance. Since it is sometimes claimed that intensive parent-child conversation is less apt to occur in lower-class families, Horner's (1968) research should be noted. In her recordings of two complete days in the life of two lower-class Black three-year-olds, Horner found that both children talked most frequently to the mother. Mother and child were together for only brief periods, but the rate of conversation during those periods was high.

Third, while infants who are fully normal in all relevant aspects of their development may cope successfully with such "noisy" environments, children with any degree of receptive disability such as deafness may be seriously affected. Friedlander seeks both to "evaluate and enrich the subjective language experience of very young children with moderate and severe hearing losses and receptive language disabilities" (Friedlander, 1970). See also Wyatt's (1969) discussion of communication disorders in children.

The "noise" that may mask language signals, or at least draw attention away from them, is not auditory noise alone. It may be tactful or visual as well. Kagan (1968) found that when mothers talk to their four-month-old infants, college-educated mothers provide more of what he calls "distinctive vocalization." When talking to their infants, these mothers less often provided simultaneous tactile or kinesthetic stimulation by touching, tickling, or picking up the infant. Because college-educated mothers generally have children whose language develops faster, a correlation can be hypothesized between distinctive vocalization by the mother and rate of language development in the child. But whether distinctive vocalization really makes any difference is not yet known.

The same kind of presumptive evidence of correlation exists for language heard over TV. Language from that source is different in many ways from language in face-to-face conversation. One difference is that language heard over TV comes in a highly nondistinctive form simultaneously with attention-grabbing visual stimuli. Because lower-class children, who watch the most TV, are also those who score lowest on language tests, a correlational relationship is assumed (3B), but (as with distinctiveness) visual noise may in fact not matter at all.

The child's own activity may also interfere with his attention by providing proprioceptive noise for the reception of verbal stimuli, but we know nothing about how this happens, or even whether it does.

Implications for Education

The picture of preschool environmental assistance, incomplete though it is, raises questions about the more deliberate assistance we call "education." Three issues will be discussed: adult attention to outward form or inward substance, sequencing instruction, and generalizability beyond language to other curriculum objectives, particularly learning to read. Additional issues are raised in Chapter 10.

OUTWARD FORM VERSUS INNER SUBSTANCE

Earlier discussion that contrasted rule-governed errors with unanalyzed chunks of superficially more mature behavior (section IB) suggested that adults may interfere with a child's learning if they press for behavior that looks or sounds "correct," regardless of its relation to the child's internal mental organization. This distinction is important not only in language. (See Glick, 1968, and Werner, 1937). Scheffler discusses the same contrast in the evaluation of classroom performance in general:

> Turning first to classroom performance, it is important to stress the subtlety and delicacy of the teacher's interchange with the student. A crude demand for effectiveness easily translates itself into a disastrous emphasis on externals simply because they are easier to get hold of than the central phenomena of insight and the growth of understanding. In an important essay of 1904, John Dewey distinguished between the inner and outer attention of children, the inner attention involving the "first-hand and personal play of mental powers" and the external "manifested in certain conventional postures and physical attitudes rather than in the movement of thought." Children, he noted, "acquire great dexterity in exhibiting in conventional and expected ways the *form* of attention to school work." The "supreme mark and criterion of a teacher," according to Dewey, is the ability to bypass externals and to "keep track of [the child's] mental play, to recognize the signs of its presence or absence, to know how it is initiated and maintained, how to test it by results attained, and to test *apparent* results by it." The teacher "plunged prematurely into the pressing and practical problem of keeping order in the schoolroom," Dewey warned, is almost of necessity going "to make supreme the matter of external attention." Without the reflective and free opportunity to develop his theoretical conceptions and his psychological insight, he is likely to "acquire his technique in relation to the ouward rather than the inner mode of attention." Effective classroom performance surely needs to be judged in relation to the subtle engagement of this inner mode, difficult as it may be to do so. (Scheffler, 1968, p. 9.)

Parents, at least when their children are young and language development is most rapid, concentrate on the inner meaning of their child's speech, sure in the conviction that as the child's capacity and need to express more complex ideas grows, so the forms in his language will change accordingly. Teachers would do well to concentrate there too.

SEQUENCING INSTRUCTION

It is natural to assume that any educational effort is more effective if the objective can be analyzed into component parts and these taught sequentially on some rational basis. But it is by no means certain that this is indeed so for all kinds of objectives.

Gagné, who developed the concept of learning hierarchies, distinguishes between intellectual skills and verbalizable knowledge, and reports research that suggests that "a learner may acquire certain intellectual skills from a presentation that is quite disorganized when viewed as a sequence of verbalizable knowledge" (Gagné, 1968, p. 4). Oral language objectives are a mixture of intellectual skills (from the discrimination of speech sounds to the ability to shift to the listener's perspective) and verbalizable knowledge (word meanings), but the former predominate.

Controversy over the role of sequence parallels the controversy between part-task and whole-task instructional procedures.

> Educators who have been influenced by the programed-instruction movement take it as self-evident that the best way to teach a complex skill is to analyze it into component subskills and subconcepts, then teach each of these in turn. Cast in different language such an approach is a part-task method, to be contrasted with the whole-task method in which the student is required to perform the terminal behavior as best he can from the very beginning of training. (Anderson, 1968, p. 207.)

In selecting among these alternatives, note that all oral language learning that takes place before the child goes to school (whether to preschool, kindergarten, or first grade) takes place on a nonsequenced, whole-task basis. The child is surrounded by examples of mature speech behavior and is encouraged to participate as best he can from the very beginning. Somehow, if he is so surrounded and if he does have the chance to participate, each child takes from his interaction with this manageable complexity (whatever that is) what he needs to build his own language system. Other than the kind of spontaneous simplification of adult language which Snow (1971) and others document, and the feedback fitted to his speech in spontaneous parental expansions and extensions, there is no sequencing of what the child hears. Whatever environmental assistance the child gets, it is clear that he never gets sequential tuition based on an analysis of component skills. When a richly supplied cafeteria is available from the beginning, no carefully prescribed diet is necessary. Oral language development therefore provides special justification for the argument that the best way to continue instruction in school is to continue on this whole-task basis. And as Anderson (1968) makes clear, the evidence for selection between these two instructional approaches is by no means conclusive in other areas of the school curriculum either.

It may be that the kind of analysis presented in learning hierarchies as a list of component skills represents the knowledge the effective teacher needs rather than a flow chart of teaching plans. This is what Resnick, herself also in the Gagné tradition, seems to suggest—

> A formal curriculum sequence has no necessary implications for the style of classroom organization. The sequence can be used, as in Bereiter and Engelmann's (1966) programs for the disadvantaged, in a manner that requires the participation of all children in all drills with little room for choice on the part of either child or teacher. However, it can be equally well used in a classroom whose organization is free and open as in the Montessori model or some modification of the progressive nursery school. In the latter situations, the child is free to move within the room, to choose his own activities within certain limitations, and to spend as long as he wishes at a

given task. The curriculum sequence need not be evident to him as a constraint. However, the teacher can use the sequence to keep careful track of each child and how he is progressing through the hierarchy of skills. (Resnick, 1967, p. 14.)

In the introduction to this book, I suggested that teachers need to know about language, beyond simply using it well themselves. Two outlets for such knowledge can now be specified. First, teachers must provide a school environment rich in both language the child hears (from people and from books) and in provocations to self-expression and communication. Such an environment seems to happen very naturally in many homes. But in schools—preschool or beyond—the language environment can be woefully meager without the teacher's deliberate attention. She needs to be self-conscious about her own language—both what she says and how she distributes her talking attention during the day. Second, teachers need to be able to listen diagnostically to the children's language and track their progress toward increasingly adequate oral and written forms, giving help as needed without imposing an arbitrary instructional sequence on a learning process we don't fully understand. (Cazden, 1971, gives many suggestions for such diagnosis at the preschool level.) Paradoxically, such diagnostic listening must not interfere with responding at the moment, fully and intently, to the ideas the child is trying to express.

GENERALIZABILITY TO OTHER EDUCATIONAL GOALS

Some critics of traditional public schools, advocates of what is now called "open education" with dangerous vagueness, contrast unsuccessful attempts to teach school subjects with the successful way children learn their native language. Quotations from John Holt, a well-known teacher and writer, and Philip Morrison, a physicist at M.I.T. who was active for many years in the Elementary Science Study curriculum development project, show how persuasive these arguments are.

First, John Holt:

> Bill Hull [*Author's note*: the teacher quoted by Bruner in Chapter 4] once said to me, "If we taught children to speak, they'd never learn." I thought at first he was joking. By now I realize that it was a very important truth. Suppose we decided that we had to "teach" children to speak. How would we go about it? First, some committee of experts would analyze speech and break it down into a number of separate "speech skills." We would probably say that, since speech is made up of sounds, a child must be taught to make all the sounds of his language before he can be taught to speak the language itself. Doubtless we would list these sounds, easiest and commonest ones first, harder and rarer ones next. Then we would begin to teach infants these sounds, working our way down the list. Perhaps, in order not to "confuse" the child—"confuse" is an evil word to many educators—

we would not let the child hear much ordinary speech but would only expose him to the sounds we were trying to teach. . . .

Suppose we tried to do this; what would happen? What would happen, quite simply, is that most children, before they got very far, would become baffled, discouraged, humiliated, and fearful, and would quit trying to do what we asked them. If, outside of our classes, they lived a normal infant's life, many of them would probably ignore our "teaching" and learn to speak on their own. If not, if our control of their lives was complete (the dream of too many educators), they would take refuge in deliberate failure and silence, as so many of them do when the subject is reading. (Holt, 1967, pp. 56–57.)

Then Philip Morrison:

First and chief of all the learned activities of man is language. The reader may perhaps recall that charming little boy who pouts a challenge to you out of the Berlitz ads. The advertisement boasts that the child can speak Ewe—difficult grammar, tonal constructions and all—at a highly practical level. "By the age of four to six," one linguist writes, "the child is a linguistic adult. He controls . . . the phonetic system of his language; he handles the grammatical core; he knows and uses the basic vocabulary of the language." Of course he has a lot to learn; but that remains true through life. It is the nearly invariable success in learning this complex and subtle tool of thought that convinces us that we tend to underestimate the abilities of children. The strong motivation a child has to learn to speak, the excellent student-teacher ratio and the long time spent at the task are certainly signposts for those who would design curricula. . . .

We are not expert at language development. Still, some observations force themselves upon us and have meant much for the style in which we seek to work. The children who learn to speak make mistakes, many of them. They try again, learning from error. They talk in all sorts of contexts, formal recitations, games, jokes, even insults and fights. They make slow progress, and they make rapid progress. They store and learn all sorts of words and forms whose utility is not clear and not soon displayed. . . .

Learning a formal subject, say Arithmetic, English, or Science, does not normally proceed along such lines. Learning is not all to be managed, it seems, by a wholly logical route. The effect is no less important. A rich context, a cheerful one, sometimes playful, sometimes earnest, sometimes austere, sometimes baroque—that is the condition for imparting not mere recall but productive use of language. Should learning about science be different? Or learning history or arithmetic or writing, for that matter? (Morrison, 1964, pp. 65–66.)

It is tempting to agree with Holt and Morrison. But in generalizing from language-learning to other subjects, we must be as clear as possible about similarities and differences among them, and then analyze the critical characteristics of a "rich" environment in each case.

Consider, as an example, the differences between learning to talk and learning to read. In oral language the child has to learn relationships between meanings and sounds. The raw material for the child's learning processes consists of a rich set of pairings of meanings and sound—for that is what language in the context of ongoing experience is. In reading, the child must learn relationships between oral language—which he now knows—and letters of the alphabet. But a rich set of pairings of oral and written language is much less available. It is available when the child is read to while sitting on an adult's lap (not when read to as part of a group in school); it is available when the bouncing ball accompanies TV commercials; it is available whenever the child points to any writing and asks *What's that say?*; and it is available whenever the child himself tries to write. Provision of a rich set of sound-word pairings can be built into deliberately planned environments—in the classroom or on TV. But the necessary pairings don't just happen for written language at school as they do for oral language at home.

In school, reading instruction that proceeds from writing to reading may be more effective than the other way around. Writing by children can take place in several ways that differ in their cognitive and motor demands. In English infant schools (Cazden, 1971), children almost always start by dictating to their teacher and then sometimes copy her transcriptions. In this case, they compose but do not write. With the Mackay and Thompson materials described in Chapter 5, the children compose sentences by selecting prewritten word cards. According to C. Chomsky's suggestions (1971a, 1971b)—and Montessori's (1965) before her, as Chomsky acknowledges—the child would compose at the level of individual letters by selecting letters made of plastic, sandpaper, or any other material. (The Mackay and Thompson materials have letter cards for a later stage, too.) All three methods minimize initial demands for the laborious and non-intellectual task of handwriting itself—though we should note that Read's (1970) preschool spellers even coped with that task when motivation was high. The relative merit of the three methods is an important but completely unresearched question.

TV or film offer particularly interesting opportunities for providing data for the acquisition of literacy. Like Holt and Morrison, Gattegno (1970) cites learning to talk as a model for successfully subordinating teaching to learning. But he has gone further to suggest very specific ways of building on the child's strengths, what he calls "the functionings of children"—such as the power of "extraction," the power to make "transformations," and the power to handle "abstractions." Gattegno's curriculum materials designed for the classroom are well known: Cuisennaire rods in mathematics and *Words in Color* (Encyclopedia Brittanica Press) in reading. More recently (*New York Times,* Jan. 6, 1971), Gattegno has worked with a Canadian film producer, Joseph Koenig, to create one-minute "pop-up" films in which animation techniques are used to present to the child raw data on how the written language system works: Its conventions about spatial arrangements, like left-to-right, top-to-bottom, and spaces between words; and the effects of transformations (Gattegno, 1969, p. 112) like insertion (*mat/mast*), reversal (nap/pan), substitution (map/mop), and addition (*mop/mops*).

Animation techniques provide a new medium for "concretizing the abstract. . . . Fundamentally, *the live-action camera represents the physical eye,* and *the animation camera represents the mind's eye* (Palmer, 1947, p. 26; emphasis in the original). More than most audiovisual technology, animation seems to epitomize one way we can validly generalize beyond language to greater success with other goals of education by taking advantage of "the functionings of children" and of adults as well.

7

Dialect Differences and Bilingualism

No language is spoken in exactly the same way by all its speakers. The most neutral, nonjudgmental label for the different ways in which a language may be spoken is "variety":

> The term variety . . . merely designates a member of a [speech community's] verbal repertoire. Its use implies only that there are other varieties as well. These can be specified by outsiders on the basis of the phonological, lexical, and grammatical differences that they (the varieties) manifest. Their functional allocations, however—as languages or as dialects—are derived only from societal observation of their uses and users rather than from any characteristics of the codes themselves. (Fishman, 1970, p. 23.)

A variety may be regional, ethnic or religious, social, functional, occupational, etc., depending on the characteristics of its speakers. The term "dialect" is properly reserved for varieties "that initially and basically represent divergent geographic origins" (Fishman, 1970, p. 22). It is in this sense that it can be applied to the language of many Black adults and children in the United States today.

> The first and most obvious generalization about the English of many Negroes is that it shows abundant characteristics of the southern United States. . . . In recent decades, as southern Negroes have surged into northern cities, they have brought along their varieties of southern speech. Since they have largely been forced to live in segregated ghettos, often shut off even more completely from association with whites than in their southern homes, their dialects have been perpetuated and passed on to their northern-born children. What had been geographically distinctive features have been converted into ethnic features. (Burling, 1970, p. 118.)

This chapter begins with dialect differences and their implications for education. Because of the social importance of questions about the education of Black children, research on dialect differences has concentrated on this group and so this chapter concentrates here too. But similar questions should be asked about children from Appalachia, rural Maine, and elsewhere. The chapter ends with a shorter section on bilingualism.

The notion of a "nonstandard" dialect raises a necessary introductory question about the validity of the concept of "Standard English" (SE). Is there in fact a single variety of English used by educated speakers throughout the country? The answer to this question depends on which aspect of language is being considered. In pronunciation, there is no single standard. Regional variations in "accent" exist and are widely accepted without social stigmatism. Taylor (1971) makes the obviously justified plea that Black speakers should be accorded the same courtesy. In syntax, by contrast, a single standard does seem to exist. With certain very minor exceptions, educated speakers around the country follow the same syntactic rules. Exceptions can be found in the case (in the grammatical sense) of pronouns. Linguistic change can be rapid, and utterances like *It is me* and *Who are you talking to?* are becoming acceptable except in the most purist circles (largely English classrooms, I suspect). Another exception in the grammatical case of pronouns is psycholinguistically more interesting. In the special sentence construction where two pronouns are conjoined, one very often hears even the most highly educated speakers utter such "errors" as the following:

I stepped between she and the police.	(MC graduate student, October 1967)
They flew my wife and I to Puerto Rico.	(College professor, September 1968)
There's very little difference between they and their South Boston peers.	(Psychologist, October 1968)

These pronoun forms constitute the only widespread instance of syntactic variability among educated speakers that I have found. In the discussion that follows, therefore, I will assume that a standard syntactic form of English does exist, and that style switching for SE speakers uses selection of vocabulary and shifts in pronunciation, as from *-ing* to *-in'*, for expressive purposes.

Black English

The most extensive research on Black dialectic patterns has been done by William Labov in New York City. He has used a variety of very carefully designed interview techniques to obtain a wide range of linguistic data from adolescent and preadolescent males in central Harlem. We will draw heavily on his findings, as reported in a two-volume monograph (Labov et al., 1968), and numerous articles supplementing them at several points with the work of other researchers.

Although Labov's work has been financed by the U.S. Office of Education because of its importance in providing a knowledge base for decisions about educational practice, it represents more than linguistic research prompted by the demands of social action. It also represents a shift in perspective and methodology within linguistics itself. There is an important contrast between Labov's view of language and that expressed by most other transformational grammarians. For instance, Katz states that "a necessary condition for something to be part of the subject matter of a linguistic theory is that each speaker be able to perform in that regard much as every other does" (Katz, 1964, p. 415). In Labov's sociolinguistic view, however, the multidimensional structure of variation across persons and across settings is an essential feature. Labov is primarily interested in language change and the factors influencing it. His goal is a "socially realistic linguistics"—a description of the structure of social and stylistic variation and an explanation of changes in that structure over time. The shift from the study of language as a homogeneous abstraction to the study of variability as an integral part of any linguistic system can be related to a corresponding contemporary shift in biological theory from typological to population models and concepts. To the typologist, differences among individuals are a kind of troublesome noise in the biological system. The populationist, on the contrary, regards diversity among individuals as the prime observable reality and the source of evolutionary possibilities (Dobzhansky, 1967). Labov's findings are extensive. This chapter can report only some of them in a fairly general form, and the reader should consult Labov's own writings for a wealth of rich detail and discussion.

The discussion is organized around eight issues; differences in meaning, differences in superficial form, the asymmetry between comprehension and production, relationships among dialects, dialect switching, dialects versus developmental change, the power of attitudes, and monitoring. Throughout, the labels Standard English (SE) and Black English (BE) will be used, except in quoting from Labov himself, where his label Negro Nonstandard English (NNE) will be retained.

DIFFERENCES IN MEANING

Labov has identified a few forms in BE which probably indicate basic differences in the deep structure of the dialect, in the underlying meaning being expressed.

> One is the use of *be* to indicate generality repeated action, or existential state in sentences such as *He be with us; They be fooling around*. . . . [A distinction which in S.E. is possible only with main verbs—*walks* (habitually) versus *is walking*—but not with the copula. —C. B. C.] Another such element is *done* to indicate an intensive or perfective meaning as in *The bullet done penetrated my body; I done got me a hat*. Both of these are part of an as-

pectual system which is plainly distinct from tense; there still remains the problem of specifying their use and limitations precisely, and then relating them to the tense system." (Labov and Cohen, 1967, p. 76.)

To date, Labov's published research has not included children younger than preadolescents. Henrie's (1969) study is one of the few careful descriptions of the speech of younger Black children. Using a story retelling technique, he elicited speech samples from three Black California kindergarten children selected as the most extreme BE speakers in their grade. In story retelling, as in sentence imitation tests, meaning is generally preserved, but the form is recoded into the speaker's own language system. (See John, Horner, and Birney, 1970, for further description of this research technique.) Henrie found that these children, like Labov's older subjects, frequently used unconjugated *be* to express habitual meaning:

Story: . . . he was always there
Child's version: He always be there.

DIFFERENCES IN SUPERFICIAL FORM

Given a certain idea to be expressed, NNE has different transformational rules governing its surface realization. One example is the deletion of the copula *be* in certain specific environments. The following are all examples of NNE (Labov, et al. 1968, Vol. 1, pp. 175–183):

Be deleted:	*Be* appears:
He fast in everything he do.	I'm not no strong drinker.
You out the game.	I was small.
They not caught.	Is he dead?
He gon' try to get up.	Allah *is* God (emphasis)
	It always somebody tougher than you are

Labov found that this alternation between the deletion and appearance of *be* is not simply random variation produced by dialect mixtures, but rather a highly structured system. Phonological influences can be specified: for example, *is* and *are* are deleted where *'m* is not because "there are no phonological processes which delete nasals" (Labov et al, 1968, Vol. 1, p. 284). An explanation can also be given of the conditions under which *is* and *are* can be deleted:

One general principle holds without exception: *wherever SE can contract, NNE can delete is and are, and vice-versa; wherever SE cannot contract, NNE cannot delete is and are, and vice-versa.* (Labov et al, 1968, Vol. 1, p. 185.)

The examples above illustrate these two phonological and syntactic rules. The rules governing SE contraction, and thereby BE deletion, follow the stress assignment rules provided by N. Chomsky and Halle (1968) and, as Labov points out, provide independent confirmation of the validity of Chomsky and Halle's work.

Question forms constitute another instance. Whereas in mature SE, the inversion transformation is what Labov calls a "categorical rule" that is rarely violated, in NNE it is a "variable rule" with certain probabilities of occurrence and considerable individual variation. So one may hear mature NNE speakers ask—

> *So why you didn't go to school?*
> *What I'm thinking of?*
> *Why I can't play?*

COMPREHENSION AND PRODUCTION

"There is strong evidence of an asymmetry between the rules which NNE speakers use in comprehension and production. When Boot hears *I asked Alvin if he knew* . . . and repeats back instantly *I ax Alvin do he know* . . . it is clear that he has understood the abstract meaning" (Labov et al., 1968, Vol. 1, p. 320).

The same translation ability was found by Baratz (1969) among third- and fifth-grade lower-class Black and lower-middle-class Caucasian children in Washington, and by Garvey and McFarlane (1968) among fifth-grade lower-class Black and Caucasian children in Baltimore. Baratz's study is particularly interesting because she gave an imitation test consisting of both SE and NNE sentences to both SE and NNE speakers. For example, with the sentences containing embedded questions—*I asked Tom if he wanted to go to the picture that was playing at the Howard* or *I aks Tom do he wanna go ta the picture that be playin' at the Howard*—both groups repeated more accurately the sentence presented in their own dialect and translated the other one.

Troike (1970) reports the same results with white Appalachian children and contrasts the knowledge of both Black and Appalachian children with that of their teachers. Parenthetically, the sentences in Troike's test deserve comment. According to Troike, they come from materials produced by Devine and Associates in Austin, Texas, designed for teaching English to speakers of other languages and later used with speakers of nonstandard English dialects. They are examples of language materials that embody superficial "middle-class values" and little intellectual interest.

Of particular interest is the response of many Negro children and white Appalachian children to the task of repeating a sentence they hear on tape while watching a coordinated colored cartoon filmstrip. Some examples follow (N indicates Negro, A indicates Appalachian white):

Model	*Response*
Mother helps Gloria.	Mother help Gloria. (N)
Gloria has a toothbrush.	Gloria have a toothbrush. (N)
She cleans her teeth with a brush.	Her cleans her teeth with a brush. (N)
David has a brush for his hair.	David has a brush for he hair. (N)
She has soap on her head.	She has soap(t) on hers head. (A)
David and Gloria are clean.	David and Gloria is clean. (A)
They are on their knees.	They are on theirs knees. (A)
The socks are on Gloria's bed.	The socks is on Gloria's bed. (A)
The children go to bed.	The children goes to bed. (A)

These examples show very clearly, I think, that the child has not merely attempted to repeat the stimulus, but has decoded it first and then re-encoded it in the form he might have used in framing the sentence as an original utterance. The rapidity with which this is accomplished suggests that the performance is closely akin to that attributed to the coordinate bilingual speaker (and might therefore be considered a type of simultaneous translation). . . . It follows that a difference between the receptive and productive competence of these children must be hypothesized. Thus they are bidialectal, with an asymmetry in their bidialectal performance, since they can presumably both understand and produce the forms of one, "non-standard," dialect, while understanding, but not producing, the forms of a second, "standard," dialect. . . .

A common complaint from white teachers is that they cannot understand their Negro pupils; from this report I think we may infer that the teachers simply lack the receptive competence which they tacitly expect of their pupils in reverse. Since most students are able to understand their teachers, it should be clear that the dialectal range of their receptive, if not their productive, competence often exceeds that of their teachers. (Troike, 1970, pp. 66–68.)

It is generally true that we understand more language than we speak. This is true throughout development. In an experiment by Fraser, Bellugi, and Brown (1963), sentences containing ten grammatical features such as *not* or the passive construction were presented to children in three tasks: imitation; comprehension, demonstrated by pointing to the correct picture; and production, demonstrated by repeating the proper sentence when the experimenter pointed to a picture. For all ten features, the sequence of sentences correct was imitation, comprehension, and then production. As adults, we also understand more words and complex structures than we use in our own speech.

The nature of this comprehension-production asymmetry remains to be explained. Presumably, production somehow makes greater cognitive demands. See McNeill (1968) and other papers in that volume on the general lag between perceiving and performing in cognitive development. In the special case of asymmetry in comprehending and speaking another dialect, attitudinal influences discussed below may also be important. One may wish to understand members of another group, but not behave like them.

When a special comprehension test of SE forms is designed on the Fraser, Bellugi, and Brown (1963) model, some BE speakers do have difficulty. Torrey (1969) gave 27 Harlem second graders such a test. Comprehension of plurals, possessives, third-person singular verb endings, and contracted *is* was tested by asking the children to match appropriate pictures to sentences with and without the inflection; for example:

> The duck nurse.
> The duck's nurse.

Torrey also taped samples of the children's spontaneous speech and evaluated their spontaneous production of these same inflections. She credited a child with an inflection if he supplied it 75 percent of the time it was required. When based on this criterion, the SE forms had a varied status: 26 of the children used plurals; nearly half of the children used possessives and the contracted *is*; only 4 children used the verb ending. Note the similarity to the developmental progression toward the more stringent criterion of 90 percent supplied, described in Chapter 3.

On the comprehension tests, some of Torrey's children did comprehend forms they never were heard to use spontaneously (the asymmetry described above); but some children did not comprehend them in this test situation. In interpreting the communicative significance of these findings, we must remember that speech is normally sufficiently redundant so that no information is carried by one grammatical morpheme alone. In fact, experimenters have a hard time creating test situations in which all normally available contextual cues are removed.

RELATIONSHIPS AMONG DIALECTS

Dialect differences are less categorical than had been believed, and are more a case of different probabilities of occurrence of particular features in specifiable social and linguistic contexts. One example is the tendency (which all speakers of English share to some extent) to simplify final consonant clusters—for example, to reduce *first* to *firs'*. This simplification depends not only on the social class of the speaker, but also on the formality or informality of the social context, whether the sound represents a separate morpheme such as past tense (*walked*) or not (*first*), and whether the subsequent sound is a consonant (*first thing*) or a vowel (*first of all*).

Figure 1 shows the variation among and within individuals for the simplification of *-t* or *-d* (Labov and Cohen,, 1967, p. 70). Following is the authors' discussion:

The percentage of simplification is given for casual speech and careful speech, for clusters followed by words beginning with a consonant K or a juncture #

Figure 1 **The Effects of Style, Class, Grammatical Status, and Phonetic Environment on the Simplification of Consonant Clusters Ending in t/d: Some Preliminary Data from Adults in South Central Harlem. (a) Monomorphemic Clusters [-t/d = *ed*]; (b) Grammatical Clusters [-t/d = *ed*]**

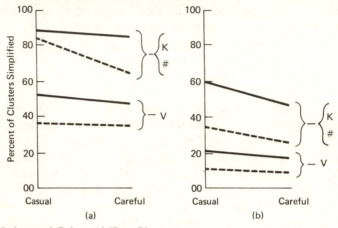

Source Labov and Cohen, 1967, p. 70

or a vowel, V. The solid lines represent the working class speakers; the dashed lines, the middle class speakers, [all Negro.] On the left, the diagram for monomorphemic clusters first shows small stylistic shift for working class speakers, with the same slope for clusters before consonants as for clusters before vowels. But the middle class line for clusters before consonants moves sharply upward, approximately the position of the working class in casual speech. Note, however, that there is no such phenomenon for the middle class use of clusters before vowels. Here the percentage of simplification is low and does not rise sharply; we can interpret this lack of parallelism by noting that a pattern of simplification before consonants but not before vowels preserves the underlying forms of the words. If we say *firs' thing* but *first of all*, there is no doubt that the underlying form is *first*.

In the right half of the diagram [where t/d = the past tense *-ed*] the same general pattern can be observed, but at a much lower level. The grammatical status of *-ed* is obviously important to both groups, since the position is lower and the slope of the lines [from casual to careful speech] is greater than for monomorphemic words. Furthermore, the middle class groups show a sharper downward shift than the working class. There is less tendency for the middle class to shift upward in casual speech to approximate the working class norm; that is, even before consonants we find no sharp stylistic increase in simplification. We can argue here that the middle class has a general constraint against the dropping of the grammatical formative *-ed* as a stylistic indicator. In these respects, the middle class group approximates the behavior of white speakers as indicated in other studies. (Labov and Cohen, 1967, pp. 69–71.)

One implication of this complex relationship among social and linguistic factors is that social-class differences in speech behavior and stylistic shifts within a social class fall on a continuum—a single continuum for the middle-class teacher and her lower-class pupil—rather than into separate categories:

> But members of a speech community are not aware of this. Their experience is limited to (a) a wide range of speech styles among ther own family and friends, and (b) the speech of a wide range of social classes in one or two styles. Thus the teacher hears the differences between middle class and working class children in classroom recitation, but does not follow his students home and hear them at their ease among their own friends. He does not realize how similar the students are to him—how they fit into the same sociolinguistic structure which governs his own behavior. Instead, teachers like most of us tend to perceive the speech of others categorically: John always say *dese* and *dose*, but Henry never does. Few teachers are able to perceive that they themselves use the same non-standard forms in their most casual speech; as we will see, almost everyone hears himself as using the norm which guides his speech production in most formal styles. In a word, the differences between speakers are more obvious than their similarities. (Labov, 1969.)

DIALECT SWITCHING

If any individual can speak in more than one dialect, what controls his selection or switching among them? Labov has identified a continuum of speech situations from most casual and excited to most formal. In research in Norway, Blom and Gumperz (in press) identified two forms of switching between a local dialect and standard Norwegian: role switching and metaphorical switching.

Two reports of role switching come from classrooms.

In Norway:

> Teachers report that they use the dialect in order to mark the transition from formal lectures in the standard, without interruption, to open discussion where the students are encouraged to speak freely. . . . there is a clear change in the actors' mutual rights and duties and in the definition of the situation. (Blom and Gumperz, in press.)

In the United States, Rainey (1969) studied the style-switching of one Headstart teacher by listening for four indicators of a switch from formal to informal style: *you→ya*; *them→'em*; *have to* and *got to→hafta* and *gotta*; *ing→in'* as in *goin'*. In two classroom situations in which the teacher was telling the story of Henny Penny and giving directions for going home, her unmarked style (as identified by the most frequent features) was formal, and she switched into a more informal way of speaking only when inserting personal comments to the children into the ongoing task, presumably in order to lessen the psychological distance between herself and them. In a third situation, when teacher and children together retold the story, the teacher's unmarked style was informal, and she switched to formal features only for the refrain of the story, "The sky is falling and I am going to tell the king."

Metamorphical switching occurs ". . . whenever two or more differently coded social relationships between the same set of individuals are relevant, [and] the use of the dialect or standard to allude to these ties serves to enrich the content of the message" (Blom and Gumperz, in press). For instance, when students who had been close friends in a Norwegian village returned home after attendance at universities in Oslo or Bergen, their conversation on local matters was in dialect, while on topics related to their Pan-Norwegian life as students, they switched to standard Norwegian. The students were not aware of this switching. Blom and Gumperz comment that "code selection may thus seem to be akin to grammatical rules. Both operate below the level of consciousness and may be independent of the speaker's overt intentions."

Even in a seemingly more homogeneous speech community, such code selection occurs. Fisher (1958) discovered switching between *-ing* and *-in'* in a semirural New England village. Children from three to ten years old varied their pronunciation, depending on the formality of the setting, changes in mood as they became more relaxed within a single interview, and even (for one boy) the formality or informality of the connotations of specific verbs: *reading, criticizing* versus *swimmin'* and *punchin'.*

Gumperz and Hernandez (in press) show how easily misunderstandings can result if teachers are insensitive to the communicative functions that dialect switching can serve—

> Imagine a child in a classroom situation who in a moment of special excitement shifts to black speech. The teacher may have learned that black speech is systematic and normal for communication in Afro-American homes. Nevertheless, intent as she is upon helping the child to become fully bilingual, she may comment on the child's speech by saying, "We don't speak this way in the classroom," or she may ask the child to rephrase the sentence in standard English. No matter how the teacher expresses herself, the fact that she focuses on the form means that the teacher is not responding to the real meaning of the child's message. The child is most likely to interpret her remark as a rebuff and may feel frustrated in his attempt at establishing a more personal relationship with the teacher. In other words, by imposing her own mono-stylistic communicative norms, the teacher may thwart her students' ability to express themselves fully. An incident from a tape-recorded language session in Black Language Arts will illustrate the point.
>
> Student: (*reading from an autobiographical essay*) This lady didn't have no sense.
> Teacher: What would be a standard English alternate for this sentence?
> Student: She didn't have any sense. But this lady *she didn't have no sense.*

DIALECTS VERSUS DEVELOPMENTAL CHANGE

One phenomenon invites misinterpretation: Some features of mature BE coincide in superficial form to stages in the language development of children in a SE-speaking community. This is true of multiple negation (*I don't want none.*), omission of the verb *to be* in certain contexts (*He sick*), omission of verb endings (*He go to the store*), and even the relationship between contraction and deletion of the copula. The easy misinterpretation is to say that BE is therefore an immature version of SE.

Brown (in press) has a careful discussion of this phenomenon. He points out that important differences also exist between the two language systems. At a general level, both children and BE speakers exhibit what Labov calls "inherent variability": any one speaker will sometimes supply syntactic features and sometimes omit them in unpredictable ways. But BE also is characterized by "contingent variability" where the probability of features can be predicted from the linguistic and social context. Labov's diagram (Figure 1) of the simplification of consonant clusters shows one example of contingent variability in pronunciation. This kind of variability has not been found in child language. At a more specific level, children are more apt to delete forms of the verb *be* after noun subjects (perhaps because they temporarily think that *it's* is a variable form of *it*, as suggested in Chapter 3), while BE speakers are more apt to delete *be* after a pronoun (as in *He sick*).

Despite these differences, important similarities exist and "challenge interpretation," in Brown's words. Wolfram (1971) suggests that certain features of a language may be particularly susceptible to modification in situations like acquisition and dialect differences. But why? And why these particular features? Brown suggests a more specific reason:

> The very fact that we were able to identify large numbers of "obligatory contexts" and score for the presence or absence of required morphemes means that these morphemes when present are often redundant. In the N + N construction the possessive inflection is usually redundant; with plural determiners like *some* or *two* the plural inflection on the head noun is redundant. . . . [etc.]. The grammatical morphemes are especially likely to be redundant in fact-to-face conversation between persons having a large fund of common experience which is the situation that obtains for child and parent and for nonliterary adult dialects. It does seem likely to me, therefore, that grammatical morphemes are especially vulnerable to deletion because they are often redundant, and their omission will not result in serious misunderstanding. . . .
>
> The meanings they convey are generally only "modulations" of the meanings carried by content words and by content word order, and these modulations may be less important than names and semantic relations. In sum, it seems probable to me that grammatical morphemes constitute an aspect of English grammar particularly susceptible to misconstruction both

in adult dialects and in child speech. We have seen, however, that there is no evidence that the stable misconstructions of particular dialects are "simpler" than the standard construction; as far as is known they are just different. (R. Brown, in press.)

THE POWER OF ATTITUDES

Labov has studied the relation of dialect differences to the attitudes of his informants toward the speech they speak and hear. The power of attitudes to influence speech behavior first came to his attention in his study of the pronunciation of vowels on Martha's Vineyard, an island off the coast of Massachusetts.

> The linguistic variable studied was the centralization of the diphthongs /ay/ and /aw/ in words such as *right, ride, my, about,* and *down.* . . . The overall social significance of this sound change was its association with a positive orientation towards Martha's Vineyard. Those who laid claim to native status as Vineyarders shared the greatest centralization, while those who were excluded from this status, or who abandoned their claims to pursue a career on the mainland, would show no centralization of these vowels. (Labov, 1966a, pp. 186–187.)

Next, Labov studied (1966c) the role of attitudes in explaining the social stratification of certain phonological features among adults and children on the Lower East Side of New York City. Consider the distribution of the presence (r–1) or absence (r–0) of final and preconsonantal /r/ as in *car* or *cards*: Regardless of their own speech patterns, 100 percent of Labov's informants between 18 and 39 years recognized the r–1 pattern as socially preferred. Only 60 percent of those over 40 did so, presumably because they grew up when r–0 was the general pattern throughout New York City, while "young people below the age of 19 or 20 have not yet acquired full sensitivity to the socially significant dialect features of their community" (Labov, 1966c, p. 421). These judgments express conformity to values imposed by the community, what Labov calls "pressure from above." But many of the very people who deprecate r–0 use the stigmatized form in their own speech. Labov hypothesized the presence of conflicting pressures from below: ". . . the need for self-identification with particular subgroups in the social complex. . . . We observe the process of increased differentiation of language behavior despite close contact of the social groups concerned, and their participation in a relatively uniform set of social norms" (Labov, 1966c, p. 450). In a pluralistic urban society, dialect differences are maintained not out of isolation and ignorance but because of "the need for self-identification with particular subgroups in the social complex" (Labov, 1966c, p. 450).

Labov's later research in Harlem confirms the power of attitudes. How any person—child or adult—speaks depends not only on who he is, but also on how he sees himself vis-a-vis others, on who he wants to be. This is a clear example of affective influences on cognitive learning. From the beginning of the language-learning process, children must pick their models. This is not done consciously. But we have seen before how powerful non-conscious knowledge can be, and attitudes are made up of knowledge plus a strong positive or negative valence. If children didn't pick their models in this sense, there would be no way to explain why Black children speak the dialect of their parents or their peers despite hours of exposure to network (usually Standard) English over TV.

The power of attitudes to affect language learning is of critical importance for education. When teachers become language planners, powerful social and political values lie behind their decisions and will affect the success of their work.

MONITORING

Finally, and more speculatively, there is the interesting cognitive process which Labov calls "monitoring," the attention that a speaker pays to his own speech. Monitoring must go on at many levels. Consider three: first, the automatic feedback processes present in all speech production whose disruption is evident in the stammering produced under experimental conditions of delayed auditory feedback; second, the largely nonconscious dialect switching described above, away from some unmarked, or neutral form, toward either "monitoring Black" or "monitoring white" (Kernan, in press), depending on the impression the speaker wishes to convey; and third, the more deliberate, conscious, stylistic choices of words and syntactic constructions for greater explicitness in the low-context situations discussed in Chapter 8.

Is there any relationship among these three processes? Is the third level related at all to either metalinguistic awareness discussed in Chapter 5 or the use of speech for intrapersonal functions discussed in Chapter 9? Is it possible that the more experience children have in conversation where such monitoring is required, the earlier they become aware of their own language, and "listen to themselves" as they solve intellectual tasks? This may seem a far-out idea, but hypotheses are sorely needed to explain how different interpersonal uses of language differentially affect the speaker's disposition to use language as an aid to thought. Perhaps investigation of this process of monitoring could be a start.

Implications for Education

In the Westinghouse study of Headstart effectiveness (Cicirelli et al., 1969) the Headstart children and their equally disadvantaged controls scored below the norms on three subtests of the Illinois Test of Psycho-linguistic Abilities. One of the three is the grammatical closure subtest, which taps knowledge of SE morphology by completion items such as

Here is a bed. Here are two _____.

In their recommendations, the authors argued that these three subtests correlate with school achievement and that "since grammatical closure tests the ability to respond automatically with proper grammatic form, more intensive training in standard English appears needed (Cicirelli et al., 1969, Vol. I, p. 249).

Here the basic non sequitur, and a shockingly prevalent one, is the leap from correlation to causation—that, because use of SE correlates with school achievement, it is a causal factor in that achievement and worth teaching for that reason. The same children probably have more dental cavities as well, but no one would claim causality there. Sometimes correlational data can support hypotheses of a causal relationship, as between smoking and cancer, but only where there is independent evidence for postulating an intrinsic connection. What is the evidence that dialect features per se carry any implications for a child's education? This question will be discussed under five headings: cognitive implications, beginning reading, social implications, strategies for nourishing bidialectalism, and the attitudes of teachers and peers.

COGNITIVE IMPLICATIONS

Differences between BE and SE are small in number and linguistic significance, no matter how socially important they may be. With the exception of a few features such as the special use of *be*, they are all matters of surface structure and affect meaning not at all. There is therefore no reason why a BE-speaking child cannot express any and all ideas in his dialect. A correlation does exist between the speaking of a nonstandard dialect and the size of a child's vocabulary, as the findings of Lesser, Fifer, and Clark (1965) and others suggest. And a small vocabulary can indeed limit educability. But there is no intrinsic connection between them. The correlation exists for historical and sociological reasons of discrimination and poverty. As Burling put it, "One cannot, in other words, characterize a language by its lexicon" (1970, p. 179).

Children can extend their vocabulary while still retaining BE patterns of grammar. One of the Black three-year-olds in my research on expansions (Cazden, 1965) showed me how easily this could be done. One of the tutors was Australian, and occasionally dropped an unusual vocabulary item into her conversations. One day she admonished a child for "*treading*" on a toy. The child promptly defended herself in fluent BE: *I ain't tread on nothing.*

A first-grade teacher in upstate New York told me that during a science lesson, one of her children excitedly told her that *The magnet brung the paper clips.* She tried to explain that we say *brought*, but the child kept saying *brung*. Finally she gave up and told the child that scientists have a special word for what magnets do, they *attract*.

Although BE and SE may not be completely mutually intelligible, BE-speaking children have considerable receptive command of SE. It seems unlikely, therefore, that their educability will be seriously affected by misunderstanding the oral language of their teacher or SE-speaking class-mates. How dialect differences between BE and SE affect the process of learning to read is a separate question, considered in more detail below. If differences do make a difference there, one solution is to change the initial teaching materials and not try (with little realistic expectation of success) to change the child.

One last question, perhaps the most interesting, is about the possible implications of functional specialization of language varieties. BE is in-trinsically usable for the full range of language functions. For example, while in a first grade in a Black neighborhood in Philadelphia, I heard BE children use language for advanced communicative purposes. One child examined a Polaroid picture I had taken earlier in the day of another child facing directly into the camera, and commented, *He looking at you*—a sophisticated example of perceptual role-taking discussed in Chapter 8. In a sharing time at the end of the morning, another child was reporting to the teacher on how many cars had been accommodated in his block-building garage: *We count them and there was nine*—an unsolicited demon-stration of verification. Clearly, these children did not seem cognitively impeded by their dialect. It may be the case, however, that among adults who control more than one dialect, their switching toward SE may be controlled by function as well as by listener and topic. We need more information on this point. But even if such a relationship does exist, the wisest course for education would seem to be concentration on the elabora-tion of language functions, letting linguistic features come out as they may.

Finally, because the relationship between dialect features and cognition is one of correlation at most, there is no basis for expecting that dialect change, even if successful, would by itself have any corresponding effect on the intellectually more important questions of vocabulary and language use.

Paul Olson, director of the Tri-University project in Elementary Educa-tion, reminds us:

A teacher must possess extraordinary knowledge and humanity if he is to distinguish what the school demands of children simply to symbolize its capacity for authority over them from what it legitimately "demands" or "woos out of them" to equip them for a niche in a technological society. (Olson, 1967, p. 13.)

In the area of verbal behavior, Labov (1970) makes a comparable distinction between all the "verbal habits" of middle-class speakers and the "verbal skills" needed for success in school. The two are not identical, and a very important job remains to be done in separating out essential verbal skills.

BEGINNING READING

Learning to read is usually judged the single most important task a child faces in school. Whether dialect differences per se interfere in that task is one specific form of general questions about the match or mismatch between some aspect of children's language and the language of their books: How much of a match does, or should, exist?

Baratz and Shuy (1969) published a set of articles urging the design of initial reading materials written in the child's native dialect. The articles focus on differences in production between Black and Standard English, saying less about how differences in comprehension interfere with reading. Since speakers of nonstandard dialects understand more Standard English than they speak, this is an important omission.

Torrey (1969) says of John, a precocious BE-speaking kindergarten boy in Atlanta, Georgia that the types of errors he made in oral reading "suggest that John expected to find in print the things he would normally say." In other words, in the process of oral reading he recoded the written text in his own dialect. For example:

(30a)   *Text*: *When do you go to school?*

(30b)   *John's Reading*: *When you go to school?*

John's response raises a critical question that will be answered only by further investigation of young readers, Black and white: A child holds certain expectations about the relation between reading and spoken language; should he expect to find in print what he would normally say? Or is it sufficient that he has heard other people say, and can understand, the kind of things he finds in print?

The first recent books in Black dialect were produced during the summer of 1965 by paraprofessionals teaching in the Headstart program—the Child Development Group of Mississippi (CDGM). One book, entitled *Pond*, from Mt. Peel, Mississippi, reads in part:

> If a toad frog hop up on you and wet on you
> he make a big blister on your feet.

Another book, *Today*, from Holly Springs and Durant, includes:

> We supposed to take a nap but we reading instead.
> My Daddy he helping make a kitchen in the schoolhouse.

Four years later, during 1969, the first sets of readers written in non-standard dialect became widely available. The Education Study Center (1970) in Washington, D.C., produced one set of these books and a companion set of "control" books with identical content and pictures written in Standard English. The first book, *Ollie* (ESC, 1970, pp. 1–3), begins as follows in the two versions:

Here go Ollie.	This is Ollie.
Ollie have a big family.	Ollie has a big family.
He have three sisters.	He has three sisters.
A sister name Brenda	A sister named Brenda . . . .

These two sets of readers are being used with different children in an attempt to determine whether these initial teaching materials in the child's native dialect aid beginning reading.

The Chicago Board of Educaion also produced a set (Davis, Gladney, and Leaverton, 1968, 1969). In books 1 through 3, each story is presented twice, first in "Everyday Talk" and then "School Talk." Books 4 through 7 are written in two editions, the "Everyday Talk" book and the "School Talk" book. All children may use both versions. Contrasting sentences from books 1 through 3 (Davis, Gladney, and Leaverton, 1969, p. 4) are:

I got a mama.	I have a mama.
My mama she pretty.	My mama she's pretty.
My mama work.	My mama works

It will not be easy to answer the important question about whether such materials do help. It is always hard to isolate aspects of a complex situation and keep all other factors controlled, and this situation is particularly complex. If the purpose of these readers is to provide a match between the oral language of the reader and his initial reading materials, how can we assume or assure such a match, given the range of variability within any Black community? Does it matter that the use of such readers will increase racial segregation during reading instruction? What will be the attitudes of children, teachers (Black and white), and parents to these materials? What are effective ways to gain acceptance for them at least for an experimental period? These questions, and more, remain. Johnson's (1971) research now in progress at the University of California at Berkeley should begin to provide answers.

Books written in nonstandard dialect are not the only answer to problems of the "match." At least four other alternatives are open: First, one can try to teach standard speech patterns before the child learns to read. So far, there is no evidence of success here. For instance, Rystrom (1968) found that neither oral language nor reading was affected by instruction in Standard English. Second, one can retain SE texts, but let the child give BE readings, as Torrey's pupil John did. Third, since dialect differences are concentrated in only a few features, one could probably write books that avoid those features entirely. Fourth, Serwer (1969) offers new arguments for using individually dictated stories and experience charts in which the teacher records each child's language as spoken in Standard English spelling. From my experience, however, a teacher trying this method will face more difficult decisions about how to do that recording than Serwer acknowledges.

Finally, one can decide that structural interference is not as important as functional interference, and that efforts to improve reading should be concentrated on content and context. Bernstein speaks to Americans from his English perspective:

> There is nothing, but nothing, in the dialect as such, which prevents a child from internalizing and learning to use universalistic meanings. But if the contexts of learning, the examples, the reading books are not contexts which are triggers for the child's imaginings, are not triggers on the child's curiosity and explorations in his family and community, then the child is not at home in the educational world. If the teacher has to say continuously, "Say it again, darling, I didn't understand you," then in the end the child may say nothing. If the culture of the teacher is to become part of the consciousness of the child, then the culture of the child must first be in the consciousness of the teacher. This may mean that the teacher must be able to understand the child's dialect, rather than deliberately attempting to change it. [Bernstein, in press (a).]

In considering content, there is a danger of assuming too narrow a definition of relevance. In a brush-shelter school in Rough Rock, Arizona, I saw a Navajo woman in a lunch line, engrossed in Marjorie Flack's book, *The Story about Ping* (Viking, 1933), the tale of a duck on a Yangtze River houseboat. I was told that the book is a favorite with Navajo children. On any superficial criterion, nothing could be more irrelevant to children living on an American desert than life on a Chinese houseboat. Yet, at some deeper level, meaning was caught. V. W. Jones (1970) speaks of "conceptual" relevance rather than "cultural" relevance, and that seems the better term. It can encompass Claudia Kernan's remark (personal communication) that Black students in her own high school English class liked Julius Caesar "because Cassius was such a great signifier." Signifying is a special speech style highly developed in the Black community in which meaning is "signified" by gesture and innuendo rather than stated explicitly in conventional terms. Evidently, recognition of this speech style helped high school students in Gary, Indiana, relate to ancient Rome. See Bloom, Waite, and Zinet (1970) for a content analysis of children's primers, including newer "multiethnic" ones.

As for context, Labov (1970) believes that cultural and social conflicts are more important than structural interference, and conducted an important study (Labov and Robbins, 1969) of the positive correlation between street gang participation and reading retardation.

Whatever the solution to the problem of the "match," teachers must understand the difference between dialect differencs in pronunciation and failures in reading readiness or reading comprehension. If a reading-readiness teacher says, "Whose name begins like *that*?" and a child says "David," it may be because he hasn't learned to attend to beginning sounds in his own speech or it may be because he does not himself produce a *d-th* contrast. Instruction to attend to sounds that the child does in fact make must be distinguished from instruction in the perception and production of phonemic contrasts that are not part of the child's dialect. The former is an educationally beneficial process of making nonconscious behavior a matter of conscious attention; the latter is an attempt at dialect change which is probably necessary only at the level of perception, not production at all.

Once reading has begun, comprehension and not pronunciation must be the critical test. One result of dialect differences in pronunciation is a set of homonyms that are different from the teacher's and may be more numerous than hers. If one has pronounced *during* and *doing* the same way all one's life, learning to read the two words and associate differential meaning with differential spelling is no different from what every English speaker does with *sun* and *son*. And even if children cannot match word to picture correctly when BE homonyms like *six* and *sick* are spoken out of context, they may respond correctly to written sentences in which that contrast in meaning is important—such as *sick cats* versus *six cats* (Paul Melmed, personal communication).

The same contrast between pronunciation and reading comprehension applies to other dialect features. Labov (1970) constructed sentences such as

When I passed by, I read the posters.

to separate pronunciation of the past tense *-ed* suffix from visual recognition and comprehension of its meaning. If a reader pronounces *read* in the past tense, he must have understood the *-ed* on *pass*, whether the latter was present in his speech or not. Labov found that whereas an adverbial phrase like *last month* did alert adolescent males in Harlem to the past-tense meaning, the *-ed* suffix was much less successful, even in generally capable readers. Instruction in such cases should concentrate on the meaning of the *-ed* suffix, not on its pronunciation.

SOCIAL IMPLICATIONS

If being able to speak SE is not an intrinsic requirement for any cognitive process or educational task, then decisions about whether to teach SE must be made on other grounds—on beliefs and values about the nature of the good life, the appropriate role of the school in achieving it, and the relevance for the United States in the 1970s of the Pygmalion effect of language on social mobility.

In applying these criteria, it is necessary to distinguish fact from folklore about what and where liabilities exist for NNE speakers in the world of jobs. Service industries are one source of expanded employment opportunities in the future, and the telephone company is one place where communication is critical. Of the 10,000 operators employed in New York City, 7000 are Black and Puerto Rican. But it is not obvious even here that dialect per se is the main problem.

> One spot check a few weeks ago disclosed some kind of "communication difficulty" in 25% of information calls. Dr. Bray [a psychologist in charge of employment and training] cited a typical example: A woman called information and asked for Korvette's. The information operator, who did not know Korvette's was a department store, asked the woman for "Mr. Korvette's first name." (*N.Y. Times,* Aug. 29, 1969, p. 18.)

Such information needs to be continuously brought up to date as social change continues over the years.

But even if all such facts were available, attitudes and values would still be important. In any nonhomogeneous speech community, decisions cannot be avoided about which language varieties to use in which aspects of public life. In his description of language planning in contemporary Norway, Haugen (1968) presents an interesting case of citizen participation in language planning. Language planning is "the activity of preparing a normative orthography, grammar and dictionary for the guidance of writers and speakers in a non-homogeneous speech community. In this practical application of linguistic knowledge, we are proceeding beyond descriptive linguistics into an area where judgment must be exercised in the form of choices among available forms" (Haugen, 1968, pp. 672–673). In Norway a deliberate attempt is being made to fuse a new national language from two competing, though linguistically very similar, languages. The Norwegian government has appointed numerous committees to investigate and make recommendations. Elected representatives debate matters of language in the Norwegian parliament; and "A system of local option administered through schoolboards has ensured that the voice of the people should be heard and has made these problems part of the daily diet of even the humblest citizen" (Haugen, 1968, p. 677).

In the United States, the same participation by people affected by decisions should take place, but the people most deeply affected are members of minority groups who are grossly underrepresented at all levels of government and educational planning. Protests against this state of affairs continue to increase across the country.

Documentation of the range of attitudes on the goals of oral language education for Black children consists of the views of two white linguists

(Sledd, 1969; Kochman, 1969); a newspaper account of a discussion among a group of civil rights workers in Mississippi, including Stokely Carmichael; and a report of research on the attitudes of parents, teachers, and community leaders in Roxbury, Massachusetts (Cazden, Bryant, and Tillman, 1970).

Two Linguists

In the U.S.A., we are being told, everybody wants approval—not approval for doing anything worth approving, but approval for doing whatever happens to be approved. Because approval goes to upward mobility, everybody should be upwardly mobile; and because upward mobility is impossible for underdogs who have not learned middle-dog barking, we must teach it to them for use in their excursions into the middle-dog world. There is no possibility either that the present middle class can be brought to tolerate lower-class English or that upward mobility, as a national aspiration, will be questioned. Those are the pillars on which the state is built, and the compassionate teacher, knowing the ways of his society, will change the color of his students' vowels although he cannot change the color of their skins. (Sledd, 1969, p. 1213.)

My first quarrel with such a program is that it does not develop the ability of a person to use language, which I would further define as performance capability in a variety of social contexts on a variety of subject matter. . . . Underlying this approach seems to be a misapplication of Basil Bernstein's terms which falsely equate *restrictive code* and *elaborated code* with, respectively, non-standard dialect and standard dialect. It ought to be noted, as Bernstein uses the term, code is not to be equated with *langue*, but *parole*, not with *competence* but *performance*. What is restrictive or elaborated is not, in fact, the *code* as sociolinguists use the term, but the message. (Kochman, 1969, p. 2.)

Civil Rights Workers, 1965

At the Waveland, Mississippi language workshop, SNCC field secretary Stokely Carmichael wrote on the left of the blackboard four sentences in the phraseology of common usage by Negroes in Mississippi. They were:
I dig wine.
The peoples wants freedom.
Whereinsoever the policemans goes, they causes troubles.
I wants to reddish to vote.

On the right side of the board, he wrote the equivalents:

I enjoy drinking cocktails.
The people want freedom.
Anywhere the officers of the law go, they cause trouble.
I want to register to vote.

Jane Stembridge, another SNCC worker recorded the colloquy:

Stokely: What do you think about these sentences, such as, *The peoples wants freedom*?

Zelma: It doesn't sound right. *Peoples* isn't right.

Stokely: Does it mean anything?

Milton: *People* means everybody. *Peoples* mean everybody in the world.

Alma: Both sentences are right as long as you understand them.

Henry: They're both okay, but in a speech class you have to use correct English.

Zelma: I was taught to use the sentences on the right side.

Stokely: Does anybody you know use the sentences on the left?

Class: Yes.

Stokely: Are they wrong?

Zelma: In terms of English they are wrong.

Stokely: Who decides what is correct English and what is incorrect English?

Milton: People made rules. People in England, I guess.

Stokely: You all say some people speak like on the left side of the board. Could they go anywhere and speak that way? Could they go to Harvard?

Class: Yes. No. (*Disagreement*)

Stokely: Does Mr. Turnbow (*a Holmes County farmer, whose idiomatic use of English is legendary. He was the first Negro in the county to attempt to register, after which his house was burned in retaliation and he was arrested for arson*) speak like on the left side?

Class: Yes.

Stokely: Would he be embarrassed?

Class: Yes . . . No!

Zelma: He wouldn't be, but I would. It doesn't sound right.

Stokely: Suppose someone from Harvard came to Holmes County and said *I want to register to vote*. Would they be embarrassed?

Zelma: No.

Stokely: Is it embarrassing at Harvard but not in Holmes County, the way you speak?

Milton: It's inherited. It's depending on where you are from. The people at Harvard would understand.

Stokely: Do you think the people at Harvard should forgive you?

Milton: The people at Harvard should help teach us correct English.

Alma: Why should we change if we understand what we mean?

Shirley: It is embarrassing.

Stokely: Which way do teachers speak?

Class: On the left, except in class.

Stokely: If most people speak on the left, why are they trying to change these people?

Gladys: If you don't talk right, society rejects you. It embarrasses other people if you don't talk right.

Hank: But Mississippi Society, ours, isn't embarrassed by it.

Shirley: But the middle class wouldn't class us with them.

Hank: They won't accept *reddish*. What is *reddish*? It's Negro dialect and
           it's something you eat.
Stokely: Will society reject you if you don't speak like on the right side of
           the board? Gladys said society would reject you.
Gladys: You might as well face it, man! What we gotta do is go out and
           become middle class. If you can't speak good English, you don't
           have a car, a job, or anything.
Stokely: If society rejects you because you don't speak good English, should
           you learn to speak good English?
Class: Nop.
Alma: I'm tired of doing what society say. Let society say *reddish* for a
           while. People ought to just accept each other.
Zelma: I think we should be speaking just like we always have.
Alma: If the majority speaks on the left, then a minority must rule society.
           Why do we have to change to be accepted by the minority group?
           If I change for society, I wouldn't be free anyway.

(W. A. Price, *National Guardian,* July 3, 1965.)

Parents, Teachers, and Community Leaders

If members of any Black community were asked about their attitudes
toward language education for young children, what would they say? A
study was conducted (Cazden, Bryant, and Tillman, 1970) in order to
tap Black attitudes toward language and language education.

Small discussion groups were arranged with preschool parents, preschool
teachers, and community leaders in Roxbury, the Black community in
Boston. All participants in all of the groups were Black. Two open-ended
questions were asked: How do you feel about the use of Standard English
and Black dialect? What kind of preschool language education do you
want for your children?

In research of this kind, two methodological questions must be raised.
What is the status of talk *about* language, and how representative is the
group of informants? We are dealing here not with samples of speech, nor
even with judgments elicited in direct response to samples of speech. We
are dealing instead in metalanguage, talk about language. We make no
assumption that what our informants say they do actually matches what
they do. Whether a mother does in fact correct her children when they
speak "as if they were hit on the end of their tongue with a hammer," or
whether she really doesn't "feel ashamed if they don't say the right thing"
—these questions have to be investigated directly. The opinions we heard
may or may not coincide with the speaker's behavior—in speaking or
responding to the speech of others. But it seems reasonable to assume that
these opinions do indicate how these individuals would respond if actually
asked to participate in decisions about present or proposed school programs.

The people who attended our discussions certainly cannot be considered
representative of the entire Black community. The parents were unrepre-
sentative first because their children attended preschools; then they were

self-selected a second time because they were willing to come to an evening meeting on an educational topic, with only token reimbursement for travel and baby-sitting expenses. Comparable selection factors affected the sample of teachers. The group of community leaders invited to come together for this purpose also undoubtedly did not reflect the entire range of opinions. The group did not include more conservative church leaders, at one end, nor any member of the Black Panthers, at the other end, though we tried to include them. It did include some of the more vocal, articulate, and militant leadership. And we believe it reflected the opinions of the larger group of community leaders who would be most likely to speak out on educational questions whenever there is opportunity to do so.

In other words, in eliciting and reporting verbal statements about language, we only claim to be dealing in what Ferguson calls "myths": "attitudes and beliefs, regardless of their truth value" (Ferguson, 1968, p. 375). In eliciting these myths from selected groups of people, we only claim that they represent those who would speak out if given the chance to make real decisions about preschool education. Since all the discussions were arranged and conducted by Melissa Tillman, a native of Roxbury, we believe that a good atmosphere prevailed in which people did honestly speak their minds.

Parents.   Discussions were held with parents of children in two preschools. The schools were picked to provide a possible contrast in degree of influence of Black Power ideology. One school is physically close to the center of Black Power activity in Roxbury, and has been more influenced by it through its personnel and educational program. For example, Black artists and musicians have come to share their skills with the children and help build their self-conscious pride in being Black. The other school is both physically farther away and less changed in personnel and program over the past few years.

Whether these Black parents reject Black English because it originated in the slave experience or appreciate it for its power of expression, they feel it has no place in school. They realize that "most of us have two faces." But since children will learn to speak Black English at home anyway, they believe the job of the school is to teach in, and teach, Standard English. Indications of the linguistic self-hatred which Labov (1966c) found in New York City appear in our protocols, both in a father's association of his own people's current speech with slavery and a mother's description of her children's pronunciation—as if "they were hit on the end of their tongue with a hammer."

Where feelings among Black parents are this deep and this negative, any programs that attempt to teach in a nonstandard dialect are likely to encounter strong opposition, even if the goal remains literacy in Standard English. Stewart (1970) narrates events in Philadelphia when the Education Study Center readers were suggested. This does not mean that such attempts should not be made if there is empirical evidence that they increase the likelihood of success with goals the parents do want, such as literacy. But it does mean that full discussion with the parents is essential. Nearly 20 years ago a UNESCO report on the use of vernacular languages in education said:

> Some people in a locality may be unmoved by the benefits to be derived from the use of the mother tongue in education and may be convinced that education in the mother tongue is to their disadvantage. We believe that educationists must carry public opinion with them if their policy is to be effective in the long run, since, in the last resort, the people of a country must always be in a position to express their free choice in the matter of the language in which their children are to be educated; and we urge that the educational authorities should make every effort to take the people into consultation and win their confidence. The problem will lose many of its elements of conflict if the people are confident that the use of languages in the educational system does not favor any section of the population at the expense of others. If the people as a whole will not accept the policy of education in the mother tongue, efforts should be exerted to persuade a group to accept it at least for experimental purposes. We believe that when the people as a whole have had an opportunity of observing the results of education in the mother tongue, they will be convinced that it is sound policy. (UNESCO, 1953, pp. 53–54.)

Teachers. Discussions were held with teachers and teacher-aides from the same two preschools. Originally we planned to talk with teachers and aides separately, since the aides represent a distinct group in social class background and social mobility. But the resulting groups were so small, and the four aides so silent, that the staff groups were combined. We wondered whether their reluctance to speak may have been at least partly because language was an area of sensitivity in their own lives. It would be important to explore whether this is generally true for this new group of educational personnel. If so, their sensitivity may influence how they respond to children. Adults—whether teachers or parents—who are themselves anxious about language forms may pay more attention to the form of children's speech and less attention to the ideas the children are learning to express.

These teachers express more conflict about language than the parents did. Survival is the main thing, and "lots of times your mouth can help you." Within the Black community, survival requires street language. Maybe it's an illusion—a myth with no basis in fact—that survival in relationship with the white community requires Standard English. And maybe we should be paying more attention to language for thinking and for creativity.

Alone among the three groups, some of the teachers referred to Black people in the third person: "*their* way of talking," "Black people, *they* also change," "*their* Black language." Not all the teachers spoke this way. Even in these excerpts, one teacher speaks of the illusion that *"we"* can't make it in this world. Use of the third person may seem an expression of psychological distance, but we cannot be sure of its real meaning to speaker or listeners.

Community leaders. A group of five community leaders assembled by invitation for an evening meeting at Melissa Tillman's apartment in Roxbury.

In their roles as leaders, community leaders are further away from the direct socialization of young children than parents and teachers. Their concern is to reflect the current needs of the group in educational policy, and at the same time to institute those changes that will move the group forward. In comparison to both parents and teachers, and closer to the Mississippi civil rights workers, these leaders were more positive in their evaluation of Black English, and more openly resentful that it is always Black people who have to change. "Survival" for them means not only economic survival in a white-dominated society but also psychological survival as a people. Language for intragroup solidarity, for "going home," is as important as language for "making it." And in education, the myth that language education is the way out is not only questioned but rejected. Control over the environment is critical. Language programs without that control are at best false hopes, and at worst insidious racism.

General comments. One of the limitations in this research is that our metalanguage is too vague to refer to specific linguistic features. We can't be sure that any two speakers agree about what Black English is, or what features they reject or value. Various features were mentioned as examples during the discussions:

Words: *Chunk* the ball.
Idioms: You're a *cool cat*. Momma *broke your face.*
Syntax: I *gots no* . . . . *Diane, she* . . . . Look at *hims hat.*
Pronunciation: ". . . hit on the end of the tongue with a hammer."
Prosodic features: rhythm; speaking "very flat and southern."

Experimental research is necessary to determine which features are most important for identification within and across groups. This information is essential for language planning.

Kochman (in press) distinguishes between two concepts of Black dialect: "the linguistic or structuralist concept, which focuses on grammar, and the social or popular concept, which focuses on rhythm, intonation, and pronunciation." He suggests that "Blacks who do not grammatically speak Black dialect still can satisfy the 'ethnicity' of the Black context by modifying the latter aspects," and cites Malcolm X's speech, Message to the Grass Roots, as an example. This seems to be the style that many national Black spokesmen have adopted, and to which the teacher refers when she describes the people seen on TV who get their message across without speaking Standard English. She is probably not referring to people who speak a pure Black dialect, but to people who have learned to speak so that their messages contain enough Standard English so that others can understand, but which at the same time signal to Blacks their credibility. Effective use of the two dialects in this manner requires the speaker to use both self-consciously. Perhaps this is the skill that parents want their children to acquire.

Discussion by the community leaders of the hustler's use of language is important and previews the discussion of communication styles in Chapter 8.

> People who have control of the language are hustlers. You know, they can really make it. You don't have to have any substance in terms of ideas— just rap a good game. In that context, language is very important.

Many researchers have commented on lower-class use of language for expressing group solidarity and contributing to it. Less often stressed is the use of language for social control and manipulation, especially in inter-group confrontations. Kochman summarizes a detailed analysis:

> The purpose for which language in *inter*-group contexts is used suggests that the speaker views those social situations as essentially agonistic, by which I mean that he sees his environment as consisting of a series of transactions which require that he be continually ready to take advantage of a person or defend himself against being victimized. He has absorbed what Horton calls 'street rationality.' (Kochman, in press.)

We need to think about how the skills of using language for group solidarity and social manipulation can be exploited in education while we also nourish language for thinking more creatively (in the teacher's words) or "using language as an instrument for the free expression of thought and feeling" (N. Chomsky, n.d., p. 66). As suggested above, questions of language use are separable from questions of dialect. One could in principle use any dialect for any purpose. But because of functional specialization, it may be easier to use Black dialect for some purposes and Standard English for others. Again, more information is needed for language planning.

Valentine (1969) suggests that the socialization of Black children must be seen as "biculturation." Mitchell discusses some of the complexities of this process:

> Socialization for many Black Americans is a process during which an individual, while acquiring his culture, is also enculturated to its disadvantaged and negatively valued status for the wider culture of which he is also a part. To the extent that an aspect of Black culture is different from some corresponding aspect of Standard Average American culture, even when it enjoys normative status intraculturally, it may become stigmatized for some individuals due to their identification and desire to participate in the wider culture. The bi-cultural status of Black Americans makes the socialization

process a time when each individual attempts to find some viable personal reconciliation to cultural patterns, values and attitudes which do not cohere or intersect in any consistent fashion. Some solutions find individuals essentially submerged in things Black, rejecting outside standards and valuations across the board. Others look outward toward the wider culture and still others straddle the two, selecting from either as the needs of the moment require. Language is an important reflector of these various positions. (Mitchell, 1969, pp. 82–83.)

Wolfram and Fasold (1969) suggested that increasing emphasis on racial pride is not yet extended to language. Obviously, changes in the social-political situation in this country will affect the biculturation process, and thereby also alter the language goals that Black people hold for their children. Ways must be found to ensure that these changes are reflected in education.

STRATEGIES FOR NOURISHING BIDIALECTALISM

If a decision is made to try to help children become bidialectal, what strategies are most likely to succeed? As Sledd (1969) makes clear, success stories are few. By-and-large, techniques have been adopted from foreign-language instruction, notably drills of all kinds. Even though American education has been largely unsuccessful in foreign-language teaching, we ignore that record and adapt the unsuccessful techniques to teaching a second dialect—and this, despite the fact that bidialectalism is probably harder to achieve than bilingualism.

One reason bidialectalism is harder is that the internal variation already present in many BE speakers' language raises important questions about what that speaker needs to learn. Ervin-Tripp [1971(c)] presented a full discussion of this point. Assume for the moment that we wish to "teach" a lower-class Black speaker to pronounce all final consonants that constitute a separate morpheme, as in *washed*, at least in formal situations. What exactly does the speaker have to "learn": a new linguistic rule, consistent mastery of a skill, or enhanced motivation for accepting a particular norm? Obviously, decisions about curriculum strategies depend on selecting among these alternatives.

A detailed analysis of curriculum attempts to teach SE is outside the scope of this book. Here, only four general questions will be raised—about priorities in linguistic features; timing; selection of staff personnel and peer-group composition; and whether the goal should be changes in oral speech or in writing.

Linguistic Features

If the purpose of teaching Standard English is for its "Pygmalion effect," then educational programs should concentrate on those nonstandard features that are most crucial in eliciting negative reactions. Shuy, Wolfram, and Riley (1967) suggest that one index of such cruciality is the degree of social stratification of the linguistic features. For instance, there are greater social class differences in the use of multiple negation (*He can't hit nobody*) than in pronominal apposition (*The playground, it has all kinds of bars and stuff*). Shuy and his associates suggest that multiple negation is therefore more important in any SE curriculum.

Timing

Separate from questions of *what* to teach and *how* is the question of *when*. How much variation in speech patterns can children of various ages control? Do the assertions that foreign languages are harder to learn after early adolescence apply to learning a second dialect—learn in the sense of automatic production without the excessive strain of careful monitoring? If attitudes play a critical role in dialect-learning, at what age are those attitudes more likely to work *for* oral language instruction rather than against it? In summary, at what age are ability at switching, flexibility of motor control of articulation and grammatical patterns, and attitudes toward SE (as influenced by peer-group identification and/or vocational hopes) at optimal values for second-dialect instruction?

Selection of Adults and Peers

If providing models of Standard English is considered desirable, important questions are raised about school personnel and the composition of the peer group. How much weight should be given to the standardness of the speech patterns of adult staff members, and how much weight to other reasons for including adults indigenous to lower-class communities—such as on-the-job training for parents and future parents, counteraction of home-school alienation, and the participation of male adults in the schools? If family day-care, in which one mother cares for several children in her own home, comes under more careful licensing, how much weight should be given to the mother's language in making licensing decisions? Criteria for selecting school personnel is shifting from dependence on formal educational credentials toward reliance on judgments of successful performance. Should there be any performance standards for speech? If so, what should they be?

And what about the composition of the peer group? We want to maximize the benefits from communication among children. How much can be gained in desegregated classrooms? Is it worth making a fight against present governmental funding policies, which usually result in preschool groups segregated by social class? So far, research evidence on the effects of heterogeneous classrooms on child language is equivocal. Perhaps children don't naturally interact across racial or social class lines as much as we hope or expect. Perhaps even if they do interact, attitudes influence which "models" are chosen. Perhaps teachers attend to and talk to the most verbal children, rather than the least verbal. We need more research in these classrooms themselves.

Speech or Writing

In other countries, attempts are also being made to teach a standard dialect. In England, one project to develop a language program for children of West Indian origin is directed by Jim Wight at the University of Birmingham. The program is planned for children from seven to nine years old because it is based in part on children's writing. It has two objectives:

> . . . to help children to write Standard English—concentrating on the places where the West Indian dialect creates special difficulties for the child; and to improve the oral fluency and general communication skills and confidence of the children. . . . (Wight and Norris, 1969, pp. 2–3.)

Only the first objective will be discussed here.

In its approach to Standard English, the Birmingham project takes an intermediate position between the extremes of "teaching English as a second language" on the one hand, and "leaving their dialect alone" on the other. In addition to the usual distinction between home language (in this case a Caribbean Creole) and school language (Standard English), Wight and Norris separate their goals for oral and written language and concentrate their efforts in trying to help children *write* Standard forms. According to Wight, no matter how you try to disguise it, if you suggest an alternative way of speaking, you are implicitly suggesting that something is wrong with what the child said in the first place. Moreover, written work is where children receive the most criticism for irregular forms. Grammatical deviations may be ignored by listeners, but the same deviations become glaringly obvious in written compositions. In Wight's program, oral drills are used for oral practice in forms needed in writing. "It is intended that these standard forms should be primarily associated in the child's mind with written English" (Wight and Norris, 1969, p. 27).

Three additional arguments in favor of practicing SE in written form can be suggested. First, as noted above, Taylor (1971) argues in favor of widening the range of pronunciations acceptable as SE to include Black English pronunciations as we now include all regional variations, thereby limiting SE to matters of grammatical structure. In print, pronunciation automatically becomes irrelevant. Second, Kernan (in press) found that Black high school students more easily accept the need for writing SE while considering as affected their peers' attempts at "proper" speech. Finally, one of the skills, discussed in Chapter 8, that working-class children most need to practice is the explicit communication of ideas without dependence on gestures or concrete referents. Written language imposes exactly that task.

Wight's project (Wight and Norris, 1969) is developing some unusual puzzlelike materials for teaching standard English morphology, such as the following for noun and verb agreement:

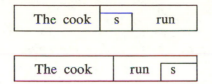

If one adds an *s* to the noun, then the only verb piece that fits is one that cannot itself take an *s*; if the noun is singular, then the matching verb piece has a space that must be filled by an *s*.

At first glance, it may seem inappropriate to use a mnemonic device to teach a linguistic rule. But as Wight pointed out (personal communication), this rule is a completely arbitrary, meaningless part of our language. If the visual shapes of words can aid learning, why not exploit them? Another good feature in the materials is that the original decision is made about the noun: is it plural or singular? Once that decision has been made, the shape of the noun determines the shape, literally, of the verb.

The incidence of nonstandard forms may not be the same in speech and writing, even for one child. De Stefano (in press) made one such comparison for a group of nine- to ten-year-old Black children in a Philadelphia summer remedial program. Written compositions were obtained after a walk around the school neighborhood and compared with speech samples from tapes and written notes on the children's talk with peers and teachers. De Stefano found significant differences between the children's language in the two media. For example, verb forms constituted a higher proportion of all nonstandard forms in speech. Most dramatically, omission of the third-person singular -*s* accounted for 45 percent of all nonstandard speech forms, as in *He act nice*, but this form did not occur once in writing. De Stefano (in press) inferred that "it is more a phonological feature of Black English than a deep structural grammatical feature, due to its evidently fairly easy inclusion in writing but with little carryover in speech habits." One cannot conclude from her data that slower, more deliberate nature of the writing process will inevitably produce fewer nonstandard forms. Some items constituted a higher proportion of nonstandard forms in writing than in speech. For example, there were no recorded nonstandard possessive pronouns, but these accounted for 4 percent of the errors in writing, as in *They car* . . . . Perhaps spelling is the source of difficulty here, which in turn may be related to a tendency to drop final consonants in pronunciation. More such research should yield both insight on the status of particular features in a child's language system, and suggestions for curriculum.

ATTITUDES OF TEACHERS

Previous sections have discussed the direct effects of a child's dialect on his intellectual and social experience. His education will also be affected indirectly through the effect of his speech patterns on his peers and his teachers. We do not know how early Black children learn that their speech patterns are stigmatized in the larger society. Given the early age at which they show such responses as preferring white dolls (Porter, 1971), we should expect an early realization of sociolinguistic facts of life as well. But children will be affected by the reactions of others, whether or not they are aware of them.

Evidence is accumulating that speech cues are one important source of the expectations teachers bulid up about their children's success in school. Williams in Chicago (1970, in press), and Shamo in Memphis (1970), found that teachers evaluate children more negatively when their speech has nonstandard pronunciation and syntax. Guskin (1970) found that Michigan teachers-in-training rated Black speakers as less likely to succeed academically than white speakers. Seligman, Tucker, and Lambert (in press) found in Montreal that a recorded speech pattern or a child's photograph had more influence on third-grade teachers' ratings than the quality of a child's composition or drawing. Holmes, Holmes, and Friedman (1968) compared the evaluations of a Headstart teacher in Coney Island with observations and IQ tests of the children in her class. The teacher's ratings of her children's intelligence were not correlated with actual intelligence test scores, and they were biased by such actual behaviors as the child's willingness to respond to directions and his general verbal skills.

We do not know how to change such ethnocentric biases. See Campbell (1967) for one analysis of the general problem. Teachers' reactions are deeply founded in their own past experience. Part of that experience is simply living in a discriminatory society; but part is also what they have read and heard from psychologists and educators (for example, Cazden, 1966) about "culturally disadvantaged children," as Labov (1970) has rightly pointed out. Although these problems were approached with the best of intentions, our analyses of cultural differences—no matter how accurate—may have contributed to teachers' lowered expectations for children's success, and thereby to self-fulfilling prophecies, by implying a causal relationship—which cannot be substantiated—between those cultural differences and school success. We have, in short, helped to "blame the victim" (Ryan, 1971).

How can teachers' perceptions of their children be changed? Perhaps the kinds of "cultural therapy" that anthropologist George Spindler (1969) advocates for teacher education in general could help. Perhaps Bruce Fraser will be successful in his current effects at the Language Research Foundation in Cambridge, Massachusetts, to develop a curriculum for teachers specifically about language—their children's and their own. At some point, there is probably a limit to what words can convey. As Landes says in her report of a teacher-education project in California, "when educators talk more *about* pupils than *with* them and their families, separateness from the objects of discussion forfeits the experiences words should mirror" (1965, p. 64).

Attitudes of linguistic chauvinism may also limit intergroup communication among children themselves. Bouchard (1969) found that on the basis of voice cues alone, middle-class fifth- and sixth-grade children ranked MC white speakers, LC white speakers, and LC Black speakers in descending order on personality characteristics such as tall, trustworthy, intelligent, helpful, and friendly. On the other hand, there is current anecdotal evidence that those same features may under some circumstances be highly valued among white peers, especially in adolescence. In either case, educational efforts toward valuing speech differences as one reflection of cultural pluralism should enhance the likelihood of all children learning from each other. O'Neil suggests that "students (urban, suburban, rural) should have understanding of the naturalness of language differences" (1968, p. 15) and tried to teach such a curriculum to Roxbury ninth graders (O'Neil, in press). We don't know at what age such efforts would be most effective.

Bilingualism

The subject of childhood bilingualism deserves book-length treatment by itself; here it is given only a section at the end of a chapter. Since thorough treatment is impossible, it seemed better not to attempt a halfway job. Therefore, only a few important issues will be raised and sources of further discussion will be suggested. Through the selected references cited, the reader can trace back to most of the important literature. Discussion is organized into three sections: becoming a bilingual child; teaching a second language; and bilingual education.

BECOMING A BILINGUAL CHILD

Some children learn two languages simultaneously; other children learn them sequentially, one language after another. There are still very few descriptions of either route toward becoming a bilingual child which match in detail and linguistic analysis the studies of first-language acquisition described in this book.

A classic study of simultaneous bilingualism is Leopold's four-volume diary (1939–1947; summarized in Leopold, 1953) of his two daughters' learning of English and German in their first two years. The pronunciation of "pretty" by Leopold's older daughter, Hildegarde, was mentioned in

Chapter 4. In a review article on child language research through 1946, Leopold (1948) cites only three other studies: Geissler, 1938; Pavlovitch, 1920; Ronjat, 1913. Since then, there is at least Burling's (1959) account of the almost simultaneous acquisition by his son Stephen of English and Garo, a nonwestern language in India.

Studies of children who successfully learn a second language when already speaking a first language should be even more relevant for educational planning. Unfortunately, studies of such sequential bilingualism seem, if anything, even rarer. One excellent study is Dato's (1970) syntactic analysis of the acquisition of Spanish by English-speaking children who went with their families to live in Madrid. As Dato points out,

> That children do indeed acquire a second language is borne out in the numerous accounts by parents visiting foreign countries for any extended periods of time.
>
> Although many of the accounts by parents are unfortunately anecdotal, we know that children learn to speak a second language, and that they do so within a relatively short time. If we were to entertain the hypothesis that a second language is learned by a child in a manner not unlike that of acquiring his first language, then we should be able, within a relatively short time, to gain a great deal of insight into second-language learning. (Dato, 1970, p. 2.)

During his first year in Madrid, Dato studied one four-year-old boy; in the second year, he added four more children (5½ to 6½ years old), all of whom were encountering Spanish for the first time. Dato's research techniques were partly derived from Brown's study of Adam, Eve and Sarah, and the analytic framework was that of transformational grammar.

For just the reasons that Dato gives, we need many more studies of natural second-language learning—both simultaneous and sequential—of English-speaking children learning other languages and of child speakers of other languages learning English. See Kelly (1969) for the proceedings of an international conference.

TEACHING A SECOND LANGUAGE

Becoming a bilingual child in the natural conversational environments described above is as dramatically successful as first-language acquisition. But the record of deliberate attempts to teach a second language in school presents an entirely different picture.

Currently, for social reasons, concern in the United States centers on teaching English to children from minority groups who speak a foreign language. The largest such groups speak Spanish or Navajo. For example, "it is estimated that more than one-sixth of the school-age population of the Southwest is Spanish-speaking [and] in New York City, Puerto Rican children . . . make up nearly one-fourth of the city's total elementary public school enrollment" (John and Horner, 1971, pp. 1–2). In a recent survey, Spolsky (1970) found that 73 percent of six-year-old Navajo children did not know enough English for success in first grade. See Fishman et al. (1966) for further demographic and historical information. So far we have failed to help these children become bilingual, without or with the latest techniques for "teaching English as a second language," and their dropout rates are high (Campbell, 1970). Hope for the future may lie in different methods of teaching a second language, or in bilingual education of which learning English would be one part, or both.

In an important article, Ervin-Tripp challenges the assumptions underlying second language teaching:

> I think two major changes have taken place in our views of language acquisition in recent years. One is that we now are beginning to see the functions of language in the life of the speaker as of far more importance in its acquisition than we had realized, and the other is that the mechanical view that practice makes perfect has given way under the impact of evidence that speechless children can have well developed language [a reference to a case study by Lenneberg]. (Ervin-Tripp, 1970, p. 314.)

At the end of Chapter 5 on the process of language development, two questions were raised about implications for education: whether adults who are trying to be helpful should attend to a child's meaning or to his superficial forms; and whether sequencing of instruction plays an important role. On these two issues, natural language acquisition and second-language teaching diverge sharply. In the former, as argued earlier in this book, the child is a full participant in conversation from the beginning, adults respond to his intended meaning, and no one attempts to segment, organize, and sequence all that he eventually must learn. In second-language teaching, by contrast, adults attend to how children talk, not what they are trying to say, and assume that "organization of input, plus practice, will have predictable results" (Ervin-Tripp, 1971, p. 315). Holt's caricature quoted in Chapter 5 is an all-too accurate description of many second-language teaching practices. It should be possible to design an educational environment that reactivates the natural language-learning abilities which all children have. Dodson, Price, and Tundo (1968) present a detailed account, including two case histories of individual children, of an infant school in Wales in which Welsh was the medium of conversation in the afternoons, but no "Welsh lessons" were given.

Reactivating language-learning abilities necessarily means harnessing children's motivations as well. Here, as much as in teaching strategies, is where the problems of minority-group children may lie. At least that seems to be the implication of one success story of second-language learning in school. Lambert, Just, and Segalowitz (1971) describe two classes of monolingual English children in Montreal who received their first years of schooling entirely in French. The kindergarten program, which the authors think may be crucial, "conducted almost entirely in French by two very skilled and experienced teachers from Europe, stressed vocabulary development and listening comprehension through art, music and play, and encouraged spontaneous verbal expression in French" (Lambert, Just, and Segalowitz, 1971, p. 233). French was the only language used from first grade on.

> The results of the experiment to date indicate that the type of bilingual training offered these children is extremely effective, even more so than was originally expected. The similarity of the findings for two different sets of classes, involving changes in teachers' methods of instruction, and modes of testing and analysis, speaks well for the stability and generality of the effects produced by the experimental program. These effects demonstrate a very high level of skill in both receptive and productive aspects of French, the major language of instruction; a generally excellent command of all aspects of English, the home language of the children; and a high level of skill in a nonlanguage subject matter, mathematics, taught through the foreign language only. (Lambert, Just, and Segalowitz, 1971, pp. 229–230.)

Furthermore, the children transferred what they had learned about reading from French to English with little trouble.

Ervin-Tripp asks the obvious question: Why does being taught in a foreign language work for these Montreal children and fail for Chicano, Puerto Rican, and Navajo children in the United States? In her words, "the differences are social" (1971, p. 314). In commenting on the same contrast, Haugen agrees—

> We need to think in terms of dominant and nondominant, but these are terms we don't like to talk about because they are ultimately political. . . . It makes a great deal of difference whether the schools are teaching the children a language that is nondominant or one that is dominant, because the children are sensitive to the pressure of society through their parents and their peers. I think the opposition of dominant and nondominant is so important that I wonder if Lambert's good results may not be accounted for by the fact that he is teaching the members of a dominant group a nondominant language which has potentialities of dominance, while in Texas or New Mexico we are teaching a dominant language to a nondominant group. This alters the educational picture totally. (Haugen, discussion in Alatis, 1971, p. 310.)

The same conclusions about the importance of attitudes was reached by Tax and his colleagues in the Carnegie Corporation Cross Cultural Education Project of the University of Chicago (Tax and Thomas [1969], Walker [1965, 1969]) which was concerned not with teaching English but with raising the literacy level of Cherokees in eastern Oklahoma. Cherokee history is particularly interesting because in the nineteenth century they had been 90 percent literate in their native language—using a writing system

developed in 1819 by Sequoyah, a Cherokee with no formal education—
and they were more literate in English than neighboring white communities
in Texas and Arkansas (Walker, 1969). Walker suggests what it would take
to regain this status:

> It seems clear that the startling decline during the past sixty years of both
> English and Cherokee literacy in the Cherokee tribe is chiefly a result of
> the recent scarcity of reading materials in Cherokee and of the fact that
> learning to read has become associated with coercive instruction, particularly
> in the context of an alien and threatening school presided over by English
> speaking teachers and controlled by English speaking superintendents and
> P.T.A.'s which conceive of Cherokee as a "dying" language and Cherokee
> school children as "culturally impoverished" candidates for rapid and "in-
> evitable" social assimilation. Indians and whites alike are constantly equating
> social competence in the school with assimilation into the middle class. . . .
> For the Cherokee community to become literate once again, Cherokees must
> be convinced that literacy does not imply the death of their society, that
> education is not a clever device to wean children away from the tribe. This
> is not a uniquely Cherokee situation. Identical attitudes toward education
> and the school no doubt can be found in Appalachia, in urban slums, in
> Afro-Asia, and, indeed, in all societies where the recruitment of individuals
> into the dominant society threatens the extinction of a functioning social
> group. (Walker, 1965, p. 10.)

BILINGUAL EDUCATION

Gaarder defines bilingual education as "a school which uses, con-
currently, two languages as mediums of instruction in any portion of the
curriculum except the languages themselves" (1967, p. 110). In reality,
the term covers a wide range of practices. See John and Horner (1970,
1971) and Gaarder (1971) for reviews of recent programs in this
country; G. R. Tucker (1970) for a description of one project in the
Phillipines; and Dodson, Price, and Tundo (1968), mentioned earlier, about
an infant school in Wales.

One important aspect of most bilingual programs is teaching initial
literacy in the child's native language. Arguments for doing this have been
made for some time. See UNESCO (1953) and Bull's (1955) critical
book review, Macnamara (1967) for a general review of the topic, and
Modiano (1968) for one comparative study in Mexico. Some arguments
for initial literacy in the child's first language apply whatever the first and
second languages may be. But similarities and differences between the two
should be considered. For instance, because Spanish orthography is simpler
than English, it is almost certainly preferable for Spanish-speaking children
to learn to read first in Spanish. For speakers of Chinese, on the other hand,
the extent of transfer or interference is less certain. C. A. Tucker (1969)
suggests that memorizing hundreds of "words" may make it harder to learn

to read with an alphabet; according to Kolers, however, "The idea that the skilled reading of even alphabetic languages involves the interpretation of symbol systems implies that the reading of Chinese and the reading of English have more in common than would at first appear" (1970, p. 118). Venezky (1970) reviews research on beginning reading materials for speakers of both nonstandard dialects and other languages.

Too often, "bilingual education" is only a euphemistic name for new means to the old goals of teaching children to speak and read the dominant language, in our case English, as fast as possible. The clue to true bilingual education is whether the concurrent use of two languages continues through the school grades, or whether the non-English language gradually drops out year by year. Many of the strongest advocates of bilingual education see it as far more than a means to such narrow ends. In the preceding quotation, Walker spoke for the goals of increased self-identity for minority people. Others, such as Fishman, stress the goal of a truly multilingual and multicultural society:

> The day is coming when more and more genuine bilingual education, for all who want it, regardless of income, mother tongue or language dominance, will be part of the variegated picture of American education. At that time it will not be a mere euphemism for programs in English as a Second Language which, though unquestionably essential, constitute only one part and one kind of dual language education. It will not be just a promissory note to the poor, nor a left-handed contribution to increasingly vocal and organized (though still exploited and dispossessed) Hispanos and Indians. It will be available to my children and grandchildren, and to yours, because it is too good to keep it from all the people. (Fishman, 1970, p. 53.)

Obviously, schools alone cannot achieve a multilingual society. Their success will depend on sociolinguistic aspects of language use in the community, and they must be evaluated in relation to that social context. That is what Ervin-Tripp and Haugen were saying about the success of Lambert and his associates in Montreal. See Fishman et al. (1968) for the study of one Puerto Rican community in New Jersey. And see O'Huallachain (1970) and Macnamara (1966) on Irish attempts to use bilingual education to revive an "ancestral" language.

But influences do operate in the other direction, too, from school to society as well as from society to school. That is what the Irish government is hoping for. And it is the point of a news item in the (London) *Times Educational Supplement* on the Welsh Language Society's campaign to deface road signs printed only in English. Evidently some teachers had been active in this campaign. After a strong statement on behalf of acts that do not violate public opinion even if they violate the law, the reporter urged the local education committees not to take action against these teachers:

> I should have thought it is ridiculous that children whose mother tongue is Welsh should grow up hearing one set of place names on the tongues of

their families but always seeing another, English form on road signs and in official use.

The same goes for all the words used in public notices and so forth. What sense does it make for an education committee to teach Welsh in its schools (unless it thinks of it as a dead language) and at the same time show no concern for the public status and use of the language. (Thomas, *Times Educational Supplement,* May 9, 1969.)

In the United States, too—through its influence on children, teachers, and parents—bilingual education can affect both speech behavior and attitudes toward language outside school as well.

8

Communication Styles

Children not only learn the structure and meanings of their native language, but also learn to use that language in actual verbal behavior. The two main categories of language functions are (Carroll, 1964, p. 4): "(1) as a system of responses by which individuals communicate with each other (inter-individual communication); and (2) as a system of responses that facilitates thinking and action for the individual (intra-individual communication)." These subsystems of language functioning must be somehow intimately related. I say "somehow related" because we do not know how overt speech becomes internalized into covert thought, particularly in the case of the growing child. And we don't know how variation in the use of language for interindividual communication affects its use as an intra-individual cognitive tool. For reasons that have to do with the intellectual history of the behavioral sciences, the two functions of language have been studied separately.

This separation should be ended. In a review of research on the language of preschool age children, LaCrosse and his coworkers recommend:

> Language has been studied by different researchers as a tool for thought, for communication, and in relation to reading. Unfortunately these studies are on different groups of children. Our suggestion is that a "language-as-a-tool" survey would be very fruitful in that it could study these important language functions in the same sample of children. A programmatic study would yield a fuller understanding of the organization of language functions within the child. (LaCrosse et al., in press.)

But for now, we're limited to separate discussions of the use of language for communication (to others) and cognition (for oneself).

It is not even clear which function should be discussed first. We don't know the order of emergence in the evolution of man or the development of children. Controversies continue on just this question. To Mead (1934) and Vygotsky (1962), inner speech is internalized dialogue, and thought has social roots. To Langer, on the other hand,

182

. . . the purely communicative aspect of language has been exaggerated. It's best to admit that language is primarily a vocal actualization of the tendency to see reality symbolically. (Langer, 1948, p. 99.)

Perhaps it is meaningless to try to place the two language functions in temporal sequence or priority of significance. In John's words, "To speak is to unite, *temporarily*, the intra-personal and interpersonal forces which simultaneously affect the speaker" (in press). For no convincing reason, therefore, this chapter considers the development of some aspects of language for communication, and some differences in communicative styles. Chapter 9 follows on the roles of language in cognition.

In a society, speech as an activity is not a simple function of the structure and meanings of the language or languages involved. Nor is speech activity random. Like the languages, it is patterned, governed by rules; and this patterning also must be learned by linguistically normal participants in the society. Moreover, the patterning of speech activity is not the same from society to society, or from group to group within societies such as our own. (Hymes, 1961, p. 57.)

The acquisition of competency for use, indeed, can be stated in the same terms as acquisition of competence for grammar. Within the developmental matrix in which knowledge of the sentences of a language is acquired, children also acquire knowledge of a set of ways in which sentences are used. From a finite experience of speech acts and their interdependence with sociocultural features they develop a general theory of the speaking appropriate in their community, which they employ, like other forms of tacit cultural knowledge (competence) in conducting and interpreting social life. (Hymes, in press.)

At any one moment, a child decides to speak or be silent, to adopt communicative intent *a* or communicative intent *b*, to express idea *x* or idea *y*, in language variety *1* or variety *2*. The options the child selects will be a combined function of the child's communicative competence and of characteristics of the situation as he perceives it on the basis of his past experience. "Sociolinguistics is the study of the characteristics of language varieties, the characteristics of their functions, and the characteristic of their speakers as these three constantly interact, change and change one another within a speech community" (Fishman, 1970, p. 4). This chapter reports studies that can be called developmental sociolinguistics—the description of language varieties in children and their functionally differentiated use. It is divided into the sections that constitute a mixed and fragmentary set. Each individual section is worthy of inclusion. But the field of developmental sociolinguistics has not proceeded far enough to make possible a more systematic presentation. The three sections are: expressive use of speech varieties; coding ability; and variations in child speech according to its social setting, including the classroom.

Expressive Use of Speech Varieties

Consciously or nonconsciously, speakers select among aspects of language which convey meaning beyond the referential meaning of the words and sentence structure alone.

> The productive competence of a speaker may range over a wide repertoire of styles and dialects, which may involve differences of lexicon, grammar, or pronunciation. In general, however, linguists have not been willing to credit children with much breadth of competence in any of these respects. While this may be true for many children, we have found that even six-year-olds are sensitive to stylistic differences. Two examples will suffice. In one instance, in which a middle-class white first-grader was interviewed, the interviewer asked her to make up a story about a picture she was shown in a magazine. At this point, the girl drew herself up, and beginning 'Once upon a time, . . . ' launched into a discourse which was very formally delivered and which was notable for containing no contractions. At the end of the story, she audibly relaxed, and from there on freely used contractions for the remainder of the interview.
>
> A second-grade Negro girl in a small East Texas town also showed stylistic shifts in phonology in going from a simple conversation to a 'storified' account of an event. Although she was not consistent in maintaining the shift, she at least showed clear sensitivity to it. The whole subject of the range of styles and dialects in the repertoire of children is only just beginning to receive attention, and a great deal yet remains to be learned. (Troike, 1970, pp. 67–68.)

Prosodic features of intonation and pitch are among the first aspects of language learned by the child in their unmarked or normal form. In a longitudinal study of three preschool children from college-educated families, Weeks looked for variation in these aspects of language, which, by contrast with unmarked utterances, "convey information or emotion beyond that conveyed by the words alone" (Weeks, 1970, p. 23). She identified 10 sources of such variation, which she called "register," in the speech of three children: three aspects of intensity (whisper, softness, and loudness); two aspects of enunciation (clarification and fuzzy speech); and five aspects of baby talk (high pitch, grammatical modification, phonetic modification, exaggerated intonation, and mimicry). She also looked for their functions, co-occurrences and social contexts of use. Here are two examples from one child:

> From about 2, 6 to 3, 1 [years and months of age], John whispered to his parents if they were visiting someone and he wanted to make a request, such as for a drink of water. He expected his parents then to make the request for him. He also uses whispering when he's concentrating, principally in private speech, where Fred uses softness. At 3, 4 John is just beginning to grasp the concept of secret-keeping but has never used whispering for secrets. . . .

The youngest age at which the clarification register was recorded was 1, 11. This seemed to be about the age at which John began to get indignant when people could not understand him. In this example, John clarified his statement principally by putting a noticeable boundary between each syllable. (Weeks, 1970, pp. 28, 29.)

Carlson and Anisfeld (1969) found similar characteristics in the speech of Carlson's son, age 21 to 33 months. When his speech seemed not intended to elicit a response, it tended to the extremes of loudness (whispering or shrieking) and sometimes had deviant pitch patterns such as shrieking or singing. At 31 months, he used "fuzzy enunciation" and a very soft voice "in situations in which he knew he would probably be forbidden to do what he was about to ask" (Carlson and Anisfeld, 1969, p. 575). Sarah, in the Harvard study, regularly used a high pitch to convey indirect discourse, as when reporting what Bugs Bunny or a doll had said.

In her conclusions, Weeks suggests:

There may be greater variation in the ages at which children learn to use the registers discussed in this paper than there is in the variation in the age at which they learn to perform other linguistic tasks such as forming plurals or putting together two-word sentences. This is not too surprising since there is probably greater individual variation in adult competence in the use of registers than in ordinary grammatical competence. (Weeks, 1970, p. 33.)

Like other aspects of language, these expressive aspects are subject to cultural patterning. Because the oral speech styles valued in Black communities (to be discussed later in this chapter) make unusual use of such prosodic features as stress and intonation, further research might show relative advancement in the features studied by Weeks among Black children.

In a direction opposite from cultural influences, it is interesting to speculate about whether some of our human manipulation of prosodic aspects of communication may be related to antecedents in our evolutionary past. For instance, whispering could be a specifically human version of a more basic adaptive behavior—that of decreasing the dimensions of an act for protective purposes. See Friedman (1968) for a provocative discussion of other examples of "evolved behavior."

Coding Ability

Any object, event, or idea can be referred to or named in many ways. A spot on the rug can be *it, that, that over there, the spot, the spot near the leg of the table*, etc. One source of variation within child language comes from the selection among such options for making meaning less or more explicit. As noted earlier, one dimension of language development is increasing ability to free language from its nonlinguistic context and communicate ideas through words alone. This has been termed "coding ability" (R. Brown, 1966).

Like intelligibility discussed in Chapter 5, coding ability must meet a shifting criterion of success. It even depends on the same two characteristics of the speech situation which were important in judgments of intelligibility: the presence or absence of a physically present nonlinguistic context, and the presence or absence of a shared "psychological context" of previously acquired information and experience. In oral speech, both are important. If, when a cat comes into the room, a mother says to her child *Get it out of here*, the pronoun *it* is not at all ambiguous because the shared focus of attention between speaker and listener substitutes for a verbally more explicit referent and eliminates the need to communicate more through words alone. In written language, where no physical context is possible, the presence or absence of a shared psychological background becomes all the more important. Salzinger and his associates (1970) report a high correlation between successful communication (as tested by the Cloze technique in which a reader guesses deleted words) and the degree of familiarity between reader and author.

Coding ability is thus taxed whenever the topic of conversation is not physically present and supplementary nonverbal communication such as pointing is impossible. Familiar occasions include describing the past, planning for the future, giving directions to strangers, talking over the telephone, and writing—especially for an unknown reader. It is often assumed (for example, by Bruner, 1965) that most talk in school is out of context in this sense, though I know of no studies to prove whether this assumption is true.

Even when the lexical and grammatical means needed for coding ability under diverse circumstances are present in a child's language system, children continue to differ in their style and effectiveness, in the "descriptive specificity" of their speech (Jones and Wepman, 1965). Most of the research on this set of speech varieties relates it only to the social class of the speaker.

Discussion of coding ability is divided into three sections: explicitness in speech, explicitness in writing, and adapting language to the needs of the listener.

EXPLICITNESS IN SPEECH

Three quite different forms of explicitness have been explored in research on child language: selecting nouns versus pronouns; giving global versus analytic descriptions; and formulating a series of questions in playing the game of Twenty Questions.

Nouns versus Pronouns

One option open to speakers in encoding meaning is the selection of nouns or pronouns. Consider the speech of one of the Black children from Roxbury in Ch. 3, Fig. 3. Gerald is the boy whose mean length of utterance is above five morphemes, almost off the top of the graph. The first speech sample was recorded when he was 33 months old. Following are all his utterances of 7 or more morphemes in the first 200 utterances of that speech sample, with the computation of number of morphemes in parentheses (unpublished speech samples from Cazden, 1965):

I'm looking for a cup. (7)
I waiting for a other cup. (7)
You put it up on there like dis. (8)
I gon' put dis one in 'nere. (7)
Look at what I made with dis one. (8)
Den gon' put dis one back in here cause it fell out. (12)
I'm gonna knock dese things in. (8)
Soon I get finish I gon' do dat way. (9)
Can I take it off and put it on? (9)

Despite Gerald's unusual grammatical development in terms of MLU, his speech is tied to its nonverbal context to an unusual extent—at least partly because he uses so many pronouns and so few nouns.

Research studies in England by Hawkins (1969), as part of Bernstein's research in London (Brandis and Henderson, 1970), and by Joan Tough in Leeds (Cazden, 1971) show large social-class differences in how this choice between nouns and pronouns is made. In Bernstein's research, the subjects were 300 children who entered 13 infant schools in a LC area of East London in 1964 and 150 comparable MC children who entered 5 infant schools in a South East Borough of London in 1965. The children were studied during their three-year stay in the infant school, ages five to seven years. Chapter 6 described some of the questions the mothers of these children were asked.

Samples of the children's speech were recorded in several structured situations. Narrative speech was elicited by asking the child to tell a story about each of three sets of pictures: a boy kicking a football that breaks a window, a boy falling into the water while fishing, and a cat stealing some fish. Descriptive speech was elicited in response to three paintings of scenes in a railway station, of a garden, and in the street. Explanatory speech was elicited by asking the child to describe and explain the workings of a mechanical toy elephant to a blindfolded experimenter.

In a subsample of 110 children, "independent of the measured ability of the children, there was a broad tendency for the middle class to use the noun and its associated forms more frequently while the working class made greater use of the pronoun" (Hawkins, 1969, pp. 125–135).

This contrast between use of nouns and pronouns was analyzed further for the two tasks that elicited the most speech (narrative and descriptive) for a larger subsample of 312 children. Pronouns were divided into those that referred to previously mentioned nouns (anaphoric reference, as in *The boy kicked the ball and it broke the window*) and those that referred outward to the situational context (exophoric reference, as in *They're playing football and he kicks it*). Both MC and LC children used anaphoric pronouns, but exophoric pronouns were used significantly more often in both situations by the LC children.

> This difference is important for two reasons: firstly, because it enables the middle-class child to elaborate—he can talk about *three big* boys but he cannot talk about *three big they*; and secondly, and more important, the middle-class child can be understood outside the immediate context, without reference to the "here and now." His speech can be interpreted on its own, without the pictures if necessary, and he makes no assumption that the listener can see the pictures in front of him and knows implicitly who is meant by *he, she, it, they*. The working-class child, on the other hand, does make these assumptions, and his speech is therefore tied to the context in which it occurs. (Hawkins, 1969, p. 134.)

In Leeds, Joan Tough did a longitudinal study (Cazden, 1971) of the language development of 48 children, half from "favored" backgrounds. The "favored" and "less favored" categories are based on the father's occupation and an interview to assess the quality of linguistic fostering provided by the home. All children were equated on mean Stanford-Binet IQ, with group means of 125–130. When the children were three years old, each child's speech was tape recorded in a one-hour play session with another child of the subject's choice.

In one analysis, all of the children's "items of representation" were rated as to whether they required the presence of the concrete situation for effective communication. This "concrete component" constituted 20.9 percent of the representations of the favored children and 34.5 percent of the representations of the less favored children. The most frequent forms of the "concrete component" were pronouns, whose only reference was to somthing pointed at in the environment. Tough contrasted such exophoric reference with anaphoric reference. The percentage of anaphoric references (which would communicate without the concrete context) was 22.8 percent for the favored children and only 7.7 percent for the less favored children. Tough's finding thus replicates Hawkins' results.

Note that these differences were found among children who are in the same range of scores on the Stanford-Binet. This means that children of equivalent intellectual ability use language in different ways. Hertzig and associates (1968) present related evidence that children equated on intelligence test scores may have different communication styles.

An older study by Schatzman and Strauss (1955) is relevant here, even though the subjects were adults, because it raises important questions about intergroup versus intragroup communication which have still not been resolved. Twenty subjects, 10 upper-status and 10 lower-status individuals selected from the extremes of income and education, were interviewed in a small Arkansas town after a tornado. The authors summarize the difference in the resulting narratives of members of the two groups:

> The difference is a considerable disparity in (a) the number and kinds of perspectives utilized in communication; (b) the ability to take the listener's role; (c) the handling of classification; and (d) the framework and stylistic devices which order and implement the communication. (Schatzman and Strauss, 1955, p. 329.)

Schatzman and Strauss express two different interpretations of their results. On the one hand, they say that the upper-status subject is better able to make his meaning explicit because he has been more often in situations where this is necessary, whereas the lower-status subject is accustomed to talking about his experiences only with people with whom he shares a great deal of previous experience and symbolism. In this view, the experience of the upper-status speaker has taught him how to encode more information. On the other hand, the authors also assert that the important variable is not how much information the speaker has encoded, but the extent to which communication of it from speaker to listener may be impeded by "differential rules for the ordering of speech and thought" (Schatzman and Strauss, 1955, p. 329). These rules, describing the structure of speech, are independent of those describing the structure of language, referred to earlier in the discussion of dialects (Chapter 7).

Degrees of explicitness do not apply only to describing a referent, the topic of a proposition. There may also be degrees of explicitness in expressing one's own stance with relation to a proposition—for instance, by a choice among alternative verb forms: I *won't, can't, shan't, wouldn't, couldn't, mustn't,* etc. (Wilbur Hass, personal communication).

Analytic versus Global Description

In social psychology experiments, coding ability has been tested in many variations of a two-person communication game. One child (the speaker) is asked to describe one of an array of objects so that another child (the listener—sometimes present behind a screen, sometimes not) can select an identical item from a rearranged array. One array that has been used in several such studies is a set of six novel abstract figures which Krauss and Glucksberg (1969) developed and someone else labeled "squiggles." These are shown in Figure 1.

One day when Adam was six years old, we played the game with him. Here are his descriptions:

    a.   A teapot. A teapot with a hole going through, going down. (#4)

Figure 1 **Abstract Designs.**

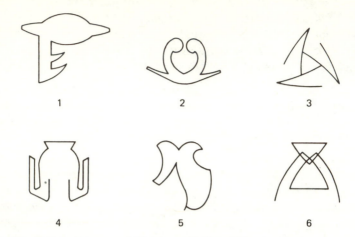

1   2   3

4   5   6

Source   Glucksberg, Krauss, and Weisberg, 1966, p. 335

  b. Triangle with a line going through it. And a little one on top. (#6)
  c. It looks like—one end an orange. Except it has two points. And a line and two sharp things with a line. (#1)
  d. One sharp end, and another sharp end, and another sharp end. Three sharp ends. With a triangle in the middle. (#3)
  e. A circle. A circle kinda like a ring. (#2)
  f. It sorta looks like a horse. With one ear, another ear. It's kinda big on one side. Just like a pig except it's square. (#5.)

In a set of experiments (Glucksberg, Krauss, and Weisberg, 1966; Krauss and Glucksberg, 1969; Krauss and Rotter, in press), Krauss and his colleagues found that children 52–63 months had trouble communicating about the squiggles in the role of both speaker and listener. Some of the child listeners could decode adult descriptions correctly, and children as young as 47 months could use their own descriptions correctly. This was so even for such seemingly confusable descriptions as "Daddy's shirt" (#4) and "another Daddy's shirt" (#5). Either children really "see" what they describe, or the act of describing itself establishes an association that is then remembered. Krauss and Rotter (in press) also found that LC 7- and 12-year-old children could neither encode nor decode descriptions of abstract figures (squiggles) as effectively as MC children.

Heider (1971) further explored social-class differences in coding effectiveness and style. The following report of her work is adapted from Heider, Cazden, and Brown (1968). The subjects were 143 10-year-old boys and girls: one-third middle class (MC) white, one-third lower class (LC) white, and one-third LC Black. The stimuli consisted of five arrays of

Krauss's figures and five arrays of the Frois-Wittmann pictures of male facial expressions. In the first session (encoding) each child was asked to describe one abstract or face out of a set of six items so that "another child" could pick out that item at a later time. In the second session (decoding) each child was read examples of descriptions given by children from each class and sex of encoder and asked to designate which figure or face in the array the speaker had been trying to describe.

Remarkably sharp and consistent differences existed between MC and LC encodings. In the first place, MC children were much more "fluent"; they gave many more images per picture than did the LC children. Beyond this difference of fluency (and even with fluency held constant), there were very reliable differences of coding style.

Heider classified images on two dimensions—Part versus Whole: whether the image referred to the whole stimulus or only a part of it; and Descriptive versus Inferential: whether the image simply described the stimulus or represented an inference going beyond it. One kind of style was common to the two social classes, the style Heider called Whole Inferential (WI). An encoding of the Whole Inferential (WI) type describes the whole picture, not physicalistically but by inference—that is, in terms of what the picture looks like. Adam's descriptions of abstract #2 as "like a ring" and of #5 as "like a house" are Whole Inferential. Of a face, Heider's subjects said: *He's mad* or *He looks surprised*; of an abstract they said *It's a flying saucer* or *It looks like two snakes are fighting at each other*. Descriptions of the WI type accounted for 80 percent of all LC images but only for 33 percent of MC images.

The MC children used also a second style, which Heider called Part Descriptive (PD). An image of this type describes some part of the picture, often a minute part, in terms of physical description. Adam's description of #3 is Part Descriptive: *one sharp end, and another sharp end, and another sharp end*. Of a face, Heider's subjects said: *One ear is dark* or *He has his left eyebrow raised more than any of the other faces*; of an abstract, they said *There's a tiny circle in the middle* or *It's a figure which is even on both of its sides and has an opening at the top and it's curved at the bottom*. Part Descriptive (PD) images accounted for only 13 percent of the LC images but for 53 percent of MC descriptions. Fluency, part descriptions, and descriptive language were all significantly correlated with one another, both within and between classes. A combination of high scores on these three variables defines the "analytic" style; and low scores, the "wholistic" style.

Communication effectiveness was measured by the accuracy of the decoders in identifying the intended figures. Figure 2 presents Heider's data. MC children were better overall encoders and decoders than LC children, but neither sex nor race had any consistent effect on either coding effectiveness or style. There was no evidence that children of one social class

Figure 2 **Decoder Accuracy: Class of Encoder x. Class of Decoder x Style of Encoding: (a) Abstracts; (b) Faces.**

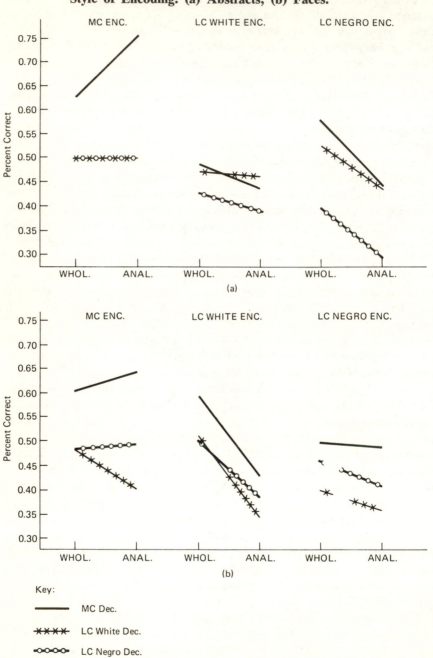

Key:

─────── MC Dec.

✻✻✻✻ LC White Dec.

-o-o-o-o- LC Negro Dec.

Source After Heider, Cazden, and Brown, 1968

communicated more accurately with each other than with children from the other group.

Style of encoding was an important variable in success of communication. Overall, those composite encodings that contained both WI and PD images were the best understood. For each class, the style of encoding most successfully decoded was the style that each class used most frequently: LC encodings composed only of WI images were better understood than LC encodings composed of PD images, while for the MC encodings, the opposite was true. But MC children were better encoders and decoders of both the wholistic and analytic style, and LC decoders were more successful with the wholistic encodings of the MC children than with their own. Communication was most accurate when MC children were decoding the analytic encodings of MC encoders.

What characteristics of either the wholistic or analytic styles might be related to their effectiveness in communication? First, the redundancy of the analytic style is striking; a typical encoding of an analytic child contains many images. Sheer length of encoding was not a decisive factor in Heider's results, however, as encodings from which some images had been removed were as well understood as intact encodings of the same style.

Second, descriptive language appears more impersonal than inferential language. *It looks like a hat* can communicate effectively only if *hat* conjures up similar images for encoder and decoder, while *It's got a point sticking out on each side on the bottom* seems less dependent for its referential import on idiosyncratic associations and imagery. One would expect, therefore, that descriptive language would be a more effective lingua franca for communication across social-class lines. In fact, it was not. WI images tend to be better understood than PD images if the social class of encoder and decoder is ignored. This may mean that American culture is sufficiently homogeneous that many associations and images have neither social-class nor individual variations. Or it may mean that PD language is a language that LC children not only rarely speak but also do not understand very well.

Other research has found related differences in coding styles. When Brent and Klamer (1967) asked college sophomores and inner-city adolescents to describe geometric figures, the inner-city subjects gave "an overwhelming number of analogical and metaphorical names" (1967, p. 4). Cohen (1968) reports correlations between such stylistic differences and a wide range of other behaviors in 16- to 17-year-olds.

Because the "concrete-abstract" contrast has been so often invoked in social-class comparisons, it is important to note that it does not apply here in the usual way. If by "concrete" is meant closer to perceptible properties of the stimulus, then the preferred LC style of using WI descriptions must be considered less concrete, not more. WI descriptions have their limitations: For the listener, the metaphor must be familiar; because a metaphor refers to each stimulus uniquely, the speaker has to start afresh to construct a metaphorical interpretation of each item. PD descriptions, by contrast, use labels for dimensions, and encode stimulus properties in terms of similarities to and differences from other items in a particular array. Be that as it may, WI descriptions are less stimulus-bound and in that sense more abstract.

What may cause such differences in preferred encoding styles? Some conceivable explanations can be set aside. First, Heider (1971) found that the WI–PD contrast was not simply an artifact of how much the child said. For any one child, the style of the first image given was highly correlated with the subsequent proportion of images in that style. Whether fluency in some sense of a basic disposition to respond verbally to the world is somehow related to the development of analytic style remains an open question. Second, an additional test (which required the children to find small differences between parts of figures) showed that LC children, when they were specifically directed to attend to parts, were almost as capable of doing so as were MC children. That is, LC children attend to parts of a stimulus when directed to do so, but are much less apt to refer to parts in their free descriptions.

Another possible explanation of stylistic differences remains untested in Heider's work. Maybe MC children are more apt to give PD encodings because they have been somehow socialized to attributize or dimensionalize their environment, even (and this is the important point) when not required to do so. They might, in other words, engage in more latent learning of the attributes underlying the categorizations of their world.

Heider, Cazden, and Brown (1968) conducted an experiment to test this hypothesis. The subjects were 18 white boys, now age 11, from the extremes of Heider's sample: 9 MC boys, whose mean percentage of PD responses = 67.5; and 9 LC boys, whose mean percentage of WI responses = 96.4. A new set of stimuli was designed, consisting of 40 cards, 8 each of 5 animals: dog, cat, lion, horse, and cow. Each subset of 8 represented 2 values each of three attributes, standing-lying, profile or three-quarter face, and 1 or 2 spots on the back. Each picture of the 40 constituted a unique conjunction of attribute values.

First, the children were shown the cards 8 at a time and asked to encode one picture to a present listener, using only one word. Since, in every instance, the target picture was the only picture of that animal in the array of 8, the child could simply say *Dog* or *Cat* or whatever, and he was not allowed to say more. Following the presentation of all 40 cards in such sets of 8, the child was asked to select one of the cards from the pack of 40 and this time to describe it for a listener so that the listener could pick out the target picture from the *entire pack* of 40. In these circumstances, of course, the name of the animal pictured would not suffice; it was necessary to specify the values of all criterial attributes. If the child did not give sufficient information—saying, for example, *It's a dog with one spot*—the listener would say *I have dogs with one spot, but I don't know which one you mean.* The conversation continued until the child gave sufficient information or gave up.

We predicted that during the first part of the experiment the MC children would gain more latent learning of the attributes on which the animals differed and would therefore be more apt to say later *It's a horse with 2 spots and he's lying down and facing straight ahead.* This hypothesis was not confirmed. The density of criterial attributes in the total number of attributes mentioned was almost identical for the two groups: The 9 MC children gave 67 attributes of which 18 were criterial, while the 9 LC children gave 69 attributes of which 16 were criterial. Of the first responses alone, 7 of the LC children gave criterial attributes, while only 5 MC children did so. With rare exceptions—one in each group—the children in both groups were evidently describing the target stimulus without regard to the array from which it came. But there was a significant social-class difference in the number of requests the listener had to make for more information before the picture was adequately specified: LC mean = 6.11 requests; MC mean = 3.56 requests.

A final piece of the puzzle to be explained is that LC behavior in general is similar to MC behavior in more informal situations. A University of California student found that college students, presumably largely MC, were more likely to give inferential or metaphorical descriptions (*It's an elephant doing push-ups*) to their close friends (Ervin-Tripp, 1969). In my own experience in demonstrating the task of describing the squiggles in a Harvard graduate class, students invariably delight in imaginative and extremely effective global descriptions. Try them out with your friends! And evidently Pablo Casals finds metaphorical expressions effective, too:

> . . . When Casals the conductor wants a certain rhapsodical kind of expression and exhorts his musicians to "play Jewish," his appeal to their intuition is more effective and more intelligent in this instance than trying to communicate with scientific precision. (Review of Pablo Casals' *Joys and Sorrows* by Donald Hanahan, *New York Times Book Review*, April 12, 1970, p. 7.)

What are the implications of this research for education? Given the potential effectiveness of both metaphorical and analytical styles, it would seem wise to direct educational efforts to encouraging greater fluency in both imaginative metaphors and informational analysis. Greater fluency seems especially important for LC children who, at least in Heider's study, were more limited in their style of response (80% WI) than the MC children (53% PD). See Leacock (in press) for further discussion.

An educational program for five- to seven-year-old children designed by Gahagan and Gahagan (1970) as part of Bernstein's research had one unanticipated result. Part of the program was designed to increase explicit language use by training communication skills in two-person communication tasks. One test then assessed the effects of the entire training program in sharpening children's perceptions of emotions and interpersonal relations, and in extending their vocabulary for this area of experience. The children were asked to describe stick figures, singly or in pairs. A high score was assigned to responses "which attributed emotion, motivation, volition or mood," while a low score was assigned to "any atomistic or fragmentary response describing parts of the figure separately." Contrary to expectations, children who had received the experimental curriculum did not give more high-score responses. On the contrary,

> . . . a small number of E1 (experimental) children, mainly boys, seemed to have given precise, meticulous descriptions of the stick figures at the expense of wholistic, relational responses. For example, they specified the exact location of each arm and each leg in relation to the body, whether the heel was turned to the left or right, and whether a foot seemed to be raised off the ground. (Gahagan and Gahagan, 1970.)

While this result was disappointing to the Gahagans, it exactly fits with Heider's results. At least in this task, the Gahagan-Bernstein language program succeeded—for better or worse—in making the children use language in more "middle-class" ways.

Playing Twenty Questions

Frequently, when we ask questions for information, one question is not enough. It is necessary to construct a series of questions, each of which takes into consideration what has been learned before. A simplified model of this information-seeking process is the game of Twenty Questions.

Readers who have played this game will realize from their own experience that one effective way to play is by continuously partitioning the array of possibilities in half. Imagine the task of finding out which of the squares on a checkerboard someone else has in mind. One could ask such questions as the following:

   a.   Is it red?
   b.   Is it in the left half facing you?
   c.   Is it in the top half facing you?

The speaker would be working on the basis of an unspoken informational analysis of the total array. The array may be present as in checkers, or only imagined—as when the game is about "I'm thinking of someone . . . ." Considered in this way, the task for the questioner requires the same informational analysis as the analytical coding style. The only difference is that now the result of that analysis is expressed in a series of questions rather than in one combined descriptive statement.

Mosher and Hornsby (1966) played the Twenty Questions game with 90 six-, eight-, and eleven-year-old boys in a suburban school. The children were shown an array of 42 pictures of common objects and asked to find out which object the experimenter had in mind. To do so, they could ask only yes-no questions. The kinds of questions asked by the children could be divided into four categories:

Constraints: Any question general enough to refer to two or more objects:

Is it a toy?

Specific Hypotheses (or Pot-Shotting):   Refers to a particular object.

Is it a hammer?

Guesses: Specific hypotheses that bear no relation to previous constraint questions, and so give an index of the unconnectedness of the child's search strategy.

Pseudoconstraints: Refers to only one item in the array but is phrased like a constraint question:

Does it have a sail?

Figure 3 gives the percentage of questions of each type asked by the three age groups.

Like the two-person communication game, Twenty Questions can be used as a medium of instruction as well as a research technique. Because Mosher and Hornsby (1966) showed so clearly that even suburban (and presumably MC) six-year-olds overwhelmingly make one specific guess after another, Bereiter's attempts to teach lower-class children in his

Figure 3   **Percent Questions of Each Type Asked by Children at Three Ages.**

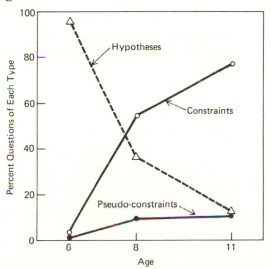

Source   Mosher and Hornsby, 1966, p. 91

Toronto kindergarten to use mature constraint strategy is all the more interesting. He has developed many versions of this game (Bereiter, Case, and Anderson, 1968). In one version, the children stand around the teacher, eyes closed and one hand outstretched. The teacher pretends to put a paper clip in each hand and then really puts it into one child's hand. Hands down and eyes open, the children start asking questions. The rules of the game specify whether on this particular occasion the teacher will answer only yes-no questions like *Is it a girl?* or only wh-questions like *What color is her hair?* As each question is asked and answered, the children who are eliminated from further consideration step back and continue asking questions until the child holding the paper clip is identified. Score is kept of how many questions are required for solution. The game can be made easier or harder—depending on the number of possibilities, whether or not they are visually present, how much help the teacher gives the children in working out the implications of each answer, and whether possibilities eliminated by an answer are physically removed.

In casual observation, I found the performance of Bereiter's children impressive. But the account of a student teacher at Wheelock College made me wonder. At my suggestion, she tried to play Twenty Questions with the children in a public school kindergarten class. When she said, *I'm thinking of an animal that's brown and fuzzy*, the children asked quite a number of constraint-type questions such as *Does it have four feet?* and *Does it live in the water?* It turned out that this class had had a circus unit during the preceding week and the children had been taught specific ways of categorizing animals—according to the number of feet, where they live, etc.

The evidence that their information-seeking ability was not generally as advanced as it had at first seemed was two-fold: First, the children frequently didn't use information from previous answers in constructing their questions; after being told *Yes, it has four legs*, a child asked *Is it a seal?* Second, the appearance of constraint-type questions was limited to this particular domain of animals. The behavior of these children is reminiscent of the inflexible routines of Adam, Eve, and Sarah at a much earlier age. One would like to see individual tests on Bereiter's children in which one could follow the connectedness of their search strategies, and observe their performance in new and unfamiliar domains. Evaluation of transfer of learning becomes especially critical when instruction has attempted to speed up the usual course of development.

EXPLICITNESS IN WRITING

All of the problems of making meaning explicit in speech are magnified in writing because nonverbal support for communicating meaning is completely absent. And if one is writing to an unknown audience, a "generalized other," all reliance on any shared background of experience is also withdrawn. In this sense, written language is the final point on the developmental dimension toward independence from nonlinguistic context, "the extreme limit of the process by which language comes to be increasingly independent of the conditions of its use" (de Laguna, 1963, p. 167). No wonder it is hard for all of us, from the elementary school years on through adult life.

Soviet psychologists such as Vygotsky (1962) and Luria (1969) argue that writing not only imposes new cognitive demands, but by so doing also yields special cognitive benefits.

> Oral speech forms during an immediately practical intercourse and its component elements long remain insufficiently conscious, unseparated by the child from general speech activity. . . . Written speech follows exactly the opposite course. It is always the product of speech training, which presupposes the separation of individual words from the flow of living speech and individual sounds from the living word. . . .
>
> Oral speech always originates in close connection with immediate experience. . . . It relies on intonation and gesture and usually becomes intelligible only if the general setting of the conversation is considered. It permits extensive abbreviation. . . . Written speech, on the other hand, is deprived of this sympractical context, and therefore it must be more detailed, contextual, or, to use Bugler's term, symsemantic. . . .
>
> It can scarcely be doubted that both oral and written speech are a most important means of communication. However, of foremost importance in written speech is another function. Written speech is bound up with the inhibition of immediate sympractical speech connections. It assumes a much slower, repeated mediating process of analysis and synthesis, which makes it possible not only to develop the required thought, but even to revert to its earlier stages, thus transforming the sequential chains of connections into a simultaneous, self-reviewing structure. Written speech thus represents a new and powerful instrument of thought.
>
> The functional and structural features of written speech have still another important feature; they inevitably lead to a significant development of *inner speech*. Because it delays the direct appearance of speech connections, inhibits them, and increases requirements for the preliminary, internal preparation for the speech act, written speech produces a rich development of inner speech which could not take place in the earliest phases of development. (Luria, 1969, pp. 141–142.)

Writing, in other words, may thus contribute to the metalinguistic awareness of language discussed in Chapter 5, and to the uses of language in intrapersonal thought to be considered in Chapter 9.

Different speech functions become highly developed in different cultural groups. Betty Bryant has discussed speech functions in Black communities. While speakers of Black English and of Standard English probably utilize context in much the same manner when engaged in everyday casual speech,

noncasual speech becomes specialized in Black communities in ways different from the specialized uses of language required in writing and in main-
stream life generally. In Black communities, the emphasis is on forms of
oral performance in which the poetic or expressive function of language
predominates (Jakobson, 1960).

The following excerpts are from Bryant's paper (1970):

> The men of words, being the most highly practiced and skilled per-
> formers, control the competence for the entire range of speech events which
> make up the verbal art form. Examples of these are: signifying, which may
> be known in various places and at different times as sounding, woofing or
> louding; playing the dozens, a method of ritualistic insult; and eloquent
> speaking of epic poems generally known as stories, toasts or jokes. There
> appears to be a developmental sequence which probably begins with younger
> children learning some form of signifying as reported by a mother talking
> about her preschool-age child:

> Parent: Well, I know that K. came home one day; an' she's only four. She's
>   the baby in our family. An' uh C. asked me for something, and
>   I said: "No." An' then K. said: *"Ha Ha, mama broke your face."*
>   And it was really good, you know. So after then, every time
>   circumstances arose where one of the children didn't have their
>   way, they knew that the other one would say it: *"Uh Oh, got your
>   face broke."* So then it really broke up that attitude, you know,
>   every time you don't get your way, you cry.
>   [*Author's note*: From the study of attitudes toward Black dialect,
>   Cazden, Bryant, and Tillman, 1970, reported in Chapter 7.]

This child uses what Mitchell (1969) has described as the concept of
indirection in Black speech. This utterance can be classified as signifying,
and the tactic can be used in many speech events. In fact, it is the strategy
which can be found in all the above-mentioned speech episodes. A literal
translation of this utterance would probably yield: "You didn't get what
you wanted, aren't you sad." In actuality, the essence of the comment does
not translate to print very well, since the rhythm, intonation, and taunting
"attitude" with which such a remark is delivered is part and parcel of the
verbal message. Also, the ability to use such utterances in appropriate
contexts implies that the child has to *know* that the words don't mean
literally what they say. Each word is part of the child's vocabulary for use
in many situations, in the more conventional referential sense. However,
here she chose to encode the message in an indirect way.

Preadolescents and adolescents, while controlling competence for the
range of speech episodes which can be designated by the term "signifying,"
employ this skill more for what is generally known as "ritual insults." H. Rap
Brown (1969) who acquired the nickname "Rap" because of his *outstanding*
verbal ability comments—

> The street is where young bloods get their education. I learned how to talk
> in the street, not from reading about Dick and Jane going to the zoo and
> all that simple shit. The teacher would test our vocabulary each week, but

we knew the vocabulary we needed. They'd give us arithmetic to exercise our minds. Hell, we exercised our minds by playing the Dozens. . . . And the teacher expected me to sit up in class and study poetry after I could run down shit like that. If anybody needed to study poetry, she needed to study mine. We played the Dozens for recreation, like white folks play Scrabble. . . . We learned what the white folks call verbal skills. We learned how to throw them words together. (H. R. Brown, 1969, pp. 25–26.)

All art forms are structured and require that the individual adhere to the structure while imbuing the performance with his unique style. Abrahams (1964) described "Kid," one of his most exciting and prolific informants, whose effectiveness stemmed from an excellent mixture of tradition and personal style:

Kid's style of rendition was very theatrical. He used as many dramatic devices as possible, changing voices for different characters or for varying situations, utilizing the full range of his voice both in regard to pitch and intensity, and he would speed up and slow down at will. He was a masterful rhymster and quipper, but he was also capable of almost endlessly embroidering a story if he wanted to. (Abrahams, 1964, p. 95.)

And as Liebow (1967) described "Sea Cat," one of the 24 street-corner men he studied—

An excellent story-teller, Sea Cat holds his audience as much by his performance as by the content of what he has to say. If he reports that "an old man was walking down the street," his body suddenly sags with the weight of age and his hands tremble and knees almost buckle as he becomes, for that moment, an old man walking down the street. If he reports that someone shouted something, he shouts that something. (Liebow, 1967.)

[*Author's note*: See Kochman, in press, for further examples.]

Several generalizations seem possible from the preceding descriptions of verbal performers: (1) the emphasis is on style, or the manner in which something is said as opposed to what is said; (2) each talker develops his unique style while operating within the traditional structure; (3) action is stressed both in words and gestures that accompany the words; (4) many forms of verbal performance use some aspect of indirection, that is, the actual spoken words do not have literal meaning; (5) children progress by stages to ability to control the highest forms of the art; and (6) since this kind of verbal activity is not recognized by the schools, children develop it solely outside the school situation (Bryant, 1970).

Oral performance, as Bryant describes it, and writing are two language functions. They both require complex planning, but of a different kind. In oral performance, where the poetic and expressive functions predominate, planning is focused on intonation, pauses, facial expressions, and gestures for maximum impact on an audience physically present and visibly responsive. That's why it was suggested earlier that LC Black children might be relatively advanced in the expressive aspects of speech which Weeks described. In written language, where the referential function of language predominates, planning is focused on what Vygotsky (1962) called "deliberate structuring of the web of meaning," the selection of words and syntactic structures to convey meaning most effectively. Thus the two kinds of verbal planning do not overlap as either ends or means.

From her research in Africa, Greenfield (1968) relates this contrast to the development of "abstract thought." Because the adjective "abstract" has so many meanings, both denotative and connotative, it is better to only say that personal literacy may be related, as Luria suggests, to particular forms of inner speech. It remains an open question as to what other forms context-independent thought—which is what Greenfield means by "abstract"—can take. See Cole and associates (1971) for an important analysis of this difficult but very important area of cross-cultural research, which overlaps with the topic of Chapter 9 as well.

School tasks that require written composition for reasons meaningful to the child may provide a very realistic context for practice in making meaning explicit, in using what Bernstein calls "an elaborated code." Some people may be able to learn to write an elaborated code even if they do not speak it, either because "speaking is a skill which requires a rapidly produced sequence of co-ordinated activity" (Robinson, 1965, p. 244), or because "he may not be able to manage the face to face requirements of the role" [Bernstein, in press (b), p. 14].

Bryant (1970) suggests that the qualitative differences between the structure of most oral speech and the structure of most written language may also explain part of the problems included under "reading comprehension." If this is so, then we have an added reason for reading aloud to children a great deal, even after they have learned to decode simple material for themselves. By reading aloud, teachers give children practice in comprehending the kinds of language structure found in books. For this purpose, pictures may be more of a hindrance than a help. As pictures in beginning reading material may short-circuit the primary task of learning to decode words, so pictures in more advanced materials may short-circuit the task of learning to derive meaning from language alone.

ADAPTING TO THE NEEDS OF THE LISTENER

An important part of coding ability is skill in adapting one's message to the listener or reader. This may require the recognition of differences in either perceptual or conceptual points of view. Here are some examples of successful role-taking behavior:

Perceptual: The three-year-old who gets his father's attention by stepping between his father's chair and the TV set.

The first grader, described in Chapter 7, who looked at a Polaroid picture of another child facing the camera and said to the picture-taker *He looking at you.*

Conceptual: The child still saying only occasional one-word utterances who says *ga-ga* for cracker to Mommy or Daddy and then utters long sequences of nonwords with English intonation directed toward his tricycle or the dog. (An intriguing and speculative interpretation from Glenda Bissex, personal communication.)

Three-year-old Eric interrupts a story about "John" to insert *He's my friend.*

A ten-year-old interrupts his second interview with a speech therapist to say *I think I already told you . . . .*

Another ten-year-old on a Sierra Club canoe trip remarks on the different baseball pictures on the cocoa cans. The person who bought the food says *You mean I should have picked the cans more carefully so you could get a complete set?* The boy says *No, you didn't know I was going to be on the trip.*

Here are some examples of the absence of role-taking:

Perceptual: A three-year-old child at a lunch counter who didn't want others to hear her singing and so covered her own ears.
Conceptual: Descriptions like "Mommy's hat" for one of the squiggles.

Such actions and speech have been labeled egocentric (Piaget, 1955). The trouble with this label is that it is ambiguous in just the way *telegraphic* is because it refers either to product or process. As a label for a particular product, "egocentric" is apt enough, but it doesn't explain how the product got that way.

Flavell and his colleagues (1968) have studied the development of role taking skills in children. Here is their description of what is required:

Where role taking does play an effective part . . . several important things are assumed to occur. First, the speaker attends very carefully to the listener, attempting to discern his powers and limitations as an audience for the data in question. Second, the resulting image of listener role attributes functions continuously to shape the organization and content of the message. The image acts as a monitor, a sort of communicative servo-mechanism, which dictates a recoding wherever the speaker's spontaneous self-coding would be likely to fail to communicate. And finally, this monitoring activity is assumed to require real vigilance and effort on the speaker's part, because a recoded message is never the path of least resistance (Flavell et al., 1968, pp. 95–96.)

The experimental tasks used by Flavell and his coworkers are ingenious: teaching a game to a blindfolded or normal partner; relaying minimally redundant information from a police chief to three subordinates each of whom knows a different part of the combination for opening a safe; switching from description of a design sufficient for reconstruction to description adequate for selection of it from an array; selecting gifts for persons who vary in age or sex. Both the tasks and their administration are described in careful detail and then discussed in admirably self-critical terms. For instance, Flavell stresses the vexing problem of experimentally separating "role taking capability per se and related capabilities, for example, that of recognizing that certain non-role taking goals demand role taking means" (Flavell et al., 1968, p. 180).

To summarize the results of this research: The six-year-old child has some awareness that differences in perspective exist, some ability to figure out what they are in the more obvious cases of visual perceptions but not in the more hidden case of information or intentions, and little awareness of a need to analyze the other's point of view if not explicitly instructed to do so. During the elementary school years, all requisite abilities develop. A child's rate of development may be affected by the range of situations in which he is forced to consider alternative points of view in order to achieve his communicative intent.

Though adults have all requisite abilities, they may not use them even when the need for such adaptation is critical. For example, I saw a concert hall usher gesture wildly to a blind student with a white cane to "show" him to the ticket office; and shouting to foreigners is not infrequent.

Teaching may be conceived as one kind of communication for which role taking—in the sense of assessing the abilities, needs, and motivations of another—is essential. Adapting one's message to individual children admittedly requires more effort than an unrecoded broadcast to a group, and looking for and using the feedback provided by the reactions of one's listener(s) is hard work too. Teachers would benefit from analyzing their own behavior in Flavell's terms. See Barnes and Britton (1969) for further discussion of the classroom language of both children and teachers.

Speech in Its Social Setting

Speech is related to its social setting in many ways. Three different relationships have been explored in this book: first, how speech becomes progressively more independent of the immediate context during development; second, how speech can itself define a situation and change it for the participants—as when the Norwegian students shifted the basis of their relationship by switching dialects, or as when a child says *You be the Mommy* during dramatic play; third, how speech is influenced by characteristics of the situation, such as its formality or informality. Here, general discussion about situational influences in the third sense is followed by more detailed comments on two particular aspects of a speech situation which are important in education: personal involvement in the topic and role relationships. This section ends with a report of research on the social setting of the classroom itself. The specific situations we call "tests" are discussed in the Appendix.

Attention to the interaction of abilities and environments is increasing in psychology, linguistics, and education. Barker coined the name "ecological psychology" and argues for its importance:

> When environments are relatively uniform and stable, *people* are an obvious source of behavior variance, and the dominant scientific problem and the persistent queries from the applied fields are: What are people like? What is the nature and what are the sources of individual differences? But today environments are more varied and unstable than heretofore, and their contribution to the variance of behavior is enhanced. Both science and society ask with greater urgency than previously: What are environments like? . . . How do environments select and shape the people who inhabit them? . . . These are questions for ecological psychology. (Barker, 1968, p. 3.)

See Stodolsky (in press) for an analysis of the ecological psychology work.

When Kagan (1967) issued a call for "relativism" in psychology, which would include the context or situation in descriptions of behavior, Psathas answered—

> When Kagan uses the term "relativistic," he says that it "refers to a definition in which context and state of the individual are part of the defining statement." The "neglected situation" as Goffman (1964) has called it and the state of the individual, particularly his internal symbol manipulating state, need to be considered. They would involve Kagan in sociology and anthropology much more than he recognizes. The "context" that he refers to is one that has *socially* defined stimulus value. The social definitions for a situation are pregiven, i.e., exist before the psychologist or experimenter enters on the scene. He must, therefore, understand what these are and how they are perceived by the subject before he can claim to understand why the subject behaves the way he does. The "state of the individual" includes not only his biological and physiological state but his interpretive structuring of the world as he experiences it, based on his previous socialization experiences as a member of the culture. (Psathas, 1968, p. 136.)

While Barker seeks an objective description of the environment—analogous to the characteristics of light or sound in the study of perception—Psathas calls for study of the environment as socially defined and perceived by individuals.

Aspects of the speech setting may be a neglected source of social-class differences in child speech. Two different relationships are possible. Differential responses according to aspects of the situation may be intensified for lower-class speakers. So, for example, all children may be constrained in a testing situation, but lower-class children especially so. Labov found this kind of "ordinal" interaction between style shifting and social stratification in his study of phonological and grammatical features. For instance, all speakers shift from *workin'* to *working* as they shift from casual speech to reading style. But the shift is much greater for lower-class speakers.

Alternatively, there may be "disordinal" interactions between language and situation in which the relationships are reversed, rather than varying in intensity, for the different social class groups. Middle-class children may be more fluent in one set of situations, while lower-class children talk more fluently in another. Bernstein reports such a contrast in his study of children's speech in London:

> . . . working-class, five-year-old children in the same contexts examined by Hawkins [for analysis of nouns and pronouns above], use fewer linguistic expressions of uncertainty when compared with the middle-class children. This does not mean that working-class children do not have access to such expressions, but that the eliciting speech context [telling a story from pictures] did not provoke them. . . .
>
> In the same way we can show that there are constraints upon the middle-class child's use of language. Turner found that when middle-class children were asked to role play in the picture story series, a higher percentage of these children, when compared with working-class children, initially refused. . . . When the middle-class children were asked "What is the man saying," or linguistically equivalent questions, a relatively higher percentage said "I don't know." When this question was followed by the hypothetical question "What do you think the man might be saying?" they offered their interpretations. The working-class children role played without difficulty. It seems then that middle-class children at five need to have a very precise instruction to *hypothesise in that particular* context. This may be because they are more concerned here with getting their answers right or correct. When the children were invited to tell a story about some doll-like figures (a little boy, a little girl, a sailor and a dog) the working-class children's stories were freer, longer, more imaginative than the stories of the middle-class children. [Bernstein, in press (a).]

As long ago as 1954, McCarthy recommended that varied situations be used to obtain a more stable index of a child's language. But what is needed is not varied settings from which numbers can be averaged to obtain a more reliable mean. Instead, in the words of one of Bernstein's colleagues, "it may be wiser methodologically to accumulate the [social class] differences within contexts and to see what higher order generalizations can be made about them" (Robinson, 1968, p. 6). This seems the only way to discover the multidimensional structure of variation across children and across settings, and eventually to understand "the effective abilities of users of a language, as manifest not in inventories of grammars, but habitual patterns of actual verbal behavior, as these relate to context both within and between groups" (Hymes, 1964, p. 39). See Hymes (1967) for an extended discussion of this area of research.

PERSONAL INVOLVEMENT IN THE TOPIC

Whether children become personally involved in the content of the school curriculum is obviously important for many nonlanguage reasons. But there are indications from research that it will also affect the extent to which a child mobilizes his full language knowledge. This seems to be true of pre-school children and of adolescents.

First of all, involvement will affect whether communication is success-fully achieved. Mueller (1971) video-taped the spontaneous conversations of children (3½ to 5½ years old) talking in pairs in a specially equipped playroom. He scored each communication from one child to the other as successful when the listener carried out the speaker's directions or replied to the speaker in a relevant manner. He then looked for properties of the speaker's utterance, or of the speaker's or listener's engagement at the time of the utterance, which best predicted such success or failure. While failure was best predicted by fragmentary or unclear properties of the utterance itself, success was most likely if the listener was watching the speaker as the utterance began, or if the utterance was itself a reply to something that the listener had said. It is notable that 85 percent of all utterances between these children received replies or at least attracted the listener's attention. Teachers who are continuously concerned with maintaining the attention and engagement of their pupils should consider these results. How often, when we seek a child's attention, are we responding to him, and how often are we intruding on his mental life with some interest of our own?

Personal involvement affects not only the likelihood of a response but also its structural complexity. Strandberg and Griffith (1968) gave four- and five-year-old children in a university laboratory school Kodak Insta-matic cameras loaded with color film and then elicited conversation about the (remarkably successful) pictures the children took. The children talked more spontaneously (that is, required fewer adult probes) and talked in longer and more complex utterances about the pictures they took at home of personally significant objects such as a favorite climbing tree or a close-up of Mother's mouth, than they did about pictures taken under adult direction during the period of orientation to the camera. Since the pictures taken at home were also frequently of only one object, the authors conclude that the difference lay in the degree of personal involvement. Although topic was compounded with order, since all the children told stories about the preselected objects first, it seems unlikely that this accounted for all the difference. Following are examples of one five-year-old's stories, first about an assigned picture and then about one of his choice:

> That's a horse. You can ride it. I don't know any more about it. It's brown, black and red. I don't know my story about the horse.
>
> There's a picture of my tree that I climb in. There's—there's where it grows at, and there's where I climb up—and sit up there—down there and that's where I look out at. First I get on this one and then I get on that other one. And then I put my foot under that big branch that are strong. And then I pull my face up and then I get ahold of a branch up at that place—and then I look around. (Strandberg and Griffith, personal com-munication, 1969.)

Labov collected narratives of TV programs and personal experience from preadolescent boys attending vacation day camps (VDC) in central Harlem. Following are two such narratives by two different 11-year-old boys, the first (from Carl, 11, VDC, #386) about "The Man from Uncle" and the second (from Norris, 11, VDC, #378) about a personal fight (Labov et al., 1968, Vol. 2, pp. 298–299):

a   This kid—Napoleon got shot.
b   and he had to go on a mission.
c   And so this kid, he went with Solo.
d   So they went.
e   And this guy—they went through this window.
f   and they caught him.
g   And then he beat up them other people.
h   And they went.
i   and then he said that this old lady was his mother.
j   and then he—and at the end he say that was the guy's friend.

a   When I was in fourth grade—no it was in third grade . . . .
b   This boy he stole my glove.
c   He took my glove
d   and said that his father found it downtown on the ground.
    (And you fight him?)
e   I told him that it was impossible for him to find downtown 'cause all those people were walking by and just his father was the only one that found it?
f   So he got all [mad].
g   So then I fought him.
h   I knocked him all out in the street.
i   So he say he give
j   and I kept on hitting him.
k   Then he started crying
l   and ran home to his father.
m   And the father told him
o   that he didn't find no glove.

Labov found that the main difference between the two sets of narratives is the absence in the TV narratives of evaluation: "the means used by the narrator to indicate the point of the narrative, its *raison d'etre*, why it was told, and what the narrator is getting at" (Labov et al., 1968, Vol. 2, p. 297). Absence of evaluation from accounts of vicarious experience reduces structural complexity. While "the syntax of the narrative clause itself is one of the simplest structures that may be found even in colloquial language" (Labov et al., 1968, Vol. 2, p. 308), explanations—one of the devices for evaluation—may be exceedingly complex. Figure 4 is the diagram for section *e* of Norris's narrative above. The symbol *S* indicates that one sentence has been embedded in another (Labov et al., 1968, Vol. 2, p. 332).

Figure 4 **Diagram for Section *e* of Morris' narrative.**

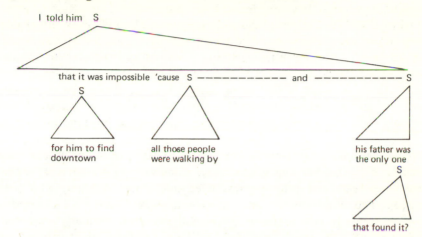

It does not seem farfetched to suggest a common element in the findings of Strandberg and Griffith (1968) and Labov et al. (1968): the greater the degree of affect or personal involvement in the topic of conversation, the greater the likelihood of structural complexity in the child's speech.

ROLE RELATIONSHIPS

While giving a seminar on child language at the University of Minnesota Institute of Child Development, I had a chance to demonstrate some testing techniques with two children from the university nursery school. It was late in June, and the summer session had just begun. One of the children, Frank, had been in school all year and had participated in many such demonstration sessions; the other child, Susan, was new to school that month. Frank came in first. As he sat down, I asked him his name. He answered and then sat quietly waiting for me to proceed. When Susan came in later, I also asked her name. She answered and then quickly asked, "What's *your* name?" to me.

At least two interpretations of this story are possible. Frank and Susan may differ in their reaction to this specific situation because of differential experience with strange adults who ask children questions. Frank had been in this situation before, was well socialized to it, and knew that his expected role was to answer questions, not ask them. Susan, on the other hand, saw this not as a specific kind of adult-child relationship but rather as another setting for pleasant conversation with an adult. Alternatively, the differences in their behavior may lie less in their differential experience in this particular setting and more in pervasive differences to which we give the name "personality." But personality differences themselves can be attributed in part at least (beyond some physiological differences in temperament) to the kinds of interaction children have been in, and the expectations about role relationships which they have learned as a result.

Horner's (1968) study of the verbal world of two LC Black three-year-olds shows how children learn to vary their communication styles according to the age of their listener. Using a wireless microphone transmitter sewn into the child's clothing, Horner taped the speech of two lower-class Black three-year-olds in Rochester, New York, for two entire days—one weekday and one week-end day. One child, Mary, just three years old, was an only child. She lived with her mother, who worked full-time for a community action agency, two teen-age uncles (brothers of the mother), and her grandmother, who cared for her during the day. Aunts, uncles, and male friends of the mother and grandmother came and went frequently. John, age three years and four months, lived next door to Mary, with both parents, two older siblings and his paternal grandfather. John's mother worked regularly as a domestic, but his father was not regularly employed. John's grandfather cared for all three children and their infant cousin.

Horner analyzed the children's speech according to a Skinnerian analysis of language functions (Skinner, 1957). Two of Skinner's functional categories are *mands* and *tacts*. Briefly, mands (which include com*mands* and de*mands*) produce some effect, verbal or nonverbal, for the benefit of the speaker; the category of "mand" is defined by its effect, not its form. But because a particular form (for example: imperatives or questions) may be closely associated with an effect in a given community, we can make a strong inference about function from form alone. *Tacts*, on the other hand, are utterances evoked by some present or imagined object or event; they inform the listener rather than manipulate him. In Horner's analysis, mands were further subdivided according to the kind of response they elicit (Horner, 1968, pp. 120–123):

Movement: Go on outside.
Attention: Hey, mama!
Information: Where is Roddie?
Permission: Can I go outside?
Repetition: Huh?
Confirmation: That's real cute, ain't it?
Continuation: What is it? (*following mand for attention*)

Table 1 shows the percentage of total mands in each functional category when John and Mary are talking with their mother (A) or with other children (B). As Horner points out, "The most important functions served by the mands of children as speakers are direct manipulation (mands for movement) and getting attention. These account for a full 65 percent of all manding by the children . . . ." (Horner, 1968, p. 147). But their distribution indicates an audience-specific pattern.

Table 1 **Percentage of Total Mands Represented by Each Functional Class when the Child Is Talking to (A) His Mother and (B) Other Children**

Mands for	Movement	Attention	Information	Permission	Repetition	Confirmation	Continuation
(A) Child and Mother							
JOHN							
As speaker	25.1	34.2	32.2	6.3	—	1.4	0.7
As addressee of Mother	52.6	3.8	26.6	—	0.6	9.2	7.1
MARY							
As speaker	20.3	56.9	4.9	8.1	6.5	2.4	—
As addressee of Mother	63.1	4.5	18.9	—	6.3	7.2	—
(B) Child and Other Children							
JOHN							
As speaker	51.7	23.3	17.2	5.2	0.9	0.9	0.9
As addressee of small children	36.0	20.3	42.2	—	—	—	1.6
MARY							
As speaker	33.7	30.3	9.1	9.1	12.9	0.9	0.5
As addressee of small children	43.9	14.6	19.9	7.8	3.5	8.4	1.7

Source: Horner (1968).

Looking only at Table 1, we see that both John and Mary ask for attention and permission from their mothers more than their mothers ask for attention or permission from the children. This difference reaches a total absence of requests for permission from mothers to children. The mothers, by contrast, make greater demands for movement than do the children. Comparing sections A and B of Table 1, we see that both John and Mary make more requests for the attention of their mothers than of other children, but they make more requests for the movement of other children. What is reflected here is the age-appropriate behavior of mothers and children, and the greater equality of relations among peers. There are no striking commonalities in the behavior of the two children shown in section B alone, which suggests that role-appropriate behavior is more standardized between children and adults than within the peer group. In the latter context, individual differences seem to be more important. Note also that—unlike the common age-appropriate patterns for manding movements, attention, and permission—manding for information varies even in this group of two.

In two important ways, learning this sociolinguistic aspect of communicative competence is similar to learning the more grammatical aspects described in Chapters 3 to 6. First, with question functions as with question forms, there are commonalities across children because they are children, and there are individual differences too. Second, as Horner points out, the age-appropriate behavior that both John and Mary had learned by the age of three years cannot have been learned by imitation because the patterns of mother and child are not the same. These patterns are also evidently not learned by explicit instruction; of the seven examples of "corrective feedback" listed by Horner, none is relevant here.

COMMUNICATION IN THE CLASSROOM

With regard to education and children, the goal of an integrated theory of sociolinguistic description would be to guide accounts of the range of settings, function, and means, and their inter-relationships, acquired by the children. Of these the school setting would be one, but not the only one; and the major purpose would be to place the school setting in the context of other settings, so as to delineate the true communicative abilities of the children and to show the extent to which the performance in school settings was not a direct disclosure of their abilities, but a product of interference between the system that they bring and the system that confronts them; or a setting simply irrelevant to the direction their abilities and competence otherwise took. In part the problem is one of conflict of values and of perceived interests. [prepublication version of Hymes, 1971.]

Much that has been said in previous sections of this book can be applied to children's speech in the special setting of the classroom. Both degree of personal involvement in the topic of discussion and role relationships among the participants are critical variables in school curriculum and organization. And the aspects of tests discussed in the Appendix apply to the mini-tests that are administered throughout the school day as teachers question children about what they have learned.

All these factors are likely to influence most adversely the classroom speech of children from powerless minorities in our society who attend schools with the most irrelevant curriculum and adults in the most authoritarian roles. Houston (1970) is undoubtedly right in arguing that many descriptions of LC Black children's verbal inadequacies are based on what she calls their "school register." Whereas Weeks (1970) limited the term "register" to prosodic features of stress and intonation, Houston includes clusters of other features that occur and shift together. Speaking specifically of Black children in rural northern Florida, she writes—

> . . . children studied had at least two distinct registers, termed by us the School register and the Nonschool register, because the first appeared primarily in school settings and with teachers and the second in other settings. However, the School register also was used with all persons perceived by the children as in authority over them or studying them in any way . . . and in formal and constrained situations. . . . characteristics of the School register include most of the observations given above [in a review of the literature on disadvantaged children's speech] as indications of disadvantaged non-fluency, notably foreshortened utterances, simplified syntax, and phonological hypercorrection. It should be added that the content expressed in this register tends to be rather limited and nonrevelatory of the children's attitudes, feelings and ideas. (Houston, 1970, pp. 952–953.)

In addition to general factors that affect all children who attend dis-advantaged schools, there may be specific cultural sources of mismatch between what teachers expect and what children have learned. Research in American Indian communities (Cazden and John, 1971) offers many examples. For example, a comment often made about Indian children is that they behave in ways we label as "shy": They withdraw from participa-tion and seem especially reluctant to talk. Such behavior in the Anglo culture would invoke explanations of retarded language development or psychological problems in interpersonal relationships. Such behavior in Indian children may be explained by cultural influences on communica-tive competence.

There are cultural influences on what children have learned about the amount and kind of appropriate conversation. For example, the Apache Indians consider too much talking as foolishness. In the Sunrise Dance, the Apache coming-of-age ceremony for girls, the young girl lies down and her grandmother places her hand on the girl's mouth to signify that she should not be a talkative woman.

There are also cultural influences on listening behavior. The child may attend in ways normal for his culture but misunderstood by the teacher. Hall describes Navajo listening behavior, at least in the 1930s:

> Unlike middle-class whites, the direct open-faced look in the eyes was avoided by Navajos. In fact, Navajos froze up when looked at directly. Even when shaking hands they held one in the peripheral field of the eyes. . . . By now some of my readers are undoubtedly thinking what it must have been like to be a small Navajo child in schools taught by whites where many teachers were frustrated by behavior they couldn't understand. . . . The teacher would raise his voice, while looking directly at the child hanging his head. "What's the matter? Can't you talk? Don't you even know your own name?" (Hall, 1969, p. 379.)

Finally, there are cultural differences in preferred ways of learning: for example, learning by looking and learning through language. Werner suggests a more general contrast between contemplation in Navajo learning and empiricism in Anglo learning:

> The Navajo approach . . . stresses the acquisition of competence as a pre-requisite for performance. Navajos seem to be unprepared or ill at ease if pushed into early performance without sufficient thought or the acquisition of mental competence preceding the actual physical activity. . . . This philosophy of learning can be summed up in the following "artificial" proverb: "If at first you don't think, and think again, don't bother trying."
>
> The Anglo approach stresses performance as a prerequisite for the acquisition of competence. . . . The comprehension of the principles is perceived as a corollary and automatic by-product of the ability to perform. This philosophy of learning can be summed up in the well-known proverb: "If at first you don't succeed, try, try again." (Werner, 1968, pp. 1–2.)

Werner found support for this contrast from a contrastive analysis of the meaning of *thought, instruction*, and *learning* in Navajo and English, and from an analysis of Navajo legends. (Cazden and John, 1971.)

Since the above report was written, there has been more research on this question, some reported in Cazden, John, and Hymes (in press). S. Phillips (in press) studied the speech patterns of children on the Warm Springs Indian Reservation in Oregon, both in and out of the classroom. Phillips refers to structural arrangements of interaction as "participant structures." In the public school classrooms on the Warm Springs reservation, teachers use four participant structures:

> In the first type of participant structure the teacher interacts with all of the students. . . . And it is always the teacher who determines whether she talks to one or to all, receives responses individually or in chorus, and voluntarily or without choice. In a second type of participant structure, the teacher interacts with only some of the students in the class at once, as in reading groups. In such contexts, participation is usually mandatory rather than voluntary, individual rather than chorus, and each student is expected

to participate or perform verbally, for the main purpose of such smaller groups is to provide the teacher with the opportunity to assess the knowledge acquired by each individual student. . . .

A third participant structure consists of all students working independently at their desks, but with the teacher explicitly available for student-initiated verbal interaction, in which the child indicates he wants to communicate with the teacher by raising his hand, or by approaching the teacher at her desk. In either case, the interaction between student and teacher is not witnessed by the other students in that they do not hear what is said.

A fourth participant structure, and one which occurs infrequently in the upper primary grades, and rarely, if ever, in the lower grades, consists of the students being divided into small groups which they run themselves, though always with the distant supervision of the teacher, and usually for the purpose of so-called "group projects." (S. Phillips, in press.)

By contrast with non-Indian children, Phillips found the Indian children reluctant to participate in the first two structures, which are the most frequent in most classrooms, but more talkative than non-Indian children in the last two contexts (a disordinal interaction in the terms used above).

Phillips explains these cultural differences as caused by sociolinguistic interference between participant structures in the school and in the children's home and community. In their homes, Indian children learn by a combination of "observation, which of course includes listening; supervised participation; and private self-initiated self-testing."

This process of Indian acquisition of competence may help to explain, in part, Indian children's reluctance to speak in front of their classmates. In the classroom, the process of acquisition of knowledge and demonstration of knowledge are collapsed into the simple act of answering questions or reciting when called upon to do so by the teacher, particularly in the lower grades. (S. Phillips, in press.)

Outside the home, in the reservation communities, the participant structure of all social (speech) events is also very different from that in school.

In summary, the Indian social activities to which children are early exposed outside the home generally have the following properties: 1) They are community-wide, in the sense that they are open to all Warm Springs Indians; 2) there is no single individual directing and controlling all activity, and to the extent that there are "leaders," their leadership is based on the choice to follow which is made by each person; 3) participation in some form is accessible to everyone who attends. No one need be exclusively an observer or audience, and there is consequently no sharp distinction between audience and performer. And each individual chooses for himself the degree of his participation during the activity. (S. Phillips, in press.)

With this degree of sociolinguistic interference, alienation instead of education will result. But with participant structures, as with the communication skills discussed in the preceding section, we do not yet know how best to use children's indigenous strengths in the classroom if our goal is to encourage them to retain their own culture while at the same time teaching them to function in a wider social context when and if they wish to do so.

9

The Roles of Language in Cognition

In a book on child language and education, a chapter on the roles of language in cognition should be the longest and most important. Everything discussed up to this point could be considered necessary preliminaries to the main show—how children use language in their own thinking. After all, thinking is what education is, or should be, all about. Sad to say, this chapter will be more modest because in this area we know least, not most, and suggestions for education must therefore be limited to good hunches based on circumstantial evidence at best. Following some introductory remarks about cognition, an overview of research findings in the field will be given, after which four important and unresolved controversies will be discussed.

"Cognition refers to all the processes by which sensory input is transformed, reduced, elaborated, stored, recovered, and used" (Neisser, 1967, p. 4). Cognitive structures supply the background ingredients for these processes:

> When we first perceive or imagine something, the process of construction is not limited to the object itself. We generally build (or rebuild) a spatial, temporal, and conceptual framework as well. . . . In general, a cognitive structure may be defined as a nonspecific but organized representation of prior experiences. . . . The cognitive approach to memory and thought emphasizes that recall and problem-solving are constructive acts, based on information remaining from earlier acts. That information is, in turn, organized according to the structure of those earlier acts, though its utilization depends also on present circumstances and present constructive skills. (Neisser, 1967, pp. 286, 287, 292.)

Bruner (1957) calls these cognitive structures "coding systems" because they represent experience in the mind, in some transformed or coded form.

Cognitive structures are wholly unobservable and are the hypothetical constructions of psychologists who infer their presence in the mind from what people (including themselves) do and report, or from the programs that must be written so that computers can simulate human intelligence (for example, see Simon and Newell, 1970). In talking about cognitive structures, we give them a reality that cannot yet be substantiated (literally) in any particular form. But because of their importance in our mental life, and therefore in education, we have to try.

Some cognitive structures have a verbal form, or cognitive structures sometimes take a verbal form—it is hard to know which way to state the importance of language. This chapter will return to the question of alternatives to words. But first consider some of the roles that language does play.

The use of language as a cognitive tool for intraindividual communication places its own demands on some special set of inner resources. Jensen sees it as depending on the existence within the individual of a hierarchical verbal network:

> . . . which environmental stimuli, both verbal and nonverbal, enter (into) and ramify. . . . A great deal of what we think of as intelligence, or as verbal ability, or learning ability, can be thought of in terms of the extensiveness and complexity of this verbal network and of the strength of the interconnections between its elements. (Jensen, 1968, pp. 125–126.)

In any network, there are at least two variables: the repertoire of elements (here, words and grammatical patterns) and the quality (which could be further subdivided at least into complexity and strength) of their connections. A repertoire can be defined by a list and is synonymous with the number of elements in the network. But network has a second attribute that repertoire does not have—the structure or relations of its parts. What do we know about the structure of children's language networks and about how they use them in various cognitive tasks?

Research Findings

To organize research on the roles of language in cognition, it is useful to adapt Jensen's (1968) categories for the various roles that language can play. Let $S, VS, R,$ and VR stand respectively for a nonverbal stimulus, a verbal stimulus, a nonverbal response, and a verbal response. Capital letters refer to behavior of the child, small letters refer to the behavior of some other object or person. If the letter V is dotted ($\dot{V}$) rather than solid (V), the verbal response is silent, or covert. Parentheses enclose alternatives. For example, S–($V,\dot{V}$) refers to the simple labeling by the child (spoken or silent) of nonverbal stimuli like "milk" or "cookie."

Relationships among these stimuli and responses include the following:

vs–VR   Word associations.

vs– R–VR   The role of silent rehearsals in serial recall, of associative
$\dot{V}$ "clustering" (or categorizing) in free recall, and "mental elaboration" in paired associative learning.

(vs, VS, S)–R   Use of the speech of another person or oneself as an
$\vee$ instruction to direct attention or guide behavior.

These roles of language in cognition—associations, mental elaboration, and
instructions—become headings for the three sections that follow. As in the
rest of the book, no attempt is made here to provide a complete research
review. Only representative research will be described. Soviet research is
included at several points because it is especially important in this field.

WORD ASSOCIATIONS: vs–VR

Related to word meanings, or semantic markers, are the associations
among words in our verbal network. While these associative links may play
little role in the acquisition or use of language, they can reveal properties
of underlying relationships. Recall the examples of associative differences
in word meanings reported in Chapter 4. See Clark (1970) for a general
discussion of word associations in terms of syntactic and semantic features.

In general, associations change with age along three dimensions: first,
from associations based on sounds, such as *stick-lick,* to association based
on meaning, such as *stick-wood*; second, from syntagmatic associations between words that follow each other in a sentence, such as *deep-hole,* to
paradigmatic associations between words that can replace each other, such
as *deep-shallow*; third, from more idiosyncratic responses to greater com-
monality among children. The developmental trend toward greater com-
monality may be a function of the shift toward paradigmatic associations,
particularly between opposites, and also of a growing attention to what the
experimenter expects.

> In such experiments, the subject is generally instructed to avoid any pur-
> poseful or directed thinking, so that a relatively unclouded view of the
> organization of memory may be obtained. However, some caution should
> be exercised in the use of the method, for this is a difficult instruction to
> follow. Many people have distinct notions about the kind of responses ex-
> pected of them in such tasks, and behave accordingly. Like other perform-
> ances, word-association depends not only on the organization of memory
> but on what the subject is trying to achieve. (Neisser, 1967, p. 289.)

Differences between ethnic or social-class groups, as between ages, may
depend on either differences in the organization of the child's language
network, or differences in how he interprets the experimental task.

A technique used in the Soviet Union for studying word associations is
less under conscious control by the subject and may thereby yield more un-
biased results. The subject is conditioned to make a particular response—
such as salivation or even blood vessel dilation—to one word, and then
is presented with other words while the degree of response generalization
or transfer is measured. The developmental shift from sound to meaning
has been replicated in these experiments. Furthermore, developmentally,

earlier associations evidently remain and can be re-elicited in adulthood under the influence of drugs. For example, adults normally generalized a conditioned response from *doktor* (doctor) to synonyms *vrach* or *lekar*; but under drugs, they will react to *diktor*, which means announcer. Luria concludes that "an entire complex of relations is hidden behind each word, but that in the normal state more elementary and less substantial vocal connections are suppressed by semantic conventions" (Luria, 1969, p. 137).

Soviet research using this conditioning procedure has also uncovered interesting details of associative structure. For example, conditioning to *violin* produces a response to *cello* and *viola* but not to *harp* (Luria and Vinogradova, 1959). This technique is one way to verify the psychological reality of the analysis of semantic structure into component features. The results for *cello* suggest that associative meanings depend on the effects of experience as much as, or more than, on formal relationships. Or perhaps one should say that the formal relationships, such as the categorization of sound production by bowing or plucking, enter into our mental organization only if they affect, as an intermediary step, the categorizations and contingencies of actual experience. Violins, cellos, violas, and harps all produce sounds in the same way, but we think of, and see, and hear the first three as members of the string section of an orchestra, whereas harps are visually and auditorially separate.

Entwisle (1966) believed that the range of a child's associations for a word and thereby—in a sense—its meaningfulness to him is important in reading comprehension. She developed a game called "giant steps" in which children take turns supplying alternatives for words in sentences such as "But he could not *escape*." Third graders who had played the game improved more than a control group in both number and meaningful quality to both game (*escape*) and nongame (*expect*) words. This suggests that part of the game's effect is to make more accessible the associations the child already in some sense knows (Entwisle, 1970).

MENTAL ELABORATION: vs–VR–VR

Some cognitive tasks are made easier if the subject silently repeats or in some way mentally elaborates the verbal stimulus before responding. Examples include experiments in serial recall, associative clustering, and paired associative learning.

Serial Recall

The simplest covert use of language is simply to verbally rehearse a list to oneself. Flavell, Beach, and Chinsky (1966) studied spontaneous verbal rehearsal in a memory task: The experimenter pointed to a series of pictures of readily nameable objects on a display board, and the subject —either immediately or after a 15-second delay—had to point to the same objects in the same order. A trained observer lip-read and recorded whatever semiovert verbal behavior the subject engaged in. The percentage of subjects showing such verbalization increased from very few in kindergarten, to about half in second grade, to nearly all in fifth grade. There was evidence among the second-graders of a relation between presence of verbalization and correct recall. In further research, Flavell hopes to find out whether spontaneous verbalization is a stable individual characteristic across various memory tasks, what are the linguistic, cognitive, and personality correlates of such verbalization, and if its development can be accelerated by training.

Associative Clustering

In some free-recall memory experiments, the experimenter reads a list of words aloud to the subject, either a random assortment or a list deliberately picked from a few preselected categories such as foods or animals. The child is asked to remember as many words as he can, and his performance is then scored for number remembered or for the degree of "associative clustering" in the order in which the words are remembered. Jensen (1969) reports that whereas there are no social-class differences in elementary school children's recall of random lists, the picture changes when categorized lists are used:

> This is shown in an experiment from our laboratory by Glasman (1968). (In this study SES and race are confounded, since the low SES group were Negro children and the middle SES group were white.) Again, 20 familiar objects are presented, but this time the objects are selected so that they can be classified into one of four categories, *animals, furniture, clothing*, or *foods*. There are five items in each of the four categories, but all 20 items are presented in a random order on each trial. Under this condition a large social class difference shows up: the low SES children perform only slightly better on the average than they did on the uncategorized objects, while the middle SES children show a great improvement in performance which puts their scores about one standard deviation above the low SES children. Furthermore, there is much greater evidence of "clustering" the items in free recall for the middle SES than for the low SES children. That is, the middle-class children rearrange the input in such a way that the order of output in recall corresponds to the categories to which the objects may be assigned. The low SES children show less clustering in this fashion, although many show rather idiosyncratic pair-wise "clusters" that persist from trial to trial. There is a high correlation between the strength of the clustering tendency and the amount of recall. Also, clustering tendency is strongly related to age. Kindergarteners, for example, show little difference between recall of categorized and uncategorized lists, and at this age SES differences in performance are nil. By fourth or fifth grade, however, the SES differences in clustering tendency are great, with a correspondingly large difference in ability to recall categorized lists. (Jensen, 1969, p. 113.)

In schematic graph form, Glasman's results would look like Figure 1.

Figure 1 **Clustering   Tendencies   as   Demonstrated   by   Glasman's Experiments.**

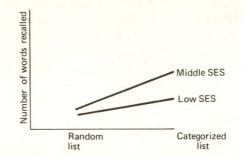

In a related experiment, Flavell and his colleagues (Moely et al., 1969) gave children from kindergarten and grades 1, 3, and 5 pictures of objects from four categories (animals, furniture, vehicles, and clothing) which they were free to arrange and rearrange and then asked to recall. There was a sharp rise between grades 3 and 5 in spontaneous categorization and in recall scores. When instructed to arrange the pictures into categories, the young children's scores also increased. Moely and his associates comment:

> Both research findings and common sense lead one to suppose, for instance, that if a child of any age knows the name of an object he is instructed to remember, and if it also occurs to him to rehearse that name a number of times prior to a recall test, then that rehearsal is very likely to help him remember the object. The problematical element in such a situation is precisely whether it will occur to him to rehearse, or for such situations generally perhaps, to engage in any planful symbolic activity that is oriented towards and adapted to subsequent goal responses.
>
> There nonetheless remain substantial problems in elucidating the factors responsible for the frequent gap between basic capacity and spontaneous production—in the above example, between knowing a stimulus label and deliberately rehearsing it in preparation for later recall. It can be supposed that there are at least two general factors which must be considered (Flavell and Wohlwill, 1969). One has directly to do with the basic capacity itself. There are surely "degrees" of possession here, vaguely describable in terms of stability, generalizability, etc., and the "degree" to which the child possesses the capacity in question must somehow help determine whether or not he will spontaneously invoke it as a mediator on appropriate occasions. The authors rather suspect, in fact, that superficial descriptive concepts like "production deficiency" (and "mediation deficiency") will simply be retired from service once more precise ways of characterizing and diagnosing the cognitive status, within the child, of the intellectual instruments he "in some sense" possesses have been found. The second factor is the task situation. It includes the various features and forces in the problem setting which, in interaction with the first factor, may facilitate or impede the passage from latent capacity to manifest production. (Moely et al., 1969, p. 32.)

Paired Associate Learning

Mental elaboration is also helpful in paired associate learning. Here, children are asked to learn to associate two words such as *shoe-clock* or *cow-hat*. After the first presentation of the pairs, the subjects are given the first word of each pair and asked to try to remember the second one. If they can't, they are told the answer and then asked again on the next trial. To help their memory and their performance, children may be instructed to make up sentences connecting the words, and then compared with children without instructions.

In one experiment, Jensen and Rohwer (1965) found that instructions to "mediate" increased effectiveness from kindergarten to sixth grade, but not later—presumably because the older children did it anyway. They noted that the younger children made up syntactically less varied and complex phrases or clauses—such as *the shoe and the clock* (in which the nouns are combined by a conjunction), while older children made up phrases like *The sleeping cow beneath the dirty hat* (in which the nouns are combined in a more distinctive way by a preposition). In another experiment, Rohwer (1966) provided sixth-grade children with verbal contexts for the eight paired associates they were required to learn. The contexts connected the words with either conjunctions, prepositions, or verbs. The largest difference in connective power was between conjunctions on the one hand and prepositions and verbs on the other. In still another experiment, Rohwer and his coworkers (1967) found that third- and sixth-grade children learned paired-associate words more rapidly when they were presented in the form of pictures rather than words. Rohwer concludes—

At this point it is appropriate to note that results such as those just reviewed have two kinds of implication for education. First, they suggest that conditions under which materials are presented for school learning determine the ease with which mastery will be attained. At least with regard to the forms of school learning that conform to the paradigms of discrimination learning, serial learning, and PA [paired-associate] learning, it seems clear that an informed and selective use of pictorial representations and verbal labels and contexts will result in more efficient performance. Second, the results suggest that some school time could be used profitably, especially during the kindergarten and even the pre-kindergarten years, to induce the habits of elaboration in children so that when confronted with unelaborated materials, as is so frequently the case in schooling, these tactics for learning can be voluntarily brought to bear. Clearly, however, there is a major limitation on the results of these studies insofar as their educational relevance is concerned: the extent to which the conclusions generalize to the learning of school subjects is entirely unknown. Additional evaluation of the effects of these variables must be conducted using materials that are like, if not identical with, those used in education. (Rohwer, 1970, p. 1435.)

INSTRUCTIONS (vs, VS, VS)–R

Instructions are words supplied by someone else or by oneself to guide action. They guide by focusing attention on particular aspects of a complex stimuli, or by actually directing behavior. Olson (1970) suggests that instruction is the primary way in which language influences thought—that is, that the influence is more on the listener than on the speaker. I feel from introspection that this contrast is less sharp than Olson suggests, and that a speaker's thought (at least, my own) is frequently clarified and even changed by the act of giving it form in words, whether in conversation or teaching or writing. But the power of instruction in the broad sense of being guided by the words of another is unquestionably important.

Luria (1961) reports an illustrative set of experiments on the redirection of attention. Children between the ages of three and seven years were taught to squeeze a balloon with their right hand for a red circle on a gray ground, and to squeeze with their left hand for a green circle on a yellow ground. If the children were then tested (Figure 2) with a red circle on a yellow ground, the figure was always the decisive element in the composite stimulus and controlled their response.

In order to see how language could be used to change the relative strength of the stimuli, two experiments were conducted. In one experiment by Martsinovskaya, the experimenter simply asked the children to squeeze with their right hand for the yellow ground. In the other experiment by Abramyan, the circles were changed to airplanes and the instructions were translated into thematic terms: "Squeeze the balloon with your right hand for a yellow ground because the plane can fly when the sun is shining and the sky is yellow" (Luria, 1961, p. 6). The difference in results is shown in Figure 3. Whereas only the oldest children, six to seven years old, could respond to Martsinovskaya's instructions, even the youngest could use the broader thematic relations to guide their attention.

In another set of experiments, Luria (1961) studied the development of the child's ability to use speech to direct his own activity. In general, he found a shift from a nonspecific impulsive effect to a more selective semantic effect. A three-year-old could follow directions to press a bulb twice when told to say "tu-tu," but not if told to "squeeze twice each time." Not until the child was 4½ to 5 years old did the meaning of the latter instruc-

Figure 2 **Luria's Experiment on Redirection of Attention.**

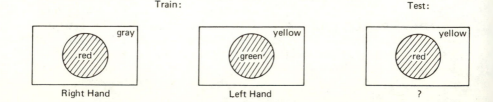

Train: Test:

Right Hand   Left Hand   ?

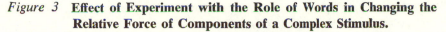

Figure 3   **Effect of Experiment with the Role of Words in Changing the Relative Force of Components of a Complex Stimulus.**

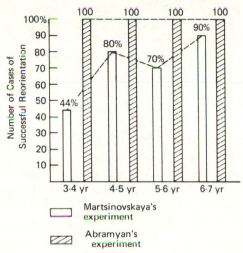

Source   Luria, 1961, p. 24

tion become effective. Attempts by American researchers to replicate these Soviet findings of an impulsive-semantic shift have yielded mixed results. Luria also found a trend from being able to follow instructions of others to being able to give them to oneself, and this has been replicated by others (for example, Denner, 1970). Wozniak (in press) gives a comprehensive review.

Instructions for action are obviously important in education. We need to understand how to give effective instructions to children, and how to help them give instructions to themselves. For example, Lauren Resnick (personal communication) reports that it is much harder for children to count out eight napkins from a larger pile than to count a pile of eight. The first task requires that the child remember the instruction (here verbal rehearsal would probably help), but it also requires that he use that remembered number to guide his actions—to count to eight and then stop. See White (1970) for a discussion of growth in children's ability to give instructions to themselves during the 5–7 age range.

According to Vygotsky, silent, self-directive speech is an internalized version of speech spoken aloud but not intended for social communication. In a series of experiments, Kohlberg, Yaeger, and Hjertholm (1968) verified Vygotsky's assertion that the amount of overt self-directive speech increases with age up to about age six and then declines, presumably because it becomes internalized into silent thought. It also increases with task difficulty: for example, a harder puzzle elicits more self-directive speech from children than an easier one. Some readers may share my experience of subvocalizing when reading an unusually complex passage or when adding an especially long list of numbers.

Educationally, the important question is whether children who do not spontaneously use inner speech to guide their actions can (and should) be trained to do so. Meichenbaum (1971) is one of several to report positive results, but how long the effect of the training lasts we do not yet know.

Controversies

In discussions of the roles of language in cognition, four issues are controversial: How much difference does the presence or absence of language make? Is a person's thought affected by the particular language forms or speech patterns with which he is familiar (L_1 versus L_2)? Which develops first, the nonverbal idea or the words to express it? And what do we know about alternative motoric or visual modes of mental representation?

PRESENCE OR ABSENCE OF LANGUAGE

In the cognitive activity discussed in the preceding section, how much difference would it make in the child's response if that child had no language at all? The weight of the argument would seem to fall heavily on the side of a "big difference" answer, but controversy continues on just which aspects of cognition are most language-dependent.

The question can't be answered by comparing children before and after learning a language because too many other developmental changes occur at the same time. So contrasts between the behavior of hearing and deaf children are made. The two sides of the controversy are represented by Furth (1966), against the critical role of language, and Blank and Bridger (1966), who argue for it.

L_1 VERSUS L_2

Turn now from questions of presence or absence of language to the effect of differences in particular language forms and speech patterns. Here we become involved in the well-argued controversy over the Whorf (1956) hypothesis that language influences our perception of and response to the world. It is not possible to review here the arguments for and against the strong (language determines) or the weak (language predisposes) versions of this hypothesis. Fishman (1970, Section VI) provides an excellent summary. It is sufficient to report the widespread agreement that evidence of differences in language, no matter how extreme, cannot be used both to suggest and to prove differences in feeling, thought, or other nonverbal behavior. The claimed effects of language or speech differences on ways of perceiving or responding must be demonstrated and not merely assumed, and their proof must involve independent measures of linguistic and non-linguistic behavior.

Carroll and Casagrande (1958) did one of the few experiments on the Whorf hypothesis with children. In Navajo verbs of handling, the verb form must be selected according to the shape of the object of the verb. Because of this obligatory categorization of objects, it seemed reasonable that Navajo-speaking children would learn to discriminate form attributes of objects earlier than their English-speaking age-mates. Stimuli for an experiment to test this hypothesis consisted of ten sets of three objects, such as a yellow stick and a blue rope, and then a yellow rope. The child was shown the first two and then asked which was like the third. Subjects were 135 Navajo children from an Arizona reservation, 3 to 10 years old, and three language groups: monolingual in Navajo or Navajo-predominant (59), balanced bilinguals (33), and English-predominant or English monolinguals (43). The hypothesis that the Navajo-dominant children would be more likely than the other Navajo children to select on the basis of form was indeed borne out by the data. But a separate control group of 47 white middle-class children in Boston also tended to group the objects by form, presumably because of previous experience with formboard types of toys.

All the research evidence supports the conclusion that language can be important in influencing the relative strength of stimuli but does not affect perceptual discrimination itself. Carroll suggests that language can be better described as a lattice than as a mold:

> It [the lattice theory] says that language structure is like a lattice or screen through which we see the world of our experience. This lattice, as it were, may obscure little bits of our experience, but it lets through the rest in larger or smaller hunks, perhaps, clarifying some parts, clouding other parts and suggesting a larger pattern for still another. All the while, however, we see the pattern of the whole and are as little bothered by the lattice as if it were a screen installed on our front porch. . . . We are predisposed to notice or pay attention to certain discriminations and neglect others, even though those other discriminations are possible for us to make and are capable of being elevated into full potency under suitable conditions of reinforcement. (Carroll, 1958, p. 33.)

Whorf was interested in the effects on thought of the syntactic structure and words of a particular language. A related version of the same hypothesis is that patterns of speech behavior also have an effect. Hymes suggests that speech patterns are in fact the more fundamental influence: "What chance the language has to make an impress upon individuals and behavior will depend upon the degree and pattern of its admission into communicative events" (Hymes, 1964, p. 20).

Part of Bernstein's theory relates speech patterns to cognitive functioning. In his earlier writings, Bernstein (1961) hypothesized that a child who could use only a restricted code would have a less differentiated perception and conceptualization of his environment. This part of his theory has been especially controversial and without empirical support until his recent work with five- to seven-year-old children. Robinson and Creed (1968) attempted the first direct test by relating language usage in the structured situations described in Chapter 8 to later performance on a discrimination task. They defined elaborated and restricted codes operationally by aspects of language that had been found previously to differentiate between social-class groups, such as number of subordinate clauses and number of modifiers. Subjects were 16 lower-class girls—eight elaborated code users and eight restricted code users. Eighteen months after the collection of speech samples, these children were asked to look at each of four paintings—dock scene, playground, living room, and child feeding a pet—for as long as they wanted. Then, when shown a second painting identical to the first except for some changes of color, position, or other detail, the children were asked first to point to the differences and then to describe them. The researchers predicted that the eight elaborated code users would "(1) study the first picture for a longer time without seeking further instruction; (2) point to more differences; (3) describe these differences more efficiently" (Robinson and Creed, 1968, p. 4). The verbal descriptions were rated 1 if the child mentioned one or both values of the variable (for example, *It's round there* or *That is red and that is green*) and they were rated 0 if the child gave neither.

Robinson and Creed found no significant differences in the time the children spent looking at the pictures. The only result that really upheld the predictions was that, in one comparison, four elaborated code users made significantly fewer pointing errors than four restricted code users. In addition, all eight elaborated code users gave more effective verbalizations than the eight restricted code users, but that could have been expected because similar measures of language were used to select the children and then evaluate their descriptions. Hopefully, this important part of Bernstein's theory can be put to a more adequate test with a larger sample of children.

In interpreting research on the relation of language or speech to cognition, it is important to remember that correlation doesn't prove causation. Differences in both language and in nonverbal behavior can be caused by something else.

WHICH COMES FIRST, IDEA OR WORD?

Woodcock (n.d.) reports examples of "pre-forms" in the speech of two-year-olds, in which the ideas expressed by *why*, *because*, and *if* are present even though the words themselves are missing.

Conditionality:
> Turn on dat, dat be hot.
> You eat your dinner, you have banana.

Causality:
> Janet don't need a coat on. Janet's too warm a coat.
> Don't sit on 'at radiator—very hot.
> I can't come now, I dus' dettin' dwessed.

Conversely, linguistic forms can be spoken with immature meaning, as when children use *because* and *if* without full understanding of causal or conditional relationships.

The controversy over which comes first—idea or word—has a long and honorable history. See Blumenthal (1970) for the historical background. Vygotsky and Piaget represent the contrasting points of view.

Vygotsky

To Vygotsky, thought and speech have separate roots until "at about the age of two the curves of development of thought and speech, till then separate, meet and join to initiate a new form of behavior" (Vygotsky, 1962, p. 43).

> The child's intellectual growth is contingent on his mastering the social means of thought, that is, language. . . .

> All the higher psychic functions are mediated processes, and signs are the basic means used to master and direct them. The mediating sign is incorporated in their structure as an indispensable, indeed the central, part of the total process. In concept formation, that sign is the *word*, which at first plays the role of means in forming a concept and later becomes its symbol. (Vygotsky, 1962, pp. 51, 56.)

Consider a concept like *brother*. It is hard to imagine how such a relational concept could be abstracted from the child's experience without a word to bind together the many instances the child encounters—his own brother, his being a brother to his sister, the brother of his father, etc. And metaphorical extensions like "all men are brothers" or "brothers under the skin" would be impossible. To Vygotsky, the word first functions as an invitation to a concept, calling attention to yet another instance. Later the word comes to symbolize the concept itself as a condensation of the child's accumulating experience.

If one has no name for a phenomenon, one may not notice it. This is as true for adults as for children, as a personal experience reminded me. A large part of learning to handle a canoe in white water is learning to read the river to tell where the dangerous rocks and safe channels are. A Maine guide once warned me to avoid the "pillows." He meant smooth, flat patches of water that signaled a rock some unknown distance beneath the surface.

Instantly, by his metaphorical application of a familiar name, I became aware of previously undifferentiated features of the moving water.

Sometimes, such metaphorical extension can transfer meanings that mislead more than they help. When explaining how Christmas tree lights worked in a circuit, a child spoke of "electrical juice." The teacher substituted the term "energy" to free both speaker and audience from the erroneous inference that juice could flow downhill but not up (Brenda Lansdown, personal communication).

To Vygotsky, "brother" is an example of a "spontaneous concept" that is saturated with experience from the very beginning. By contrast, he suggests, scientific concepts like "slavery," "exploitation," or "civil war" are learned first in school through words and then gradually acquire rich meaning, particularly through reading. Spontaneous concepts and scientific concepts thus develop in different directions, the former "upward" from concrete experience and the latter "downward" from a verbal definition. According to Vygotsky, scientific concepts—and by inference school, where they are learned—play a particular role in the child's cognitive development:

> School instruction induces the generalizing kind of perception and thus plays a decisive role in making the child conscious of his own mental process. Scientific concepts, with their hierarchical system of interrelationships, seem to be the medium within which awareness and mastery first develop, to be transferred later to other concepts and other areas of thought. Reflective consciousness comes to the child through the portals of scientific concepts. (Vygotsky, 1962, p. 92.)

Vygotsky's distinction between spontaneous and scientific concepts offers a useful way of conceiving two important and complementary objectives in education. Cole and Bruner (1971) suggest that the "relevant" curriculum is one that starts with events or materials or concepts in which a child spontaneously demonstrates his competence, and then helps him generalize and extend that competence into other areas of performance. That's the direction of spontaneous concepts to scientific concepts, upward from concrete experience. Conversely, scientific concepts, initially taught with a verbal definition, need to be grounded downward to that experience. A six-year-old boy taped by Labov (personal communication) while talking to a rabbit said to the rabbit, "The more he get nervous, the more he die, the more Harold gonna hafta pay the doctor bills." That, in essence, is the concept of correlation. But even graduate students may fail to connect this abstract concept to the everyday relationship expressed in our language by such phrases as "the faster, the better."

Piaget

In contrast to Vygotsky, Piaget and his colleagues in Geneva hold that the child's thought derives from internalized actions. Language is not irrelevant; it "may increase the powers of thought in range and rapidity" by representing a string of actions very rapidly, by liberating thought from immediate space and time, and by representing simultaneously the elements of an organized structure that in action proceeds step by step (Piaget and Inhelder, 1969, p. 86). But basically, the child's use of language is determined by the developmental level of his nonverbal cognitive structures and not the other way around.

The work of Sinclair-de-Zwart (1969; Inhelder et al., 1966) on the relationship between language and conservation is often cited as evidence for this position. The term "conservation" here refers to the fact that number, volume, and weight remain unchanged when the items or substance are distributed into perceptionally different arrangements. Four pennies remain four, whether spaced close together or far apart; one cup of water remains one cup, whether distributed among tall glasses or low saucers; a wad of clay weighs the same in one big ball or three little ones. Sinclair-de-Zwart's research had two phases: first, to explore differences in descriptive language use between children who had or did not have the concept of conservation of liquids; second, to see whether verbal training would accelerate this aspect of cognitive development.

When Sinclair-de-Zwart asked conservers and nonconservers to describe the difference between two pencils (a short, thick one and a long, thin one) or the difference between two dolls (one with four big marbles and one with two small marbles), she found three differences in their speech.

(1) Conservers used relational terms such as *One has more than the other*.

Nonconservers said only *One has got a big bit, the other has a small bit*.

(2) Conservers used more differentiated terms, like *long/short* and *fat/thin*.

Nonconservers were more restricted to the use of *big* and *small* for all differences in size.

(3) Conservers used coordinated descriptions to talk about two dimensions: *He has more marbles but they are smaller*.

Nonconservers tended to mention only one of the dimensional differences: *One has got a lot of marbles and the other only has two*.

Despite these differences, all the children could understand the more differentiated language when given directions by the teacher.

Sinclair-de-Zwart then tried to teach the nonconservers to use the more advanced language. It was easiest to teach them the more differentiated vocabulary items (2, above); comparatives (1, above) were harder; and the coordinated sentence structure (3, above) was hardest. In general, the verbal training did direct the children's attention to pertinent aspects of the problem, such as a higher level of liquid in a narrower glass, but only 10 percent of the children so trained actually achieved conservation. Inhelder and associates conclude:

> Language learning does not provide, in our opinion, a ready-made "lattice" or lens which organizes the child's perceptual world. Rather the lattice is constructed in the process of the development of intelligence, i.e., through the actions of the child on the environment and the interiorization of these actions to form operational structures. (Inhelder et al., 1966, p. 163.)

To ask whether the idea or the word comes first may seem a useless example of the chicken-and-egg game. But, in practical terms, different points of view over the relative importance or optimal timing of verbal and nonverbal experience underlie many controversies about education, particularly in early childhood (See Kohlberg, 1968).

ALTERNATIVE MODES OF REPRESENTATION

Recall the qualification stated at the beginning of this chapter with respect to the relationship between language and cognition: Not all cognitive structures take a verbal form all of the time. Even though this book is about child language and education, the picture of children's cognitive processes must not become distorted by overemphasizing the role of language and ignoring the roles that other modes of representation play.

Alternatives to the verbal mode of representation are usually categorized as either visual or motoric ("enactive," in Bruner's, 1965 terms). Einstein wrote introspectively of fusing all three processes:

> The words or the language, as they are written or spoken, do not seem to play any role in my mechanism of thought. The psychical entities which seem to serve as elements in thought are certain signs and more or less clear images which can be "voluntarily" reproduced and combined.
>
> There is, of course, a certain connection between those elements and relevant logical concepts. It is also clear that the desire to arrive finally at logically connected concepts is the emotional basis of this rather vague play with the above mentioned elements. But taken from a psychological viewpoint, this combinatory play seems to be the essential feature in productive thought—before there is any connection with logical construction in words or other kinds of signs which can be communicated to others.
>
> The above mentioned elements are, in my case, of visual and some of muscular type. Conventional words or other signs have to be sought for laboriously only in a secondary stage, when the mentioned associative play is sufficiently established and can be reproduced at will. (Einstein, 1955, p. 43.)

Einstein spoke of muscular as well as visual elements. Sometimes the two may be related. Flavell and his colleagues (Daehler et al., 1969) conducted an experiment on the use of gestures, rather than words, as an aid to serial recall. Colored lights having distinct spatial locations were illuminated sequentially and subjects were asked to remember the sequence. As the authors suggest, the activity analogous to verbal rehearsal could be either covert "visual gesture" (eye movements) or more overt (manual pointing). Either could contribute to some inner cognitive map.

Nursery school teachers have told me that when a child can't find the piece of a puzzle for a certain shaped hole, it helps if the child runs his fingers around the edge of the empty space. Presumably this contributes to the image in the child's mind, which then guides his search.

Pantomime and sign language as used by the deaf are forms of motoric representation highly developed to serve for communication with others as well as oneself. Do the deaf think in inner signs rather than inner speech?

Four questions about implications for education come to mind: Do children differ in their disposition to use one mode of representation or another? Can we help all children improve their nonverbal as well as their verbal ways of thinking? What is the value of the nonverbal communication used in encounter groups? Is there a general trend, as McLuhan and others claim, toward a more visual culture?

Lesser, Fifer, and Clark (1965) found that Chinese six-year-olds had highest scores on a Spatial-Conceptualization Test in comparison both with other ethnic groups and with their own scores on tests of vocabulary, number, and reasoning. To my knowledge, these particular mental ability tests have not been administered to American Indian children, but there is other evidence (reviewed by Cazden and John, 1971) that children in at least some Indian tribes excel in visual skills. It is not easy to think through the implications of these differences for education. In selecting goals, one has to decide how much education should build on children's strengths and how much it should strengthen children's weaknesses. In selecting means, one has to find ways to maximize ability-instruction interaction. Stodolsky and Lesser (1967) and Farnham-Diggory (1970) discuss these issues.

All children would probably benefit from more help than they usually get in using visual means as an aid to thinking. I found one Soviet suggestion helpful in teaching first-grade arithmetic. According to Slavina (1957) Voya could do simple sums if he had objects to manipulate, but could not do the sums in his head. An intermediate stage was introduced: After manipulating the objects and counting out loud, Voya was asked to do the same operations out loud but without looking at the objects, which were still arrayed before him; that is, he was helped to form a mental schema of visual representation. Only later was he asked to try the completely mental process, using the mental schema with covert responses. One advantage of visual representation is that relationships can be presented simultaneously rather than sequentially. Diagrams are a good example. Children could be encouraged to play with the relationships that particular diagrammatic forms can best express: outlines, Venn diagrams with intersecting circles, matrices, tree diagrams, etc. For further discussion of these important topics of visual thinking and visual education, see Arnheim (1969) and Kepes (1965).

Encounter groups emphasize nonverbal ways of dealing with emotion. As Webb (in press) points out, it is undoubtedly true that language can all too easily provide us with clichés that provide only a "pseudo-accommodation" to new experiences. "One can learn what to say about a new experience rather than how to deal with it" (Webb, in press, p. 13). Encounter groups may successfully use nonverbal activities to break through these clichés, which interfere with true learning. But Webb insists, contrary to many encounter group proponents, that while use of language may be part of the problem, it also retains an indispensable role in the solution:

> The attempts of group practitioners to deal with "body language" or "nonverbal communication" actually represents attempts to re-educate participants in the use of language. Given all its limitations, we are stuck with language as our major means of communication. The number of unambiguous statements that can be made with language far exceeds that possible in any other form of communication, and there is simply no way to get inside the other fellow's skin and feel with him. However, if they are done well, group exercises can become a form of poetry in which new language is continually being created to express more subtle nuances of meaning. (Webb, in press.)

According to Webb, it is the novel experiences that the group provides, and the pressures to talk about them in novel ways, which are conducive to psychological growth—not any nonverbal activity per se. This is an important idea. If it is true, then—as Webb suggests—as a group culture emerges and group activities (no matter how nonverbal) become conventionalized, they will lose their therapeutic value.

Finally, what about "McLuhanism"? The notion that we are shaped by the media through which we communicate can be considered a related version of the Whorf hypothesis. Socrates, in the *Phaedrus*, worried that invention of the alphabet "will create forgetfulness in the learners' souls, because they will not use their memories." True to his prediction, there are reports of superior memory abilities in nonliterate societies. Whether increasing use of television and other nonlinear, visual modes of communication will have any long-term effects on our cognitive abilities remains to be seen.

In the meantime, it is certainly the case that, as with diagrams, television and films can present some ideas more powerfully than any sequence of oral or written words can do. Many visitors to "Expo '67" in Montreal had their first exposure to the provocative juxtaposition of ideas presented on multiple-split screens. Many modern films accomplish the same juxtaposition on a single screen by nonlinear, nonnarrative editing. Animation is another technique for presenting information that is not simply a copy of objects and events in the real world. Chapter 6 included a report of how animation is being used to teach beginning reading.

We will probably all tend to value those modes of representation we use best ourselves. Goodnow (in press) warns against the danger of "building theories that contained a cultural bias towards the value of solutions achieved with 'no hands' and a well-turned phrase." The same danger exists in education. Like psychologists, teachers as an occupational group are self-selected partly on their ability with words. We need, therefore, to free ourselves deliberately from this bias and play with alternatives to words, for our own benefit as well as the children's. But recall Einstein's distinction between combinatory play and some later stage of communication with others. For the analysis and evaluation of ideas, separate from their initial generation, in an increasingly multimedia world we will have more need for language, not less.

10

On Language Education

Eight boys from a working-class community on a hillside near Florence, Italy, have written a remarkable book (*Letter to a Teacher*), attacking an educational system that perpetuates class differences by failing those who need help most. About the goals of education, they write—

> The right goal is to give oneself to others.
>
> In this century, how can you show your love, if not through politics, the unions, the schools? We are the sovereign people. The time for begging is gone; we must make choices—against class distinctions, against hunger, illiteracy, racism and colonial wars.
>
> This is the ultimate goal, which should be remembered from time to time. The immediate one, which must be remembered every minute, is to understand others and to make oneself understood. . . .
>
> We must become amateurs in everything and specialists only in the ability to speak. (Schoolboys of Barbiana, 1970, p. 89.)

How does one teach "the ability to speak"? Or in the terms used in the introductory chapter of this book, how can we improve a student's communicative adequacy?

No complete answer can be provided here. What follow are three notes toward a design for oral language education—how philosophers analyze a human behavior like speaking, the paradoxical role of knowledge in skilled behavior, and whether school should attempt to inculcate norms whereby using particular skills becomes a habit or way of life. In short, from an adaptation of Scheffler's (1960) threefold distinction, these notes are about "learning how," "learning that," and "learning to."

Learning How

The goals of language education are normally stated in behavioral terms. We want students to do certain things with language—comprehend particular materials or speak in certain ways. These behavioral goals can be considered as verbal skills. Discussions of skilled performance by philosophers all include speaking as one example—along with other behaviors as diverse as spelling, playing chess, swimming, bicycling, and playing the piano (Polanyi, 1964; Ryle, 1949; Scheffler, 1965). Scheffler and Polanyi distinguish between two levels of skilled performance—levels in the sense of a set of nested hierarchies in which a skill at one level is a component of a skill at the next level. Scheffler uses the terms "facilities" and "critical skills" to contrast them. Polanyi discusses the same distinction as two kinds of awareness: subsidiary and focal. When hammering in a nail, the nail is the focal object of our attention, while the hammer is the subsidiary instrument of it.

> Subsidiary awareness and focal awareness are mutually exclusive. If a pianist shifts his attention from the piece he is playing to the observation of what he is doing with his fingers while playing it, he gets confused and may have to stop. This happens generally if we switch our focal attention to particulars of which we had previously been aware only in their subsidiary role. . . . This scheme can be easily reformulated and expanded in terms of *meaning*. If we discredit the usefulness of a tool, its meaning as a tool is gone. All particulars become meaningless if we lose sight of the pattern which they jointly constitute.
>
> The most pregnant carriers of meaning are of course the words of a language, and it is interesting to recall that when we use words in speech or writing we are aware of them only in a subsidiary manner. This fact is usually described as the *transparency* of language. . . . (Polanyi, 1964, pp. 56–57.)

Everything said about language and speech in previous chapters justifies applying this distinction between "facility" and "critical skill" here. We can consider knowing how to speak and comprehend sentences as a facility —attended to only in a subsidiary way—as it constitutes a part of or is used in the service of some higher-order unit of behavior that can be called a critical skill and to which we give our focal attention. Examples of critical speech skills include language functions such as complimenting, persuading, giving directions, or arguing.

Curriculum planners have to decide at which level to focus instruction. Should we focus on particular "facilities," or should we undertake to strengthen many facilities simultaneously by setting problems in which they are instrumental to the accomplishment of a particular purpose?

The work of John Mellon (1969) and James Moffett (1968a, 1968b) provide a useful contrast. Mellon devised a curriculum for seventh-grade students in transformational sentence-combining—the use of grammatical options available in English for packing more information into a single sentence. For example, the following sentences in "A" can all be combined into sentence "B" (Mellon, 1969, p. 96):

    A.   A volume of poetry lay unguarded near the library exit.
         The volume was thin.
         The volume was brown.
         The volume was leather-bound.
         The volume was compiled by Dr. Johnson.
         The volume was a rare first edition.
    B.   A thin brown leather-bound volume of poetry compiled by Dr. Johnson,
        a rare first edition, lay unguarded near the library exit.

Moffett, by contrast, conceptualized a curriculum sequence at the level of critical skills on two dimensions of increasing abstraction. The "I-thou" dimension is based on increasing distance between speaker and audience—from reflection to oneself through conversation and written correspondence to publication. The "I-it" dimension is from perception of what *is happening* (drama) through narrating *what happened*, to generalizing about *what happens,* and finally theorizing about *what may happen.* Moffett suggests curriculum activities for narration, for example, which include writing monologs, letters, diaries, autobiographies, the narrative of an observer, biographies, and the combining of these in fiction.

Only Mellon's curriculum has been subject to experimental test, by Mellon himself. His seventh-grade pupils did indeed learn to pack more information into their sentences, and in this sense gained more "syntactic fluency" than a control group. But when compositions of a subset of the students were given to teachers for the kind of stylistic judgments made by the College Entrance Examination Board, the experimental group was not rated more highly than the control group. Even if one questions the basis of the teachers' judgments, one must also consider whether practice at the level of facility does not omit the important question of deciding when using such a facility is advisable on some criterion of functional effectiveness or esthetic taste. Otherwise, as Brown puts it in his introduction to Moffett's book, "A student is likely to learn something more absolute than the teacher intends" (R. Brown, 1968b, p. vii). Even though Moffett's curriculum has not been tested experimentally, I think it is the most interesting curriculum proposal for the language arts, and best carries out the implications of what we know about child language and child speech.

In interesting ways, selection of particular purposes in language use may entail a shift in frequency of certain grammatical constructions. In other words, particular tasks at the level of critical skills require particular behaviors at the level of facility. Moffett speaks of how describing scientific experiments affected children's use of complex sentences:

> While watching some third-graders write down their observations of candle flames—deliberately this time, not merely in note form—I noticed that sentences beginning with if—and when—clauses were appearing frequently on

their papers. Since such a construction is not common in third-grade writing, I became curious and then realized that these introductory subordinate clauses resulted directly from the children's *manipulation of what* they were observing. Thus: "If I place a glass over the candle, the flame goes out." And: "When you throw alum on the candle, the flame turns blue." Here we have a fine example of a physical operation being reflected in a cognitive operation and hence in a linguistic structure. . . . (Moffett, 1968b, p. 180.)

Halliday describes a similar effect from explaining how to play games with intent to teach them to someone else:

> To start with, certain features of sentence structure are associated with the fact that the rules of the game are being explained—high frequence of "ifs" and "whens" and formulations like "it depends on whether," and there are many rather complex sentence structures in this passage which are associated with precisely this field, the explaining of rules and principles. (Halliday, 1965, p. 16.)

One characteristic of critical skills is that the attainment of one's purpose can be evaluated against some kind of functional criterion. In fact, the distinction between facilities and critical skills offers a new opportunity to characterize the nature of feedback in natural conversations. Compare the skills of playing the piano, playing chess, and speaking in terms of the nature of the criterion, or standard, on which feedback can be based. In the case of piano playing, the criterion must be supplied by some internalized auditory model (except for the few times one practices for a teacher). Such an internal model must guide Anthony Weir's bedtime monologs (Weir, 1962) and the covert rehearsals we all engage in while waiting for our turn to speak. But speech is also like chess in being behavior in the context of interaction. It thus shares the sources of feedback of both piano playing and playing chess—models internalized from listening, and the reactions of another person. In the reactions of other people, isn't all feedback at the higher-level units? We say, or hear, "I don't get it" or "Tell me again" or "Touché." We don't say or hear, "That's not a complete sentence" or "What's the referent for that pronoun?" There must be a big difference in effectiveness between feedback against a criterion derived from one's own purpose, and correction about some picayune aspect of behavior of concern only to someone else (like a teacher).

In planning a curriculum to educate "specialists in the ability to speak," can we provide consistent and detailed feedback to the speaker (or writer) to enhance his functional effectiveness? If so, then we can agree with the Duchess who said to Alice in Wonderland, "and the moral of *that* is— 'Take care of the sense, and the sounds will take care of themselves'." Or to paraphrase her advice, "Take care of the functions, and the forms will take care of themselves."

Learning That

In any curriculum aimed at increasing proficiency in skilled performance, what is the role of knowledge? English teachers have traditionally ignored a child's tacit knowledge and taught afresh—as substantive information—a set of prescriptive statements about language. Partly, this was done out of special intent to "correct"—to substitute what *ought* to be said on some criterion, for what *is* said. Partly, it was done out of ignorance that tacit knowledge of language structure already exists in the mind of every school-age speaker. Is anything likely to be gained by a curriculum that aims to make such nonconscious knowledge conscious?

Three linguists, O'Neil (1968), Keyser (1970), and Hale (1970), advocate the study of linguistics by children as an intellectual activity in its own right, as an example of rational inquiry and theory construction in a domain where every student has rich personal data available. After all, our language is as significant a subject for scientific study as are our senses or our digestive system, and is an easier subject because the data are in our own heads. Hale is currently working with native speakers of several American Indian languages to develop their ability to analyze their own language and then to design curriculum materials in linguistics for children in their tribes. Such materials would focus on discovering patterns at the level of "facilities" like phonology and syntax.

Such curriculum efforts are properly labeled "linguistics," the study of language as a science. Whatever the intellectual benefits of that study (and they may be related to "metalinguistic awareness" discussed in previous chapters), it should not be confused with currently fashionable "linguistic approaches" to language education. There is no evidence that learning to be aware of one's tacit grammatical knowledge makes any difference in verbal behavior—oral or written. O'Neil (1968) speaks of the danger of "tying one's tongue and one's pen." Mellon (1969), in a lengthy review of the literature on the teaching of grammar, found no evidence of any enabling effect. Roger Brown, in his introduction to Moffett's theoretical rationale for his language arts curriculum, says—

> By what means can communication skills be taught: I agree with Mr. Moffett that it is extremely improbable that they should be affected at all by instruction in explicit grammar, whether that grammar be traditional or transformational circa 1958, or transformational circa 1965, or on the current transformational frontier. Study of the theory of language is probably completely irrelevant to the development of skill in the use of the language. (R. Brown, 1968b, p. vii.)

An interesting paradox is posed by these assertions. There is general agreement that grammatical performance is based on grammatical knowledge, and simultaneous agreement that explicit teaching of that knowledge has no effect on that performance. However the initial acquisition of that knowledge takes place, teaching any of it explicitly seems to put it in a form unusable to the learner. One reason why language is a special and difficult subject for curriculum planning is that we don't yet understand the relationship between what is in some sense "learned" and what can in some sense be "taught."

Polanyi's discussion of maxims, or rules of art, is helpful:

> Maxims are rules, the correct application of which is part of the art which they govern. The true maxims of golfing or of poetry increase our insight into golfing or poetry and may even give valuable guidance to golfers or poets; but these maxims would instantly condemn themselves to absurdity if they tried to replace the golfer's skill or the poet's art. Maxims cannot be understood, still less applied by anyone not already possessing a good practical knowledge of the art . . . Once we have accepted our commitment to personal knowledge, we can also face up to the fact that there exist rules which are useful only within the operation of our personal knowing, and can realize also how useful they can be as part of such acts. (Polanyi, 1964, p. 31.)

Later, in a discussion of the unspecifiability of the elements of skilled performance, Polyani says—

> If [the performer's own muscular actions which may subserve his purpose] are experienced only subsidiarily, in terms of an achievement to which they contribute, its performance may select from them those which the performer finds helpful, without ever knowing these as they would appear to him when considered in themselves. This is the usual process of unconscious trial and error by which we *feel our way* to success and may continue to improve on our success without specifiably knowing how we do it. . . . All these curious properties and implications of personal knowledge go back to what I have previously described as its logical unspecifiability; that is to the disorganizing effect caused by switching our attention to the parts of the whole. We can now appreciate this effect too in dynamic terms.
>
> Since we originally gained control over the parts in question in terms of their contribution to a reasonable result, they have never been known and still less willed in themselves, and therefore to transpose a significant whole into the terms of its constituent elements is to transpose it into terms deprived of any purpose or meaning. Such dismemberment leaves us with the bare relatively objective facts, which had formed the clues for a supervening personal fact. It is a relatively destructive analysis of personal knowledge in terms of the underlying relatively objective knowledge. (Polanyi, 1964, pp. 62–63.)

This "destructive analysis" is probably what O'Neil meant when he spoke of tying one's tongue and one's pen.

If we accept Polanyi's view, it does not follow that nothing can be done to teach maxims of the art of effective communication, but only that the maxims selected for curriculum inclusion should be at the level of critical skills—questions of style as related to functional effectiveness—in referential communication, logical argument, etc.

It may be argued that these are matters of style to which English teachers have always given some consideration: unambiguous reference for pronouns, selection of coordinating and subordinating pronouns to convey differentiated relationships, or the organization of sentences in a paragraph. But it is all too easy to ignore the curriculum implications of Polanyi's insistence on intentionality in providing the only context in which maxims can be incorporated into personal knowledge and thereby assimilated into skilled performance. Neither practice for practice's sake, nor maxims for maxims' sake, will suffice. Both have to serve a personal purpose, an intentionality that alone provides the personal meaning which binds the parts into the whole. See Bruner (1970) for further discussion of the role of intentionality in behavior.

As a context for assimilating maxims, written language may offer some advantages. Tying one's pen is quite different from tying one's tongue. While writing, one can stop, consider, and revise without annoyance to others or embarrassment to oneself. Furthermore, writing is available for overt manipulation and explicit evaluation, not only by one person, but also by a group. *Letter to a Teacher* was written by eight students at the school in Barbiana, working collectively. Moffett emphasized the importance of students speaking and writing not just for the teacher, but for their peers as well. The students of Barbiana engaged in collaborative effort in even more of the creative and critical process:

This is the way we do it:

To start with, each of us keeps a notebook in his pocket. Every time an idea comes up, we make a note of it. Each idea on a separate sheet, on one side of the page.

Then one day we gather together all the sheets of paper and spread them on a big table. We look through them, one by one, to get rid of duplicates. Next, we make separate piles of the sheets that are related, and these will make up the chapters. Every chapter is subdivided into little piles, and they will become paragraphs.

At this point we try to give a name to each paragraph. If we can't it means either that the paragraph has no content or that too many things are squeezed into it. Some paragraphs disappear. Some are broken up.

While we name the paragraphs we discuss the logical order for them until an outline is born. With the outline set, we reorganize all the piles to follow its pattern.

We take the first pile, spread the sheets on the table and we find the sequence for them. And so we begin to put down a first draft of the text.

We mimeograph that part so we each can have a copy in front of us. Then, scissors, paste, and colored pencils. We throw everything back up into the air. New sheets are added. We mimeograph again.

A race begins now for all of us to find any word that can be crossed out, any excess adjectives, repetitions, lines, difficult words, overly long sentences, and any two concepts that are forced into one sentence.

We call in one outsider after another. We prefer that they have not had too much school. We ask them to read aloud. And we watch to see if they have understood what we meant to say.

We accept their suggestions if they clarify the text. We reject any suggestions made in the name of caution.

Having done all this hard work and having followed these rules that anyone could use, we often come across an intellectual idiot who announces, "This letter has a remarkable personal style." (Schoolboys of Barbiana, 1970, pp. 120–122.)

One kind of "learning that" more open to direct, explicit assistance is knowledge of word meanings, as argued in Chapter 6. Our mental dictionary catalogs more than our knowledge of language; it catalogs our personal knowledge of the world. We should incite children to delight in the exploration of word meanings throughout the school day, not try to teach them in some pallid context labeled "language arts." That schools differ in their success here is shown in Coleman's (1966) survey of equality of educational opportunity. Coleman found that vocabulary tests, which he initially considered ability tests, were more influenced by school differences like reading or arithmetic. He suggests an explanation for this surprising result:

What is the explanation for the fact that the ability test scores show more school-to-school variation, and appear to be more affected by differences in school characteristics than achievement test scores? The answer seems to lie in the fact that achievement tests cover material that is nearly the same in all school curriculums, toward which all schools teach alike, while the ability tests [namely, vocabulary] cover material that the school teaches more incidentally, and thus with more differential success. (Coleman, 1966, p. 294.)

Learning To

Is the job of education to teach skills or is it also to inculcate the norms that control behavior so that the exercise of a skill becomes a habit, propensity, consistent pattern of behavior? If we agree with Scheffler that "teaching is *not* just deliberate equipping" (1960, p. 99), then we must be concerned with the values and motivation that guide action.

One way to think about this problem is in terms of sources of reinforcement. Chapter 6 argued that reinforcement seems impotent in affecting the child's learning of grammatical rules. But reinforcement can, and probably does, affect the frequency with which language, once learned, is activated in actual verbal behavior. In other words, reinforcement for particular speech behaviors may get built into the sociolinguistic rules that govern

when and how that behavior is inhibited, reactivated, or changed. Mc-
Clellan—like Sheffler and Polanyi, a philosopher—discusses the learning-
performance distinction as the learning of different levels of rules:

> Rules come not only in different kinds, i.e., apply to different classes of
> events—horse judging, figure skating, etc.—but also in different grades or
> orders. . . . I suspect that further analysis would reveal sharp differences in
> the sense of "teach" and "learn" appropriate to different orders or grades
> of rules. . . . It would seem that if one learns the rules of, say, the judging
> of horses, one is still not prepared to face the world as a judge of horses,
> for one must learn a set of further rules governing when and how to apply
> the rules of judging horses. . . . One learns a rule, or one follows a rule.
> But learning to follow a rule in Green's sense, i.e., with discrimination,
> acumen, and freedom, is a more complex affair, governed by higher order
> rules which are structural to the whole enterprise of life. (McClellan, 1965,
> p. 201.)

The sociolinguistic interference on the Warm Springs reservation, described
in Chapter 8, is one example of conflict between "higher-order" rules of
language use.

Havighurst suggests a threefold distinction between sources of reinforcement, depending on whether the subjective experience of the learner is
affected via his id, superego, or ego. Reinforcement via the id would include,
according to Havighurst, what Herbert Kohl (1967) did with his *36
Children*. Kohl was able

> . . . to get the id behind their learning experience, that is, to give their
> "natural drive to learn," their "native curiosity," free play, and to count
> on their learning "creatively" in this way throughout their school ex-
> perience. (Havighurst, 1970, p. 319.)

Kohl's sixth-grade Harlem children had remarkable experiences with
language. For instance, starting from a question about the meaning of
psyche when one child cursed another by saying *What's the matter, psyches,
going to pieces again?*, the class went on to "the study of language and
myth, of the origins and history of words, of their changing uses and
functions in the human life" (Kohl, 1967, pp. 23–24). And all for the
excitement of learning for its own sake. Perhaps only the unusual teacher
can do as much.

Reinforcement via the id would also include playing on the "language
jungle gym" in philosopher Thomas Green's play school:

> Language, too, has its structure, its logical operators, its functors and
> modals, its peculiar metaphors. This is no less true of the "language of the
> street"; its structure, too, is already there. What is often lacking in the school,
> however, is the recognition that language can be played with, modified and
> enjoyed. This sense of enjoyment and play in the use of language becomes
> increasingly difficult to develop, in proportion as the function of the school

becomes more heavily laden with the necessity of certifying achievement in a particular standard of linguistic usage. The focus must then fall on the outcome—standard good usage—rather than on the enjoyment of the language. While the ultimate goal of teaching might be viewed as the attainment of a certain level of skill, the immediate function of learning language is to introduce the child to the structure and properties of language so that he can enter it as something to enjoy. It is to help him to become more self-conscious in the management of a skill that he has to some degree already acquired. Learning, understood in this way, has its own immediate motivation and it cannot be understood or controlled by the need to attain some standard of certification. The value of teaching and of learning, in this view, is like the value of play; it is intrinsic and immediate and directly related to the characteristics of leisure. (Green, 1968, p. 15.)

It is interesting to note that Green agrees with arguments presented in Chapter 7 against spending school time on teaching Standard English, but for him the significant reason is that such teaching detracts from the enjoyment of language for its own sake.

Havighurst questions whether a teacher can depend on the id as a source of reinforcement for all necessary school learnings. He suggests supplementing the id with the superego, by praise and perhaps material rewards, and the ego "by putting order and consistency into the school situation so that the child can learn how to control his environment on the basis of the reality principle" (Havighurst, 1970, p. 322).

Risley and his associates at the University of Kansas have taught particular speech behaviors via the superego. They have used reinforcement—in the form of teacher attention, M&M's, or access to materials—"to teach children to talk more frequently, to talk only on some occasions and not to talk on others, to use appropriate social speech, to narrate longer and more complex accounts, to readily match what another person had said or done" (Risley, Reynolds, and Hart, in press); and to use more nouns, adjective-noun combinations, or compound sentences (Hart and Risley, in press). Can these children be said to have acquired the norms of behaving in these ways? It doesn't seem so, for two reasons: First, the behavior is only maintained under the effect of the reinforcement; when the reinforcement is removed, behavior patterns revert toward the pre-reinforcement level. Second, the reinforcement works in a highly specific way. When use of nouns is reinforced, use of adjectives is not affected. While this specificity of the effect attests to the impressive operation of the reinforcement technique (Hart and Risley, in press, p. 31), it raises questions about its more general educational significance.

The facilities-critical skills contrast may be helpful here. Risley and his colleagues reinforced particular facilities—like nouns or compound sentences. Can we provide reinforcement instead for particular critical skills? Life in school could be arranged to make this possible. Labov (personal communication) described the demands made on a morning kindergarten class which had to communicate explicitly, via dictated messages, with the afternoon class (which they never saw) about the details of caring for a rabbit both groups shared. Children of all ages can hypothesize, argue, plan, and evaluate—and receive feedback on their efforts—if there are aspects of school life that are sufficiently important to them and that are subject to their control.

Role-playing situations may contribute too. Smilansky (1968) and Shaftel and Shaftel (1967) have developed role-playing curricula for younger children. Older children and even adolescents could role play more complex interactions such as jury deliberations or draft board hearings. Moffett is now working on such "case" material as a way of helping teachers carry out the ideas in his books (Moffett, 1968a, 1968b).

If we agree with Havighurst that the ego is the best source of strength for the norms we wish to inculcate, we are led back to the role of intentionality and to questions about the use of language in the world outside school, from which the ultimate reinforcement will come.

On a small scale, why should a child want to learn to convey explicit information to strangers if his world continues to be limited to members of a small social group? Why should he want to learn to write with clarity and style if writing has no instrumental value in his life? Why should he want to learn a second dialect if there are few occasions when speaking it makes any difference?

On a broader scale, some young people are turning away from the use of words for rational dialogue, and one important reason is the hypocrisy of much speech and writing in our society today. Whether deliberately or not, words are often used to mask meaning, divert attention, and incite only mindless consumer action. An excerpt from "The Talk of the Town" in *The New Yorker* can speak for many such observations:

> In the language used in discussing this nation's involvement in Vietnam, there is a growing number of words by which meaning, instead of being underlined and made memorable, is hidden and by-passed. Pale words, delivered in swift, precise syllables, move us painlessly past reality after reality. We march to Vietnam under such bannerets as "escalate," "defoliate," "pacification," "counter-force concept," "controlled responses," "damage-limitation forces," "benevolent incapacitators," "targeting lists." Our current Vietnam vocabulary seems to aspire to a destruction not only of the meaning but also of the feeling that language should naturally express. The language of the crisis is one of estrangement, not communication; of censorship, not information. Its concern is with non-feeling rather than conviction, and with computerizing rather than patriotism. It is the language of anesthesia. (*New Yorker*, May 8, 1965, p. 35.)

Rejection of this hypocrisy, this "language of anesthesia," takes various forms. These forms vary in both the role of language and in their psychological consequences. Four of them can be placed on a continuum with a major division between the first two and the last two: use of language in political activity to change society; interest in alternate modes of symbolic communication—such as films and popular music (including song lyrics of considerable relevance and power); reliance on nonverbal communication in interpersonal relationships, as in encounter groups; and drugs.

I hope these ideas will not be dismissed by the reader without serious thought. Intruding political and social issues, of which language use is a symptom, into a book on child language and education is required by the pragmatics of language use in the United States of the 1970s.

Ultimately, solution lies in a change in society. Brandis and Henderson suggest that schools can become "a growing point in the consciousness of a community" (1970, p. 121). Greenberg's (1969) documentary history of the Mississippi Headstart program, *The Devil Has Slippery Shoes,* is the story of one attempt to help the school play exactly that role. Older students themselves, like the schoolboys of Barbiana, may find their strongest motivation in using language for social change.

In the meantime, we needn't retreat to the more limited goal of school as "deliberately equipping." We can follow Havighurst's suggestion and start by trying to change the child's environment over which we ourselves have most control—the school. People concerned with language education —as teachers or researchers—must at least be concerned with the pragmatics of language use in the total school environment.

Appendix: Methods of Analyzing Child Language

"An answer—spoken, written, drawn, or acted out in gesture—is the datum from which we ordinarily infer cognitive process. . . . Psychology uses public performance to make wise guesses about these processes" (Kagan and Kogan, 1970, p. 132). The need to describe and evaluate a child's language through his "public performance" arises in both research and education whenever we want to compare children. Sometimes we want to compare the same children at Time$_1$ versus Time$_2$, whether the intervening period is filled with natural development or deliberate education. Sometimes we want to compare Children A versus Children B, who differ in some way: sex; ethnic group, social class, native language; normality versus an abnormality such as deafness or schizophrenia. Beyond restating that one child said X and another child said Y, how can we more economically and informatively describe how they differ?

Linguists and psycholinguists are interested in what people *can* do with language. Sociolinguistics insist on attention to what people *do* do with language. And teachers and educational researchers want to describe both. In other words, we are interested in both knowledge and behavior. In fact, the gap between the two may yield important suggestions for education.

Teachers and researchers can learn about children's language by deliberately eavesdropping, preferably with tape recorder, as children talk among themselves in school and out; they may listen as the children respond in conversation with adults—parent, teacher, or experimenter; and they may set up structured situations, which we call "tests." With adults, one can also tap linguistic or sociolinguistic intuitions about language by asking them to evaluate sentences on some criterion of grammaticality or appropriateness, but this technique is seldom successful with young children. And even with adults, Bever (1970) suggests that intuitive judgments about sentences should be considered only one form of language performance rather than the purest access to linguistic competence.

Analyses of spontaneous speech have at least two limitations. First, not all behaviors appear spontaneously, even if they have been learned. For example, it is hard to find out whether children can say and understand passive sentences by listening to natural conversations because passive sentences are rare, even in the talk of adults. In this case, analyses confined to spontaneous speech would probably underestimate a child's linguistic knowledge. Second, even if certain behaviors are present, the natural situation is usually not sufficiently controlled so that inferences about the child's knowledge can be made. If the adult says *Please bring me the napkins from the kitchen table*, and the child correctly brings two napkins, one cannot conclude that the child attended to and understood the meaning of the plural *-s*. He may have been responding simply to the presence of two napkins on the table and have seen no reason to leave one behind. In this case, analyses confined to spontaneous speech may óverestimate a child's linguistic knowledge.

For both reasons, tests are useful. But sometimes criticisms of analyses of spontaneous speech make it seem as if tests were always preferred. This is not the whole story. It is important to understand both what new information tests can add and what new problems they pose.

Readers who are more interested in education than in research may want to skip some details of the first section, on analyses of spontaneous speech. But teachers and researchers alike should read the second section, on tests. Because language is the medium of evaluation as well as of instruction, teachers are continuously administering mini-tests whenever they ask a child a question in class, and we need to think very carefully about all the factors that may influence his response.

See Berko and Brown (1960) and Slobin (1967) for reviews of methods for child language research; see Cazden (1971) for more practical suggestions for evaluating the language of young children.

Analyses of Spontaneous Speech

The most complete description of spontaneous speech would be provided by writing a grammar for each child's language. But as soon as this proposal is made, it must be eliminated as unfeasible for all but a few specialists. See R. Brown (in press) for one example. Most researchers have neither the linguistic expertise nor the time for such a task. More feasible descriptions reduce particular aspects of child speech to numbers. Three examples are mean length of utterance, weighted scales, and frequency counts.

MEAN LENGTH OF UTTERANCE

A traditional measure, still widely used, is obtained by computing the mean length of a child's utterances (MLU). A natural sequence of utter-

ances is used, usually 50 or 100. Rules for what to count have been codified
[as in Slobin (1967)] so results from different investigators can be compared. In the past ten years, the unit counted has been the morpheme
rather than the word.

For a sample computation, take a corpus of eight utterances from
Bloom's subject, Kathryn, at two times in her development. See Table 1.
Utterances on the left are from recording I when Kathryn was 21 months
old (when she uttered *Mommy sock*); utterances on the right are from
recording VII when she was 30 months old. Intervening adult utterances
and all contextual information have been omitted. The number after each
utterance gives my judgment of utterance length in morphemes. MLU for
each set of eight utterances is computed at the bottom. (Bloom herself
computed MLU for Kathryn I as 1.32 morphemes, a more reliable estimate
than mine because it is the average of a larger number.)

Questions about MLU can be raised about its validity, reliability, and
informativeness. In evaluation terminology, validity refers to the relationship between any method or instrument for assigning numbers to behavior
and what it is designed to measure. Reliability refers to the consistency
with which that method would yield the same result if applied repeatedly.
Informativeness refers nontechnically to the amount of information that we
obtain.

Table 1 **Length of Child Utterances**

Kathryn I (20 mos.)*		Kathryn VII (30 mos.)†	
UTTERANCE	NO. MORPHEMES	UTTERANCE	NO. MORPHEMES
ə pull	2	You came here last night	6
		When my mother was	
ə pull hat	3	ironing	6
pull	1	Yes	1
		My mother my mother	
Mommy pull	2	ironed	4
Mommy bounce	2	Yes	1
		Oh she ironed some	
push	1	clothes	6
push	1	Oh I played with you	6
Mommy push	2	Yes	1
Total	14	Total	31
14 ÷ 8 = 1.75 MLU		31 ÷ 8 = 3.75 MLU	

Source: Bloom (1970).

   * Table 3.5, pp. 46–47.

   † Page 229.

Validity

When we compute MLU, we do so not because we value utterance length in itself, but because increasing length is an index of increasing linguistic complexity. MLU is an indirect measure of complexity, as the height of a column of mercury in a thermometer is an indirect measure of temperature. The validity of MLU as a measure of child speech rests on the widespread finding that it increases with age, and on more recent discoveries of a correspondence between mean length and the emergence of specific grammatical features. Brown and Fraser (1964) found that children whose MLU was less that 3.2 morphemes formed the progressive verb without the auxiliary (*I going*); with less than 3.5 morphemes, they still omitted modal auxiliaries (*I park the car*). Bellugi (in press) also found consistent relationships between length and complexity in her study of the development of negation; the four stages in negation which she identified appeared in three children's languages when they were at the same developmental level as measured by MLU.

While there are adequate grounds for using MLU for comparing the speech of young children up to about four years of age, questions about validity must be kept in mind. Computing MLU in morphemes requires decisions about what is an utterance and what is a morpheme. Determining the boundaries of an utterance has proven to be no problem. For Kathryn's utterances, I follow Bloom's punctuation, which presumably was based on obvious cues of intonation and pauses.

Determining what is a morpheme is harder. A morpheme is not a word. A word may include more than one morpheme, as in *something* or *going*, or more than one word may be combined into a single morpheme, as a proper name like *Santa Claus* probably is to young children. Morphemes can be divided into free morphemes like *go* and *red*, which can appear alone, and bound morphemes like *-ing* and *-ly*, which never appear alone. Determination of morpheme boundaries is a problem just because a morpheme is defined as the smallest meaningful unit, and meaningfulness is relative to the individual speaker. In the study of child language, this relativity is especially important. For bound morphemes such as the plural *-s*, we should determine whether a particular child's use is spontaneous or imitative, whether the child uses the singular form as well as the plural, whether he recognizes a contrast in meaning between the two forms, and whether the suffix can be added productively to new nouns (Ervin and Miller, 1963). In computing MLU for Kathryn, this information was not available and therefore typical arbitrary decisions had to be made; for instance, that for Kathryn *came* includes a past tense, but that *clothes* is probably an unseparated and uncontrasted unit.

More importantly, and increasingly so at older ages, length and complexity are not matched exactly, although they are highly correlated. For example, in spontaneous production, tag questions such as *We'll go won't we* are short but develop later than other question forms (Bellugi, in press; Brown and Hanlon, 1970). In a sentence imitation test, Menyuk (1969) found that MLU did not predict order of difficulty. She asked a group of preschool and kindergarten children to repeat in normal and reversed word order a set of well-formed sentences previously obtained from child speech. Sentences ranged in length from *Are you nice?* to *Peter is over here and you are over there.*

> The most significant finding was that the structure of a particular sentence determined whether or not it was repeated, not its length. The correlation between sentence length and nonrepetition of sentences in their correct grammatical order is .03. For reverse word order utterances, on the other hand, the correlation is .87. The results of these studies indicated that repetition was dependent on structure rather than just imitation up to the limits of memory capacity. With sentences up to nine words in length, the length of the sentence was not the factor which determined successful repetition even for children as young as 3 years. The differences in the ability of children of varying ages to repeat sentence types was dependent on the particular rules used to generate these sentences, not length. When the structure was broken down completely, however (sentence in reverse word order), sentence length was a highly significant factor. Under this condition subjects imitate without comprehension, for the most part, and therefore repeat up to limits of their memory capacity. (Menyuk, 1969, pp. 113–114.)

The trouble with length is that one counts units (in this case morphemes) as if they were beads on a string and all alike. This is true of numbers in a digit-span test or words in a reversed sentence, but it is not true of words in normal sentences. A sentence is special precisely because it has an internal structure, and the morphemes in a sentence must have differential cognitive weight, depending on structural complexity. How, then, can structural complexity be described more directly? Psycholinguists are hard at work on this question. In research on the readability of written texts, the same question is important (Bormuth, 1967).

In some child language research, an adaptation of MLU has been used. Instead of an utterance, Hunt (1965) substituted a "minimal terminal unit," or "T-unit" for short. A T-unit is one main clause with all subordinate clauses attached to it. Hunt himself and Mellon (1969) computed the average length of T-units and the average number of clauses per T-unit for samples of children's written language; O'Donnell, Griffin, and Morris (1967) applied the same measures to children's speech. But mean length of T-units, like MLU, remains at best a superficial index of language maturity.

Reliability

If questions about the validity of MLU seem to affect only unusual utterances, questions of reliability are more pervasive. MLU is related to aspects of the speech situation which affect the pattern of conversation. Even with the very young child, MLU will vary as a function of the density of answers to questions. Note the effect on MLU of the *yes* answers in Kathryn VII (Table 1).

A situational influence on MLU is noticeable in tests as well. For instance, Cowan et al. (1967) presented elementary school children of mixed socioeconomic status with ten colored pictures from magazine covers. The effect of the particular picture on MLU was strong across age, sex, socioeconomic class, and experimenter. One picture of a group standing around a new car elicited significantly shorter MLUs, and one picture of a birthday party elicited significantly longer MLUs, whereas the other eight pictures were undifferentiated between the two extremes. Although the authors could not specify the source of the stimulus effect, they conclude that "the implicit assumption that magnitude of MLR [mean length of response, same as MLU] is a property of the subject independent of his setting should be permanently discarded" (Cowan et al. 1967, p. 202).

Leler (1970) discusses the problems she encountered in using MLU in her research on the relationship between mother-child interaction and the language of lower-class Black children, 2½ to 3½ years old, in California. To obtain spontaneous speech samples for each child, white speech therapists taped a conversation with each child in the child's home. Some of the children had had little previous contact with Caucasians, or even with strangers at all, and either talked in one-word answers or asked one-word questions like *Huh* or *What*. Some of the therapists had trouble understanding the children's speech, because of age and dialect factors, and they varied in ability to stimulate child speech rather than depress it. Then, when the tapes were given to supposedly well-qualified linguists for transcribing, they, too, had a hard time understanding the children's speech. It is not surprising, therefore, that Leler questions the reliability of the resulting MLU scores and recommends against its use in other research. Her problems are recounted here not as a criticism of her work but rather, as she intended, as a warning to others of what can easily happen. These problems can be overcome by familiarity—best acquired in a relationship sustained over time between child and adult researcher. But too little research makes such a relationship possible.

Measurement can be construed broadly as a link between nature and knowledge. Decisions about measurement are made in order to separate some "figure" from the total "ground" of complex human behavior. In developmental research, the intent is to separate the "figure" of developmental change from the "ground" of all other influences—situational, interpersonal, emotional—which affect a child's speech at any given moment. It is important that researchers be aware of the effects of situations on child speech and, perhaps cumulatively, on child language as well.

Informativeness

After validity and reliability, there is the question of informativeness. If two children differ in MLU, we can rank them accordingly. But what else have we learned about their speech? We can say nothing about what they can or cannot do with language. Conversely, similarity of MLU may mask interesting individual differences in child language. Chapter 3 documented how complexity summarized by a certain MLU is not the same in all details for all children. In current evaluation terminology, MLU is a norm-referenced rather than a criterion-referenced measure (B. Bloom, Hastings, and Madaus, 1971).

WEIGHTED SCALES

Hopefully, research on the acquisition of language will eventually make possible developmental scales that will be more valid measures than MLU. Such scales have not been established, much less standardized on any large sample of children. But attempts have been made. Details of two such attempts may highlight some of the problems others are likely to encounter.

Research on the effects of two kinds of adult-child conversation on two- and three-year-old children (Cazden, 1965; discussed in Chapter 6), required a measure of syntactic development in finer detail than MLU would provide. So a scale for noun phrases and verb phrases was worked out, based largely on the sequence with which particular forms are acquired, and then numbers were assigned to points on that scale.

From Brown and Bellugi's (1964) study of the development of noun phrases in Adam and Eve, we knew that, at first, any modifier was combined with any noun. When the differentiation process began, articles were separated out of the category of modifiers. The children said *a blue flower* but not *blue a flower*. Only later did the children use two modifiers other than articles before a noun, as in *my blue flower*. Therefore, on a weighted scale, utterances like the following could be scored from 1 to 4:

> Flower, 1
> Nice flower, 2
> A blue flower, 3
> My blue flower, 4

No objective difference in linguistic complexity dictated this separation of articles from other modifiers, but the developmental sequence was clear.

Verb forms presented more trouble. The following sequence represents sequence of emergence in Adam and Eve's speech, and the forms were scored 1 to 3, respectively:

> I drop, 1
> I dropping, 2
> I'm dropping, 3

But what about the past tense *dropped*? Its emergence was definitely later than *dropping*, but how much later wasn't certain. Therefore it had to be assigned a number on the basis of the number of morphemes in the verb phrase, and so *dropped*, like *dropping*, was given 2 points.

How well did these scales work? Except in special instances, we can assume that any developmental characteristic will either stay at the same level or increase. Therefore, a valid measure of that characteristic will yield increasing numerical scores to the extent that it taps the hidden currents of developmental change; conversely, fluctuation in the scores over time indicates the presence of more superficial influences. We cannot assume that the perceived gain is the true gain, but we can assume that it is closer to a true picture of growth than fluctuating scores would be.

Evaluated in this way, the NP index turned out to be more valid than the V index. Verbs are a particularly complex part of English syntax, and we still lack detailed information on how they develop. Further, there may be greater individual and dialectal variation in the development of verb forms than in noun phrases, and a scale works best for changes all children share. Miner (1969) describes and recommends a length-complexity index that is based partly on MLU and partly on these NP and V scales.

Frank and Osser (1970) devised a scale for evaluating the complexity of an entire utterance. Based on a "modified transformational grammar," it makes possible both qualitative and quantitative analyses. Qualitatively, an utterance can be categorized according to whether it is simple or complex and according to the type of transformation it assumes; quantitatively, the number of elements plus the operations that the transformations require can be counted and compared. For example:

> One unit is given for each of the components of the nucleus (i.e., NP & VP) present; thus "That man is sick" (a simple kernel) gets a score of two. In the expanded sentence "That man from the office is very sick" (a complex kernel) an extra unit is given for each of the two additions "from the office" (adj.-prep. phrase) and "very" (intens.), so that this sentence has a total complexity of four units. . . .
>
> Sentences which include transformations can be broken down operationally into combinations of the operations of addition, subtraction, transposition, and intonational change. Each of these four types of change has been assigned one unit of complexity (1 for NP, 1 for VP, and 1 for a transposition, i.e., the inversion transformation). (Frank and Osser, 1970, pp. 43–44.)

Frank and Osser (1970) include an interesting comparison of the application of this scheme with three others. They conclude, "In a group of pre-school subjects under investigation (Osser, Frank, and Wang, 1967), as well as in the sample sentences cited above, the authors' system corroborated common-sense notions of relative complexities of syntax, whereas the other three methods did not" (Frank and Osser, 1970, p. 45). In a study of parent-child interaction using this scale, Baldwin and Frank (1969) also obtained results that were reasonable and consistent with the results of Slobin and Phillips, reported in Chapter 6. While the mean complexity score for the mothers was 13 in an adult interview, it dropped to 5 in conversation with children. And, in turn, 5, was higher than the mean of about 3 for the three-year-old children themselves.

But questions about validity remain. Just as the NP and V scales (Cazden, 1965) depended on our understanding of developmental sequences, so Frank and Osser's scale depends on our understanding of syntactic complexity. Three reasons can be suggested why number of transformations may not be a valid index of complexity. First, there is empirical evidence from psycholinguistic research that the number of transformations in the structural description of an utterance does not correspond to psychological complexity as measured, for example, by the time needed for some demonstration of comprehension (Fodor and Garrett, 1967). Second, transformations are now construed as formal representations of sentence relationships which may not enter into the cognitive processes of sentence production and comprehension at all (Bever, 1970). Third, even if they are psychologically real, there is no more reason to believe that all transformations are of equal psychological complexity than to believe that all morphemes add equivalent cognitive loads to MLU (Brown and Hanlon, 1970). These criticisms do not apply to Frank and Osser's scale alone. They do show how child language research can only proceed in symbiotic relationship to research in linguistics itself.

In addition to problems posed by limitations on our understanding of both development and complexity, weighted scales pose two more problems, one about numbers and the other about differences among dialects. When numbers were assigned to points on a scale (Cazden, 1965; Frank and Osser, 1970), it was done without assuming that equal intervals existed between them. In the NP index, for example, there is no reason to believe that the intervals between being able to say a single N, ART + N, ART + MOD + N, etc., are in any sense the same. Yet, when a mean is computed from those numbers, all increments must be considered equivalent, as they are in measurements of height. In technical terms, arithmetical operations were applied to an "ordinal" scale that were strictly appropriate only to an "interval" scale.

Even more serious is the problem of differences among dialects. These problems affect both scales. For example, in developing the NP and V scale (Cazden, 1965), I wanted to evaluate the developmental progress of the lower-class Black children without in any way "penalizing" them for speaking a nonstandard dialect. But conformity to Standard English did intrude. Sometimes deviations from Standard English left the meaning ambiguous. If the child said *Her go upstairs,* clearly *her* was being used in the subject position. But if the child said *He wet him bed,* it was not equally clear whether *him* was being used as a possessive pronoun. Sometimes nonstandard forms raised problems in scoring even when the meaning was clear. The children in my sample often used an auxiliary with an unmodified verb, such as *He's go* or *I'm put*. These patterns hadn't been anticipated, since they had not appeared in Brown and Bellugi's data, and it was not clear how they should be scored.

Dialect differences also made it impossible to measure the use of negation. Basis for such an analysis existed in Bellugi's study (in press) of the sequence of emergence of particular negative forms, but many of the utterances of the subjects in my study could not be placed on Bellugi's scale. The frequent use of *got* and *ain't got* produced a construction in which the negation appeared after the verb, as in *I got no crayons*. And multiple negatives (*I not kiss no people*) were more frequent and seemed to appear at earlier stages than in Bellugi's data.

Ideally, a child's language development should be evaluated in terms of his progress toward the norms for his particular speech community. Reliance on complexity more than on developmental sequence as a criterion for evaluation may make the transfer from one dialect to another easier. A scale that accepts alternate forms of the complexity on which it is based can be applied cross-culturally more appropriately than one based on sequence of emergence. Though the latter is probably otherwise the superior criterion, it is more likely to penalize departures from a preconceived norm. This issue of "dialect-fair" scales of language development may become as significant in the future as that of "culture-fair" tests of intelligence has been in the past.

At the moment, four solutions seem possible. First, Ervin and Miller (1963) suggest limiting the scale to those features of language which are shared by all dialect groups. Problems arose in developing the NP and V scale (Cazden, 1965) partly because the study dealt with inflections, linguistic features where dialect differences are concentrated. Second, Osser, Wang, and Zaid (1969) tried to work out "equivalencies" for certain forms. Knowing that Black nonstandard English frequently does not include a possessive -*s* and has different pronoun forms, they counted *His sister hat* as the equivalent of *His sister's hat*, and *He washes herself* as the equivalent of *She washes herself*. Third, one could attempt to establish multiple, dialect-specific scales. Fourth, Fraser (1969) suggests a new way of conceptualizing the whole problem. Although he was talking about a new kind of language test, applicable across dialect (or even language) communities, his ideas also provide a new framework for analyzing what children say spontaneously.

Fraser's research plan (unpublished) is to define a set of functions for which all language must provide in some way: topicalization (which was discussed in Chapter 2), modification, asking questions, etc.; determine how these functions are expressed in particular languages or dialects such as

Black English (BE); and finally, assess a child's ability to comprehend and produce the particular forms these functions take in his native dialect.

In identifying the relevant properties of linguistic competence we are not so concerned whether or not a dialect has a passive form or adverbial pre-posing, etc., but rather in identifying the more basic functional concepts of language, concepts such as topicalization, contrast, anaphoric reference, deletion of redundant elements, subject-verb agreement, negative concord, conditionality, coordination, comparison, and so forth. The question is usually whether a dialect has a particular construction or morphological process; we suggest that the really important question is what such a construction or process is representing in terms of a more basic language concept. . . .

It is clear, for example, that at some point in the language development of a child learning standard English, he learns the concept of topicalization. In standard English this function is accomplished by a number of devices: formation of the passive sentence (e.g., "John was seen by Mary"), forma-tion of a cleft sentence (e.g., "It was John that Mary saw"), formation of a pseudo-cleft sentence (e.g., "Who Mary saw was John"), by emphatic stress (e.g., "Mary saw JOHN"), adverbial preposing (e.g., "At five o'clock, I'll go to the store"), to name a few. . . .

We must determine, for example, to what extent the possible devices for topicalization in English occur in BE [Black English]. Recent studies of BE indicate that the *got* passive predominates (e.g., "I got seen by Mary"), and that cleft and pseudo-cleft sentences are rarely used. Therefore, while the concept of topicality certainly exists in BE, its form is not identical to that in SE in all cases. Moreover, many speakers of BE topicalize using a con-struction not generally held acceptable in SE, namely, noun phrase preposing (e.g., "John, he a cool cat"). Thus, before one can begin to determine how to test a child's linguistic competence, he must know in what form this competence can be expected to occur. . . .

Once we know what we might ultimately expect in the adult speaker of the dialect, we must determine at what point these features appear in the speech and understanding of the child learning this dialect. We might schematize this task in the following way:

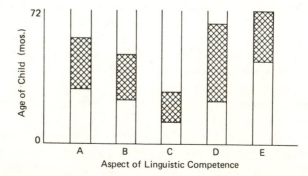

where the shaded areas represents the period of transition for the average child—where some children have this concept as indicated by the presence of a specific construction, etc. The lower unshaded area denotes where this concept is rarely found; the upper unshaded area where it is nearly always found. Certainly, this knowledge, whether represented in this form or otherwise, is a prerequisite to determining what concepts to test at what age and how they should appear. (Fraser, 1969.)

FREQUENCY COUNTS

Many research studies have counted the frequencies of specific linguistic features. The informativeness of such counts depends on the linguistic and psychological validity of the features counted, and on the kind of inferences that are made. After a description of three kinds of research which are largely based on frequency counts, the problem of inference will be considered.

Least interesting are counts of deviations from Standard English. For instance, Templin (1957), Thomas (1962), and Loban (1963) all find that verb usage is the most frequent source of nonstandard forms—specifically, violation of subject-verb agreement; deviant use of the verb *to be* "especially for Negro subjects whose parents have migrated from the rural South" (Loban, 1963, p. 52); use of present for past tense; and use of *got* for *have*. Such analyses violate two essential characteristics of language. First, the language of any group or individual is a system, and specific features in that system can be understood only as integral parts of a whole. Second, the language system of any group or individual has internal variability whose realization is related in predictable ways to aspects of the linguistic or nonlinguistic context—for instance, to whether a speech situation is casual or formal. Counting deviations from Standard English is usually justified in order to pinpoint targets for educational efforts. At least, efforts should be made to determine which particular "deviations" are socially most significant. Even then, the systematicity and contextuality of any child's language must be incorporated into instructional plans.

In research on the language of Adam, Eve, and Sarah, Brown and his associates made frequency counts of many syntactic elements: noun and verb inflections [Cazden, 1968(a)]; prepositions (Brown, Cazden, and Bellugi, 1969); questions of various types (R. Brown, 1968a; Brown and Hanlon, 1970); and others. Examples were given in Chapter 3.

Finally, Labov's research on the language of Black English, described in Chapter 7, was based largely on frequency counts. Many of his counts are of phonological variables, such as the pronunciation of -r after vowels as in *car* or *four*, and the simplification of consonant clusters at the end of words, as *tes'* for *test*. Labov has also counted syntactic units such as the presence or absence of forms of the copula *be*. As Labov points out, phonological variables have a great advantage for the researcher. They appear more frequently, and so a smaller corpus of speech yields sufficient numbers for statistical analysis. But studying them requires particularly good recording equipment and technical skill in phonetic analysis.

Related to frequency counts are type-token ratios (TTR) for comparing diversity over time, or among children, within some category of linguistic forms. Traditionally, TTRs have measured lexical diversity by expressing the number of different words (types) in a sequence of, say, 1000 words (tokens). Wilbur Hass (1967) has developed a system for computing a TTR for diversity of grammatical constructions. In comparing TTRs, it is essential that they be computed on the same absolute number of tokens because the likelihood of new types decreases with an increase in the number of tokens in the total sample.

Once frequency counts have been made, questions of inference arise. How should these data be scored? How does one decide when to credit a child with a particular bit of linguistic knowledge? Psychologists are accustomed to dealing with frequencies and mean scores, but for assessing whether a child knows or doesn't know, such methods raise serious questions. For linguists, by contrast, one example may be accepted as sufficient evidence of knowledge and all instances to the contrary explained by interferences of performance factors such as momentary inattention. This, too, seems wrong. Take the case of chess, often used to explain the distinction between knowledge (of rules) and behavior (actual moves in a game). Suppose one set up an experimental situation where two people were faced with the same board and then compared in their next moves. Let us say further that both people made the same move. Can one then infer the same knowledge, even in reference only to this part of the total game of chess? May not one person have a more complete understanding of the relation of this move to all other moves? What are the criteria of "understanding"?

One is reminded of controversies in Piaget-type research on the development of such cognitive schema as conservation. For example, after examining contradictory results on both the age at which conservation is acquired and its susceptibility to instruction, Gruen concludes that the results are related to differences in criteria and these in turn to differences in definition, to "the psychological processes that one assumes underlie conservation" (Gruen, 1966, p. 982).

The work of Brown and his associates (discussed in Chapters 3, 4 and 5), and of Labov and his associates (discussed in Chapter 7) illustrate two different but equally valid reasons for counting. Brown and coworkers studied the language acquisition process. They wanted to be able to describe the sequence with which children gradually acquire mature English syntax. For example, which verb inflection do children learn first: *-ing* or *-ed*? To answer this question, one must be able to say that at a certain point in time, a child knows X but does not yet know Y. What appears in the data essentially as a continuous variable has to be transformed into a dichotomous yes-no statement. Brown, Cazden, and Bellugi discuss this methodological problem:

> In certain facts about construction frequency there lies a major trap for the student of child speech who is interested in the development of knowledge of grammar: there seems to be something like a standard frequency profile for mother-to-child English, a profile that children match within their competence at any given time, and in this profile great inequalities exist even among very simple and familiar constructions. . . .
>
> Consider two examples in detail: major sentence types and expressions of possession. If we set an arbitrary frequency in child speech as a criterion of emergence—for example, the occurrence of three instances of a given type of sentence in each of three consecutive samples of seven hundred utterances—we find a high rank order correlation between parental sentences—affirmative, declaratives, negatives, yes-no interrogatives and Wh interrogatives using, respectively, lexical verbs or *have* or *be* or *will* or *can* or *may*. Lexical and be-verbs in declarative sentences are the most common in all three mothers and appear first in the speech of all three children. But suppose we entertain the extreme hypothesis that all twenty-four verbs enter the child's competence simultaneously. Because the probability that a given construction will attain an arbitrary criterion varies with its standard frequency in mother-to-child English, and because these frequencies are grossly unequal, lexical and *be*-verbs would appear first on a strict probability basis. The student of child speech might then conclude that the hypothesis of simultaneous development was false when it could indeed still be true. Highly stable orders of construction emergence, in terms of an arbitrary frequency criterion, are not inconsistent with the possibility that the children in question know how to form all the constructions from the start but produce them with unequal frequency. . . .
>
> There are various ways out of the trap, all involving data that are better indexes of knowledge or competence than is an arbitrary frequency of production. One can consider child frequencies against a background of known stable adult frequencies and so set frequency criteria that are not entirely arbitrary; one can consider frequencies of forms in contexts that make them obligatory; one can consider the pattern of omissions in the total distributional range of a form; one can consider the adequacy of the child's responses to adult questions and assertions; and above all, one can use the child's analogical errors of commission. (Brown, Cazden, and Bellugi, 1969, pp. 64–66.)

Brown and his colleagues have used all the "various ways out of the trap." Brown and Hanlon (1970) established a criterion of acquisition for question types based on output rate for the mothers; the study of inflections (Cazden, 1968a) considered frequencies in obligatory contexts; Brown and Hanlon departed from a frequency criterion in the one case where a child's very frequent use of the question opener *D'you want* was not accompanied by related forms such as *Does he want* or *D'you see*.

And analyses of spontaneous speech were supplemented as often as possible by indications of what the child understood.

Labov's purposes were quite different, and so the inferential process is different too. Labov was not trying to determine sequence of emergence in a developmental progression. He only rarely made statements about the presence or absence of some feature in the linguistic knowledge of a person or group. His aim was to describe speech performance, and so the pattern of frequencies themselves were of primary interest. From these patterns, Labov made inferences about the sociolinguistic knowledge that speakers have of language use—in short, about their communicative competence.

Much of the research on social-class differences in child language is like Labov's—frequency counts of particular linguistic features in particular situations. Studies in England by Hawkins (1969) and Tough (Cazden, 1971) on the relative frequencies of nouns and pronouns are excellent examples. No inferences from these speech data were made by these investigators, or should be made by others, about differences in purely linguistic knowledge. The data represent differences in options selected by speakers in actual speech performance. We need to know about both child language and child speech. And we must not get the two mixed up.

Tests

Interpreting a child's response in any test situation poses special problems to teachers and researchers alike because any test is a complex situation that makes multiple intellectual and interpersonal demands on the child. Aspects of this complex situation which can influence a child's response are discussed under five headings: intellectual processes, test content, aspects of the test task outside the intended focus, attending behaviors required, and the interpersonal relationship between adult and child.

INTELLECTUAL PROCESSES OR KNOWLEDGE

Any test is designed to evaluate some intellectual knowledge or process. The focus may be an aspect of language knowledge such as discriminations among sounds; explanation of vocabulary meanings; or comprehension of parts of English syntax such as passive sentences. Or it may be some ability important in communication and cognition, such as designing a sequence of cumulative questions to obtain information in the Twenty Question game; adapting one's message to the needs and background of particular listeners, called "role taking"; or supplying verification for particular facts.

TEST CONTENT

In any specific test, these processes are applied to specific content, and this content may be differentially familiar to children, individually or by group. An auditory discrimination test may include a distinction between *pin* and *pen*, which is made in only some dialects of English. A test of English morphology may ask children to supply verb endings such as the past *-ed*, which are frequently omitted in their dialect. A vocabulary test may ask about objects that are unknown (*toboggan* or *vests*) or known under a different name (*sun glasses* versus *shades*). A sentence imitation test may contain syntactic constructions differentially familiar to groups of children being tested. (See Ervin-Tripp, 1971(c), for further discussion.) Children may be asked to engage in dramatic play with unfamiliar props; for instance, after asserting that Oriental Jewish children in Israel don't engage in dramatic play, Smilansky admits that "We found no kindergarten teacher or experimenter guiding and demonstrating among a group of boys a gathering of men in the local coffee house or the Turkish-Bath, which almost certainly was a weekly experience in the lives of the boys' fathers and known and familiar to the boys but unknown, unexperienced and unfamiliar to the experimenters and kindergarten teachers" (1968, p. 132).

Some aspects of the test content may pose problems of a more general sort. For example, tests for children frequently use pictures. Sometimes they play no intrinsic role; Berko's (1958) test of English morphology could be given without pictures, if children's attention could be maintained. But often interpretation of pictures is required by the test iself. Then the researcher must assume that all children have the same understanding of pictorial representation. Yet Sigel, Anderson, and Shapiro (1966) found that in a test situation, lower-class Black preschool children had more trouble categorizing pictures of objects than the objects themselves, while for middle-class Black children the level of representation made no difference.

Correct interpretation of test pictures also frequently depends on acceptance of particular conventions. Recently, a group at the Educational Testing Service did an item analysis of the answers given on the Peabody Picture Vocabulary Test (PPVT) by 120 children, of which 60 were lower-class predominantly Black (LSES), and 60 middle-class predominantly white (LSES), from ages four to six years old:

> On all items the MSES scores are better than the LSES. On most items the two groups share similar patterns of option choice, and the "distractors" [wrong pictures] seem to be working in similar ways. There are notable exceptions, however.
>
> Item 47—"yawning." The two groups are quite different on this item. No MSES children chose distractor option 3; 11 LSES children selected it. The girl in option 2 (correct choice) is shown to be yawning in the stereotyped way (hand over mouth)—a middle class mannerism that has come to be the accepted cartoon for depicting yawning. . . . The girl in option 3 also has her mouth open and certainly might be yawning, and therefore— so the interpretation goes—is the choice of children who are less aware of convention in pictorial representation. More generally, recognition of con-

ventions in pictures and words must be a factor in many items. (E. Chitten-den, personal communication, 1970.)

Even older children may not share the same conventions. A student at Harvard, Kristine Rosenthal, noticed that middle-class ten-year-old white children said that black-and-white pictures in which coloring was shown by dots were "colored" or "shaded," while lower-class white children of the same age said the pictures had "dots" or "dirt" or "stuff" in them.

The same kind of general difference may arise when children are asked to operate with nonsense words, or actual words that become "nonsense" to children to whom the words are unfamiliar. For example, in research on children's perceptions of the sounds of English, discussed in Chapter 5, Read tested kindergarten children's discrimination of the sounds /s/ and /z/ by asking them which of a pair of words rhymed with a third one—e.g., whether *face* or *days* rhymed with *plays*. In evaluating his test, Read comments:

> The item that made use of unfamiliar words also produced a disproportionate share of errors; *blaze*, for instance, seemed to puzzle the children. Ideally, the unfamiliarity of a word—even nonce words—should not prevent an accurate judgment of rhyming, but in practice, familiarity made a difference . . . even to those children who had performed perfectly on the rhyming subtest of the pre-reading test. The item that produced the fewest answers was *cease: grease—bees*. Fewer than one-third answered this correctly, so one might speculate that some children heard an unfamiliar word (*cease*) as a more familiar one—*seize*. If this guess proved correct, the result would be another illustration of the extent to which expectations can interact with the actual acoustic stimulus to produce perceptions. (Read, 1970, p. 147.)

The values implicit in test questions are another source of culturally specific content. In an analysis of standardized tests, Roberts points out two examples of questions on the Wechsler Preschool and Primary Scale of Intelligence (WPPSI) which reflect particular cultural norms:

> On the WPPSI comprehension subtest, for example, the question "Why do you need to wash your face and hands?" presupposes that you *do* need to wash your face and hands, which may not be a cultural universal. A good response is: "to get clean" or "so you won't get germs"; a less acceptable response is "they're dirty"; an even lower-rated response is: "Mother tells you to . . . ."
>
> On the same test the question "Why are criminals locked up?" is considered well-answered if the child includes the idea that locking up criminals is a deterrent, that it is for the protection of society, for punishment, revenge, rehabilitation and/or segregation. A bad response is: "they're bad, they kill people (in the present tense) . . . they're dangerous." (Roberts, 1970, pp. IV-21–22.)

In an item-analysis of errors on a multiple-choice reading comprehension test, a student at Harvard, Louise Smith, found that lower-class children were apt to say that *to confess* is *foolish*—a response behaviorally often realistic even if "wrong."

The actual dialect of the examiner may not itself be a critical aspect of the test situation. Quay (1971) studied the effects of translating the Stanford-Binet into Black nonstandard English. For instance, the tester showed a paper doll and said, "Now show me where de doll hair at." William Stewart made the translation and approved tapes of Quay's testers using his translation. Subjects were disadvantaged Black four-year-olds in Philadelphia. No difference was found between scores on dialect and standard versions of the test, nor between different reinforcement (motivation) conditions. Dr. Quay (personal communication) then replicated the study with nine-year-old children. Her interpretation of the results (which are in the opposite direction from any experimenter bias), is that Black children have more ability to comprehend Standard English than has been assumed.

TASK REQUIREMENTS

Separate from test content, particular requirements of the test task may affect the child's response. If children are asked to answer questions in complete sentences, their willingness to adopt temporarily an unnatural conversational pattern becomes important. If an experimenter shows the child an object and says, "Tell me about it," (as in the "verbal expression" subtest of the Illinois Test of Psycholinguistic Abilities) the child's answers will vary with his understanding of these directions as a request for extended verbal display. When Menyuk asked children three to six years old to imitate sentences containing grammatical immaturities such as *He wash his dirty face*, the number of spontaneous corrections to *He washes* (or *washed*) *his dirty face* decreased with age (Menyuk, 1969, p. 113); evidently, the older children understood the directions more literally and were more willing to accede to them. Sometimes more specific metalinguistic operations are required, in which language is manipulated as an object of intellectual activity as well as its medium. For instance, on the Wepman Auditory Discrimination Test, children are asked to demonstrate their sound-discrimination ability by judging pairs of words as "same" or "different."

In all these tests, evidence about the child's language becomes confounded with something else, and valid inferences becomes correspondingly more difficult. Jakobson wrote about testing aphasic patients, but his words apply as well to children:

> The methodology of clinical tests is likewise an intricate and cardinal linguistic problem. What is obtained by such tests from the patient very often proves to be not his proper language but his so-called metalinguistic operations with language, his exercises in intralingual and interlingual translation. He works under constraint. Here we must heed Niels Bohr's wise

warning: when we have to do with an observer and an object under observation, we must take into account the distortion of the object by the observer.
We must measure and analyze such a distortion. And when an aphasic is
being tested, the distortion may be quite high. . . . There can be no
monopolizing solution which would eliminate the necessity of a qualitative
linguistic analysis based primarily on the unconstrained speech of the patient.
(Jakobson, 1964, pp. 44–46.)

Research can be done in which the effect of task requirements is isolated.
Four examples follow. First, in their research on mental abilities in different
ethnic and social-class groups, Lesser and his colleagues paid exemplary
attention to the possible influence of variables not under substantive study:

Groups must be equated or group differences measured for a host of test
influences, including such variables as extent and quality of formal schooling,
language handicaps, interest, effort, attention span, ability to understand and
follow verbal directions, ability to read and write, familiarity with the test-
taking situations, general desire to excel, test-taking motivation, rapport
with the examiner, and speed of response. Failure to control or assess these
and several similar test influences would make observed social-class and
cultural-group differences in mental-ability patterns virtually uninterpretable.
(Lesser, Fifer, and Clark, 1965, p. 14.)

Second, a student of Carl Bereiter's (Thompson, 1968) tested the
Bereiter-Engelmann claim that lower-class children speak in "giant words"
by asking lower-class (LC) and middle-class (MC) preschool children to
repeat backwards certain three-word phrases, such as *a higher tree* and *he
took it*. He found that the LC children needed a longer training period in
order to learn to make the reversals (a matter of the metalinguistic task),
but once learned, that process was applied with equivalent ease to the
test phrases by both groups of children (a matter of the organization of
linguistic knowledge in each child's mind). Burling (1970, p. 137) suggested using the game of talking in pig Latin for the same purpose of
studying children's word boundaries. Following Thompson, the adult should
allow time to learn the game to vary as needed.

Third, Williams and Naremore (1969a, 1969b) analyzed 40 interviews
with Black and Caucasian fourth to sixth graders at the extremes of the
socioeconomic distribution from a larger group of 20 interviews in a Detroit
dialect study (Shuy, Wolfram, and Riley, 1967). All informants had responded to three topics: games (*What kinds of games do you play around
here?*); TV (*What are your favorite TV programs?*); and aspirations
(*What do you want to be when you finish school?*). Williams and Naremore
scored the interviews by the type of question asked by the interviewer and
the corresponding type of child response.

Question
    Simple: Do you play baseball?
    Naming: What television programs do you watch?
    Elaboration: How do you play kick-the-can?

Response
> *Simple*: Yeah.
> *Naming*: Baseball.
> *Qualified naming*: I usually watch the Avengers and lots of
> cartoons.
> *Elaboration*: Last night the Penguin had Batman trapped on top
> of this tower . . . .

They found that following the "simple" or "naming" questions, "the lower status children had more of a tendency to supply the minimally acceptable response, whereas their higher status counterparts had a greater tendency to elaborate their remarks." Following the question for elaboration, however, these differences disappeared. "The mark of a lower-status child was that he had some tendency to provide the type of response which would minimally fulfill the fieldworker's probe, [but] not go on to assume a more active role in the speech situation, including elaboration of more of his own experience" (Williams and Naremore, 1969b).

Fourth is Heider, Cazden, and Brown's (1968) study, reported in Chapter 8, of the ability of 10-year-old LC and MC white children to discover the four attributes on which a set of 40 animal pictures differed. Our conclusions from that research apply more widely:

> . . . we received virtually the same information from the two social class groups when amount of probing or feedback was deliberately decontrolled. This finding raises questions about social class differences which arise in experimental situations or classrooms where such controls usually exist. There are undoubtedly class differences in dispositional and motivational variables; and there are undoubtedly class differences in cognitive abilities as well. One important problem—in research as well as in education—is how not to get the two mixed up. (Heider, Cazden, and Brown, 1968, p. 10.)

ATTENDING BEHAVIORS AND MOTIVATION

If tests are administered to children in a group, attending behaviors are particularly important. Each child must focus his attention at the right place and keep up with a group pace, waiting when necessary and attending on demand. If tests are timed, children unaccustomed to schedules and time pressures will be at a disadvantage in both group and individual administrations. There is some evidence that this is particularly true for American Indian children.

Even when a child is in some sense attending, his full intellectual ability may not be engaged. For instance, two researchers (Isaacs, 1930 and Oettinger and Marks, 1969) caution against using children's comprehension of questions as an indication of their level of intellectual or linguistic development. Usually, we think that children's competence is more adequately displayed in a test situation where, for example, the adult asks questions and the child is supposed to answer them. But as Isaacs pointed out in criticism of Piaget, the child may care little about the topic selected by the adult and may not do his best thinking in response.

> It is a complete error to equate the situation in which we ask children "why" questions, with that in which they ask us. The seeming precaution of putting to them their own kind of question is irrelevant, and only serves to hide from us the total difference of the two situations *functionally*. It allows only for the subject-matter, and hides the controlling features of attitude and function. . . . "Why," in questions addressed to the child, interpreted informationally and without any special significance for him, tap those earlier levels of merely applied organization, without any learning stimulus or effort. The child's own epistemic "why's," on the other hand, represent some of his most significant learning situations, forced or voluntary, with genuine interest or effort. (Isaacs, 1930, pp. 328, 331.)

When the child asks his own question, according to Isaacs, he is more apt to be operating with the full extent of his ability, and a more valid assessment can therefore be made.

While visiting a junior high mathematics class, Oettinger and Marks (1969) made a similar observation. After a student interrupted a teacher to ask how it could be that a line has length when the points that make it up have no length at all, Oettinger and Marks comment:

> Although students seemed extraordinarily apathetic and stupid in answering questions posed to them by the teacher, they exhibited great acumen and intelligence in raising questions that would divert the teacher from the path of the syllabus. These questions were frivolous in intent, but by no means frivolous in content: they showed a keen appreciation not only of human relations and of techniques for screwing up a teacher, but also of the unpleasant loose-ends of geometry. The matter of the unidimensional point making up a dimensional line was the best example of this kind. (Oettinger and Marks, 1969, p. 243.)

In an unusual experiment, Elkind, Deblinger, and Adler (1970) found that degree of motivation changed as a function of the contrast between the test task and the task that the children were engaged in when interrupted to take the test. They first suspected this effect when children from all the elementary grades in a highly innovative school in Rochester, New York, the World of Inquiry School (WOR), did not score as high on creativity tests as children from traditional public schools. The effect was confirmed in a second experiment with WOR pupils only. Some of the children were interrupted when following their own interests in the usual WOR fashion; others were interrupted while engaged in dreary busy work which Elkind and his colleagues had made up. The latter group gave three times as many "creative responses," presumably because they found the test more stimulating than their previous work.

The role of the situation in arousing or depressing a child's attention applies to all teaching as well as testing. The yearbook of the National Society for the Study of Education (NSSE), *Theories of Learning and Instruction* (1964) includes two chapters on readiness. One is on the more familiar "developmental readiness": the child's abilities, knowledge, motivation, etc. The other is on "immediate readiness": those factors in the immediate situation which will influence whether the child's attention is engaged and sustained.

INTERPERSONAL RELATIONSHIPS

Of all aspects of human behavior, speech is probably the most susceptible to subtle situational influences, especially the interpersonal relationships inherent in any kind of testing situation. And it is especially true for subtests who are at any social disadvantage vis-a-vis the tester—for example, patient to doctor, child to adult, minority group member to majority group member, outsider to formal bureaucratic institution.

A recent report, "*Perspectives on Human Deprivation,*" prepared for the National Institute of Child Health and Development, cautioned that "a great deal of the testing of children's verbal abilities has taken place in the same environment as the school situation itself, and such tests therefore register the child's reaction to the social context primarily and only secondarily his actual verbal skills" (Birren and Hess, 1968, p. 135).

Labov provides a dramatic example of the effect of the test situation on an older child. Attacking the conditions under which much of the data on "verbal deprivation" is collected, he quoted an entire interview with a preadolescent boy in a New York City school:

> The child is alone in a school room with the investigator, a young, friendly white man, who is instructed to place a toy on the table and say "Tell me everything you can about this." The interviewer's remarks are in parentheses. [Italics inserted for time intervals.]
> (Tell me everything you can about *this*.) (Plunk).
>   (*12 seconds of silence*)
> (What would you say it looks like?)
>   (*8 seconds of silence*)
> A space ship.
> (Hmmm.)
>   (*13 seconds of silence*)
> Like a je-et.
>   (*12 seconds of silence*)
> Like a plane.
>   (*20 seconds of silence*)
> (What color it is?)
> Orange.   (*2 seconds*)   An' whi-ite.   (*seconds*)   An' green.
>   (*6 seconds of silence*)

(And what could you use it for?)
  (*8 seconds of silence*)
A jet.
  (*6 seconds of silence*)
(If you had two of them, what would you do with them?)
  (*6 seconds of silence*)
Give one to some-body.
(Hmmm. Who do you think would like to have it?)
  (*10 seconds of silence*)
Clarence.
(Mm. Where do you think we could get another one of these?)
At the store.
(O-ka-ay!)

The social situation which produces such defensive behavior is that of an adult asking a lone child questions to which he obviously knows the answers, where anything the child says may well be held against him. It is, in fact, a paradigm of the school situation which prevails as reading is being taught (but not learned). (Labov et al., 1968, vol. 2, pp. 340–341.)

Good interpersonal relationships are often labeled "rapport." That's an easy-sounding name for a hard job—creating an interpersonal setting in which the child's communicative competence is most likely to be evoked. This requires time and care. Kagan reports the experience of Francis Palmer in New York City:

Dr. Palmer administered mental tests to middle and lower class black children from Harlem. However, each examiner was instructed not to begin any testing with any child until she felt that the child was completely relaxed, and understood what was required of him. Many children had five, six, or even seven hours of rapport sessions with the examiner before any questions were administered. Few psychological studies have ever devoted this much care to establishing rapport with the child. Dr. Palmer found few significant differences in mental ability between the lower and middle class populations. This is one of the first times such a finding has been reported and it seems due, in part, to the great care taken to insure that the child comprehended the nature of the test questions and felt at ease with the examiner. (Kagan, 1969, p. 276.)

Rapport may be increased by the presence and participation of the parent or by doing the testing in the children's homes, as Carroll and Casagrande did in their study of the relationship of verb structure to categorization in Navajo and English: "Most of the testing was done in the children's home, usually Navajo hogans of the traditional sort—and in the presence of parents, grand-parents, siblings, and other interested and very curious onlookers" (1958, p. 28).

Rapport may be helped by including other children, to dilute the intensity of the one-to-one adult-child relationship. Labov contrasts the meager interview data reported above with richer results. ". . . when we change the social situation by altering the height and power relations, introducing a close friend of the subject, and talking about things we know he is interested in, we obtain a level of excited and rapid speech (Labov et al., 1968, vol. 2, pp. 340–341). More complex language was also obtained in peer discussions by Smith (1970) for Headstart children in Buffalo, and by Williams and Legun (1970) for five- and nine-year-old Black children in the Watts area of Los Angeles. Well replicated birth-order differences on measures of language and general intelligence may not be due solely to the cognitive benefits of adult-child interaction. "Oldest" children and "only" children may perform better on these tests at least partly because the adult-child conversation required in the test situation is itself more familiar to them.

Blount's (1969) study of the language development of Luo children in Kenya faced these same problems. As is often the case, they command our attention more forcefully when writ large in cross-cultural terms. Blount's work is part of a cross-cultural study of the acquisition of communicative competence based at the University of California at Berkeley and directed by an interdisciplinary team of Ervin-Tripp (speech), Gumperz (anthropology) and Slobin (psychology). (See Slobin, 1967, for the manual that guided this research.) Blount focused on the social setting in which child language is both generated and collected. He showed that, for the researcher, the culturally specific sociolinguistic rules of language use are not simply another part of what children learn as they become mature members of their culture. In addition, those rules affect the extent to which the child's grammatical competence, or underlying knowledge, will be expressed in, and therefore can be inferred from, his performance in actual speech behavior. In other words, the contextual dependency of speech behavior is not only a focus of research interest, but also a problem in research methodology at the same time.

> In the present study, any description of competence must follow an account of the major rules governing children's speech. The basic rules are: (1) children do not interact with strangers; (2) children interact only ritually with visitors; (3) children interact formally with adults in the presence of other adults, according to a prescribed manner; and (4) children interact "freely" (with minimum constraint) with peers. (Blount, 1969, p. 43.)

The combined effect of these social rules is to depress the child's speech in the researcher's presence and make the researcher's assessment of the child's knowledge of his language very difficult.

The social constraints that regulate the child's speech, and thereby also the data-collection process, affect not only quantity but types of utterances as well. In Luo grammar, there are two basic types of sentences: predicative (or narrative) sentences with noun-phrase and verb-phrase (*Mama went to work.*), and nonpredicative (or equational) sentences with Noun +

Noun (*It shoes.*), Noun + Locative (*She here.*), or Noun + Adjective (*They black.*). In Blount's protocols, nonpredicative sentences seemed to develop before predicative constructions, but he suggests that this may be more a function of social constraints than of limitations in the child's grammar:

> The major restriction on the children's speech by the controlled conditions is that most of their speech in our presence consisted of answers to questions, particularly to "what" and "where" questions. The expectation of the adults as to the linguistic ability of the children, i.e., the adults' cultural attitudes, then had an effect on the type of speech provided by the children. The early appearance of non-predicative constructions in the speech record is directly attributable to this interplay between the child's capacity and the adults' attitudes. This is not to argue that there is a direct one-to-one correspondence between the acquisition of language by the children and the adults' expectations, but the latter had the effect of channeling the children's speech in the contexts in which the speech was collected. (Blount, 1969, pp. 154–155.)

The relationship between eliciting context, sociolinguistic rules, and valid inferences is critical whenever children's speech is being collected and evaluated. This applies not only in all child language research, but in all education as well—in everyday classroom events in which children's words are taken as indicators of what they have learned.

References

AARONS, A. C., GORDON, B. Y. and STEWART, W. A. Linguistic-cultural differences and American education. *The Florida FL Reporter*, 1969, 7 (whole No. 11).

ABRAHAMS, R. D. *Deep down in the jungle: Negro narrative folklore from the streets of Philadelphia.* Hatboro, Pa.: Folklore Associates, 1964.

ALATIS, J. E. *Twenty-first annual round table: bilingualism and language contact.* Monograph Series on Languages and Linguistics, No. 23, Washington, D.C.: Georgetown University Press, 1970.

AMMON, P. R., & AMMON, M. Effects of training young black children in vocabulary vs. sentence construction. Paper presented at meeting of American Educational Research Association, Minneapolis, March 1970.

ANDERSON, R. C. Part-task versus whole-task procedures for teaching a problem-solving skill to first graders. *Journal of Educational Psychology*, 1968, *59*, 207–214.

ANGLIN, J. M. *The growth of word meaning.* Cambridge, Mass.: M.I.T. Press, 1970.

ARNHEIM, R. *Visual thinking.* Berkeley: University of California Press, 1969.

BALDWIN, A. L., & FRANK, S. M. Syntactic complexity in mother-child interactions. Paper presented at meeting of Society for Research in Child Development, Santa Monica, March 1969.

BAR-ADON, A. Primary syntactic structures in Hebrew child language. In Bar-Adon, A., & Leopold, W. F. (Eds.), *Child language: a book of readings.* Englewood Cliffs, N.J.: Prentice-Hall, 1971. Pp. 433–472.

BAR-ADON, A., & LEOPOLD, W. F. (Eds.) *Child language: a book of readings.* Englewood Cliffs, N.J.: Prentice-Hall, 1971.

BARATZ, J. C. A bi-dialectal task for determining language proficiency in economically disadvantaged Negro children. *Child Development*, 1969, *40*, 889–901.

BARATZ, J. C., & SHUY, R. W. *Teaching black children to read.* Washington, D.C.: Center for Applied Linguistics, 1969.

BARATZ, S. S., & BARATZ, J. C. Early childhood intervention: the social science base of institutional racism. *Harvard Educational Review*, 1970, *40*, 29–50.

BARKER, R. G. *Ecological psychology.* Stanford, Calif.: Stanford University Press, 1968.

BARNES, D., & BRITTON, J. *Language, the learner and the school.* Baltimore, Md.: Penguin Books, 1969.

BEE, H. L., et al. Social class differences in maternal teaching strategies and speech patterns. *Developmental Psychology*, 1969, *1*, 726–734.

BEE, H. L., et al. Deficits and value judgments: a comment on Stroufe's critique. *Developmental Psychology*, 1970, *2*, 146–149.

BEILIN, M., & SPONTAK, G. Active-passive transformations and operational reversibility. Paper presented at the biennial meeting of the Society for Research in Child Development, Santa Monica, Calif., March 1969.

BELLUGI, U. The development of interrogative structures in children's speech.

In K. Riegel (Ed.), *The development of language functions.* Ann Arbor: Michigan, Language Development Program Report No. 8, 1965.

BELLUGI, U.   Simplification in children's language. In R. Huxley & E. Ingram (Eds.) *Language acquisition: models and methods.* New York: Academic Press, 1971. Pp. 95–119. (a)

BELLUGI, U.   The language of signs and the signs of language. Paper presented at the Third Annual Michigan conference on Applied Linguistics, Ann Arbor, Mich., Jan. 30, 1971. (b)

BELLUGI, U.   *The acquisition of the system of negation in children's speech.* Cambridge, Mass.: M.I.T. Press, in press.

BELLUGI, U., & BROWN, R. (Eds.)   The acquisition of language. *Monograph of Social Research in Child Development,* 1964, *29* (whole No. 1).

BEREITER, C., CASE, R., & ANDERSON, V.   Steps toward full intellectual functioning. *Journal of Research and Development in Education,* 1968, *1* (3), 70–79.

BERKO, J.   The child's learning of English morphology. *Word,* 1958, *14,* 150–177. Also in S. Saporta (Ed.), *Psycholinguistics.* New York: Holt, Rinehart and Winston, 1961.

BERKO, J., & BROWN, R.   Psycholinguistics research methods. In P. H. Mussen (Ed.), *Handbook of research methods in child development.* New York: Wiley, 1960.

BERLIN, B., & KAY, P.   *Basic color terms and their universality and evolution.* Berkeley: University of California Press, 1969.

BERNSTEIN, B.   Social class and linguistic development: a theory of social learning. In A. H. Halsey, Floud, & C. A. Anderson (Eds.), *Education, economy and society.* Glencoe, Ill.: Free Press, 1961. Pp. 288–314.

BERNSTEIN, B.   A critique of the concept "compensatory education." In C. B. Cazden, D. Hymes, & V. John (Eds.), *Functions of language in the classroom.* New York: Teachers College Press, in press. (a)

BERNSTEIN, B.   A socio-linguistic approach to socialization: with some reference to educability. In J. Gumperz & D. Hymes (Eds.), *Research in sociolinguistics.* New York: Holt, Rinehart and Winston, in press. (b)

BERNSTEIN, B., & HENDERSON, D.   Social class differences in the relevance of language to socialization. *Sociology,* in press.

BEVER, T. G.   The cognitive basis for linguistic structures. In J. R. Hayes (Ed.), *Cognition and the development of language.* New York: Wiley, 1970. Pp. 279–362.

BIRREN, J. E., & HESS, R.   Social and biological deprivation influences on learning and performance. In *Perspectives on human deprivation: biological, psychological, and social.* Washington, D.C.: U.S. Department of Health, Education and Welfare, National Institute for Child Health and Development, 1968.

BLACK, M.   *Models and metaphors.* Ithaca, N.Y.: Cornell University Press, 1962.

BLANK, M., & BRIDGER, W. H.   Conceptual cross-modal transfer in deaf and hearing children. *Child Development,* 1966, *37,* 30–34.

BLOM, G. E., WAITE, R. R., & ZIMET, S. G.   A motivational content analysis of children's primers. In H. Lavin & J. F. Williams (Eds.), *Basic studies in reading.* New York: Basic Books, 1970.

BLOM, J., & GUMPERZ, J. J.   Some social determinants of verbal behavior. In J. J. Gumperz & D. Hymes (Eds.), *Directions in sociolinguistics*. New York: Holt, Rinehart and Winston, in press.

BLOOM, B. S., HASTINGS, T., & MADAUS, G.   *Formative and summative evaluation of student learning*. New York: McGraw-Hill, 1971.

BLOOM, L. M.   *Language development: form and function in emerging grammars*. Cambridge, Mass.: M.I.T. Press, 1970.

BLOUNT, B. G.   Acquisition of language by Luo children. Unpublished doctoral dissertation, University of California at Berkeley, 1969.

BLUMENTHAL, A. L.   *Language and psychology: historical aspects of psycholinguistics*. New York: Wiley, 1970.

BORMUTH, J. R.   New developments in readability research. *Elementary English*, 1967, *44*, 840–845.

BOUCHARD, E. L.   Psycholinguistic attitude study. Ann Arbor: University of Michigan Center for Research on Language and Language Behavior, Progress Report No. VIII, February 1969.

BRANDIS, W., & HENDERSON, D.   *Social class, language and communication*. Beverly Hills, California: Sage Publications, 1970.

BRENT, S. B., & KLAMER, P.   The naming and conceptualization of simple geometric forms: a cross-cultural study. Paper presented at the meeting of the Society for Research in Child Development, New York, March 1967.

BRONOWSKI, J., & BELLUGI, U.   Language, name and concept. *Science*, 1970, *168*, 669–673.

BRONSON, M.   An exploration of the abilities of children between the ages of three and six to appreciate the abstract distinction between nouns and verbs. Unpublished term paper, Harvard University, 1971.

BROWN, H. R.   *Die Nigger die*. New York: Dial Press, 1969.

BROWN, R.   *Social psychology*. New York: The Free Press, 1965.

BROWN, R.   From codability to coding ability. In J. Bruner (Ed.), *Learning about learning: a conference report*. Washington, D.C.: U.S. Department of Health, Education and Welfare, 1966. Pp. 185–195.

BROWN, R.   The development of wh-questions in child speech. *Journal of Verbal Learning and Verbal Behavior*, 1968, *7*, 279–290. (a)

BROWN, R.   Introduction. In J. Moffett, *Teaching the university of discourse*. Boston: Houghton Mifflin, 1968. Pp. v–ix. (b)

BROWN, R.   The first sentences of child and chimpanzee. In *Psycholinguistics: selected papers by Roger Brown*. New York: Free Press, 1970. Pp. 208–231.

BROWN, R.   *A first language*. Cambridge, Mass.: Harvard University Press, in press.

BROWN, R., & BELLUGI, U.   Three processes in the child's acquisition of syntax. *Harvard Educational Review*, 1964, *34*, 133–151.

BROWN, R., CAZDEN, C. B., & BELLUGI, U.   The child's grammar from I to III. In J. P. Hill (Ed.), *1967 Minnesota symposium on child psychology*. Minneapolis: University of Minnesota Press, 1969. Pp. 28–73.

BROWN, R., & FRASER, C.   The acquisition of syntax. In U. Bellugi & R. Brown (Eds.), The acquisition of language. *Monographs of the Society for Research in Child Development*, 1964, *29* (1), 43–79.

BROWN, R., & HANLON, C.   Deprivational complexity and order of acquisition in child speech. In J. R. Hayes (Ed.), *Cognition and the development of language.* New York: Wiley, 1970. Pp. 11–53.

BRUNER, J. S.   Going beyond the information given. In *Contemporary approaches to cognition.* Cambridge, Mass.: Harvard University Press, 1957. Pp. 41–69.

BRUNER, J. S.   The growth of mind. *American Psychologist,* 1965, *20* (13), 1007–1016.

BRUNER, J. S.   *Toward a theory of instruction.* Cambridge, Mass.: Harvard University Press, 1966.

BRUNER, J. S.   The skill of relevance or the relevance of skills. *Saturday Review,* April 18, 1970, 66–68ff.

BRYANT, B.   The relationship between language usage and reading skill. Unpublished term paper, Harvard University, 1970.

BULL, W. A.   The use of vernacular languages in fundamental education. *International Journal of American Linguistics,* 1955, *21,* 288–294. Reprinted in D. Hymes (Ed.), *Language in Culture and Society.* New York: Harper & Row, 1964. Pp. 527–533.

BURLING, R.   Language development of a Garo and English-speaking child. *Word,* 1959, *15,* 45–68. (Reprinted in Bar-Adon & Leopold, 1971.)

BURLING, R.   *Man's many voices: language in its cultural context.* New York: Holt, Rinehart and Winston, 1970.

BURT, M. K.   *From deep to surface structure: an introduction to transformational syntax.* New York: Harper & Row, 1971.

CAMPBELL, D. T.   Stereotypes and the perception of group differences. *American Psychologist,* 1967, *22,* 817–829.

CAMPBELL, D. T., & STANLEY, J. C.   Experimental and quasi-experimental designs for research on teaching. In N. L. Gage (Ed.), *Handbook of research on teaching.* Chicago: Rand McNally, 1963. Pp. 171–246.

CAMPBELL, R. N.   English curricula for non-English speakers. In J. E. Alatis (Ed.), *Twenty-first annual roundtable: bilingualism and language contact.* Washington, D.C.: Georgetown University Press, 1970.

CARLSON, P., & ANISFELD, M.   Some observations on the linguistic competence of a two-year-old child. *Child Development,* 1969, *40,* 569–575.

CARROLL, J. B.   Some psychological effects of language structure. In P. Jock & J. Zubin (Eds.), *Psychopathology of communication.* New York: Grune & Stratton, 1958.

CARROLL, J. B.   *Language and thought.* Englewood Cliffs, N.J.: Prentice-Hall, 1964.

CARROLL, J. B.   Some neglected relationships in reading and language learning. *Elementary English,* 1966, *43,* 577–582.

CARROLL, J. B., & CASAGRANDE, B.   The function of language classifications in behavior. In Maccoby, Newcomb, & Hartley (Eds.), *Readings in social psychology* (3rd ed.). New York: Holt, Rinehart and Winston, 1958. Pp. 18–31.

CARSON, A. S., & RABIN, A. I.   Verbal comprehension and communication in Negro and white children. *Journal of Educational Psychology,* 1960, *51,* 47–51.

CAZDEN, C. B.   Environmental assistance to the child's acquisition of grammar. Unpublished doctoral dissertation, Harvard University, 1965.

CAZDEN, C. B.   Subculture differences in child language. *Merrill-Palmer Quarterly,* 1966, *12,* 185–219.

CAZDEN, C. B.   On individual differences in language competence and performance. *Journal of Special Education,* 1967, *1,* 135–150. (a)

CAZDEN, C. B.   The role of parent speech in the acquisition of grammar. *Project Literacy Reports* No. 8. Ithaca, N.Y.: Cornell University, 1967, pp. 60–65. (b)

CAZDEN, C. B.   The acquisition of noun and verb inflections. *Child Development,* 1968, *39,* 433–448. (a)

CAZDEN, C. B.   Review of W. Labov: The social stratification of English in New York City. *Contemporary Psychology,* 1968, *13,* 320–322. (b) Reprinted by permission of the American Psychological Association.

CAZDEN, C. B.   Some implications of research on language development for preschool education. In R. D. Hess & Roberta M. Bear (Eds.), *Early education.* Chicago: Aldine, 1968. Pp. 131–142. (c)

CAZDEN, C. B.   Three sociolinguistic views of the language of lower-class children—with special attention to the work of Basil Bernstein. *Developmental Medicine and Child Neurology,* 1968, *10,* 600–612. (d)

CAZDEN, C. B.   Review of D. Lawton: Social-class, language and education. *Contemporary Psychology,* 1969, *14,* 445–446. (a)

CAZDEN, C. B.   Suggestions from studies of language acquisition. *Childhood Education,* 1969, *46,* 127–131. (b)

CAZDEN, C. B.   Children's questions: their forms, functions and roles in education. *Young Children,* 1970, *25,* 202–220. (a)

CAZDEN, C. B.   Language in early childhood and reading: a review for 1969/70. Washington, D.C.: ERIC Clearinghouse for Linguistics, May 1970. (b)

CAZDEN, C. B.   The neglected situation in child language research and education. In Frederick Williams (Ed.), *Language and Poverty: perspectives on a theme.* Chicago: Markham, 1970. Pp. 81–101. Expanded version in *Journal of Social Issues,* 1970, *26,* 35–60. (c)

CAZDEN, C. B.   Review of J. H. Flavell et al.: *The development of role-taking and communication skills in children;* and S. Smilansky, *The effects of sociodramatic play on disadvantaged preschool children. Harvard Educational Review,* 1970, *40,* 137–141. (d) Copyright © 1970 by President and Fellows of Harvard College.

CAZDEN, C. B.   The hunt for the independent variables. In R. Huxley & E. Ingram (Eds.), *Language acquisition: models and methods.* New York: Academic Press, 1971. Pp. 41–47. (a)

CAZEN, C. B.   Language programs for young children: notes from England and Wales. In C. B. Lavatelli (Ed.), *Preschool language training.* Urbana, Ill.: University of Illinois Press, 1971. Pp. 119–153. (b)

CAZDEN, C. B.   Evaluating language and learning in early childhood education. In B. S. Bloom, T. Hastings & G. Madaus (Eds.), *Handbook for formative and summative evaluation of student learning.* New York: McGraw Hill, 1971. Pp. 345–398. (c)

CAZDEN, C. B.   Review of A. C. Aarons, B. Y. Gordon, & W. A. Stewart (Eds.), *The Florida FL Reporter* special anthology issue: Linguistic-Cultural Differences and American Education. *Modern Language Journal,* 1971, *55* (5), 331–333. (d)

CAZDEN, C. B.   The psychology of language. In L. E. Travis (Ed.), *Handbook of speech, hearing and language disorders.* (Rev. ed.) New York: Appleton, in press. (e)

CAZDEN, C. B., BRYANT, B. H., & TILLMAN, M. A.   Making it and going home: the attitudes of Black people toward language education. *Harvard Graduate School of Education Association Bulletin,* Spring 1970, *14,* (3), 4–9.

CAZDEN, C. B., & JOHN, V. P.   Learning in American Indian children. In M. L. Wax, S. Diamond, & F. O. Gearing (Eds.), *Anthropological perspectives in education.* New York: Basic Books, 1971. Pp. 252–272. Copyright © 1970 by Basic Books, Inc., Publishers, New York.

CAZDEN, C. B., JOHN, V. P., & HYMES, D. (Eds.).   *The functions of language in the classroom.* New York: Teachers College Press, in press.

CHOMSKY, C. S.   *The acquisition of syntax in children from 5 to 10.* Cambridge, Mass.: M.I.T. Press, 1969.

CHOMSKY, C.   Reading, writing and phonology. *Harvard Educational Review,* 1970, *40,* 287–309.

CHOMSKY, C.   Invented spelling in the open classroom. Cambridge, Mass.: Radcliffe Institute & Harvard Graduate School of Education, unpublished manuscript, 1971. (a)

CHOMSKY, C.   Write now, read later. *Childhood Education,* 1971, *47,* 296–299. (b)

CHOMSKY, N.   *Aspects of the theory of syntax.* Cambridge, Mass.: M.I.T. Press, 1965.

CHOMSKY, N.   *Language and mind.* New York: Harcourt, 1968.

CHOMSKY, N.   Phonology and reading. In H. Levin & J. Williams (Eds.), *Basic studies in reading.* New York: Basic Books, 1970. Pp. 3–18.

CHOMSKY, N.   *Form and meaning in natural language.* Amsterdam: North-Holland, n.d.

CHOMSKY, N., & HALLE, M.   *The sound pattern of English.* New York: Harper & Row, 1968.

CHUKOVSKY, K.   *From two to five.* Berkeley: University of California Press, 1963.

CICIRELLI, V., et al.   The impact of Head Start: an evaluation of the effects of Head Start on children's cognitive and affective development. Vols. I and II. Bladensburg, Md.: Westinghouse Learning Corp., 1969. (Distributed by Clearinghouse for Federal Scientific and Technical Information.)

CLARK, H. H.   The primitive nature of children's relational concepts. In J. R. Hayes (Ed.), *Cognition and the development of language.* New York: Wiley, 1970. Pp. 269–278. (a)

CLARK, H. H.   Word associations and linguistic theory. In J. Lyons (Ed.), *New Horizons in Linguistics.* Baltimore: Penguin Books, 1970. Pp. 271–286. (b)

CLINCHY, B., & ROSENTHAL, K.   Analysis of children's errors. In G. S. Lesser (Ed.), *Psychology and educational practice.* Glenview, Illinois: Scott, Foresman, 1971. Pp. 90–129.

COHEN, R. The relation between socio-conceptual styles and orientation to school requirements. *Sociology of Education,* 1968, *4,* 201–220.

COLE, M., & BRUNER, J. S. Preliminaries to a theory of cultural differences. *American Psychologist,* 1971, *26,* 867–876.

COLE, M., GAY, J., GLICK, J., & SHARP, D. W. *Culture and cognitive processes.* New York: Basic Books, 1971.

COLEMAN, J. S. *Equality of educational opportunity.* Washington, D.C.: U.S. Department of Health, Education and Welfare, Office of Education, 1966.

COMPTON, A. J. Generative studies of children's phonological disorders. *Journal of Speech and Hearing Disorders,* in press.

COWAN, P. A., WEBER, J., HODDINOTT, B. A., & KLEIN, J. Mean length of spoken response as a function of stimulus, experimenter, and subject. *Child Development,* 1967, *38,* 191–203.

CREMIN, L. A. *The transformation of the school.* New York: Knopf, 1961.

CROMER, R. F. The development of temporal reference during the acquisition of language. Unpublished doctoral dissertation, Harvard University, 1968.

CROMER, R. "Children are nice to understand": surface structure clues for the recovery of a deep structure. *British Journal of Psychology,* 1970, *61,* 397–408.

DAEHLER, M. W., HOROWITZ, A. B., WYNNS, F. C., & FLAVELL, J. H. Verbal and nonverbal rehearsal in children's recall. *Child Development,* 1969, *40,* 443–452.

DATO, D. P. *American children's acquisition of Spanish syntax in the Madrid environment* (preliminary ed.). U.S. Department of Health, Education and Welfare, Office of Education, May 1970. (Available from Georgetown University Bookstore, Washington, D.C.)

DAVIS, O., GLADNEY, M., & LEAVERTON, L. *The psycholinguistics reading series, Books 1–7.* Chicago: Board of Education, 1968.

DAVIS, O., GLADNEY, M., & LEAVERTON, L. *The psycholinguistics reading series: a bidialectal approach. Teachers Manual.* Chicago: Board of Education, 1969.

DE LAGUNA, G. *Speech: its function and development.* Bloomington, Ind.: Indiana University Press, 1963. (First published by Oxford Univ. Press, 1927.)

DENNER, B. Representational and syntactic competence of problem readers. *Child Development,* 1970, *41,* 881–887.

DE STEFANO, J. S. Productive language differences in fifth grade Black students' syntactic forms. *Elementary English,* in press.

DIXON, J. *Growth through English.* Reading, England: National Association for the Teaching of English, 1967. (Also available from the National Council of Teachers of English, Champaign, Ill.)

DOBZHANSKY, T. Of flies and men. *American Psychologist,* 1967, *22,* 41–48.

DODSON, C. J., PRICE, E., & TUNDO, I. *Towards bilingualism: studies in language teaching methods.* Cardiff: University of Wales Press, 1968.

DONALDSON, M., & WALES, R. On the acquisition of some rational terms. In J. R. Hayes (Ed.), *Cognition and the development of language.* New York: Wiley, 1970. Pp. 235–268.

EDUCATION STUDY CENTER. *Ollie.* Washington, D.C.: Author, 1970.

EIMAS, P. D., SIQUELAND, E. R., JUSCZYK, P., & VIGORITO, J.　Speech perception in infants. *Science*, 1971, *171*, 303–306.

EINSTEIN, A.　Letter to Jacques Hadamard. In B. Ghiselin (Ed.), *The creative process: a symposium.* New York: The New American Library (Mentor books), 1955.

ELKIND, D., & FLAVELL, J. H. (Eds.)　*Studies in cognitive development.* New York: Oxford University Press, 1969.

ELKIND, D., DEBLINGER, J., & ADLER, D.　Motivation and creativity: the content effect. *American Educational Research Journal*, 1970, *7*, 351–357.

ELKIND, D.,　Piaget and Montessori. *Harvard Educational Review,* 1967, *37,* 535–545.

ENTWISLE, D. R.　*Word associations of young children.* Baltimore: The Johns Hopkins Press, 1966.

ENTWISLE, D. R.　Semantic systems of children: some assessments of social class and ethnic differences. In F. Williams (Ed.), *Language and poverty.* Chicago: Markham, 1970. Pp. 123–139.

ERVIN, S. M.　Imitation and structural change in children's language. In E. Lenneberg (Ed.), *New directions in the study of language.* Cambridge, Mass.: M.I.T. Press, 1964. Pp. 163–189.

ERVIN, S. M., & MILLER, W. R.　Language development. In H. Stevenson (Ed.), *Child psychology*, 62nd yearbook of the National Society for the Study of Education. Chicago: University of Chicago Press, 1963.

ERVIN-TRIPP, S.　Language development. In L. W. Hoffman & M. L. Hoffman (Eds.), *Review of child development research.* Vol. 2. New York: Russell Sage Foundation, 1966.

ERVIN-TRIPP, S.　Sociolinguistics. In L. Berkowitz (Ed.), *Advances in experimental social psychology.* Vol. 4. New York: Academic Press, 1969. Pp. 91–165.

ERVIN-TRIPP, S.　Discourse agreement: how children answer questions. In J. R. Hayes (Ed.), *Cognition and the development of language.* New York: Wiley, 1970. Pp. 79–107. (a)

ERVIN-TRIPP, S.　Structure and process in language acquisition. In J. E. Alatis (Ed.), *Twenty-first annual round table: bilingualism and language contact.* Washington, D.C.: Georgetown University Press, 1970. Pp. 313–344. (b)

ERVIN-TRIPP, S.　Social background and verbal skills. In R. Huxley and E. Ingram (Eds.), *Language development: models and methods.* New York: Academic Press, 1971. Pp. 29–39. (a)

ERVIN-TRIPP, S.　Social dialects in developmental sociolinguistics. In R. Shuy (Ed.), *Sociolinguistics: a cross-disciplinary perspective.* Washington, D.C.: Center for Applied Linguistics, 1971. Pp. 35–64. (b)

FARNHAM-DIGGORY, S.　Cognitive synthesis in Negro and White children. *Monographs of the Society for Research in Child Development*, 1970, *35* (whole No. 2).

FERGUSON, C. A.　Baby talk in six languages. In J. G. Gumperz & D. Hymes (Eds.), The ethnography of communication. *American Anthropologist*, 1964, *66* (6), 103–114.

FERGUSON, C. A.　Myths about Arabic. In A. F. C. Wallace (Ed.), *Men and cultures.* Philadelphia: University of Pennsylvania Press, 1956. (Reprinted in J. Fishman (Ed.) *Readings in the sociology of language*. The Hague: Mouton, 1968. Pp. 375–381.)

FISHER, J. L.   Social influence in the choice of a linguistic variant. *Word*, 1958, *14*, 47–56. Reprinted in D. Hymes (Ed.), *Language in culture and society*. New York: Harper & Row, 1964. Pp. 483–488.

FISHMAN, J. A.   The status and prospects of bilingualism in the United States. *Modern Language Journal*, 1965, *49*, 143–155.

FISHMAN, J. A.   *Sociolinguistics*. Rowley, Mass.: Newbury House, 1970. (a)

FISHMAN, J. A.   The politics of bilingual education. In J. E. Alatis (Ed.), *Twenty-first annual round table: bilingualism and language contact*. Monograph Series on Language and Linguistics, No. 23. Washington, D.C.: Georgetown University Press, 1970. Pp. 47–54. (b)

FISHMAN, J. A., et al.   *Language loyalty in the United States*. The Hague: Mouton, 1966. (Summarized briefly in Fishman, 1965.)

FISHMAN, J. A., et al.   *Bilingualism in the barrio*. 2 vols. U.S. Department of Health, Education and Welfare, Office of Education, August 1968.

FLAVELL, J. H., BEACH, D. R., & CHINSKY, J. M.   Spontaneous verbal rehearsal in a memory task as a function of age. *Child Development*, 1966, *37*, 283–299.

FLAVELL, J. H., & WOHLWILL, T. F.   Formal and functional aspects of cognitive development. In D. Elkind & J. H. Flavell (Eds.), *Studies in cognitive development*. New York: Oxford University Press, 1969. Pp. 67–120.

FLAVELL, J. H., et al.   *The development of role-taking and communication skills in children*. New York: Wiley, 1968.

FODOR, J. A., & GARRETT, M,   Some syntactic determinants of sentential complexity. *Perception and Psychophysics*, 1967, *2*, 289–296.

FRANK, S. M., & OSSER, H.   A psycholinguistic model of syntactic complexity. *Language and Speech*, 1970, *13*, 38–53.

FRASER, B.   Unpublished proposal. Cambridge, Mass.: Language Research Foundation, 1969.

FRASER, C., BELLUGI, U., & BROWN, R.   Control of grammar in imitation, comprehension and production. *Journal of Verbal Learning and Verbal Behavior*, 1963, *2*, 121–135.

FREIRE, P.   Cultural action and conscientization. *Harvard Educational Review*, 1970, *40*, 452–477.

FRIEDMAN, D. G.   Personality development in infancy: a biological approach. In S. L. Washburn & P. G. Jay (Eds.), *Perspectives on Human Evolution*. New York: Holt, Rinehart and Winston, 1968. Pp. 258–287.

FRIEDLANDER, B. Z.   Identifying and investigating major variables in receptive language development. Paper presented at biannual meeting of Society for Research in Child Development, Santa Monica, Calif., March 1969.

FRIEDLANDER, B. Z.   Receptive language development in infancy. *Merrill-Palmer Quarterly*, 1970, *16*, 7–51.

FRIEDLANDER, B. Z.   Listening, language and auditory environment. In J. Hellmuth (Ed.), *Exceptional infant, Vol. 2: studies in abnormality*. New York: Brunner/Mazel, in press.

FRIEDLANDER, B. Z., CYRALIK, A., & DAVIS, B.   Time-sampling analysis of infants' natural language environments in the home. Madison: University of Wisconsin, unpublished manuscript, n.d.

FURTH, H.   *Thinking without language: psychological implications of deafness.* New York: Free Press, 1966.

GAARDER, A. B.   Organization of the bilingual school. *Journal of Social Issues,* 1967, *23,* 110–120.

GAARDER, A. B.   The first seventy-six bilingual education projects. In J. E. Alatis (Ed.), *Twenty-first annual round table: bilingualism and language contact.* Washington, D.C.: Georgetown University Press, 1971. Pp. 163–175.

GAGNÉ, R. M.   Learning hierarchies. Presidential address to Division 15, American Psychological Association, San Francisco, August 1968. (Reprinted in *Educational Psychologist,* Division 15 Newsletter, November 1968, 1–9.)

GAHAGAN, D. M., & GAHAGAN, G. A.   *Talk reform: explorations in language in the primary school.* Primary socialization, language and education, Vol. III. Sociological Research Unit Monograph Series directed by B. Bernstein. Beverly Hills, California: Sage Publications, 1970.

GARDNER, R. A., & GARDNER, B. T.   Teaching sign language to a chimpanzee. *Science,* 1969, *165,* 664–672.

GARVEY, C., & MCFARLANE, P. T.   A preliminary study of Standard English speech patterns in the Baltimore city public schools. The Johns Hopkins University Center for the Study of Social Organization of Schools, Report No. 16, 1968.

GATTEGNO, C.   *Towards a visual culture: education through television.* New York: Outerbridge & Dienstfrey, 1969.

GATTEGNO, C.   *What we owe children: the subordination of teaching to learning.* New York: Outerbridge & Dienstfrey, 1970.

GEISSLER, H.   *Zweisprachigkeit deutscher Kinder in Ausland.* Stuttgart, 1938.

GINSBERG, H., & OPPER, S.   *Piaget's theory of intellectual development: an introduction.* Englewood Cliffs, N.J.: Prentice-Hall, 1969.

GLASMAN, L. D.   A social-class comparison of conceptual processes in children's free recall. Unpublished doctoral dissertation, University of California, Berkeley, 1968.

GLEASON, J. B.   Do children imitate? Paper read at International Conference on Oral Education of the Deaf, Lexington School for the Deaf, New York City, June 1967.

GLICK, J.   Cognitive style among the Kpelle of Ligeria. Paper presented at symposium on cross-cultural cognitive studies. American Educational Research Association, Chicago, February 1968.

GLUCKSBERG, S., KRAUSS, R. M., & WEISBERG, R.   Referential communication in nursery school children: method and some preliminary findings. *Journal of Experimental Child Psychology,* 1966, *3,* 333–342.

GOODENOUGH, W. H.   *Description and comparison in cultural anthropology.* Chicago: Aldine, 1970.

GOODNOW, J. J.   The role of modalities in perceptual and cognitive development. In J. P. Hill (Ed.), *1970 Minnesota symposium on child psychology.* University of Minnesota, in press.

GREEN, T. F.   Teaching, acting and behaving. *Harvard Educational Review,* 1964, *34,* 507–524.

GREEN, T. F.   *Work, leisure and the American schools.* New York: Random House, 1968.

GREENBERG, P. *The devil has slippery shoes: a biased biography of the Child Development Group of Mississippi.* New York: Macmillan, 1969.

GREENFIELD, P. M. Oral and written language. Paper presented at annual meeting of American Educational Research Association, Chicago, February 1968.

GRUBER, J. S. Topicalization in child language. *Foundations of Language,* 1967, *3,* 37–65. Reprinted in Bar-Adon & Leopold (1971).

GRUEN, G. E. Note on conservation: methodological and definitional considerations. *Child Development,* 1966, *37,* 977–983.

GUMPERZ, J. J., & HERNANDEZ, E. Bilingualism, bidialectalism and classroom interaction. In C. B. Cazden, D. Hymes, & V. John (Eds.), *The functions of language in the classroom.* New York: Teachers College Press, in press.

GUSKIN, J. T. The social perception of language variations: Black and white teachers' attitudes towards speakers from different racial and social class backgrounds. Unpublished doctoral dissertation, University of Michigan, 1970.

HALE, K. Navajo linguistics. Paper prepared for Hunter's Point Workshop, Summer 1970. Massachusetts Institute of Technology, unpublished manuscript, 1970.

HALE, K. A note on a Walbiri tradition of antonymy. In D. Steinberg & L. Jakobvits (Eds.), *Semantics: an interdisciplinary reader in philosophy, psychology, and anthropology.* Urbana: University of Illinois Press, in press.

HALL, E. T. Listening behavior: some cultural differences. *Phi Delta Kappan,* 1969, *50,* 379–380.

HALLIDAY, M. Speech and situation. In A. Wilkinson (Ed.), *Some aspects of oracy.* Huddersfield, Yorkshire, England: National Association for the Teaching of English, Bulletin II, No. 2, 1965, pp. 14–17.

HART, B., & RISLEY, T. R. The use of preschool materials for modifying the language of disadvantaged children. *Journal of Applied Behavior Analysis,* in press.

HASS, W. A. A manual for syntactic analysis of children's connected discourse. University of Chicago, Speech and Language Research Laboratory (mimeo), December 1967.

HATCH, E. Four experimental studies of syntax in young children. Inglewood, Calif.: Southwestern Regional Laboratory for Research and Development. TR 11, October 1969. (a)

HATCH, E. The syntax of four reading programs compared with language development of children. Inglewood, Calif.: Southwestern Regional Laboratory for Educational Research and Development. TR 21, 22, December 1969. (b)

HAUGEN, E. Language planning in modern Norway. *Anthropological Linguistics,* 1959, *1* (3), 8–21. Reprinted in J. Fishman (Ed.), *Readings in the sociology of language.* The Hague: Mouton, 1968. Pp. 673–687.

HAVIGHURST, R. J. Minority subcultures and the law of effect. *American Psychologist,* 1970, *25,* 313–322.

HAWKINS, P. R. Social class, the nominal group and reference. *Language and Speech,* 1969, *12,* 125–135.

HEIDER, E. R. "Focal" color areas and the development of color names. *Developmental Psychology,* 1971, *4,* 447–455. (a)

HEIDER, E. R. Style and accuracy of verbal communications within and between social classes. *Journal of Personality and Social Psychology*, 1971, *18*, 33–47. (b)

HEIDER, E. R., CAZDEN, C. B., & BROWN, R.   Social class differences in the effectiveness and style of children's coding ability. *Project Literacy Reports*, No. 9. Ithaca, N.Y.: Cornell University, 1968.

HENRIE, S. N., JR.   A study of verb phrases used by five year old nonstandard Negro English-speaking children. Unpublished doctoral dissertation, University of California at Berkeley, 1969.

HERTZIG, M. E., BIRCH, H. G., THOMAS, A., & MENDEZ, O. A.   Class and ethnic differences in the responsiveness of preschool children to cognitive demands. *Monographs of the Society for Research in Child Development*, 1968, *33* (whole No. 1).

HESS, R. D.   Parental behavior and children's school achievement: implications for Head Start. In E. Grotberg (Ed.), *Critical issues in research related to disadvantaged children*. Princeton, N.J.: Educational Testing Service, 1969. Seminar #5, pp. 1–76.

HESS, R. D., & SHIPMAN, V.   Maternal influences upon early learning. In R. D. Hess and R. M. Bear (Eds.), *Early education*. Chicago: Aldine, 1968. Pp. 91–103.

HESS, R. D., et al.   *The cognitive environments of urban preschool children*. Vol. 1. University of Chicago Graduate School of Education, November 1968. Vol. 2, *Follow-up phase*. University of Chicago Graduate School of Education, June 1969.

HOLMES, M. B., HOLMES, D., & FRIEDMAN, A.   Interaction patterns as a source of error in teacher's evaluations of Head Start children. Final report to OEO. New York: Associated YM-YWHAs of Greater New York, August 1968.

HOLT, J.   *How children learn*. New York: Pitman, 1967.

HORNBY, P. A.   The differential effect of word order, syntactic structure, and contrastive stress on one aspect of sentence meaning as a function of age. Unpublished doctoral dissertation, University of Chicago, 1970.

HORNBY, P. A., & HASS, W. A.   Use of contrastive stress by preschool children. *Journal of Speech and Hearing Research*, 1970, *13*, 395–399.

HORNER, V. M.   The verbal world of the lower-class three-year-old: a pilot study in linguistic ecology. Unpublished doctoral dissertation, University of Rochester, 1968.

HOUSTON, S. H.   A reexamination of some assumptions about the language of the disadvantaged child. *Child Development*, 1970, *41*, 947–963.

HUNT, K. W.   Grammatical structures written at three grade levels. Resident report No. 3. Champaign, Ill.: National Council of Teachers of English, 1965.

HUTTENLOCHER, J., & STRAUSS, S.   Comprehension and a statement's relation to the situation it describes. *Journal of Verbal Learning and Verbal Behavior*, 1968, *7*, 300–304.

HUXLEY, R., & INGRAM, E. (Eds.)   *Language acquisition: models and methods*. New York: Academic Press, 1971.

HYMES, D.   Functions of speech: an evolutionary approach. In F. C. Gruber (Ed.), *Anthropology and education*. Philadelphia: University of Pennsylvania Press, 1961. Pp. 55–83

HYMES, D. Directions in (ethno-) Linguistic theory. In A. K. Romney & R. G. D'Andrade (Eds.), Transcultural studies in cognition. *American Anthropologist*, 1964, *66* (3), part 2, 6–56.

HYMES, D. Models of the interaction of language and social setting. *Journal of Social Issues*, 1967, *23*, 8–28.

HYMES, D. Competence and performance in linguistic theory. In R. Huxley and E. Ingram (Eds.), *Language acquisition: models and methods*. New York: Academic Press, 1971. Pp. 3–28.

HYMES, D. Sociolinguistics and the ethnography of speaking. In E. Ardener (Ed.), *Linguistics and social anthropology* (approximate title). London: Tavistock Press, in press.

INHELDER, B. Memory and intelligence in the child. In D. Elkind & J. H. Flavell (Eds.), *Studies in cognitive development*. New York: Oxford University Press, 1969.

INHELDER, B., BOVET, M., SINCLAIR, H., & SMOCK, C. D. On cognitive development. *American Psychologist*, 1966, *21*, 160–164.

ISAACS, N. Appendix on children's 'why' questions. In S. Isaacs, *Intellectual growth in young children*. London: Routledge, 1930. Pp. 293–349.

ISTOMINA, Z. M. Perception and naming of color in early childhood. *Soviet Psychology and Psychiatry*, 1963, *1*, 37–45.

JACOBS, R. A., & ROSENBAUM, P. S. *English transformational grammar*. Waltham, Mass.: Blaisdell, 1968.

JAKOBSON, R. Closing statement: linguistics and poetics. In T. Sebeok (Ed.), *Style in language*. Cambridge, Mass.: M.I.T. Press, 1960. Pp. 57–69.

JAKOBSON, R. Discussion. In CIBA Foundation Symposium, *Disorders of language*. Boston: Little, Brown, 1964. Pp. 42–46.

JAKOBSON, R. *Child language, aphasia, and phonological universals*. The Hague: Mouton, 1968.

JAKOBSON, R. Why "mama" and "papa"? In R. Jakobson, *Selected writings*. The Hague: Mouton, 1939. (Reprinted in Bar-Adon & Leopold, 1971.)

JAKOBSON, R., & HALLE, M. *Fundamentals of language*. The Hague: Mouton, 1956.

JENSEN, A. R. Social class and verbal learning. In M. Deutsch, I. Katz, & A. R. Jensen (Eds.), *Social class, race and psychological development*. New York: Holt, Rinehart and Winston, 1968. Pp. 115–174.

JENSEN, A. R. How much can we boost IQ and scholastic achievement? *Harvard Educational Review*, 1969, *39*, 1–123. Copyright © 1969 by President and Fellows of Harvard College. All Rights Reserved. Reprinted by permission of the author, Dr. Arthur R. Jensen, and the President and Fellows of Harvard College.

JENSEN, A. R., & ROHWER, W. D., JR. Syntactical mediation of serial and paired-associate learning as a function of age. *Child Development*, 1965, *36*, 601–608.

JOHN, V. P. Language and educability. In E. Leacock (Ed.), *Culture of poverty: a critique*. New York: Simon and Schuster, in press.

JOHN, V., & HORNER, V. M. Bilingualism and the Spanish-speaking child. In F. Williams (Ed.), *Language and poverty: perspectives on a theme*. Chicago: Markham, 1970.

JOHN, V. P., & HORNER, V. M.   *Early childhood bilingual education.* New York: Modern Language Association, 1971.

JOHN, V., HORNER, V., & BERNEY, T.   Story re-telling. In H. Levin and J. P. Williams (Eds.), *Basic studies in reading.* New York: Harper & Row, 1970. Pp. 246–262.

JOHN, V., & MOSKOVITZ, S.   Language acquisition and development in early childhood. In A. H. Marckwardt (Ed.), *Linguistics in school programs*, 69th yearbook, Part II. Chicago, Ill.: National Society for the Study of Education, 1970.

JOHNSON, K.   A report on research to determine if Black children can read dialect with fewer errors and greater comprehension than standard English dialect. Paper presented at annual meeting of Teachers of English to Speakers of Other Languages, New Orleans, March 1971.

JONES, V. W.   The Alaskan reading and language development program. Paper read at meeting of American Educational Research Association, Minneapolis, 1970.

JONES, L. V., & WEPMAN, J. M.   Grammatical indicants of speaking style in normal and aphasic speakers. Chapel Hill, N.C.: The Psychometric Laboratory, University of North Carolina, No. 46, December 1965.

KAGAN, J.   On the need for relativism. *American Psychologist*, 1967, *22*, 131–142.

KAGAN, J.   On cultural deprivation. In D. C. Glass (Ed.), *Environmental influences.* New York: Rockefeller University Press and Russell Sage Foundation, 1968. Pp. 211–250.

KAGAN, J.   Inadequate evidence and illogical conclusions. *Harvard Educational Review,* 1969, *39*, 274–277.

KAGAN, J., & KOGAN, N.   Individual variation in cognitive processes. In P. H. Mussen (Ed.), *Carmichael's manual of child psychology*, Third edition, Vol. 1. New York: Wiley, 1970. Pp. 1273–1365.

KATZ, J.   Semi-sentences. In J. Katz & J. Fodor (Eds.), *The structure of language.* Englewood Cliffs, N.J.: Prentice-Hall, 1964.

KATZ, J. J., & FODOR, J. A.   The structure of a semantic theory. In J. Katz and J. Fodor (Eds.), *The structure of language.* Englewood Cliffs, N.J.: Prentice-Hall, 1964.

KELKAR, A. R.   Language: linguistics: the applications. Bloomington, Indiana: *Language Sciences* No. 4. February 1969.

KELLY, L. G. (Ed.)   *Bilingualism: description and measurement*—an international seminar. Toronto: University of Toronto Press in association with the Canadian National Commission for UNESCO, 1969.

KEPES, G. (Ed.)   *Education of vision.* New York: Braziller, 1965.

KERNAN, C. M.   On the status of Black English for native speakers: an assessment of attitudes and values. In C. B. Cazden, V. P. John, and D. Hymes (Eds.), *Functions of language in the classroom.* New York: Teachers College Press, in press.

KERNAN, K. T.   The acquisition of language by Samoan children. Unpublished doctoral dissertation, University of California at Berkeley, 1969.

KEYSER, S. J.   The role of linguistics in the elementary school curriculum. *Elementary English*, 1970, *47*, 39–45.

KLIMA, E. S., & BELLUGI, U. Syntactic regularities in the speech of children. In J. Lyons and R. J. Wales (Eds.), *Psycholinguistics papers*. Edinburgh: University Press, 1966. Pp. 183–208.

KOCHMAN, T. Social factors in the consideration of teaching standard English. Paper read at convention of Teachers of English to Speakers of Other Languages (TESOL). Chicago: March 1969.

KOCHMAN, T. Black English in the classroom. In C. B. Cazden, D. Hymes, and V. John (Eds.), *The functions of language in the classroom*. New York: Teachers College Press, in press.

KOHL, H. *36 children*. New York: New American Library, 1967.

KOHLBERG, L., YEAGER, J., & HJERTHOLM, E. The development of private speech: four studies and a review of theory. *Child Development*, 1968, *39*, 691–736.

KOLERS, P. A. Three stages of reading. In H. Levin & J. P. Williams (Eds.), *Basic studies in reading*. New York: Basic Books, 1970. Pp. 90–118.

KRAUSS, R. M., & GLUCKSBERG, S. The development of communication: Competence as a function of age. *Child Development, 1969, 40*, 255–266.

KRAUSS, R. M., & ROTTER, G. S. Communication abilities of children as a function of status and age. *Merrill-Palmer Quarterly*, in press.

LABOV, W. Linguistic research on the non-standard English of Negro children. Paper read at New York Social Experiment Study of Education, April 1965. (a)

LABOV, W. Stages in the acquisition of standard English. In R. W. Shuy (Ed.), *Social dialects and language learning*. Champaign, Ill.: National Council of Teachers of English, 1965. Pp. 77–103. (b)

LABOV, W. The effect of social mobility on linguistic behavior. *Sociological Inquiry*, 1966, *36*, 186–203. (a)

LABOV, W. On the grammaticality of every-day speech. Paper given at the meeting of the Linguistics Society of America, New York, Dec. 18, 1966. (b)

LABOV, W. *The social stratification of English in New York City*. Washington, D.C.: Center for Applied Linguistics, 1966. (c)

LABOV, W. The logic of non-standard English. *The Florida FL Reporter*, 1969, 7(1), 60–74. (a)

LABOV, W. Some sources of reading problems for Negro speakers of non-standard English. In J. C. Baratz and R. W. Shuy (Eds.), *Teaching Black children to read*. Washington, D.C.: Center for Applied Linguistics, 1969. Pp. 29–67. (b)

LABOV, W. *The study of non-standard English*. Washington, D.C.: Clearinghouse for Linguistics, Center for Applied Linguistics, 1969. (c) (Available from the ERIC Document Reproduction Service.)

LABOV, W. The reading of the *-ed* suffix. In H. Levin & J. P. Williams (Eds.), *Basic studies in reading*. New York: Basic Books, 1970. Pp. 222–245.

LABOV, W., & COHEN, P. Systematic relations of standard and non-standard rules in the grammars of Negro speakers. *Project Literacy Reports* No. 8. Ithaca, N.Y.: Cornell University, 1967. Pp. 66–84.

LABOV, W., COHEN, P., ROBINS, C., & LEWIS, J. A study of the non-standard English of Negro and Puerto Rican speakers in New York City. Vol. 1.

Phonological and grammatical analysis. Vol. 2. The use of language in the speech community. Final report of Cooperative Research Project No. 3288. Columbia University, 1968. (To be distributed through ERIC.)

LABOV, W., & ROBINS, C.   A note on the relation of reading failure to peer-group status in urban ghettos. *The Record—Teachers College*, 1969, *70*, 395–405.

LACROSSE, E. R., JR., LEE, P. C., LITMAN, F., OGILVIE, D. M., STODOLSKY, S. S., & WHITE, B. L.   The first six years of life: a report on current research and educational practice. *Genetic Psychology Monographs*, in press.

LAMBERT, W. E., JUST, M., & SEGALOWITZ, N.   Some cognitive consequences of following the curricula of the early school grades in a foreign language. In J. E. Alatis (Ed.), *Twenty-first round table: bilingualism and language contact*. Washington, D.C.: Georgetown University Press, 1970.

LANDES, R.   *Culture in American Education*. New York: Wiley, 1965.

LANGACKER, R. W.   *Language and its structure*. New York: Harcourt, 1967.

LANGER, S. K.   *Philosophy in a new key*. New York: New American Library (a Mentor book), 1948. (First published in 1942.)

LASHLEY, K. S.   Learning. In C. Murchison (Ed.), *The foundations of experimental psychology*. Worcester, Mass.: Clark University Press, 1929. Pp. 524–563.

LASHLEY, K. S.   The problem of serial order in behavior. In L. A. Jeffress (Ed.), *Cerebral mechanisms in behavior*. New York: Wiley, 1951. Pp. 112–136. (Reprinted in S. Saporta (Ed.), *Psycholinguistics*. New York: Holt, Rinehart and Winston, 1961. Pp. 180–198.)

LAVATELLI, C. S.   *Piaget's theory applied to an early childhood curriculum*. Boston, Mass.: American Science and Engineering, 1970.

LAWTON, D.   *Social class, language and education*. London: Routledge & Kegan Paul, 1968.

LEACOCK, E. B.   Abstract versus concrete speech: a false dichotomy. In C. B. Cazden, V. P. John, & D. Hymes (Eds.), *The functions of language in the classroom*. New York: Teachers College Press, in press.

LELER, H.   Language development of socially disadvantaged preschool children. Unpublished doctoral dissertation, Stanford University, 1970.

LENNEBERG, E. H.   Understanding language without ability to speak: a case report. *Journal of Abnormal and Social Psychology*, 1962, *65*, 419–425. (Reprinted in Bar-Adon & Leopold, 1971.)

LENNEBERG, E. H.   *Biological foundations of language*. New York: Wiley, 1967.

LENNEBERG, E. H.   On explaining language. *Science*, 1969, *164*, 635–643.

LEOPOLD, W. F.   *Speech development of a bilingual child: a linguistic record*. 4 vols. Evanston, Ill.: Northwestern University Press, 1939–1947.

LEOPOLD, W. F.   The study of child language and infant bilingualism. *Word*, 1948, *4*, 1–17. (Reprinted in Bar-Adon & Leopold, 1971.)

LEOPOLD, W. F.   Patterning in children's language learning. *Language Learning*, 1953, *5*, 1–14. (Reprinted in Bar-Adon & Leopold, 1971.)

LESSER, G. S., FIFER, G., & CLARK, D. H.   Mental abilities of children in different social and cultural groups. *Monograph of Social Research and Child Development*, 1965, *30*, No. 4 (Serial No. 102).

LÉVI-STRAUSS, C. *The savage mind*. Chicago: The University of Chicago Press, 1966.

LEWIS, M. M. *Language, thought and personality*. New York: Basic Books, 1964.

LIEBOW, E. *Tally's corner: a study of Negro streetcorner men*. Boston, Mass.: Little, Brown, 1967.

LOBAN, W. D. *The language of elementary school children*. Champaign, Ill.: National Council of Teachers of English, 1963.

LUNDSTEEN, S. W. Manipulating abstract thinking as a subability to problem solving in the context of English curriculum. *American Educational Research Journal*, 1970, *7*, 373–396.

LURIA, A. R. *The role of speech in the regulation of normal and abnormal behavior*. New York: Liveright, 1961.

LURIA, A. R. Speech development and the formation of mental processes. In M. Cole & I. Maltzman (Eds.), *A handbook of contemporary Soviet psychology*. New York: Basic Books, 1969.

LURIA, A. R. The functional organization of the brain. *Scientific American*, 1970, *222*(3), 66–78.

LURIA, A. R., & VINOGRADOVA, O. S. An objective investigation of the dynamics of semantic systems. *British Journal of Psychology*, 1959, *50*, 89–105.

LYONS, J. Introduction. In J. Lyons (Ed.), *New horizons in linguistics*. Baltimore: Penguin Books, 1970. Pp. 7–28.

MACDONALD, J. W. A critique of developmental phonology from the point of view of transformational theory. Unpublished qualifying paper, Harvard University, 1967.

MACKAY, D., & THOMPSON, B. The initial teaching of reading and writing: some notes toward a theory of literacy. Programme in linguistics and English teaching, Paper No. 3. London: University College and Longmans, 1968.

MACNAMARA, J. *Bilingualism and primary education: a study of the Irish experience*. Edinburgh: Edinburgh University Press, 1966.

MACNAMARA, J. The effects of instruction in a weaker language. *Journal of Social Issues*, 1967, *23*(2), 121–135.

MACNAMARA, J. Review of C. Chomsky: *The acquisition of language in children from 5 to 10*. Cambridge, Mass.: M.I.T. Press, 1969. *General Linguistics*, in press.

MAYR, E. Cause and effect in biology. *Science*, 1961, *134*, 1501–1506.

MARATSOS, M. P. The development of definite and indefinite reference. Unpublished doctoral dissertation, Harvard University, 1972.

MCCARTHY, DOROTHEA. Language development in children. In L. Carmichael (Ed.), *A manual of child psychology*. Second edition. New York: Wiley, 1954. Pp. 492–630.

MCCLELLAN, J. E. Discussion of "Teaching, acting and behaving." *Harvard Educational Review*, 1965, *35*, 199–203.

MCNEILL, D. Developmental psycholinguistics. In F. Smith and G. A. Miller (Eds.), *The genesis of language: a psycholinguistic approach*. Cambridge, Mass.: M.I.T. Press, 1966. Pp. 15–84.

MCNEILL, D. Production and perception: the view from language. In D. R. Olson and S. M. Pagliuso (Eds.), From perceiving to performing: an aspect of cognitive growth. *Ontario Journal of Educational Research*, 1968, *10*, 181–185.

MCNEILL, D. *The acquisition of language: the study of developmental psycholinguistics.* New York: Harper & Row, 1970. (a)

MCNEILL, D. The development of language. In P. H. Mussen (Ed.), *The manual of child psychology.* (3rd ed.) Vol. I. New York: Wiley, 1970. Pp. 1061–1161. (b)

MCNEILL, D., YUKAWA, R., & MCNEILL, N. B. The acquisition of direct and indirect objects in Japanese. *Child Development*, 1971, *42*, 237–249.

MEAD, G. H. *Mind, self, and society.* Chicago: University of Chicago Press, 1934.

MEICHENBAUM, D. H. Paper presented at biennial meeting of Society for Research in Child Development, Minneapolis, April 1971.

MELLON, J. C. *Transformational sentence-combining: a method for enhancing the development of syntactic fluency in English composition.* Champaign, Ill.: National Council of Teachers of English, 1969.

MENYUK, P. *Sentences children use.* Cambridge, Mass.: M.I.T. Press, 1969.

MENYUK, P., & BERNHOLTZ, N. Prosodic features and children's language production. *Quarterly Progress Report* No. 93, M.I.T. Research Laboratory of Electronics, April 1969, 216–219.

MILLER, G. A., & CHOMSKY, N. Finitary models of language users. In R. D. Luce, R. R. Bush, and E. Galanter (Eds.), *Handbook of mathematical psychology.* Vol. III. New York: Wiley, 1963.

MILLER, G. A., GALANTER, E., & PRIBRAM, K. H. *Plans and the structure of behavior.* New York: Holt, Rinehart and Winston, 1960.

MILLER, G. A., & MCNEILL, D. Psycholinguistics. In G. Lindsey and E. Aronson (Eds.), *Handbook of social psychology.* (2nd ed.) Vol. III. Reading, Mass.: Addison-Wesley, 1969. Pp. 666–794.

MILLER, W., & ERVIN, S. The development of grammar in child language. In U. Bellugi and R. Brown (Eds.), The acquisition of language. *Monograph of Social Research and Child Development*, 1964, *29*, 9–34.

MINER, L. E. Scoring procedures for the length-complexity index: a preliminary report. *Journal of Communication Disorders*, 1969, *2*, 224–240.

MITCHELL, C. I. Language behavior in a black urban community. Unpublished doctoral dissertation, University of California at Berkeley, 1969.

MODIANO, N. National or mother language in beginning reading: a comparative study. *Research in the Teaching of English*, 1968, *1*, 32–43.

MOELY, B. E., OLSON, F. A., HALWES, T. G., & FLAVELL, J. H. Production deficiency in young children's clustered recall. *Developmental Psychology*, 1969, *1*, 26–34.

MOERK, E. Principles of interaction in language learning. *Merrill-Palmer Quarterly*, in press.

MOFFETT, J. *An integrated curriculum in the language arts, K-12.* Boston, Mass.: Houghton Mifflin, 1968. (a)

MOFFETT, J. *Teaching the universe of discourse.* Boston, Mass.: Houghton Mifflin, 1968. (b)

MONTESSORI, M. *The Montessori method.* Cambridge, Mass.: Robert Bentley, Inc., 1965.

MOORE, D. Competence and performance factors in the development of copulative sentences in children of different social classes. Unpublished term paper, Harvard University, 1967.

MOORE, D. A comparison of two methods of teaching specific language skills to lower-class pre-school children. Unpublished doctoral dissertation, Harvard University, 1971.

MORRISON, P. The curricular triangle and its style. *ESI Quarterly Report*, 1964, *3*(2), 63–70. Reprinted by permission of Education Development Center.

MOSHER, F, A., & HORNSBY, J. R. On asking questions. In J. S. Bruner, R. R. Oliver, & P. M. Greenfield (Eds.), *Studies in cognitive growth.* New York: Wiley, 1966.

MOSKOWITZ, A. I. The acquisition of phonology. Berkeley, Calif.: Language-Behavior Research Laboratory, University of California, Working Paper No. 34, July 1970.

MUELLER, E. C. An analysis of children's communications in free play. Unpublished doctoral dissertation, Cornell University, 1971.

MYRDAL, G. *Objectivity in social research.* New York: Pantheon, 1969.

NATIONAL SOCIETY FOR THE STUDY OF EDUCATION. *Theories of learning and instruction.* 63rd Yearbook, Part I. Chicago: University of Chicago Press, 1964.

NEISSER, U. *Cognitive psychology.* New York: Appleton, 1967.

NELSON, K. Pre-syntactical strategies for learning to talk. Paper presented at biennial meeting of the Society for Research in Child Development, Minneapolis, April, 1971.

NESHER, P. Deep and surface structure in arithmetic. Unpublished term paper, Harvard University, 1970.

O'DONNELL, R. C., GRIFFIN, W. J., & NORRIS, R. C. *Syntax of kindergarten and elementary school children.* Champaign, Ill.: National Council of Teachers of English, 1967.

OETTINGER, A. G. The uses of computers in science. *Scientific American*, 1966, *215*, 161–172.

OETTINGER, A. G., & MARKS, S. *Run, computer, run.* Cambridge: Harvard University Press, 1969.

O'HUALLACHAIN, C. Bilingual education program in Ireland: recent experiences in home and adult support, teacher training, provision of instructional materials. In J. E. Alatis (Ed.), *Twenty-first round table: bilingualism and language contact.* Washington, D.C.: Georgetown University Press, 1970. Pp. 178–193.

OLDS, A. R. A study of syntactic and semantic factors in children's comprehension of sentences. Unpublished doctoral dissertation, Harvard University, 1970.

OLSON, P. A. Introduction. *The craft of teaching and the school of teachers.* Report of the first national conference, U.S. Office of Education Tri-University Project in Elementary Education, Denver, September 1967.

OLSON, D. R. Language and thought: aspects of a cognitive theory of semantics. *Psychological Review*, 1970, *4*, 257–273.

O'NEIL, W. A. The spelling and pronunciation of English. In *The American heritage dictionary of the English language*. Boston: Houghton Mifflin, 1969. Pp. xxxv–xxxvii.

O'NEIL, W. A. Paul Roberts' rules of order: the misuses of linguistics in the classroom. *The Urban Review*, 1968, *2*(7), 12–16.

O'NEIL, W. A. *On the way to M.I.T. one day: essays on linguistics and education*. Englewood Cliffs, N.J.: Prentice-Hall, in press.

OPIE, I., & OPIE, P. *The lore and language of school children*. London: Oxford University Press, 1959.

OSSER, H., WANG, M. D., & ZAID, F. The young child's ability to imitate and comprehend speech: a comparison of two subcultural groups. *Child Development*, 1969, *40*, 1063–1075.

PALMER, C. Cartoon in the classroom. *Hollywood Quarterly*, 1947, *3*(1), 26–33.

PAVLOVITCH, M. *Le langage enfantin: acquisition du serbe et du francais par un enfant serbe*. Paris, 1920.

PHILLIPS, J. R. Formal characteristics of speech which mothers address to their young children. Unpublished doctoral dissertation, The Johns Hopkins University, 1970.

PHILLIPS, S. U. Acquisition of rules for appropriate speech usage. In C. B. Cazden, D. Hymes, and V. P. John (Eds.), *The functions of language in the classroom*. New York: Teachers College Press, in press.

PIAGET, J. *The language and thought of the child*. (Originally published 1926.) Cleveland, Ohio: World, 1955.

PIAGET, J., & INHELDER, B. *The psychology of the child*. New York: Basic Books, 1969.

POLANYI, M. *Personal knowledge: towards a post-critical philosophy*. New York: Harper & Row (Torchbooks), 1964.

PORTER, J. D. R. *Black child, white child: the development of racial attitudes*. Cambridge, Mass.: Harvard University Press, 1971.

PRIBRAM, K. H. (Ed.) *On the biology of learning*. New York: Harcourt, 1969.

PSATHAS, G. Comment. *American Psychologist*, 1968, *23*, 135–137.

QUAY, L. C. Language, dialect, reinforcement, and the intelligence-test performance of Negro children. *Child Development*, 1971, *42*, 5–15.

RAINEY, M. Style switching in a Head Start class. University of California at Berkeley, Language and Behavior Research Laboratory, Working Paper No. 16, 1969.

READ, C. Preschool children's knowledge of English phonology. *Harvard Educational Review*, 1971, *41*, 1–34.

READ, W. C. Children's perceptions of the sounds of English: phonology from three to six. Unpublished doctoral dissertation, Harvard University, 1970.

REEVES, J. W. *Thinking about thinking*. London: Secker & Warburg, 1965.

RESNICK, L. B. Design of an early learning curriculum. Working Paper No. 16. University of Pittsburg Learning Research and Development Center, 1967.

RISLEY, T., REYNOLDS, N., & HART, B. Behavior modification with disadvantaged preschool children. In R. Bradfield (Ed.), *Behavior modification: the human effort*. San Rafael, Calif.: Dimensions Press, in press.

ROBERTS, E. An evaluation of standardized tests as tools for measuring language development. In *Language Research Report No. 1.* Cambridge, Mass.: Language Research Foundation, 131 Mt. Auburn St., May 1970.

ROBINSON, W. P. The elaborated code in working-class language. *Language and Speech*, 1965, *8*, 243–252.

ROBINSON, W. P. Restricted codes in sociolinguistics and the sociology of education. Paper presented at Ninth International Seminar, University College, Dar es Salaam, December 1968.

ROBINSON, W. P., & CREED, C. D. Perceptual and verbal discriminations of 'elaborated' and 'restricted' code users. *Language and Speech*, 1968, *11*, 182–193.

ROHWER, W. D., JR. Constraint, syntax and meaning in paired-associate learning. *Journal of Verbal Learning and Verbal Behavior*, 1966, *5*, 541–547.

ROHWER, W. D., JR. Cognitive development and education. In P. H. Mussen (Ed.), *Carmichael's manual of child psychology.* (3rd ed.) Vol. I. New York: Wiley, 1970. Pp. 1379–1454.

ROHWER, W. D., JR., LYNCH, S., LEVIN, J. R., & SUZUKI, N. Grade level, school strata and learning efficiency. *Journal of Educational Psychology*, 1967, *5*, 294–302.

RONJAT, J. *Le dévelopment du langage observé chez un enfant bilingue.* Paris, 1913.

RYAN, W. *Blaming the victim.* New York: Pantheon, 1971.

RYLE, G. *The concept of mind.* New York: Barnes & Noble, 1949.

RYSTROM, R. The effects of standard dialect training on Negro first-graders learning to read. Concord, Calif.: Diablo Valley College. Final Report, 1968.

SALZINGER, K., HAMMER, M., PORTNOY, S., & POLGAR, S. K. Verbal behavior and social distance. *Language and Speech*, 1970, *13*, 25–37.

SAPIR, E. *Language.* New York: Harcourt (Harvest Books), 1947. (First published in 1921.)

SAPON, S. Sapon intelligibility function test. Rochester, N.Y.: Mono Press, in press.

SCHATZMAN, L., & STRAUSS, A. Social class and modes of communication. *American Journal of Sociology*, 1955, *60*, 329–338.

SCHEFFLER, I. *The language of education.* Springfield, Ill.: Charles C Thomas, 1960.

SCHEFFLER, I. *Conditions of knowledge.* Chicago: Scott, Foresman, 1965.

SCHEFFLER, I. University scholarship and education of teachers. *The Record-Teachers College*, 1968, *70*, 1–12.

Schoolboys of Barbiana, *Letter to a Teacher.* Translation by N. Rossi and T. Cole. New York: Random House, 1970.

SELIGMAN, C. R., TUCKER, G. R., & LAMBERT, W. E. The effects of speech style and other attributes on teachers' attitudes toward pupils. *Language in Society*, in press.

SERWER, B. L. Linguistic support for a method of teaching beginning reading to Black children. *Reading Research Quarterly*, 1969, *14*, 449–467.

SHAFTEL, F., & SHAFTEL, G. *Words and action.* New York: Holt, Rinehart and Winston, 1967.

SHAMO, G. W. The psychological correlates of speech characteristics of sounding "disadvantaged", a southern replication. Paper presented at Annual

Convention of American Educational Research Association, Minneapolis, March 1970.

SHIPLEY, E. F., GLEITMAN, C. S., & SMITH, L. R.   A study of the acquisition of language: free response to commands. *Language*, 1969, *45*, 322–342.

SHUY, R. W., WOLFRAM, W. A., & RILEY, W. K.   Linguistic correlates of social stratification in Detroit speech. Final report, Cooperative Research Project 6–1347, Wayne State University, 1967. (To be distributed through ERIC.)

SIGEL, I. E., ANDERSON, L. M., & SHAPIRO, H.   Categorization behavior of lower- and middle-class Negro pre-school children: differences in dealing with representation of familiar objects. *Journal of Negro Education*, 1966, *35*, 218–229.

SILBERMAN, C. E.   *Crisis in the classroom.* New York: Random House, 1970.

SIMON, H. A., & NEWELL, A.   Human problem solving: the state of the theory in 1970. *American Psychologist*, 1970, *7*, 145–159.

SINCLAIR, H.   The transition from sensory-motor behavior to symbolic activity. *Interchange*, 1970, *1*(3), 119–126.

SINCLAIR-DE-ZWART, H.   Developmental psycholinguistics. In D. Elkind & J. H. Flavell (Eds.), *Studies in cognitive development: essays in honor of Jean Piaget.* New York: Oxford University Press, 1969. Pp. 315–336.

SKINNER, B. F.   *Verbal behavior.*   New York: Appleton, 1957.

SLAVINA, L. S.   Specific features of the intellectual work of unsuccessful pupils. In B. Simon (Ed.), *Psychology in the Soviet Union.* Stanford University Press, 1957, 205–212.

SLEDD, J.   Bi-dialectalism: the linguistics of white supremacy. *English Journal*, 1969, *58*, 1307–1315.

SLOBIN, D. I. (Ed.)   *A field manual for cross-cultural study of the acquisition of communicative competence.* (Second draft.) Barkeley, Calif.: University of California, 1967.

SLOBIN, D. I.   Questions of language development in cross-cultural perspective. Paper prepared for symposium on "Language learning in cross-cultural perspective," Michigan State University, September 1968.

SLOBIN, D. I.   Early grammatical development in several languages, with special attention to Soviet research. Working Paper No. 11, [University of California] Language-Behavior Research Laboratory, Berkeley, 1969.

SLOBIN, D. I.   Suggested universals in the ontogenesis of grammar. University of California Language-Behavior Research Laboratory, Working Paper No. 32, April 1970.

SLOBIN, D. I.   *Psycholinguistics.* Glenview, Ill.: Scott, Foresman, 1971.

SLOBIN, D. I., & WELSH, C. A.   Elicited imitation as a research tool in developmental psycholinguistics. Department of Psychology, University of California, Berkeley, unpublished paper, 1967.

SLOBIN, D. I., & WELSH, C. A.   Elicited imitation as a research tool in developmental psycholinguistics. In C. S. Lavatelli (Ed.), *Language training in early childhood education.* Urbana: University of Illinois Press for the ERIC Clearinghouse on Early Childhood Education, 1971. Pp. 170–185.

SMILANSKY, S.   *Effects of sociodramatic play on disadvantaged pre-school children.* New York: Wiley, 1968.

SMITH, D. R.   The effect of four communication patterns and sex on length of verbalization of four year old children. Buffalo, New York: State University of New York, unpublished report, March 1970.

SNOW, C. E. Language acquisition and mothers' speech to children. Unpublished doctoral dissertation, McGill University, 1971.

SPEIER, M. The organization of talk and socialization in family household interaction. Unpublished doctoral dissertation, University of California at Berkeley, 1969.

SPINDLER, G. D. The transmission of American culture. *The Florida FL Reporter*, 1969, 7(1), 1–9.

SPOLSKY, B. Navajo language maintenance: six-year-olds in 1969. *Language Sciences*, No. 13, December 1970, 19–24.

SROUFE, L. A. A methodological and philosophical critique of intervention-oriented research. *Developmental Psychology*, 1970, 2, 140–145.

STEWART, W. A. Current issues in the use of Negro dialect in beginning reading texts. *The Florida FL Reporter*, 1970, 8(1–2), 3–7ff.

STODOLSKY, S. S. Maternal behavior and language and concept formation in Negro preschool children: an inquiry into process. Unpublished doctoral dissertation, University of Chicago, 1965.

STODOLSKY, S. S., & LESSER, G. Learning patterns in the disadvantaged. *Harvard Educational Review*, 1967, 37, 546–593.

STODOLSKY, S. S. Essay review: ecological psychology or what's been going on at Kansas? *School Review*, in press.

STRANDBERG, T. E., & GRIFFITH, J. A study of the effects of training in visual literacy on verbal language behavior. Eastern Illinois University, 1968.

STROSS, B. Language acquisition by Tenejapa Tzeltal children. Unpublished doctoral dissertation, University of California at Berkeley, 1969.

TAX, S., & THOMAS, R. K. Education "for" American Indians: threat or promise. *The Florida FL Reporter*, 1969, 7(1), 15–19ff.

TAYLOR, O. L. Social dialects and the field of speech: response to F. Williams. In R. Shuy (Ed.), *Sociolinguistics: a cross-disciplinary perspective*. Washington, D.C.: Center for Applied Linguistics, 1971. Pp. 13–20.

TEMPLIN, M. C. *Certain language skills in children: their development and interrelationships*. Minneapolis: University of Minnesota Press, 1957.

THOMAS, D. R. Oral language, sentence structure and vocabulary of kindergarten children living in low socio-economic urban areas. Unpublished doctoral dissertation, Wayne State University, 1962.

THOMPSON, J. W. The implicit unit of linguistic analysis used by advantaged and disadvantaged children. Unpublished doctoral dissertation, University of Illinois, 1968.

TINBERGEN, N. *The herring gull's world: a study of the social behavior of birds*. New York: Basic Books, 1960.

TIZARD, B., COOPERMAN, O., JOSEPH, A., & TIZARD, O. Environmental effects on language development: a study of young children in long-stay residential nurseries. *Child Development*, in press.

TORREY, J. W. Learning to read without a teacher: a case study. *Elementary English*, 1969, 46, 550–556. (a)

TORREY, J. W. Teaching Standard English to speakers of other dialects. Paper presented at Second International Congress of Applied Linguistics, Cambridge, England, September 1969. (b)

TROIKE, R. C.   Receptive competence, productive competence, and performance. In J. E. Alatis (Ed.), *Report of the twentieth annual round table meeting on linguistics and the teaching of Standard English to speakers of other languages or dialects.* Washington, D.C.: Georgetown University Press, 1970. Pp. 63–69.

TUCKER, C. A.   The Chinese immigrant's language handicap: its extent and its effect. *The Florida FL Reporter,* 1969, 7(1), 44–45ff.

TUCKER, G. R.   An alternate days approach to bilingual education. In J. E. Alatis (Ed.), *Twenty-first annual round table: bilingualism and language contact.* Washington, D.C.: Georgetown University Press, 1970. Pp. 281–295.

TULKIN, S. R.   Mother-infant interaction in the first year of life: an inquiry into the influences of social class. Unpublished doctoral dissertation, Harvard University, 1970.

TULKIN, S. R., & KAGAN, J.   Mother-child interaction: social class differences in the first year of life. Paper presented at Annual Convention of American Psychological Association, Miami Beach, Florida, September 1970.

UNESCO.   *The use of vernacular languages in education.* Paris: Author, 1953, pp. 53–54.

VALENTINE, C. A.   Deficit, difference, and bicultural models of Afro-American behavior. *Harvard Educational Review,* 1971, *41,* 137–157.

VENEZKY, R. L.   Nonstandard language and reading. *Elementary English,* 1970, *47,* 334–345.

VYGOTSKY, L. S.   *Thought and language.* Cambridge, Mass.: M.I.T. Press, 1962.

WALES, R. J., & MARSHALL, J. C.   The organization of linguistic performance. In J. Lyons & R. J. Wales (Eds.), *Psycholinguistic papers.* Edinburgh: University Press, 1966. Pp. 29–80.

WALKER, W.   An experiment in programmed cross-cultural education: the import of the Cherokee primer for the Cherokee community and for the behavioral sciences. Wesleyan University, Middleton, Connecticut. Mimeo, March 1965.

WALKER, W.   Notes on native writing systems and the design of native literacy programs. *Anthropological Linguistics,* 1969, *11,* 148–165.

WARBURTON, F. W., & SOUTHGATE, V.   *I.T.A.: an independent evaluation.* London: W. R. Chambers & John Murray, 1969.

WARDHAUGH, R.   *Reading: a linguistic perspective.* New York: Harcourt, 1969.

WATT, W. C.   Comments on the Brown and Hanlon paper. In J. R. Hayes (Ed.), *Cognition and the development of language.* New York: Wiley, 1970. Pp. 55–78.

WEBB, R. A.   Learning, emotion and language in group experience: some speculations on why group procedures work. Albany: State University of New York Press, in press.

WEEKS, T. E.   Speech registers in young children. In *Papers and reports on child language development No. 1,* Stanford, Calif.: Stanford University Committee on Linguistics, March 1970. Pp. 23–42.

WEIR, R. H.   *Language in the crib.* The Hague: Mouton, 1962.

WERNER, H. Process and achievement: a basic problem of education and developmental psychology. *Harvard Educational Review*, 1937, *7*, 353–368.

WERNER, H. The concept of development from a comparative and organismic point of view. In D. B. Harris (Ed.), *The concept of development*. Minneapolis: University of Minnesota Press, 1957. Pp. 125–148.

WERNER, O., & BEGISHE, K. Styles of learning: the evidence from Navajo. Paper prepared for conference on styles of learning in American Indian children, Stanford University, August 1968.

WHITE, S. Some general outlines of the matrix of developmental changes between five and seven years. *Bulletin of the Orton Society*, 1970, *20*, 41–57.

WHORF, B. L. The relation of habitual thought and behavior to language. (Originally published 1941.) Reprinted in J. B. Carroll (Ed.), *Language, thought and reality: selected writings of Benjamin Lee Whorf*. Cambridge, Mass.: M.I.T. Press, 1956. Pp. 134–159.

WIGHT, J., & NORRIS, R. A. *Teaching of English to West Indian children*. Report No. 2, University of Birmingham School of Education, 1969.

WILLIAMS, C. E., & LEGUM, S. E. *On recording samples of informal speech from elementary school children*. TR 25. Inglewood, California: Southwest Regional Laboratory, May 6, 1970.

WILLIAMS, F. Language, attitude, and social change. In F. Williams (Ed.), *Language and poverty*. Chicago: Markham, 1970.

WILLIAMS, F. Psychological correlates of speech characteristics: on sounding "disadvantaged." *Journal of Speech and Hearing Research*, in press.

WILLIAMS, F., & NAREMORE, R. C. On the functional analysis of social class differences in modes of speech. *Speech Monographs*, 1969, *36*, 77–102. (a)

WILLIAMS, F., & NAREMORE, R. C. Social class differences in children's syntactic performance: a quantitative analysis of field study data. *Journal of Speech and Hearing Research*, 1969, *12*, 777–793. (b)

WILLIAMS, F., CAIRNS, H. S., CAIRNS, C. E., & BLOSSER, D. F. *Analysis of production errors in the phonetic performance of school-age Standard-English speaking children*. Austin, Texas: Center for Communication Research, University of Texas, December, 1970.

WOLFRAM, W. Social dialects from a linguistic perspective: assumptions, current research, and future directions. In R. Shuy (Ed.), *Sociolinguistics: a cross-disciplinary perspective*. Washington, D.C.: Center for Applied Linguistics, in press. 1971. Pp. 86–135.

WOLFRAM, W. A., & FASOLD, R. W. Toward reading materials for speakers of black English: three linguistically appropriate passages. In J. C. Baratz & R. W. Shuy (Eds.), *Teaching black children to read*. Washington, D.C.: Center for Applied Linguistics, 1969. Pp. 138–155.

WOODCOCK, L. P. *When children first say why, because, if*. New York: Bank Street Publications, n.d.

WOZNIAK, R. H. Verbal regulation of motor behavior—Soviet research and non-Soviet replications: a review and explication. *Human Development*, in press.

WYATT, G. L. *Language learning and communication disorders in children*. New York: Macmillan, 1969. (See Chap. 15 especially.)

ZIPF, G. K. *Human behavior and the principle of least effort*. Cambridge, Mass.: Addison-Wesley, 1949.

Glossary

agent–action–object A sentence or independent clause ordered such that the actor is the first noun mentioned, the verb follows next, and the object of the verb is the last noun mentioned.

Example: Mary   hit   the ball.
         agent action object

ambiguous sentence A sentence which a native speaker of the language understands as having more than one meaning; correct interpretation of the sentence requires use of the linguistic or non-linguistic context to select among alternative meanings.

Example: Visiting relatives can be a nuisance.
         a. It is a nuisance to visit relatives.
         b. Relatives who visit us are a nuisance.

anaphoric pronoun A pronoun referring to some other noun or nounphrase already given in the sentence. Compare *exophoric pronoun*.

Example: The boy kicked the ball and *it* broke the window.

aphasia Partial or total loss of the ability to produce or understand speech, usually due to an injury to the brain.

anomalous sentence A sentence that is considered meaningless because the meaning of the sentence as given is absurd, irrational, or in some way deviant.

Examples: The little pie with mud eyes was making a red girl.
          Colorless green ideas sleep furiously.

apical A consonant articulated or produced by the tip of the tongue.

Example: "t" in *t*ip of the *t*ongue.

articulation Pronunciation of a speech sound.

aspirated A sound whose pronunciation involves a strong release of air from the oral cavity.

Example: *h* in "heart."

associative clustering The tendency for a subject, when asked to recall a list of words, to recall two words in succession because of some association between them even though they were separated in the original presentation of the list.

branching, left Sentences where modifying words, phrases, or clauses are attached (or refer to) the subject.

branching, right Refers to sentences where the modifying words, phrases, or clauses are attached (or refer to) the object of the verb.

Examples: left branching—That big red truck is mine.
          right branching—I saw that big, red, truck.

catenative A link or chain; used by Brown (in press) as a label for *gonna, wanna,* and *hafta* in the speech of young children.

Example: I hafta eat my ice cream.

cleft sentence A transformed sentence that can be defined most easily by examples. The sentence *Germs cause diseases* has two synonymous cleft transformations
What germs cause are diseases.
What causes diseases are germs.

communicative competence Hymes' (1971) term for the nonconscious, tacit knowledge underlying communicative behavior; it includes both knowledge of language in the more usual and narrow sense of syntax, phonology, and semantics, and knowledge of the social world and of rules for using language in that world so that speech is appropriate as well as grammatical, creative within both linguistic and sociolinguistic rules.

consonant cluster   A group of two or more consonants in a sequence.
  Examples: "thr" and "st" in *thrust*.

content word or *contentive*   A noun, verb, adjective, or adverb having semantic content and conveying information. Compare *functors*.
  Examples: she, red

comment   See "*topic-comment*."

competence   The nonconscious, tacit knowledge for fuller definition underlying behavior. See *communicative competence*. Compare *performance*.

confounded results   When two or more variables being studied change together so that their effects cannot be separated.
  Example: If middle-class white children are compared with lower-class black children, the effects of class and race are confounded.

connotative meaning   The nuances of meaning, based on factors such as emotion, that a word has for an individual speaker. Compare *denotative meaning*.
  Example: Different reactions to the phrase "law and order" in the United States today.

conservation   In psychology, understanding that a characteristic such as number, weight, or volume remains the same despite different physical arrangements of matter.
  Example: . . . . is the same number as : :

contingent variability   Defined by Labov et al. (1968) as fluctuation in the speech patterns of any one speaker that is due to, and predictable from, the linguistic and/or social context. Compare *inherent variability*.
  Example: The tendency to shift from *going* to *goin'* in more informal contexts.

contrastive stress   Emphasis in speech on a certain word which, by departing from the usual pattern, conveys additional information.
  Example: The bóy chased the dog. (The important idea is that the chasing is done by the boy and not someone else.)

co-occurrence   The grammatical or appropriate combining of words in an utterance.
  Example: In a subject-verb relationship, *boy* can co-occur with *sleeps*, but *chair* cannot co-occur with *talks*.
  In Blom and Gumperz's (in press) research on the use of Norwegian dialects, shifts between dialects co-occurred with shifts among topics.

copula   A form of the verb "be" linking subject and predicate.
  Example: Silver *is* heavy.

corpus   A sample of utterances that have been gathered for the purpose of linguistic analysis.

correlation   An arithmetical procedure for determining the relationship between two variables. If an increase in one variable produces an increase in the other, the correlation is positive; if an increase in one variable produces a decrease in the other, the correlation is negative.
  Example: Scholastic Aptitude Test scores and success in college as measured by grade point average are positively correlated; family income and infant mortality are negatively correlated.

count noun   A noun that may be pluralized. Compare *mass noun*.
  Example: stick-sticks

decode   The psychological process by which a hearer derives meaning from a verbal message. Compare *encode*.

deep structure   The underlying and abstract form of each sentence which represents the basic semantic relationships—such as actor-action-object—being expressed. Compare *surface structure*.

Example: The boy was hit by the car.
        object   action   actor

delayed auditory feedback   An experimental condition in which speech is temporarily impaired by forcing the speaker to listen to his own voice after a brief delay.

denotative meaning   The generally accepted "dictionary definition" of a word. Compare *connotative meaning*.

dependent variable   The condition that is being predicted in an experiment. Compare *independent variable*.

Example: In an experiment to determine the effect of social class on vocabulary test scores, the test score is the dependent variable.

dialect   A variety of a spoken language that initially represented divergent geographic origins, but may now represent social groups within a community.

Example: The language of some Black adults and children had its origins in the Southern United States.

dialect switching   An individual speaker's shift from one dialect to another. See *role switching* and *metamorphical switching* for two forms.

diphthong   Two vowel sounds joined in one syllable to form a single speech sound.
Example: The "ou" in out and the "i" in ice.

disadvantaged child   A term frequently applied to a child whose family is below some standard of adequacy on objective indices, such as income or nutrition.

distinctive feature   An elementary component by which speech sounds are distinguished from one another; each distinctive feature is expressed as a contrast between opposites such as voiced-voiceless.

Example: *b* (voiced) and *p* (voiceless)

egocentric speech   The term used by Piaget (1955) to describe the speech of young children who do not yet take into account the point of view of another person.

elliptic form   Omission from a sentence of one or more words which are obviously understood.

Example: That's Daddy's! (omitting object that belongs to Daddy)

embedded   One construction inserted into another.

Example: The boy *who wore the red hat* plays baseball.
        (The adjective clause *who wore the red hat* is embedded within the sentence *The boy plays baseball*.)

encode   The psychological process by which the speaker converts meaning or proposition into a spoken utterance. Compare *decode*.

enculturation   Or socialization, the process by which a child learns to be a competent participant member of his society and culture.

enunciation   The manner of pronouncing, or articulating, speech sounds and words.

exophoric pronoun   A pronoun referring outward to something in the situational context. Compare *anaphoric pronoun*.

Example: *They*'re playing football and *he* kicked it.
        (if antecedents for these pronouns are not supplied in preceding utterances)

expansion   An adult verbal response which is contingent on the child's previous utterance and which expresses in syntactically complete form the meaning of the child's utterance as the adult understands it. Compare *extension*.

Example: child: "Dog bark."
        adult: "Yes, the dog is barking."

extension An adult verbal response which is contingent on the child's previous utterance, and which presupposes a particular expansion but then builds out from it along some dimension of meaning. Compare *expansion.*

> Example: child's utterance: "Dog bark."
> adult's extension: "Yes, and the kitty is running after him."

feature, distinctive, see *distinctive feature*

feature, prosodic, see *prosodic feature*

flow chart A schematic diagram illustrating a sequence of operations to be followed—as used, for example, in computer programming.

fricative A consonant produced by friction caused by air passing through a sustained narrow passage in the mouth.

> Examples: *f* and *v*

functor A small closed class of words including inflections, articles, and prepositions which are necessary to the interpretation of meaning of the sentence but do not have referential meaning themselves. Compare *content words.*

> Examples: possessive 's, the, on

gain score The amount of gain, for example in test scores, from one time to another.

generative grammar A description of a language which consists of a set of rules which can "generate" all, and only, the sentences of a language considered grammatical by a native speaker.

gerund The *-ing* form of a verb when used as a noun.

> Example: *Swimming* is fun. *Having* done my homework tired me.

grammar Description of a language written by linguists.

grammatical closure subtest One of subtests of the Illinois Test of Psycholinguistic Abilities; it taps knowledge of standard English morphology by asking for the completion of items.

> Example: "Here is a bed. Here are two _____ ."

grapheme The smallest unit of writing or printing which distinguishes one meaning from another.

> Examples: b, c, d, e

hierarchical structure In language the characteristic that makes a sentence divisible into progressively smaller constituents.

holophrase A one-word utterance expressing an idea or meaning; the holophrastic stage in children's acquisition of language is a period in which the child utters mainly one-word sentences.

iconic A sign or symbol that resembles in some way what it represents.

> Examples: A word like *buzzing* where sound resembles its meaning.
> A sentence like *The boy took off his boots and then walked in,* in which order of words reflects order of events.

independent variable The condition that is varied in an experiment, from which predictions about effects on dependent variables are made. Compare *dependent variable.*

> Example: In an experiment to determine the effect of social class on vocabulary test scores, social class is the independent variable.

inflections The addition of certain endings to the base of a word to express such meanings as number and tense.

> Example: the possessive or plural *'s* on nouns, the past tense *ed* on verbs.

informant A native speaker of a language from whom a linguist gathers samples of speech.

inherent variability   Defined by Labov et al. (1968) as fluctuations in the speech patterns of any one speaker in unpredictable ways. Compare *contingent variability*.
　Example: In child speech, the oscillation between supplying and omitting plural endings.

interval scale   A numerical scale which assumes equal distances between the units. Compare *ordinal scale*.
　Example: Fahrenheit scale for temperature.

intonation   The rise and fall of the speaking voice as an utterance is pronounced.
　Example: It's warm out. *vs.* It's warm out?

ITA, or Initial Teaching Alphabet   An alphabet of 44 symbols designed to regularize the correspondence between English sounds and letters in beginning reading texts.
　Example: "serve" written as "serv," "word" written as "wurd."

inner speech, see *private speech*

intransitive verb   A verb that does not take an object.
　Examples: The bird flies.
　　　　　　 The dog runs.

labial   A consonant produced with one or both lips.
　Examples: *p, b, m*

langue   A term used by Ferdinand de Saussure to refer to the system (grammatical and semantic) which makes speech possible. *Langue* is distinguished from *parole* which refers to the actual vocal output of the speaker. Langue *vs.* parole is an historical antecedent of the current distinction between competence and performance.

lax vowel   A vowel sound pronounced with less muscular tension in the speech organs.
　Examples: *i* in "hit."

learning, serial recall, see *serial recall learning*

learning, paired associate, see *paired associate learning*

learning hierarchies   Refers to the learning of one aspect of a skill, which depends on the degree of mastery achieved in some lesser or lower aspect of the same skill.
　Example: Counting depends at least on a knowledge of the order of number names and an understanding of one-to-one correspondence.

left branching sentences, see *branching, left*

lexicon   The totality of words and morphemes in a given language. May refer to the language of an individual or a community.

linguistics   The scientific study of language.

locative   A word or phrase which refers to some place or location.
　Examples: It's *there*.
　　　　　　 He's *at home*.

mand   A term used by Skinner (1957) for an utterance which produces an effect (verbal or nonverbal) on someone else for the benefit of the speaker. Compare *tact*.
　Example: "Give me the book."

marked   That member of a pair of linguistic units which is distinguished by the presence of a particular feature.
　Example: In the pair "pin" and "bin," *b* is marked by the presence of the "voice" feature, while *p* is unmarked. Extended by some linguists to semantic features such as singular *vs.* plural.

mass noun   A noun that can not be pluralized because its meaning refers to an extended substance. Compare *count noun*.
　Examples: sugar, rice

mean length of utterance, or *MLU*   The average number of words or morphemes in an utterance; found by dividing the total number of words or morphemes in a speech sample by the total number of utterances in the sample.

meaning, connotative, see *connotative meaning*

meaning, denotative, see *denotative meaning*

metalinguistic awareness   The ability to reflect upon language as well as comprehend and produce it.

metamorphical switching   A speaker's shift from one language variety to another in order to allude to alternative social relationships between speaker and listener(s) and thereby enrich the content of the message.

> Example: Blom and Gumperz (in press) found that when students who had been close friends in a Norwegian village returned home after attendance at universities in Oslo or Bergen, their conversation on local matters was in dialect, whereas on topics related to their Pan-Norwegian life as students they switched to standard Norwegian.

minimal terminal unit, or *T unit*   Hunt's (1965) name for one main clause with all subordinate clauses attached to it.

> Example: *The big girl who had on a blue scarf walked down the road,* and *her brother followed close behind her* (= 2 T units).

monomorphemic cluster   A consonant cluster which is part of a simple morpheme, as in *first*—as opposed to *asked* where the consonant cluster contains an additional morpheme -ed ending.

morpheme   The smallest meaningful unit of speech. "Free" morphemes like *chair* can occur alone. "Bound" morphemes like -*ed* must be attached to other morphemes.

morphology   That part of a grammar which consists of the rules for combining morphemes into words.

multiple negation   A negative meaning stated more than once in a sentence.

> Example: I *don't* want *none.*

nominalization   The process of fulfilling the function of a noun by a word or group of words.

> Example: nounphrase—*The one with the red shirt* left.

noun, count, see *count noun*

noun, mass, see *mass noun*

noun phrase, or *NP* or *N*   A group of two or more associated words which can be substituted for a noun.

> Example: *A tall, handsome boy* walked in.

obligatory context   A linguistic environment in which certain linguistic forms are required.

> Example: Plurality is required after numbers larger than one:
>   Two cookie*s.*

ontogenetic development   The history of an individual organism. Compare *phylogenetic development.*

operational definition   Identifies a phenomenon by specifying the procedures or operations used to measure it.

> Example: A particular intelligence test, such as the Stanford Binet, supplies one operational definition of the meaning of "intelligence."

ordinal scale   A series of numbers which do not assume equal distances between them. Compare *interval scale.*

> Example: house numbers on a block.

orthography   Spelling; the conventional written representation of a word.

paired associate learning   A learning task involving the formation of associations between a list of pairs of verbal items, where one member of each pair is the stimulus and the other member is the response. Using flash cards to learn the vocabulary of a foreign language is a similar real-life task.

paradigmatic   An association between words—usually the same part of speech—that can replace each other in a sentence. Compare *syntagmatic*.
> Example: deep-shallow

parole   Defined by Ferdinand de Saussure as the actual speech or vocal output of the speaker. See *langue* for fuller discussion.

participant structures   Phillips' (in press) name for the structural arrangements of a social interaction.
> Example: The teacher interacts with only some of the students in the class at one time, as in reading groups.

performance   Actual speech production or comprehension. Compare *competence*.

phoneme   The traditional name for speech sounds which distinguish one word from another in a given language.
> Example: *top vs. pot*.

phonology   That part of a grammar which consists of rules for combining speech sounds.

phylogenetic development   The history, or evolution, of a species or group.

pooled data   Combining research data from two or more sources (e.g., boys and girls).

private speech or *inner speech*   Silent speech; an internalized modification of speech spoken aloud, not intended for communication to others.

prosodic features   Aspects of speech which include stress, intonation, and pauses.

protocol   Raw data collected in a research project, such as the transcription of speech before any analysis has been made.

psycholinguistics   Study of the psychological processes underlying speech performance.

Pygmalion effect   The way speech marks a person's social identity. From George Bernard Shaw's play about how Henry Higgins taught Eliza Doolittle to talk "like a lady."

reinforcement   Any event that increases the probability of a particular response.
> Example: If a child receives a reward every time he makes his bed, then the number of times he makes his bed should increase.

reliability   The extent to which a measure would produce the same score if the measure were applied again under the same conditions.
> Example: How many utterances are needed for a *reliable* measure of a child's mean length of utterance?

right branching sentence, see *branching, right*

role switching   The speaker's shift of language variety when there is a change in the relationship among the participants and in their definition of the situation.
> Example: Blom and Gumperz (in press) report that Norwegian teachers use standard Norwegian in formal lectures, but switch to a local dialect in open discussion with students.

rule   A formal statement which describes how the units of a language are related.

SAAD   A *s*imple, *a*ctive, *a*ffirmative, *d*eclarative sentence.
> Example: Mary hit the ball.

scale, interval, see *interval scale*

scale, ordinal, see *ordinal scale*

segmentation error   An error in which the speaker fails to divide a linguistic form into its proper units.
   Example: A child's use of *thas* (*that's*) as a variation of *that: Thas is mine.*

semantics   The study of meaning in language, including the relationship between linguistic symbols and the objects, events, or ideas to which they refer.

sensory?motor-intelligence   According to Piaget (e.g., Piaget and Inhelder, 1969), the first stage in the development of intelligence, reached at 12–18 months. The child perceives and acts upon his world in purposeful ways but without any means of internally representing it.

serial recall learning   A learning task in which a list of verbal items is learned.

signal-to-noise-ratio   The relationship between an audible message and background noise.

signifying   A special speech style highly developed in the Black community in which meaning is "signified" by gesturing and innuendo rather than stated explicitly in conventional terms.

social class   A type of social stratification in which an individual's general position in society is determined by criteria such as income and occupation.

sociolinguistics   The study of characteristics of language varieties and their relationship to speakers, topics, settings, functions, etc., within a speech community.

spectograph   An instrument for making a visual representation of the physical characteristics of speech sounds (pitch, loudness, and duration).

speech, egocentric, see *egocentric speech*

speech, inner, see *private speech*

speech, private, see *private speech*

speech, telegraphic, see *telegraphic speech*

status verbs   Verbs like *know, need* and *want* which refer to a state rather than a process or action; in the United States, the present progressive inflection *-ing* is never added to status verbs.

stop   A consonant that momentarily stops the flow of breath.
   Example: The *b*ad *d*og *t*ore the *p*ocketbook.

stress   The amount of muscular energy put into the articulatory movements.

stress, contrastive, see *contrastive stress*

structure, deep, see *deep structure*

structure, surface, see *surface structure*

style switching   An individual speaker's shift from one mode of expression or style to another. Can refer to shifting among dialects or any other set of language varieties.

surface structure   The superficial and perceptible form of a sentence which represents the grammatical relationships such as subject of verb and object of verb in the sentence as spoken. Compare *deep structure.*
   Example: The boy   was hit   by   the car
   ————————   ————   ——————————————
   subject   verb   object of preposition *by*

switching, dialect, see *dialect switching*

switching, metaphorical, see *metaphorical switching*

switching, role, see *role switching*

switching, style, see *style switching*

synchronization More than one process operating at the same time.

synonymous sentences Sentences that have approximately the same meaning for speaker and hearer.
Example: The car hit the boy. *and* The boy was hit by the car.

syntagmatic The association between words usually not the same part of speech that follow each other in one sentence. Compare *paradigmatic*.
Example: deep–hole

syntax That part of the grammar that consists of rules for combining words into sentences.

tacts A term used by Skinner (1957) for an utterance elicited by some object or event, either present or imagined, that informs the hearer. Compare *mand*.
Example: That is a chair.

tag question Formed by adding a "tag" to a declarative sentence; semantically simple, but grammatically complex.
Example: Joe and I are playing, *aren't we?*

telegraphic speech Brown and Bellugi's (1964) label for a form of speech characteristic of young children in which length is limited, content words are present whereas functors are absent, and normal word order is preserved.
Example: Daddy shoe (for Daddy's shoe).

topic-comment The topic is the psychological subject, and the comment is the psychological predicate defined contextually as new information the speaker wishes to convey.
Example: The boy | ran to the store.
          topic | comment

topicalization Manipulating the relationship between topic and comment.

transcription The rendering of speech in writing.

transition probabilities In language, the statistical likelihood that one word will follow another in a string of words.
Example: In English, there is a high probability that "cat" will follow "the" while there is a low probability that "cat" will follow "lagoon."

transitive A verb that can have an object.
Example: Mary *hit* the ball.

tree diagram In language, an analysis of a sentence into its constituent units in a way that graphically illustrates the essential relationships between the units.

truncated Shortened, or cut off, as when a passive sentence does not tell the agent.
Example: The glass was (or got) broken.

type-token-ratio, or *TTR* A measure of the variability of language. In words, for example, the TTR for a passage would equal the number of different words (types) divided by the number of total words (types) in that passage. For this definition (A measure . . . passage) the TTR is .79.

utterance Any self-sufficient meaningful unit of spoken language preceded and followed by a pause; may or may not be a grammatical sentence.

validity The extent to which a measure taps the characteristic it is supposed to measure.
Example: Is mean length of utterance a valid measure of a child's syntactic maturity?

variable, dependent, see *dependent variable*

variable, independent, see *independent variable*

variability, contingent, see *contingent variability*

variability, inherent, see *inherent variability*

vernacular The current, everyday, speech of a group of people in a specific geographic area.

voiced Sounds produced by vibration of the vocal cords.

Example: *b, d, z,* as opposed to *p, t, s*

word association The tie between two words demonstrated when one word prompts the thought of the next.

Example: words linked by sound–stick-lick; or linked by meanings–stick-wood.

Index